DATE DUE			

THIRD EDITION

ORGANIZATIONS
Structure and Process

Richard H. Hall

State University of New York

at Albany

Prentice-Hall, Inc.
Englewood Cliffs, New Jersey 07632

Library of Congress Cataloging in Publication Data

HALL, RICHARD H., (DATE)
  Organizations: structure and process.

  Includes bibliographical references and index.
  1. Organization. 2. Organizational change. I. Title.
HM131.H237 1982   302.3'5   81-15899
ISBN 0-13-641993-3   AACR2

For Sherry

3 0 2.3 5
H 1 4 0
1 2 2 2 9 9
July 1982

PRENTICE-HALL SERIES IN SOCIOLOGY
Neil J. Smelser, Editor

© 1982, 1977, 1972 by Prentice-Hall, Inc.,
Englewood Cliffs, N.J. 07632

Printed in the United States of America

10 9 8 7 6 5 4 3 2 1

Editorial/production supervision
and interior design: Jeanne Hoeting
Cover design: Carol Zawislak
Manufacturing Buyer: John Hall

ISBN 0-13-641993-3

Prentice-Hall International, Inc., *London*
Prentice-Hall of Australia Pty. Limited, *Sydney*
Prentice-Hall of Canada, Ltd., *Toronto*
Prentice-Hall of India Private Limited, *New Delhi*
Prentice-Hall of Japan, Inc., *Tokyo*
Prentice-Hall of Southeast Asia Pte. Ltd., *Singapore*
Whitehall Books Limited, *Wellington, New Zealand*

Contents

Preface
to the
Third Edition

This is the second revision of this book. Readers familiar with the earlier editions will note some strong continuity with the earlier editions, such as the emphasis on organizational structure and the processes within organizations. There are also some major changes. These changes have been incorporated to reflect developments within the field of organizations. The role of the environment is emphasized even more than in the past. Interorganizational relations are given extensive treatment in a separate chapter. Organizational effectiveness is considered after the analysis of organizational characteristics and the environment. The chapter on effectiveness focuses on the contradictions inherent in effectiveness considerations. Unlike most other current treatments of effectiveness, the importance of organizational goals is emphasized. Goals are brought into the analysis at several other points, also. The book ends with a chapter on organizational theory. This chapter is intended to tie together the various issues which have been discussed. It is also intended as a criticism of much of the current thinking on organizations.

The field of organizations has changed rapidly in recent years. At the same time, troublesome issues remain. I have tried to point these out, as in the section on typologies. Fortunately, through the hard work of Charles K. Warriner, typological or taxonomic efforts are being rejuvenated as they must be if we are to make sense out of the subject matter.

This edition is an attempt to reflect the current understanding of organizations, primarily from the sociological perspective. The field of organizations, of course, does not have disciplinary boundaries, and I have tried to incorporate the best knowledge regardless of its disciplinary base. The references and index indicate my intellectual debts, which are high. I would like especially to thank Joe Morrissey and Mike Lindsey for helping bring some order into the analysis of interorganizational relationships.

Billie Albrecht was prompt, efficient, and accurate in typing the manuscript and I want to thank her for her effort. Gloria Swigert and Eileen Crary of the Sociology Department at the State University of New York at Albany also provided indispensible help at critical points in the preparation of this work. Ed Stanford and Jeanne Hoeting of Prentice-Hall also provided encouragement and hard work in getting this volume prepared. Ed, in particular, was instrumental in getting me moving on this revision. A year spent as Acting Vice President for Research and Dean of Graduate Studies at Albany provided me with insights into the real workings of organizations that I did not have as a scholar on the outside looking in and I would like to thank President Vincent O'Leary for the opportunity to have that experience. My colleagues in the Department of Sociology continue to provide a congenial and enjoyable place to work. Finally, I want to thank Sherry and Tom and Julie for their warm support.

I

The Nature of Organizations

The purpose of this first section of the book is to introduce the subject matter of organizations. The discussion begins with an analysis of the role of organizations in society, starting with the topic of organizations and individuals and moving through analyses of organizations in communities and the wider society. In this analysis we will consider the role of organizations in social change. Organizations are the change agents in society. Paradoxically, they are also the major resistors of change and their role in the resistance of change will be documented. The analysis will then proceed to a set of specific research findings in regard to the role of organizations in society with the purpose of indicating specific organizational impacts. The role of powerful multinational organizations will be considered at the end of the first chapter.

The second chapter in this part of the book begins with a consideration of the sticky issue of defining what organizations are. As will be seen, this is not a simple task. The analysis then moves to consider the important question of whether or not organizations are real and can be studied and understood apart from the individuals which comprise them. The answer taken here is that, yes, organizations are real. This point serves as the core of the analysis in the balance of the book. The analysis in this section concludes with a consideration of the issue of organizational typologies or taxonomies. Since all thought requires classification, the issue of classifying the subject matter under investigation is an important one. We will conclude that there is not an adequate typology or taxonomy now available after reviewing the existing efforts in this direction. The purpose of this examination is to sensitize the reader to the fact that premature generalizations can be very misleading if we mix inappropriate types as in the case of the proverbial apples and oranges.

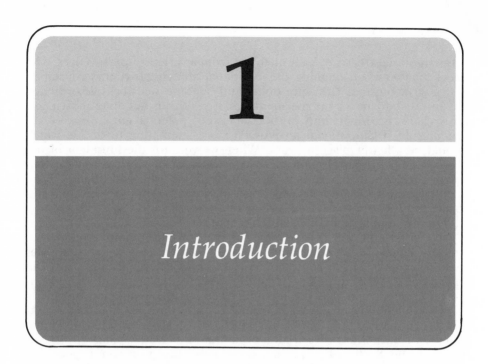

Introduction

It has become a cliché to note that we live in an organizational society. Organizations surround us. We are born in them and usually die in them. The space in between is filled with them. They are just about impossible to escape. They are as inevitable as death and taxes.

The pervasiveness of organizations can be seen by thinking through an average day of an average person. The day starts with awakening to the music on a clock radio. Obviously, the radio was built by an organization, and the radio station is an organization. The music being played was selected with a particular market in mind, probably on the basis of consumer research carried out by an organization. If we shower or shave or otherwise prepare ourselves for the day ahead, we use products manufactured, marketed, and sold by organizations. We have been convinced by organizations that certain scents are better than others, so that we perfume or after-shave ourselves on the basis of tastes generated by the marketers of products. When we eat our breakfast, the food is on the table as a consequence of the vast network of agricultural organizations which enable an urban society to exist. Here again, our tastes and even our appetite are colored by marketing, since it is bad to eat too much for fashion's sake and certain things are breakfast foods and others are not. We next ride a bus to work, and we are now really in the hands of an organization. So it proceeds through the day and into the evening. Just about the only escape from organizations comes when we go back to sleep.

This overly simplified example was intended to suggest that the analysis of organizations is not trivial. It is also not just an academic exercise.

Organizations are continually analyzed from a variety of perspectives. The stock market is an ongoing organizational analysis. Investors constantly assess how business firms are doing and buy and sell stocks accordingly. As in other forms of organizational analyses, this is not an exact science. If we have the opportunity to choose between potential employers, we are making an organizational analysis. We are attempting to decide which would be a better place to work. When we vote for the President of the United States in an election, it is an assessment of an organization to a surprising extent. There is a large organization which has handled the campaign and we estimate what kind of organization the individual will bring to office.

Organizational analysis also occurs at other levels. Organizational management has the job of assessing the state of the organization. Labor unions, themselves organizations, analyze the operations of the companies with which they have contracts. As customers or clients, we assess the quality of stores and their merchandise. When I buy a pair of skis, I want to be fairly certain that the manufacturer has the reputation of quality and the likelihood of staying in business. I also want to know that the ski shop can handle any problems which arise. More serious individual concern comes when we select an organization like a hospital.

Hart and Scott (1975, p. 261) have noted that whatever is good for humanity can only be achieved through modern organization. The reverse is also true, since it is organizations that discriminate, pollute, and wage wars. The study of organizations is thus not trivial. In this introductory chapter we will examine the impact of organizations on individuals, on categories of individuals, on communities, and on society. The rest of the book will be concerned with the analysis of organizational characteristics. The book is based on research on organizations and interpretations of that research. It is also based on theoretical analyses which have developed over the years.

Organizations and the Individual

The focus of most of this analysis will be on work organizations. In contemporary society almost all work is organizational work. Table 1-1 indicates the rapid decline in self-employment. While agricultural employment has remained relatively constant, the proportion of the labor force in agriculture has declined dramatically. Moreover, agricultural employment is increasingly organizational in form, as agribusiness becomes more and more dominant.

Work is carried out in organizations. It is also carried out in large organizations. Table 1-2 demonstrates this. About 5 percent of the organizations account for about 60 percent of the employment. Even more startling is the fact that $3/10$ of 1 percent of all organizations employ over 25 percent of the workers. Since most organizations are small, they do not account for much employment. The focus of the analysis in this book is the larger organization—the dominant form in contemporary society.

The fate of the individual in the organization is a hotly debated topic.

Table 1-1   The Large Majority of People Are Employees (in percent)

Year	Total Self-employed	Self-employment Agriculture	Self-employment Nonagriculture	Proportion of Labor Force in Agriculture
1900 25		53	8	38
1910 22		53	8	31
1920 21		56	8	27
1930 19		58	8	21
1940 19		58	11	17
1950 18		58	12	13
1960 14		49	10	9
1970 9		52	7	4
1975 9		51	7	4

Sources: *Statistical Abstract of the United States*, 1976, 1965, 1961; *United States Census of Population, U.S. Summary*, 1960, Final Report PC(1)-1C; U.S. Bureau of the Census, *Historical Statistics of the United States: Colonial Times to 1957*. Curt Tausky, *Work Organizations: Major Theoretical Perspectives* (Itasca, Illinois. F. E. Peacock, Publishers, 1978), p. 2.

Table 1-2   The Very Many Small Organizations Account for Limited Employment (in percent)

Employee Size Class	Reporting Units, 1973 Employees	Reporting Units, 1973 Employing Organizations*
0–3	5.0	47.3
4–7	6.8	21.9
8–19	12.6	17.6
20–49	14.8	8.1
50–99	11.0	2.7
100–249	14.1	1.6
250–499	10.2	0.5
500 or more	25.5	0.3

* Organizations here represent reporting units to the Old-Age and Survivors Insurance Bureau. Because there are more reporting units than employers, these figures understate the extent of employment by large organizations. However, from the point of view of the worker, the reporting unit data reflect the size of the work organization which is daily experienced (Tausky, p. 4).
Source: Bureau of the Census, *County Business Patterns*, 1973.

Several recent analyses have examined how individuals react to their lives as employees of organizations (Terkel 1974; Rosow 1974; Aronowitz 1973; *Work in America* 1973; Hall 1975). These analyses agree that work that is highly routinized, repetitive, and dull is highly alienating for the individual. This is not to say, of course, that work in pre-organizational societies was *not* alienating. Subsistence farming or hunting and gathering is hardly enlightening. Romanticized imageries of the pre-organizational system forget that people starved to death and froze to death. Early industrialization, with its exceedingly low pay, child labor, and absence of worker protection, was also alienating, but in a truer Marxian sense than the social-psychological alienation felt by today's worker in a routine job.

The studies of individual reactions to work also reveal that work which provides challenge, potential for advancement, and the use of creative or expressive capabilities is enjoyable and even enlightening. The ways in which people react to their work results from their own expectations and the characteristics of the organization (Lorsch and Morse 1974). Although organizational characteristics will be discussed at length at a later time, at this point it should be noted that there are limits to the variation possible in organizational characteristics, given the constraints of size, the technology employed, the market conditions, and other environmental factors. Organizations cannot change simply to be more pleasant places in which to work.

There is another side to working in organizations. In an important study, Kohn (1971) found small but consistent tendencies for people who work in more bureaucratized organizations to be more intellectually flexible, more open to new experiences, and more self-directed than those working in nonbureaucratized settings. Kohn and Schooler (1978) suggest that people's occupational conditions both affect and are affected by their psychological functioning. In regard to work in a bureaucratized setting, Kohn attributes the findings to the fact that bureaucratized organizations require their work force to be better educated and also provide more job protection, higher salary, and more complex work. The implication of this study is that work in organizations is not necessarily deadening to the individual. Indeed, it is likely that for exactly the same work some organizations demand more creativity and flexibility than other organizations do. The work of a secretary or an executive can be challenging and have potential for advancement in one organization and not in another. Here again, organizational characteristics are critical variables as they interact with those of the individual.

People not only work in organizations, they have extensive contacts with them as customers or clients. The recent growth of consumer and client-advocacy organizations is testimony to the fact that those who come to the organization for products or services were not totally satisfied with what they receive. Aside from the frequently ignored fact that advocacy organizations share the same pitfalls as the very organizations they are fighting, relatively little is known about how people react to their meetings within organizations.

A recent study by Katz et al. (1975) sheds some light on how people react to their encounters with organizations. In a survey of people's reactions to their contacts with government agencies in the areas of employment, job training, workmen's compensation, unemployment compensation, welfare services, hospital and medical services, and retirement services, it was found that the majority of these clients were satisfied with the service and treatment they received. Thus, widespread discontent with the "system" in this regard appears to be a myth, because common stereotypes about encounters with government bureaucracies are contradicted by the data. Nevertheless, the fact that most people are satisfied does not mean that the organizations are operating as effectively as possible. Katz et al. note:

A majority of satisfied clients may leave a sizable minority dissatisfied. Even a 75 percent level of satisfaction may be low for some programs in which 90 percent or higher is desirable and feasible. In a population of 200 million, small percentages are large numbers. (p. 115)

In a related study of the same phenomenon, this time among juveniles who have had contact with the juvenile justice system, Giordano (1974) found "something less than a seething rage against the professionals who staff the juvenile justice system." Apparently even in this population, which is thought to have very negative encounters with the establishment, organizations are not viewed with the distaste that is generally believed to be present.

An element in the Giordano research is worth noting: if a client feels close to an individual in an organization, his or her interpretation of the total organization appears to be affected. Individuals coming to an organization do so as individuals. The person in the organization may or may not be able to respond in a personal way. Many organizations prescribe the manner in which their employees are to respond to outsiders. Even if the prescribed manner is warm and friendly, as is the case of airline cabin attendants, it is still an organizational prescription. In the case of the professional staffs with which Giordano dealt, and which formed the bulk of the services studied by Katz et al. (1975), the professional is granted some latitude in interpersonal interactions. Such latitude is less likely at the clerical or retail sales level, where many individual contacts with organizations are made.

The analysis of individuals in organizations is incomplete unless economic factors are considered. Sociologists have a tendency to ignore the economic, but it is a mistake to do so. Focusing on factors such as morale and satisfaction deflects attention away from the fact that economic factors are a major consideration for management and workers. Hage (1980) notes that "on the one hand managerial elites and owners of capital want to drive costs down by means of policies of low wages and uniform tasks. On the other hand workers want to increase their standard of living and have interesting work. There is an inherent conflict of interest between these two perspectives" (p. 7). Hage goes on to suggest that the inherent conflict can be handled by either fighting or quitting, as suggested by

Hirschman (1972). While fighting or quitting are two important options—Hage does not deal with the option of continuing while dissatisifed because there are not other feasible economic options for the worker—Hirschman also suggests that loyalty to the organization can be developed. Hage's own analysis leads him away from economic considerations, but the original point regarding a conflict between workers and management should not be lost. People do have an economic stake in the organizations in which they work. Organizations affect the economic well-being of workers and hence their dependents. This is true for the individual as well as classes of individuals.

Classes of Individuals

The processes of differentiation and stratification have been abiding concerns of sociologists. The past decade has witnessed a flood of studies of the process of status attainment. These studies have primarily used occupational categories as the measure of status attainment. Recently there has been a realization that employers (organizations) are the primary mechanisms by which individuals are distributed among occupations and by which earnings are distributed among persons (Stolzenberg 1978; see also Baron and Bielby 1980). By understanding the process by which people attain positions within organizations, a more complete understanding of the overall stratification process is possible.

Rosenbaum (1979) has examined the mobility patterns within a single organization and reports some interesting patterns. Promotions occur most frequently at younger ages, with mobility unlikely after individuals are in their forties. Persons with college educations are more likely to receive promotions, which is not, of course, surprising, but even among this group, the decline at middle age occurs. Rosenbaum also examined the effect of growth or decline in the organization studied and the mobility process. When an organization is growing, there is greater promotional opportunity for all groups. When the organization is in a period of declining growth, the college-educated younger persons are the least affected. This organization, like others, sorts people into status categories on a nonrandom basis. The organization is the stratifier.

The recognition that organizations are at the core of the stratification process is incomplete unless it is also recognized that categories of individuals are differentially affected by organizations. Miles, Snow, and Pfeffer (1975) and Kanter (1977) have demonstrated the manner in which organizations discriminate against women. These studies suggest that even when women are promoted, there are detrimental consequences. Miller, Snow, and Pfeffer suggest that women who advance lose friendship and respect. Their influence declines as does their access to information. Kanter finds that advancing women face responses to themselves in stereotypical categories. What holds true for women would also hold true for minority-group members, perhaps to a greater degree. Thus, organizations reflect the divisions in society and reinforce them. Obviously, also, organizations are the only means by which women and minorities can advance. Affirmative action policies are organizational policies. If such policies work, then the categories of individuals which have suffered discrimination may be able to experience the same mobility patterns as the dominant white males.

In concluding that affirmative action policies might benefit categories of individuals, the fact that organizations are the mechanisms of stratification should not be forgotten. Organizations sort their members into levels. These levels are the individuals' places in the stratification system.

Organizations and the Community

Organizations are not benign in their impact on individuals and classes of individuals. The same is true for the communities or localities in which they operate. This can be seen dramatically in a study reported by Seiler and Summers (1979). They examined the consequences of the decision by a major steel manufacturing firm to locate a major new plant in a small town in the middle western United States. This company did not want to be identified in the community power structure as such, but their actions clearly had a major impact on the community.

The steel company, Jones and Laughlin, engaged in unilateral actions, such as buying land for their plant through ghost buyers and having a policy of hiring workers from surrounding counties, rather than in the home county. The company also co-opted the local community leaders, through such means as using key bankers and lawyers as their local representatives. No Jones and Laughlin personnel were active in the community, but their operatives were. The company also directly intervened in plans for a new high school in the community, forcing the building of a less expensive, and more practical, school and thus reducing their tax liability.

Seiler and Summers do not suggest that all of the results of the company's actions were either good or bad for the local community. Indeed, some were recognized as positive and others as negative. The important point is that this organization had a direct and dramatic impact on this local community. The impact of a single organization can thus be great. This is easily seen in other settings. The college or university town is dominated by that organization as much as any "company town" is dominated by a single industry.

Most communities have more than a single dominant organization. This does not dilute the power of organizations in the community, however. Perrucci and Pilisuk (1970) and Galaskiewicz (1979) have examined patterns of interorganizational relationships in local communities. Local power structures reflect interorganizational competition and thus the interests of powerful actors. We will consider interorganizational linkages in detail in Chapter 12. For our purposes here we can note that the interorganizational power linkages can work to the advantage or disadvantage of a community. Crittenden (1978) reports that Minneapolis, Minnesota is blessed with an extraordinarily high level of corporate philanthropy. Much of this is based on the interorganizational linkages among the business firms there. Most other cities are less fortunate. Some have been literally destroyed as businesses move to other areas. Still others receive virtually nothing from their organizational inhabitants.

These studies have been concerned with organizations in the private sector. Public organizations also have an obvious community effect, through such mechanisms as the placement of hospitals—in the central city or in the suburbs—and the provision of municipal services. Communities reflect the organizations that they contain.

Organizations and Society

Organizations affect the societies of which they are a part in obvious and more subtle ways. In the first part of this section, we will deal with some ways in which organizations contribute to and resist social change.

We will begin with the caveat that the analysis is hampered by the absence of good data. Most of the information comes from the limited number of published case studies. Examples of attempts to change society typically deal with successful efforts—as in the case of studies of politicians; we know very little about the losers. While we are concerned with change, and ineffective attempts at change therefore are not a central concern, it would be useful to be able to compare successful and unsuccessful efforts.

Organizations are both agents of change and major sources of societal stability. Dill (1965) notes:

> In countries like the United States and Canada, most of the nations of Western Europe, Australia, or Japan, business organizations are the most powerful. They provide the major source of employment and income and some of the major bases for determining social status. They decide in large measure what shall be produced and how much. (p. 1101)

In other societies, government organizations perform the same functions. Regardless of the form of the economy, organizations are the major decision makers for the priorities and actualities of the society.

There is another way in which organizations are important for the social structure. Since modern work is almost exclusively organizational work, and since total life styles are decreasingly influenced by the ascriptive components of age, sex, race, ethnicity, or other such factors, occupational roles and the interrelationships between these roles are a major component in determining the overall social structure. (For a discussion of this point, see Hall 1975.) The organizations set occupational rewards of all sorts.

Organizations are change agents in two ways. The first involves internal changes in respect to organizational membership, while the second involves direct attempts by organizations to intervene in the social system.

Internal Change and the Social Structure

Internal organizational changes can affect the social structure in two ways. The first is by changing membership patterns. If an organization alters its stance toward minority-group members, women, or the aging, there is a direct impact on the social structure. Moreover, by the hiring of more women or minority-group members (a condition usually brought about by such external pressures as affirmative action programs) the patterns of the surrounding communities are affected as needs for child-care facilities are increased or as more minority-group members move into the area. If the minority-group members are at anything other than the low-skill levels, residential patterns are affected, since ghetto residences are not sought by minority professionals or executives. Similarly, the importation of low-skill minority-group members has traditionally led to the creation of ghettos.

The second way in which internal changes affect the social structure is through altered patterns of work. Although it is unclear whether or not a person's attitude toward the job work affects his or her outlook on life, or vice versa, there is certainly a relationship. Thus, changes in the manner in which work is performed—such as through programs of participative management, job enlargement or enrichment, or through other such mechanisms—would appear to be related to other important social relationships. Alteration of superior-subordinate patterns, such as making them more egalitarian or by otherwise altering the reward structure, would appear to have an important carry-over effect for the society. This is said not on the basis of firm evidence, but rather on the basis of our knowledge of the power role of organizations in society.

Two additional aspects of the impact of organizations on their members and their relationship to the overall social structure deserve mention. While it is not clear whether a dull or exciting position in an organization leads to a dull or exciting life outside the organization, it is evident that a person's occupation has important consequences for other aspects of personal life. For example, political outlook, patterns of family life, and general life style have been shown to be linked to an individual's occupation. Organizations with occupations encouraging dissent and controversy, as opposed to conformity and acceptance of the status quo, would have members who carried this style of life outside the organization. Since organizations affect the way in which their various constituent occupations are oriented, there is an organizational effect on the way people view and act toward the world around them (Kohn 1971). This effect is balanced by nonorganizational factors as well, but the organization does make a difference. Here again, comparative research is needed to determine exactly how much membership in various forms of organizations contributes to the variance in people's approaches to life.

Voluntary Organizations The final point in this discussion involves organizations that are designed to have an impact on the behaviors and attitudes of their members. The voluntary organization, in most cases, is established to be a force affecting the lives and behaviors of its members. People belong to voluntary organizations because they believe in what the organization stands for and would like to see it promoted. (This ignores that element of voluntary-organization membership that is present for nonnormative reasons.) It is probably very safe to assume that the voluntary-organization membership of an individual is a good indicator of some of his or her salient values. Even when this assumption is made, however, the question remains as to whether the membership itself has any effect on individual attitudes and behaviors. The answer is that such memberships undoubtedly reinforce predispositions already present when the person joins the organization.

This answer is not very useful, however, since there are insufficient indications of the extent to which such memberships are balanced against other facts of the individual's life. Research into the impact of membership in religious organizations, for example, has led to largely inconclusive results regarding the impact of such membership as opposed to that of the person's place in the social stratification system, his or her occupation, place of origin, and so on. (Lenski 1963; see also Shuman 1971.) Without an extended discussion of the importance of such memberships vis-a-vis other important considerations, it is sufficient for our purposes here to note that voluntary-organization memberships have some consequences for the people involved, but it would appear that such consequences are not as strong as those of other conditions under which the person is living. Voluntary-organization memberships thus appear to be modifiers of attitudes and behaviors formed by individuals through their life histories.

THE ORGANIZATION AS A CHANGE AGENT

Besides affecting society (largely unintentionally) through their structuring of social life and impacts on members, organizations are also active participants in the social-change process. This can be most easily seen in the political arena, as organizations lobby and fight for legislation and rulings favorable to their own programs. A favorable decision for one organization leads to programs that in turn affect the society. Whenever a government agency is established to carry out a new program, it becomes a social-change agent. We will begin the analysis of change agents with this point, moving from this rather established, accepted form of social change to a consideration of organizations as revolutionary agents.

A classic example of the organization as a change agent is provided by Selznick's (1966) study of the Tennessee Valley Authority (TVA) during its formative years. In addition to its pertinence to the analysis of change, this study is also very important for its contribution to the topic of the environmental impact on the organization. There is a reciprocal relationship between organizations and their environments. Each affects the other as they interact.

The TVA Act was passed by the U.S. Congress in 1933. As Selznick notes:

> A great public power project was envisioned mobilizing the "by-product" of dams built for the purpose of flood control and navigation improvement on the Tennessee River and its tributaries. Control and operation of the nitrate properties, to be used for fertilizer production, was also authorized, although

this aspect was subordinated to electricity. . . . A new regional concept—the river basin as an integral unit—was given effect, so that a government agency was created which has a special responsibility neither national nor state-wide in scope. (p. 4–5)

That the TVA has had an effect on the physical environment is evident. Of greater interest for our purposes here is its effect on the social system into which it was placed. An important consideration in understanding the social effects of the TVA is the fact that the organization was designed to be decentralized. Not only were decisions within the organization to be made at the lowest reasonable levels with participation by members, but local organizations and even local citizens were also to be brought into the decision-making process. For example, the agricultural-extension services of the land-grant colleges were intimately involved with the TVA. This, of course, is one of the prime examples of a co-optation, or "the process of absorbing new elements into the leadership or policy-determining structure of an organization as a means of averting threats to its stability or existence" (p. 13).

Co-optation, however, is a two-way process. The organization is affected by the new elements brought into its decision-making process; Selznick documents the manner in which some activities of the TVA were deflected from the original goals because of the new elements in the system. At the same time, the co-optation process affects the system from which the elements were co-opted. The presence of the agricultural-extension element from the land-grant colleges gave this part of the local system much more strength than it had had in the past. The American Farm Bureau Federation was also brought into the process at an early point. In both these cases, the inclusion of one group was associated with the exclusion of another. Black colleges and non-Farm Bureau farm organizations either lost power or did not benefit to the degree that co-opted organizations did. In addition, the strength of the Farm Bureau in the decision-making process led to the exclusion from the area of other federal government farm programs. Regardless of their merits, these programs were therefore unavailable to the system. Selznick notes, "This resulted in the politically paradoxical situation that the eminently New Deal TVA failed to support agencies with which it shared a political communion, and aligned itself with the enemies of those agencies" (p. 263). This becomes a rather complex analysis when one considers the fact that the other government programs involved were also part of the same larger organization, so that internal politics in one large organization were affected by the external relationships of some of its component parts.

An organization like the TVA affects the surrounding social organization. Some elements prosper while others suffer. New social relationships arise as alliances among affected individuals and organizations are formed. Thus, an organization specifically designed to be a change agent is exactly that, but in ways that can be most inconsistent with the original intent of the planners. The dynamics of the interactions with the environment affect both the organization and its environment.

In a later reexamination of the study, Selznick (1966) notes that the TVA has recently been attacked by conservationists for strip mining. The need for coal for its power productions and the strength of those supporting an expansion of this function within the TVA has led to a further environmental impact. Selznick attributes the current state of the TVA to the internal struggles that occurred in its early history—struggles to obtain environmental support. Since such support is selective, a strong organization such as this rearranges the world around it. If the groups in power in the TVA see the need for a greater capacity for generating electrical power as more important than soil conservation, the internal decision-making process, affected as it is by external pressures, makes a further impact on the social and physical environment.

The Organizational Weapon   In another analysis of organizations as change agents, Selznick (1960) studied the Bolshevik revolution in Russia. Here he analyzes the nature and role of the "organizational weapon." In defining what he means, Selznick states:

> We shall speak of organizations and organizational practices as weapons when they are used by a power-seeking elite in a manner unrestrained by the constitutional order of the arena within which the contest takes place. In this usage, "weapon" is not meant to denote any political tool, but one torn from its normal context and unacceptable to the community as a legitimate mode of action. Thus the partisan practices used in an election campaign insofar as they adhere to the written and unwritten rules of the contest—are not weapons in this sense. On the other hand, when members who join an organization in apparent good faith are in fact the agents of an outside elite, then routine affiliation becomes "infiltration." (p. 2)

An important component of the organizational weapon is the "*distinctive competence to turn members of a voluntary association into disciplined and deployable political agents.*" (p. xii).

The Organization as the Requisite of Social Change   Before turning to some elements of Selznick's analysis, we must point out that the organizational weapon cannot be regarded as a tactic of the Bolsheviks alone. Indeed, it is the vital component of most major social changes and of change within the organization itself. In other words, in order to achieve change, *there must be organization.* This organization requires the kind of commitment to which Selznick refers. Spontaneous demonstrations or collective emotional responses may be sincere and well intended, but longer-lasting movements toward change must come about through the organizational mode. And Selznick's reference to "constitutionality" can be translated into the *offical* and accepted set of organizational arrangements that make up the "constitution" of any organization. The concern here is thus with the organizational weapon as it seeks to change any ongoing societal or organizational arrangement.

The scope of the organization as a weapon is determined by its aims. Even if the change sought is a limited one and one that will not upset the basic system under attack, the change agent still must be viewed as a weapon, although of lesser scope than one that seeks total organizational or societal change. The aim of Bolshevism was total societal change. The basic means of accomplishing the movement's goal was the "combat party." Cadres of dedicated men are a basic component of such parties. This dedication requires that the individuals be totally committed to the cause, insulated from other concerns, and absorbed in the movement. Once a core of dedicated personnel is available, the party must protect itself from internal dissension, banning power centers that might threaten the official leadership. The party must be capable of mobilization and manipulation; it must be protected from possible isolation from the people it hopes to convert and also from possible liquidation at the hands of the existing authorities; and it must struggle for power in every possible area of action. This struggle can take place through seeking official recognition, as well through conspiratorial or illegal practices. And at all times, the basic ideology must be kept at the forefront of the members' minds (pp. 72–73).

The operation of these principles can be seen in the history of the movement that Selznick carefully traces. This manifesto for an organizational weapon is potentially applicable at any point in history, in any social setting, and at either the total societal or more microcosmic levels. A revolt of junior high school students exhibits the same characteristics as the Bolshevik movement, and so does the history of early Christianity.

For our purposes, the important thing is not the cause being advanced, but rather the fact having a cause is not enough for social change. The cause must be organized if it is to be successful. The organization can be a successful change agent if it is capable of maintaining dedication and gaining power in the system. The specific means of gaining power will depend on the situation. Political or military power is successful only where it is relevant. Selznick says:

> We must conclude, therefore, that in the long view political combat plays only a tactical role. Great social issues such as those which divide communism and democracy are not decided by political combat, perhaps not even by military clashes. They are decided by the relative ability of the contending systems to win and to maintain enduring loyalties. Consequently, no amount of power and cunning in the realm of political combat can avail in the absence of measures which rise to the height of the times. (p. 333)

The implication is that the specific tactics used in the Bolshevik movement may not be effective in another setting, but that the need for a dedicated membership and the concern for power are central to the change process.

Societal Support   We have stressed the reciprocal nature of the relationship between an organization and its environment. This is seen in clear relief in the consideration of organizations as change agents. The basic processes are the same in all effective change situations: to be successful an organizational weapon must gain power and support in the society it is attempting to change. The pages of history are filled with abortive efforts that did not gather sufficient support from the society they were trying to change. The basic set of ideas underlying the change effort must therefore be compatible—or become compatible—with the values of the population as a whole. These values of the wider community can be altered during the change process to become more congruent with those of the change agent. At the same time, the change agent itself can become altered as it seeks support from the wider community.

The importance of this form of support can be extrapolated from Joseph Gusfield's (1955, 1963) analysis of the Women's Christian Temperance Union. This organization was highly successful in its attempts to change society through the passage of legislation prohibiting the sale of alcoholic beverages. Its tactics were appropriate for the values of the times, and it succeeded in mobilizing support from a sufficiently large segment of the population. But later, as it became evident that Prohibition was not accomplishing what it was intended to do—and indeed had some unintended consequences that have lasted until the present—and as the originally supportive society changed, the WCTU was faced with a decision regarding its future. It could have altered its stance toward alcohol to keep it in line with the prevailing opinions or maintained its position in favor of total abstinence. The latter course was selected as the result of decisions made within the organization. The consequences of the decision were to isolate the movement from the population, reducing it to virtual ineffectiveness as a force in the wider society.

It is difficult to predict what might have happened if the stance had been altered to one of temperance rather than abstinence. It well might be that the whole antialcohol movement was one whose time had passed. It might also be that the WCTU would have had a greater educational and social impact if its position had shifted with the times. At any rate, what was once an important social movement became a small, socially insignificant organization.

The social system around it thus affects the social-change agent as much as it does any other form of organization. While such organizations can appear to be revolutionary, deviant, martyred, or to fit any other emotion-laden category, the fact remains that they are organizations. The critical aspect is the acceptance of the organization by society. This is obviously important for any organization, since to survive it must receive support in one form or another, but for these change-oriented ones it is even more so. Unfortunately (or fortunately in some cases), because organizational analysts, decision makers, and politicans have not figured out exactly how to determine when an idea's time has come, the organization embarking on a change mission is in a precarious position at best.

There are other, more subtle ways in which organizations are change agents. As Perrow (1970b) notes:

> We tend to forget, or neglect, the fact that organizations have an enormous potential for affecting the lives of all who come into contact with them. They control or can activate a multitude of resources, not just land and machinery and employees, but police, governments, communications, art, and other

areas, too. That is, an organization, as a legally constituted entity, can ask for police protection and public prosecution, can sue, and can hire a private police force with considerably wider latitude and power than an individual can command. It can ask the courts to respond to requests and make legal rulings. It can petition for changes in other areas of government—zoning laws, fair-trade laws, consumer labeling, and protection and health laws. It determines the content of advertising, the art work in its products and packages, the shape and color of its buildings. It can move out of a community, and it selects the communities in which it will build. It can invest in times of imminent recession or it can retrench; support or fight government economic policies or fair employment practices. In short, organizations generate a great deal of power that may be used in a way not directly related to producing goods and services or to survival. (pp. 170–71)

Rather obviously, the power potential of organizations is often used to thwart change, as will be seen in the next section. Even when an organization is an active change agent, if the change is accomplished, the organization tends then to resist further changes. The labor union movement, which was once considered revolutionary, is now viewed by some as reactionary. National revolutions lead to established governments that in turn are attacked as opponents of social progress. Industries that alter the composition of a society resist new technologies and social patterns.

Constraints Organizations do not change the society around them at will. All the environmental influences on organizations also constrain it as a change agent. This point is most graphically seen in the case of organizations in developing nations. If development is a national goal, then almost all organizations in such a society are designed to be change agents. A basic problem, however, is that the organizational forms that work in developed societies do not necessarily work in the case of those just developing. For example, Milne (1970) notes that there is a strong tendency for superiors not to delegate authority to subordinates. This is seen as a result of the lack of shared values among the different ranks, differing conceptions of authority, incompetence or lack of training among the subordinates, and the fear of loss of opportunity to earn income corruptly. Similarly, subordinates seem unwilling to accept power. Studies in the Philippines and Latin America have noted the unwillingness of middle-level administrators to make decisions. Milne states that in addition to the shortage of skills, deficiencies in training, lack of resources, and poor communications, the general culture precludes effective adminstration. Loyalty to the organization, for example, is an alien notion and thus is not present to supplement the formal channels. Milne concludes that effective administration cannot be achieved unless the general cultural conditions also change.

Because of the cultural and other environmental constraints, organizations in developing societies must take a different form from those in more developed situations. It is generally suggested that such an organization must operate in a less formalized manner, taking into account the particular environment in which it is trying to operate.

But despite the constraints, organizations in developing societies do affect those societies. They do things that were not done before, in terms of yielding goods and services and arranging social relationships, and this simple fact alone affects the surrounding society. Not all such societies will become Westernized or bureaucratized, but they will be different from what they were before the advent of organizations. As in many other situations, the exact direction and extent of the organizational impact is not known, but the impact itself can be seen on the immediate alterations of the social fabric. A more subtle effect can occur between generations. Each succeeding generation will tend to be more accepting of the presence of organizations, creating generation gaps and also altering the organizational environment. A previously hostile environment may become accepting. Here again, the reciprocity of the organizational-societal relationship can be seen.

Before we turn to the discussion of organizations as resisters of change, it should be reiterated that organizations have a wide variety of impacts on the environment. These range from the exciting examples of revolution or pollution to the more mundane but equally important matters of establishing and maintaining equilibrium in the system. In a comprehensive analysis, organizations must be viewed as a major stabilizing factor in society. Each kind of output has an impact on society, from the production of goods to the development of ideas. Since an organizational society contains a multitude of values, it must also be recognized that what is of value to one segment of the society may be violently opposed by another segment. Thus, organizations that provide drugs or prostitutes are still organizations and can only be understood as such.

Because organizations do have outputs that in either intent or effect are opposed to those of other organizations, another point is raised about the organizational impact on society. Organizations are the source of much of the conflict in society. While individual conflict in the form of fights, debates, shoot-outs, and so on are the stuff of which movies and newspaper headlines are made, it is conflict between organizations that really alters the fabric of society. The ability to wage a successful conflict is largely tied to the organizational capacities of the parties involved. The outcome of a conflict is usually alteration of the situation that existed before the conflict. Since organizations are such an important component of conflict in society, it follows that organizations are central to social change through this mechanism.

ORGANIZATIONS AS RESISTERS OF CHANGE

An earlier section began with the point that organizations are a major structuring component in society. This structuring takes place through the work roles of the members of the organizations and the values that organizational membership can impart. Organizations are a means of structuring the activities of the members. This in and of itself is a structuring element. Since our concern in this chapter is with change, it is important to go beyond the basic fact of organizational contributions to social stability. Organizations also actively resist change. This resistance is directed toward change introduced from outside the organization. The organization attempts to protect itself. Obviously, changes that are not important to the organization will not bring an organizational response.

Again, organizations by their very nature are conservative. This is seen in the political stances taken and in economic policies. When the focus is shifted to how the organization itself operates, the point becomes even more clear. *Organizations operate conservatively regardless of whether they are viewed as radical or as reactionary by the general population.* Seymour Martin Lipset's (1950) analysis of populist rural socialism in Saskatchewan, Canada provides an example of this point. In 1944, the Cooperative Commonwealth Federation (CCF) came to power in the province. The objective was "the social ownership of all resources and the machinery of wealth production to the end that we may establish a Cooperative Commonwealth in which the basic principle regulating production, distribution and exchange will be the supplying of human needs instead of the making of profits" (p. 130). This aim has been only partially realized. One reason has been continued political opposition to the movement; another, consistent with the argument here, is that the movement itself apparently became more conservative as power was achieved. An additional important consideration is the fact that the new socialist government utilized the existing government structures in attempting to carry out its program. In explanation Lipset notes:

Trained in the traditions of a laissez-faire government and belonging to conservative social groups, the civil service contributes significantly to the social inertia which blunts the changes a new radical government can make. Delay in initiating reforms means that the new government becomes absorbed in the process of operating the old institutions. The longer a new government delays making changes, the more responsible it becomes for the old practices and the harder it is to make the changes it originally desired to institute. (pp. 272–73)

The reason for this blunting is quite simple. The new ruling cabinet had to rely on the system already in operation.

The administratively insecure cabinet ministers were overjoyed at the friendly response they obtained from the civil servants. *To avoid making administrative blunders* [emphasis added] that would injure them in the eyes of the public and the party, the ministers began to depend on the civil servants. As one cabinet minister stated in an interview, "I would have been lost if not for the old members of my staff. I'm only a beginner in this work. B_____ has been at it for twenty years. If I couldn't go to him for advice, I couldn't have done a thing. Why now (after two years in office) I am only beginning to find my legs and make my own decisions. . . . I have not done a thing for two years without advice." (p. 263)

It is important to note that the aims of the movement can be blunted without malice or intent. It is not a personal matter, but an organizational one. Certainly, personal motivations can enter the picture in an important way, but the crucial factor is that the new leaders did not understand the organizations they were to head. The organization itself contained rules and procedures that had to be learned along the way, so that the organization became the instrument that deflected the party in power from its goals.

The organization trains its members to follow a system for carrying out its activities. It would require a complete resocialization before the takeover of a new party if this sort of thing were to be prevented. This, of course, is impossible in government organizations. An alternative practice would be to purge the entire system, replacing the original members with ones of the appropriate ideology. This would in essence mean that the organization would have to start de novo and that nothing would be done until the organizational roles were learned and linkages to the society were established. Since the organization has clients and customers, as well as a broader constituency in the case of government organizations, the expectations of nonmembers would also have to be altered. For these reasons, the likelihood of success is slim, regardless of the technique selected. The tendency for the organizaton to operate as it has in the past is very strong.

Most government organizations in Western democracies operate with a civil service system. An extension of Lipset's analysis suggests, therefore, that changes in the party in power will have less impact on the operation of the government agencies than political rhetoric would suggest. In non-Western societies, the same principles seem to hold. The potentiality for major social change through change in government is therefore modified by the organizational realities that exist. Since social systems do change, of course, the organization must be viewed as something that does not change overnight, but will change with time. The changes that occur may not be in phase with the change in political philosophy of the government in power. A "liberal" party in power may over time be able to introduce more of its adherents into the civil service system. These people can remain in office after a change in the party in power, blunting the efforts of a conservative party, but at the same time increasing the "liberalness" of the agencies involved. In whatever political direction a state, county, or nation is moving, organizational conservatism will remain an important consideration.

Government organizations are not the only example of organizational conservatism. In the United States, automobile manufacturers persisted in making large, fuel-inefficient automobiles, despite several kinds of warnings that the market for these cars would soon dwindle. While much higher profits were made with the large cars in the short run, rapidly shrinking markets soon brought financial losses and layoffs for workers. Janowitz (1969) has documented the manner in which urban educational systems persisted in maintaining traditional academic programs while the population around the schools shifted and the needs of students changed. In later analyses we will examine some of the reasons why organizations are resistant to change. Their very resistance is a source, desirable or not, of social stability.

SOME SPECIFIC ORGANIZATIONAL IMPACTS

Up to this point our analysis of the impact of organizations on society has been rather general. In this section we will consider some specific research findings to demonstrate the variety of ways in which organizations have societal repercussions.

Organizations serve the interests of individuals or groups. These controlling interests shape the directions which organizations take. In an historical analysis, Antonio (1979) examined the organizational context of the Roman Empire. According to Antonio, the Roman bureaucracy was controlled by the ruling class whose orientation was to dominate the masses. Rather than emphasizing production of goods and services, the emphasis on domination "preserved, and even intensified, conditions which contributed to the erosion and eventual destruction of the socio-economic substructure of the bureaucracy" (p. 906). Antonio notes that the Roman organization was successful in achieving domination. This study also suggests that contemporary organizational forms have the same potential, since the large modern bureaucracy is largely closed to external scrutiny, much as the Roman version was.

The implication in the Antonio study is that the bureaucracy serves the interest of the ruling elite. This has been a point of contention for organizational analysts for some time. In 1932 Berle and Means claimed that the ownership of private corporations had become so widely distributed that ownership per se no longer was of central importance in the control of organizations. Control was passed to corporate management, which in turn appointed people to boards of directors. Boards of directors were viewed as tools of management, rather than of the stockholders.

Aldrich (1979) has noted that this point of view has now been severely challenged on several grounds. First, there is some evidence that families such as the Mellons, who have controlling interests in Gulf Oil, Alcoa, Koppers Company, and Carborundum Company in the manufacturing sector, also have controlling interests in the First Boston Corporation, the General Reinsurance Corporation, and the Mellon National Bank and Trust Company in the financial sector (Zeitlin 1947). The Mellon National Bank, in turn, owns almost 7 percent of Jones and Laughlin Steel. The Rockefeller family has similar points of linkage among financial institutions and insurance companies. Patterns of interlock like these have also been found outside the United States. Aldrich (1979) suggests that while there is not direct evidence that such family control has direct economic implications, the fact of family ownership indicates the potential for organizational control.

There is a remarkable degree of interlock among the boards of directors of corporations. This means that members of the board of directors of one corporation are likely to serve on the boards of other corporations. Such interlocks are believed to give a corporation access to capital and to co-opt or control sources of pressure in the environment. Pennings (1980b) states:

> We have investigated one aspect of the 797 largest American corporations: the relationships among the organizations' strategic interdependence on firms in their environment, their economic effectiveness, and their propensity to form interlocking directorates. Our survey of these organizations showed that only 62 of them have no interlocks with the remaining 735 and that financial firms are disproportionately active in interlocking. (p. 188)

In general, the more interlocks the more effective was the organization. A specific finding of interest in the Pennings study was that firms that are well interlocked with the financial community enjoyed lower interest rates for their debts than their more poorly interlocked fellow firms. Burt, Christman, and Kilburn (1980) have found similar relationships between interlocks and profitability.

There are two basic ways in which findings such as these can be viewed. They can be viewed as sound management. Interlocks, with or without family ties, are a means to achieve a competitive edge. The other view is conspiritorial. Such interlocks permit a ruling class to maintain its power and wealth at the expense of the rest of the population. If the first view is taken, the impact on society is beneficial; if the second is taken, the impact is detrimental. In my opinion a position between the extremes seems most warranted, with both benefits and harm resulting from these arrangements. Analysts who have looked carefully at these findings have not demonstrated a direct societal effect. The implications drawn result largely from the political orientation of the analyst.

There are some additional interpretations of the impact of corporate power in society. Useem (1979) notes that an "inner group" of business elites are selected to assist in the governance of other institutions, such as governmental advisory boards, philanthropic organizations, colleges and universities, and so on. The same pattern of interlocking directorates is found in the noncorporate sector of society. Useem concludes that this permits the promotion of the more general interests of the entire capitalist class. Again, this political interpretation could be challenged by the claim that these institutional interlocks are merely a means by which able people are brought to the boards of directors of organizations that provide benefits for society. Whichever interpretation is taken cannot deny the importance or presence of the interlocks.

In yet another examination of the impact of business corporations on society, Hicks, Friedland, and Johnson (1978) examined the consequences of the presence of large business corporations and labor unions for governmental redistribution to the poor. The presence of business corporations was negatively related to such redistribution, while the presence of labor unions was positive.

Organizations are thus not inert masses in society. They act in their own or their owners' or members' behalf. As the Hicks et al. findings suggest, it is not just business firms which can have an important impact. The studies most recently described all share the political orientation that there is a ruling elite behind business firms. Conclusions in the other directions are equally political.

Government organizations also affect society by more than just the coordination or services that they provide. Altheide and Johnson (1980) have documented the manner in which government agencies present themselves to the public, making statements of "fact" which may well be self-serving interpretations. "Official information" in forms as varied as crime rates or inflation indices can be used to serve the purposes of office holders and civil servants.

Moving to a very different direction, Needleman and Needleman (1979) have suggested that organizations can also contribute to crime. They suggest that some organizations are "crime-coercive." These organizations force their members or customers to engage in illegal activities. Farberman (1975) found, for example, that some franchised automobile dealers are forced into illegal practices such as kickbacks and unrecorded income to survive financially. Needleman and Needleman propose that there are also crime-facilitative organizations. Fire insurance companies facilitate the "torching" of buildings by arsonists. The arsonist owns the building, which is rundown and unsalable. After it burns, the arsonist collects the insurance on the building. The insurance companies facilitate the arsonist, but do not benefit themselves. More vigorous investigations of slum ownership and insurance patterns could be conducted, but apparently insurance companies believe that vigorous background investigation might offend or drive away legitimate customers. Organizations can thus contribute to crime. In the case of arson, of course, there is the potential for the loss of life, making it more than a simple financial matter.

It is well recognized that organizations attempt to shape the tastes of the public. The advertising industry is devoted to such activities. Perrow (1979) has analyzed research regarding the popular music industry and concludes that organizations in this industry, such as recording companies, try to stabilize public tastes through controls over the creative process and marketing. The organization makes moves for its own behalf, but perhaps not that of the society.

The research which has been cited in these recent pages has largely been critical of organizations and particularly of business organizations. The field of organizational analysis has moved from a rather unquestioning acceptance of organizations as nonpolitical actors without economic and social implications for society. Benson (1977) labels this the administrative-technical orientation. Some contemporary analysts have moved to the opposite extreme, sighting the ruling capitalist elite behind every organizational bush. In the presentation here, the attempt has been to provide a balanced interpretation not by ignoring the harmful effects of organizations on societies, but by also considering alternative interpretations of the patterns which have been identified.

Organizations, at least in some cases, apparently consider what they are doing to the society around them. It appears that corporate philanthropy is associated with patterns of corporate interlocks. Thus, the same empirical condition which serves as the basis for conclusions regarding control by an elite and for community power structures also contributes to corporate philanthropy. In this regard, Alexander and Buchholz (1978) found little relationship between organizational performance and corporate social responsibility. Local conditions apparently have a strong influence on the direction that organizational actions take.

The impact of organizations on the societies in which they are imbedded is great. There is little likelihood of this condition being reversed. Morris (1972) has pointed out that organizational growth is organizational success. Even in a no-growth economy, private and public organizations try to grow at one another's expense. Growth is a major way in which organizational decision makers or elites demonstrate their contributions to the organization.

In addition to their size, there is another factor that gives contemporary organizations their unprecedented role in contemporary society: the modern organization is a *legal* entity, just like the individual person. In a perceptive set of essays, Coleman (1974) has indicated that legality is granted by the state, itself a legal creation. While the individual is given a set of rights and responsibilities by the state, rights and responsibilities are extended to organizations. These rights, coupled with size, give organizations an enormous amount of power within the state. Coleman also points out that the state or government is more comfortable dealing with other organizations than with individual persons, and thus tends to provide more preferential treatment to organizations in areas as diverse as taxation or rights to privacy.

The recognition of organizations as legal entities is not a trivial matter. Organizations, rather than individuals, can be held responsible for certain actions. Air New Zealand, for example, was held responsible for a crash that killed 257 people (*New York Times* 1981). A new flight plan was put into effect which led to a collision course with a volcano. The crew had not been informed. The judge in the case also accused airline officials of attempting to conceal their mistakes. Swigert and Farrell (1980–81) analyzed the case of the Ford Motor Company which was charged with homicide. They found that the mass media shifted its orientation from the recognition of harm based on mechanical defects to an attribution of nonrepentance on the part of the offender. Swigert and Farrell concluded that a shift in public attitudes had occurred in which an organization was believed to have engaged in criminality in a form previously reserved for individuals. The fact that Ford was found not guilty does not alter the importance in the shift in public attitude.

The consideration of the legal status of organizations raises an issue which will be considered directly in the next chapter—can organizations be considered as objects or entities in their own right, apart from the individuals which comprise them? This is a complex question which involves more than their legal status.

Organizations Across Societies: The Multinational Corporation

The analysis of the impact of organizations thus far has moved from the individual to the society. It is also clear that organizations can have important implications across societies. This is easily seen in the myriad accounts of international spy rings and terrorist groups and in the case of extractive industries which take natural resources away from developing nations and give little in return, aside from low wages to workers. The multinational corporation is less visible, but perhaps more important in the long run.

There have been international organizations for probably as long as there have been nations. The Roman Empire and the Catholic Church exemplify this as do the imperialist organizations that were at the heart of the British Empire. The multinational corporation is a different matter, however. This organizational form involves much more than simply having branch offices in more than one nation. In the case of the multinational firm, the total operation of things as diverse as the production and sales of automobiles or chocolate candy is in the hands of a subsidiary or equal firm in another nation. As McMillan (1973) suggests, multinational firms are not just the outgrowth of developments in the United States. German, Dutch, British, French, Swedish, and Japanese firms are an important part of this international scene.

There are many explanations for the emergence of the multinational corporation. All have a strong element of truth. The first such explanation is imperialism, or the attempt to expand corporate markets and reduce costs through the use of economic power over a weaker nation. The nation could be weaker in terms of pay scales and thus provide cheap labor; it could be weaker in terms of political dependence and thus give corporations of the more powerful nations tax breaks and incentives. Heilbroner (1974) sees technology as the key to the growth of multinationals. Mass-production systems and computer information handling have pushed all societies to larger and larger units of production. An inevitable consequence of this is expansion to overseas markets and production facilities.

Toynbee (1974) offers another explanation: multinational firms overcome the problem that sovereignty is dispersed over 140 local states, many of which can have antiquated political arrangements. Toynbee believes that because local economic independence is impossible for many nations, the multinational firm could become the dominant economic and political form of organization, superseding the traditional nation-state.

McMillan's (1973) explanation is more complex. He suggests that the multinational corporation is a consequence of corporate choices made to implement product-market strategy: as corporations begin to produce a complex range of products, these are to be sold in different markets through multiple channels of distribution. McMillan's explanation, which, as will be seen later, is solidly within contemporary organizational theory, suggests that multinational corporations are in essence inevitable. Even in a no-growth economic situation, the desire to cut costs or maintain the share of the market would lead to international expansion.

Each of the above explains part of the international growth of organizations. Each also explains why organizations in general seek to expand their influence over the environment as a means of protecting their flanks and expanding their operations.

Multinational firms have several kinds of impacts on their host countries and governments. Clegg and Dunkerly (1980) claim:

> It must be recognized that multi-national organizations are different from the kind of organization traditionally studied by organizational theorists. Their size and complexity and their capacity for capital investment in countries of their choice makes them able to control their environment in hitherto unknown ways. The fact of being independent of national governments in many instances enable them to pursue their goals in a ruthless and unaccountable manner. (pp. 390–91)

Clegg and Dunkerly go on to note instances in which the Ford Motor Company influenced many governments to pass laws or to provide investment capital in order to attract Ford installations. The most dramatic instance of multinational influence came in Chile in 1970 when the Marxist Allende government was in power. In addition to the United States's CIA, multinational firms such as ITT and Ford played a significant part in the downfall of that government.

Clegg and Dunkerly also note several other consequences of multinational corporations. Considerations of what is best for a national economy are secondary to considerations of what is best for the corporation as a whole. Although the multinational is frequently welcomed in areas of high unemployment, their presence can create a situation of extremely high dependence on the firm. Once the local economy is dependent on such a firm, the firm itself has a great deal of power. The multinational is also often able to avoid paying taxes at the rate paid by domestic corporations through reporting profits in countries with lower tax rates and other forms of financial shifts.

There is an aura of inevitability in most discussions of multinational firms. This aura is generally warranted, but there are conditions which could drastically affect the operations of multinational firms. National revolutions or elections can turn the host country to the point that all industries are nationalized or all foreign investments confiscated. The case of Iran and the United States is a graphic illustration here. Not all multinational ventures are successful. Nonetheless, the multinational corporation appears to be an increasing part of the international scene and will continue to influence international events.

Society and Organizational Theory

The review of the impact of organizations on our lives is essentially depressing. Yet, there are organizational theorists who see organizations as the only way by which desirable ends such as peace, prosperity, and social justice can be achieved. Etzioni (1968) uses organizations as the basis for his call for an "active" society. Based on his analysis of French society, Crozier (1973) sees the modern organization, if it can be democratic, as the means by which the now less rigid populace can make choices by which creativity and innovation can be captured. This kind of optimism must be tempered by the realism seen in Child (1976) that organizations will undoubtedly continue to grow, bureaucratize, and centralize. The pressure for participation and democratization appears to run counter to what are perhaps inevitable organizational processes.

Organizational theory cannot, as its present state of development, provide prescriptions for peace, prosperity, and social justice. It can point out those organizational conditions and practices which lead toward or away from those ends. It also can point out the contradictions which exist in organizations, since a move toward prosperity might be a move against peace. Most organizational theory does not concern itself with such issues, focusing instead on more micro matters within organizations. In the analysis to be presented here, we will try to demonstrate that organizations themselves contain a set of contradictions which interfere with organizational attempts to achieve their version of peace, prosperity, and justice.

Brown (1978) has noted: "The more we are able to create worlds that are morally cogent and politically viable, the more we are able, as workers and as citizens, to manage or resist" (p. 378). An understanding of organizations is imperative if we are to understand and be involved in the society around us.

SUMMARY AND CONCLUSIONS

The purpose of this chapter has been a simple one—to indicate the importance of organizations at every level of human life. Thus, the individual, classes of individuals, the community, the society, and the international order were examined in terms of the manner in which organizations impact upon them. Organizational analysis is dull until the crucial and central role of organizations is understood. If organizations are understood, then individuals have a tool by which they can deal with the reality that they face.

The astute reader has no doubt noticed that the subject matter of this book, organizations, has not been defined or delineated. It is to this that we now turn.

2

On the Nature and Types of Organizations

This chapter will first define the subject matter—organizations. It will then consider the issue of whether or not organizations can be considered as realities in their own right, involving something more than the individuals of which they are comprised. Finally, the issue of typologies or types of organizations will be considered.

Definitions

Discussions of definitions can be quite deadly. This one may be deadly, also, but it is necessary. Although some writers (for example, March and Simon 1958, p. 1) argue that definitions of organizations do not serve much purpose, a more reasonable approach would appear to be that definitions provide a basis for understanding the phenomena to be studied. Here we will consider the definitions developed by some classical writers in the field and then offer our own approach to the subject.

Weber   Like any other field of study, and like organizations themselves, organizational analysis has a tradition. The tradition centers heavily on Max Weber, who is known for his analyses of bureaucracy and authority, topics which will be considered later, but he also concerned himself with the more general definitions of organizations. Weber first distinguishes the "corporate group" from other forms of social organization (Weber 1947). The corporate group involves: "a social relationship which is either closed or limits the admission of outsiders by rules, . . . so far as its order is enforced by the action of specific individuals whose regular function this is, of a chief or 'head' and usually also an administrative staff" (pp. 145–46).

This aspect of the definition contains a number of elements requiring further discussion, since they are basic to most other such definitions. In the first place, organizations involve social relationships. That is, individuals interact within the organization. However, as the reference to closed or limited boundaries suggests, these individuals are not simply in random contact. The organization (corporate group) includes parts of the population and excludes others. The organization itself thus has a boundary. A major component of this definition, the idea of order, further differentiates organizations from other social entities. Interaction patterns do not simply arise; a structuring of interaction is imposed by the organization itself. This part of the definition also suggests that organizations contain a hierarchy of authority and a division of labor in carrying out their functions. Order is enforced with specific personnel designated to perform this function.

To the idea of the corporate group, Weber adds some additional criteria for organizations. In organizations, interaction is "associative" rather than "communal" (pp. 136–39). This differentiates the organization from other social entities, such as the family, which share the other, aforementioned characteristics of the corporate group. Weber also notes that organizations carry out continuous purposive activities of a specified kind (pp. 151–152). Thus, organizations transcend the lives of their members, and have goals, as "purposive activities" suggests. Organizations are designed to do something. This idea of Weber's has been retained by most organizational analysts.

Weber's definition has served as the basis for many others, in part because it is close to reality. His focus is basically on legitimate interaction patterns among organizational members as they pursue goals and engage in activities.

Barnard   A different focus has been taken by Chester Barnard and his followers. While in agreement with Weber on many points, Barnard stresses a different basis for organizations. His basic definition of an organization is "a system of consciously coordinated activities or forces of two or more persons" (Barnard 1938, p. 73), that is, activity accomplished through conscious, deliberate, and purposeful coordination. Organizations require communications, a willingness on the part of members to contribute, and a common purpose among them. Barnard stresses the role of the individual. It is they who must communicate, be motivated, and make decisions. While Weber emphasizes the system, Barnard is concerned with members of the system. The relevance and implications of these contrasting approaches will be taken up later.

Organizations and Social Organization

One of the major problems in discussing or thinking about organizations is that the term is so similar to the broader term of "social organization." Most analysts conceive of social organization as the "networks of social relations and the shared orientations . . . often referred to as the social structure and culture, respectively" (Blau and Scott 1962, p. 4). Social organization is the broader set of relationships and processes of which organizations are a part. The analysis of social organization can be at the macro or total-societal level or at the micro, or interpersonal or intergroup, level. Experimental analyses of dyads or triads, for example, contribute to the understanding of social organization. Organizations, as we are using the term here, are part of the more general social organization, being affected by it and, reciprocally, affecting it in turn (see Coleman 1974).

Other Definitions   Some writers have attempted to alleviate these terminological problems by adding the adjective "complex," "large-scale," or "formal" as a prefix to organizations. As Peter M. Blau and W. Richard Scott (1962), for example, note:

> Since formal organizations are often very large and complex, some authors refer to them as "large-scale" or as "complex" organizations. But we have eschewed these terms as misleading in two respects. First, organizations vary in size and complexity, and using these variables as defining criteria would result in such odd expressions as a "small large-scale organization" or a "very complex complex organization." Second, although formal organizations often become very large and complex, their size and complexity do not rival those of the social organization of a modern society, which includes such organizations and their relations with one another in addition to other nonorganizational patterns. (Perhaps the complexity of formal organizations is so much emphasized because it is man-made, whereas the complexity of societal organization has slowly emerged, just as the complexity of modern computers is more impressive than that of the human brain. Complexity by design may be more conspicuous than complexity by growth or evolution.) (p. 7)

While few would argue with Blau and Scott's points regarding the difficulties in the use of "complex" or "large-scale," the same criticism can be made of "formal" as a prefix. Organizations also vary in their formalization, and we would thus have to talk about more-or-less-formal formal organizations, which is not a great leap forward. With these considerations in mind, the simple term "organization" will be used here. "Social organization" will refer to the broader context.

The discussion becomes more concrete when we consider Amitai Etzioni's and W. Richard Scott's definitions and examples. Etzioni (1964) states:

> Organizations are social units (or human groupings) deliberately constructed and reconstructed to seek specific goals. Corporations, armies, schools, hospitals, churches, and prisons are included; tribes, classes, ethnic groups, and families are excluded. Organizations are characterized by: (1) divisions of labor, power and communication responsibilities, divisions which are not

randomly or traditionally patterned, but deliberately planned to enhance the realization of specific goals; (2) the presence of one or more power centers which control the concerted efforts of the organization and direct them toward its goals; these power centers also continuously review the organiztion's performance and repattern its structure, where necessary, to increase its efficiency; (3) substitution of personnel, i.e., unsatisfactory persons can be removed and others assigned their tasks. The organization can also recombine its personnel through transfer and promotion. (p. 3)

Scott's (1964) definition contains some additional elements. He says:

... organizations are defined as collectivities ... that have been established for the pursuit of relatively specific objectives on a more or less continuous basis. It should be clear, ... however, that organizations have distinctive features other than goal specificity and continuity. These include relatively fixed boundaries, a normative order, authority ranks, a communication system, and an incentive system which enables various types of participants to work together in the pursuit of common goals. (p. 488)

This definition appears to correspond quite well with reality. Two problems are evident, however, in this and the other definitions: the place of goals in the nature of organizations and the issue of the distinctiveness of boundaries.

The issue of goals is a critical one in organizational analysis (see Mohr 1973 and Hannan and Freeman 1977b for contrasting approaches to the goal issue). Goals will be considered in depth later in this analysis, but at this point several considerations should be noted. First, there are many activities in organizations that are hardly goal related by any stretch of the imagination. Some activities are sheerly administrative, such as filling out forms which assure that the organization is complying with some set of government regulations. Other activities are sheerly social, such as people idly chatting over coffee. Still other activities are reactions to pressures on the organization from outside, such as designing automobile engines which deliver fewer pollutants into the atmosphere as a result of government pressures.

Secondly, goals can be considered to be reifications or as Simon (1964) notes: "treating it [goals] as a superindividual entity having an existence and behavior independent of the behavior of its members" (p. 2). The analysis here accepts such reification as necessary and correct. Interestingly, Simon then goes on to note:

In the decision-making situations of real life, a course of action, to be acceptable, must satisfy a whole set of requirements or constraints. Sometimes one of these requirements is singled out and referred to as the goal of the action. But the choice of one of the constraints, from many, to a large extent is arbitrary. For many purposes it is more meaningful to refer to the whole set of requirements as the (complex) goal of the action. This conclusion applies both to individual and organizational decision-making (p. 7).

Simon is suggesting, and I agree, that goals serve as constraints on decision making. In this analysis we will consider them as independent of the human actors in the organization. The final aspect of goals to be considered here should be evident from the fact that we are using the term "goals" in the plural. Organizations have multiple goals. For the most part, these multiple goals also tend to be contradictory. Thus, issues such as quality versus quantity, teaching versus research, and so on are part of the very fabric of organizations.

The problem of the distinctiveness of organizational boundaries is interesting in its own right and raises an additional critical issue for organizations. The boundary issue can be exemplified by the example of the local political party. The party organization frequently has a small paid staff to answer phones, collect mail, and so on. The true power, however, belongs to nonpaid members. During election campaigns, membership in the organization swells as people are enlisted to make phone calls, distribute literature, and make speeches. The addition of voluntary and part-time personnel throws the issue of the boundary up in the air. This is most easily seen in the case of voluntary organizations, but the boundary issue also is problematic in the nonvoluntary situation. For example, the company that manufactured the computer which is used in my university has personnel permanently assigned to the university facility. In many ways, they are more a part of the university than the computer manufacturer. (They have a better place to park than I do.) The boundary thus is not something that is totally impermeable.

The notion of boundary also suggests that there is something outside of the organization, namely, its environment. Organizational theory is currently in the throes of an almost overwhelming emphasis on the environment. This emphasis will be critically evaluated at a later point. Here it is sufficient to note that the environment of organizations is truly critically important. The conception of environment to be used here includes everything "outside of" or beyond the boundary of a particular organization. The social environment of organizations, including other organizations, is of major concern, although the physical environment is perhaps more important than most analysts have noted. The State University of New York at Albany is affected by climate more than a comparable university in a more moderate climate. The climate interacts with the social environment, of course, since fuel costs are affected by international relationships and the operations of petroleum firms.

Environmental factors affect organizations from two directions. First, environmental factors are a major part of an organization's input. The organization, as described in the definitions above, then does something to or with this input, producing an output. The output goes back into the environment, thus affecting the organization as the output is consumed, utilized, and evaluated in the environment (this "systems"-like approach follows Thompson 1967 and Katz and Kahn 1978). Both organizational outputs and inputs also affect the environment, of course.

With all of these considerations in mind, the definition of organizations to be used in this analysis can now be stated. *An organization is a collectivity with a relatively identifiable boundary, a normative order, ranks of authority, com-munications systems, and membership-coordinating systems; this collectivity exists on a relatively continuous basis in an environment and engages in activities that are usually related to a set of goals.*

This is a cumbersome definition. The discussion thus far has indicated the reasons for this. Organizations are complex entities that contain a series of elements and are affected by many diverse factors. To convey an understanding of the nature and consequences of these internal and external factors is the task of the remaining chapters of this book.

Some Other Organizational Characteristics

The definition that was developed is an attempt to get at the substance of organizations. As such it is designed to be comprehensive and inclusive. At the same time it does not reveal certain organizational attributes which are important for our consideration.

Rothschild-Witt's (1979) work provides a useful overview of organizational characteristics. Her work was intended to demonstrate the critical differences between traditional bureaucratic organizations, the dominant form in Western society, with alternative or collectivist organizations. Her comparison, shown in Table 2-1 permits an overview of most of the major organizational characteristics which will be considered in this analysis. Most of the present analysis will be concerned with the traditional bureaucratic side of her distinctions.

The analysis thus far has emphasized the organization as a whole. As will be seen, it is reasonable to do this. It is also reasonable to consider

Table 2-1   Comparisons of Two Ideal Types of Organization

Dimensions	*Bureaucratic Organization*	*Collectivist-Democratic Organization*
1. Authority	1. Authority resides in individuals by virtue of incumbency in office and/or expertise; hierarchal organization of offices. Compliance is to universal fixed rules as these are implemented by office incumbents.	1. Authority resides in the collectivity as a whole; delegated, if at all, only temporarily and subject to recall. Compliance is to the consensus of the collective which is always fluid and open to negotiation.
2. Rules	2. Formalization of fixed and universalistic rules; calculability and appeal of decisions on the basis of correspondence to the formal, written law.	2. Minimal stipulated rules, primacy of ad hoc, individuated decisions; some calculability possible on the basis of knowing the substantive ethics involved in the situation.

Table 2-1 *(Continued)*

Dimensions	Bureaucratic Organization	Collectivist-Democratic Organization
3. Social Control	3. Organizational behavior is subject to social control, primarily through direct supervision or standardized rules and sanctions, tertiarily through the selection of homogeneous personnel especially at top levels.	3. Social controls are primarily based on personalistic or moralistic appeals and the selection of homogeneous personnel.
4. Social Relations	4. Ideal of impersonality. Relations are to be role-based, segmental and instrumental.	4. Ideal of community. Relations are to be wholistic, personal, of value in themselves.
5. Recruitment and Advancement	5.a. Employment based on specialized training and formal certification.	5.a. Employment based on friends, social-political values, personality attributes, and informally assessed knowledge and skills.
	5.b. Employment constitutes a career; advancement based on seniority or achievement.	5.b. Concept of career advancement not meaningful; no hierarchy of positions.
6. Incentive Structure	6. Remunerative incentives are primary.	6. Normative and solidarity incentives are primary; material incentives are secondary.
7. Social Stratification	7. Isomorphic distribution of prestige, privilege, and power; i.e., differential rewards by offics; hierarchy justifies equality.	7. Egalitarian; reward differentials, if any, are strictly limited by the collectivity.
8. Differentiation	8.a. Maximal division of labor; dichotomy between intellectual work and manual work and between administrative tasks and performance tasks.	8.a. Minimal division of labor; administration is combined with performance tasks; division between intellectual and manual work is reduced.
	8.b. Maximal specialization of jobs and functions; segmental roles. Technical expertise is exclusively held; ideal of the specialist-expert.	8.b. Generalization of jobs and functions; wholistic roles. Demystification of expertise: ideal of the amateur factotum.

Source: Joyce Rothshild-Whitt, "The Collectivist Organization: An Alternative to Rational Bureaucratic Models," *American Sociological Review,* 44 (August 1979), 519.

organizations in terms of parts or units within them as is done in intraorganizational comparisons. Organizations should also be understood as political entities, with various parties struggling for control. Writers with a Marxian perspective, such as Benson (1977) and Heydebrand (1977), have alerted us to the presence of contradictions within organizations. These writers focus on class interests in the contradiction process, but the class emphasis is not necessary for inclusion of the notion of contradiction. Organizations do contain oppositional forces. These forces vie for control. The nature of organizations is such that those in power tend to remain in power, but the fact that organizations contain internal oppositional forces is an important consideration.

Just as there is internal differentiation within organizations, so too should distinctions be made at the boundaries of organizations. Hage (1980) notes that there are many "multi" organizations. These are organizations of such scope that it is wise to consider their component parts as separate organizations. Hage uses the former United States Department of Health, Education, and Welfare as his example. The Public Health Service and the Department of Social and Rehabilitation Services are better treated as separate organizations. According to Hage, it is not a matter of whether or not diversified products or services are involved, since a single organization can involve such multiple outputs, but rather the important distinction is the operating technology of the multiple organizations. The notion of operating technology will be considered at a later point. For the purposes here, it is sufficient to note that an autonomous unit of a larger organization can be considered an organization in its own right (Warriner 1980). If the unit can provide its own input and throughput and can distribute its outputs, it can be considered to be an organization. Thus, a new-car dealership that is dependent upon the manufacturer for its input would not qualify as an organization on its own. A used-car dealership which relies totally on cars that it buys and sells and does not rely on a wholesaler would be an organization. This is a technical distinction, therefore, and one which actually interferes with some useful comparisons. It does point out, however, the importance of clear boundary specifications.

The new-car dealership—used-car dealership distinction also highlights the importance of the way in which we go about classifying organizations. On one basis—selling cars—they are very similar, but on another—the degree of autonomy from a single supplier—they are not. The less autonomous might be more profitable, however, while the more autonomous might be less ethical. There are thus many dimensions along which organizations can be classified. Before considering classifications of organizations, however, an important but often overlooked question must be considered.

Are Organizations Real?

This question may seem inane. From the outset we have been considering the organizations that surround us and of which we are a part. We have examined some of the impacts of organizations on individuals and on society. A careful consideration of the question, however, reveals one of the basic dilemmas in sociology and in philosophy.

Most theorists have addressed this question one way or another. Simon (1964), for example, argues against reifying the concept of organization or treating it as something more than a system of interacting individuals. Approaching the issue from the standpoint of exchange theory, Blau (1964) notes:

> Within the organization, indirect exchange processes become substituted for direct ones, although direct ones persist in interstitial areas, such as informal cooperation among colleagues. The development of authority illustrates the transformation of direct into indirect exchange transactions. As long as subordinates obey the orders of a superior primarily because they are obligated to him for services he has rendered and favors he has done for them individually, he does not actually exercise authority over the subordinates, and there is a direct exchange between him and them, of the type involving unilateral services. The establishment of authority means that normative constraints that originate among the subordinates themselves effect their compliance with the orders of the superior—and indirect exchanges now take the place of the former direct ones. The individual subordinate offers compliance to the superior in exchange for approval from his colleagues; the collectivity of subordinates enforces compliance with the superior's directives to repay its joint obligations to the superior; and the superior makes contributions to the collectivity in exchange for the self-enforced voluntary compliance of its members on which his authority rests. (p. 329)

Blau continues:

> in return for offering services to clients without accepting rewards from them, officials receive material rewards from the organization and colleague approval for conformity with accepted standards. The clients make contributions to the community, which furnishes the resources to the organization that enable it to reward its members. (p. 330)

This analysis places primacy on the interaction between individuals as the heart of the organization. Other analysts, such as Benson (1977), are even more individualistic, claiming that reality is a social construction in the minds of organizational actors. The position taken in the present analysis is that these individualistic approaches are incomplete in two ways.

Organizations and the Individual   In the first place, individuals in organizations frequently behave *without* engaging in direct or indirect exchange. There are many routine behaviors that are learned in an exchange situation but are then carried out without mental reference to the interaction process. The behavior becomes a type of learned stimulus-response mechanism, with the intervening interaction variable deleted as a consideration. Department store clerks are trained to input each transaction into the store's computer. Bank tellers routinely check the status of a customer's account. Much behavior in organizations is of this type. The organization trains, indoctrinates, and persuades its members to respond on the basis of the requirements of their position. Responses become quite regularized and routinized and do not involve the interaction frame of reference.

The argument that behavior in organizations is organizationally, rather than individually or interactionally, based is not intended to mean that *all* behavior in organizations is so determined. There clearly are many times when individual discretion is called for, times when the individual is crucial for organizational survival. The point is that the organization can be the major determinant of individual actions in some situations and an important determinant in others. In discussing the factors that contribute to the kinds of role expectations one organizational member holds toward another (role expectations are of vital importance in any interaction situation), Kahn et al. (1964) note:

> To a considerable extent, the role expectations held by the members of a role set—the prescriptions and proscriptions associated with a particular position—are determined by the broader organizational context. The organizational structure, the functional specialization and division of labor, and the formal reward system dictate the major content of a given office. What the occupant of that office is supposed to do, with and for whom, is given 'by these and other properties of the organization itself. Although other human beings are doing the "supposing" and rewarding, *the structural properties of organization are sufficiently stable so that they can be treated as independent of the particular persons in the role set.* For such properties as size, number of echelons, and rate of growth, the justifiable abstraction of organizational properties from individual behavior is even more obvious [italics added]. (p. 31)

Clegg and Dunkerly (1980) approach this issue from a power perspective. They suggest that the "capacity of management to impose its hegemony on the members of the organization" means that organizations assume a real existence for the people who are oriented to the organization. If an organization has power over the individual, then it is real (pp. 209–10).

The perspective taken here is that organizations are real to the extent that strictly organizational factors account for part of the behavior of individuals at all times in organizations. The exact proportion of the variation in individual behavior accounted for by organizational factors, as opposed to interactional or individual factors, cannot be exactly specified at the present time. The position taken here is that organizational factors can account for *all* of the variation in behavior in some circumstances (this is the purpose of training and indoctrination programs in many kinds of organizations). In others, organizational factors interact with other behavioral determinants. It is hoped that research in organizations will provide data on the conditions under which these factors operate. At present, unfortunately, the analysis must rest on these incomplete descriptions.

Organizations as Actors The treatment of organizations as realities thus far has been concerned with the behavior of individuals. An even more basic issue is whether organizations have an existence of their own, above and beyond the behavior and performance of individuals within them. The question becomes, Do organizations act? The answer again is in the affirmative and is the second reason that viewing organizations just as interacting or reality constructing individuals is too narrow a conceptualization.

Some characteristics of the definitions discussed above provide indications of the existence of organizations. The fact that organizations persist over time and replace members suggests that they are not dependent upon particular individuals. Universities outlive the generations of students and faculty which pass through their gates. The General Motors Corporation has been in existence for a long time. Organizations may indeed have a life cycle which includes decline and death (Kimberly and Miles 1980), but the fact is that our dominant organizations persist across generations of members. When members enter an organization for the first time, they are confronted with a social structure, which includes the interaction patterns among organizational members and these members' expectations toward them, and a set of organizational expectations for their own behavior. It does not matter who the individuals are; the organization has established a system of norms and expectations to be followed regardless of who its personnel happens to be, and it continues to exist regardless of personnel turnover. Individuals establish the norms and expectations, to be sure, but they persist long past the persons who established the policies in the first place.

Organizational factors influence decision making in organizations. Routine decisions can be preprogrammed, such as when computerized inventory records show that a particular item is becoming in short supply and an order for additional such items is generated. More important decisions about future organizational directions and policies are also strongly influenced by organizational factors. Decisions are strongly influenced by the power of the individuals making the decisions. Power in turn is the result of occupying an organizational position. Decisions are also based on tradition and precedent, as well as the organization's relationships with its environment. These organizationally based considerations have an impact on how individuals within the organizational hierarchy make decisions on behalf of the organization.

When we hear statements such as "It is company policy," "The White House today announced . . . ," or "Z State University does not condone cheating," these are recognizable as being about organizations. Organizations have policies, make announcements, and may or may not condone cheating. They also manufacture goods, administer policies, and protect the citizenery. These are organizational actions and involve properties of organizations, not individuals. The actions are carried out by individuals—even in the case of computer-produced letters, which are programmed by individuals—but the genesis of the actions remain in the organization.

The argument being made here has certain philosophical assumptions that should be noted. Following Burrell and Morgan (1979, pp. 4–7) it can be noted that in terms of ontology, we are taking a realist as opposed to a nominalist position. The nominalist position is that reality is constructed through individual cognition, with the external world made up of artificial creations formed in people's minds.The realist position claims that the world external to individual cognition is a real world made up of hard, tangible, and relatively immutable structures. Warriner (1956) has taken the realist view toward groups and we are taking it toward organizations.

Epistemologically, the position taken is a positivist one in that we seek to explain and predict what happens in the organizational world by searching for regularities and causal relationships among the elements related to organizations. Antipositivists suggest that the world is relativistic and can only be understood from the points of view of the actors in a particular situation. Again, this analysis is based around a positivist perspective.

Burrell and Morgan also suggest that assumptions about human nature must be considered in organizational analyses. They contrast the voluntarist position with the determinist perspective. Voluntarism sees humans as totally autonomous and free willed, while determinism sees people as totally controlled by the situation or environment in which they are located. The analysis here leans toward the determinist perspective without embracing it totally.

There is also a methodological issue, according to Burrell and Morgan. On the one hand, there is the ideographic approach which stresses detailed analyses of the meanings which social actors attach to situations and emphasizes that social actors meanings should be stated in their own terms. The nomothetic approach emphasizes testing hypotheses with scientific rigor and the use of systematic research protocols. The nomothetic approach will be stressed in this analysis, with the realization that ideographic studies can provide useful insights and contribute to the development of rigorous tests of the insights.

Part of the difficulty that arises around the issue of organizational reality comes from the methodologies that have been employed. There is a long tradition of obtaining information about organizations from respondents in organizations. This is done through data collected from "key informants" or from samples of personnel in the organizations. Lazarsfeld and Menzel (1961; see also Barton 1961) have suggested that it is possible to construct organizational properties from data gathered from individuals, through the use of averages, standard deviations, correlation coefficients, and other such figures. It is also possible to obtain data from individuals *about* the organization. Lincoln and Zeitz (1980) have demonstrated a technique by which data from individuals can be aggregated to the organizational level with strong explanatory power.

This rather lengthy expedition into the issue of organizational reality was conducted for the purpose of specifying the perspective that the analysis in this book takes. As Roberts, Hulin, and Rousseau (1978) conclude, social scientists vary in their interests, with some concerned with individual phenomena, some with group phenomena, and some with organizational phenomena. Each is a legitimate interest.

Organizational characteristics are crucial determinants of the behavior of individuals in them. That is, if organizations have characteristics of their own, and if these characteristics affect the behavior of their members, then organizational characteristics must be understood if we are to understand human behavior. By the same token, if we are to understand society, we must understand its organizations.

Types of Organizations

The discussions of the different definitions of organizations and of the reality of organizations could lead to the conclusion that all organizations share common characteristics and are thus of one class or type. In one sense this is true, just as there are defining characteristics that enable us to differentiate humans from other forms of life. In many cases, only the simple classification of human versus nonhuman is required for thought or action. In other cases, this simple classification does not tell us enough and we begin to classify.

Classification schemes are designed to indicate a meaningful difference between the types or classes identified. Classification enables a person to view the world; without classification the individual is surrounded by a chaos of stimuli. Without classification a person would be unable to function at all.

There is a basic difficulty in classifying anything: a classification that works marvelously in one situation might be disastrous in another. For example, the typology based on sex is one of the most useful that we have available. It is nice to be able to distinguish between women and men. This distinction becomes useless, however, if we need to distinguish between a qualified or unqualified person as a lawyer, accountant, chef, or automobile mechanic. Here, a different classificatory scheme is required.

The same problem is faced when organizations are considered: a usable classification system in one instance may be unusable in the next. In some instances, knowing whether an organization is a good place to work or not is sufficient. In others, we may want to classify on the basis of which parties benefit from the actions of the organization. In still others it is useful to know how formalized or structured the organization is so that we can understand or predict the amount of autonomy given to individual workers.

Organizational analysts are well aware of the need for typologies. But at the same time they are convinced that the relatively simple, prima facie typologies probably add more confusion than clarity. Perrow (1967), for example, notes that

> types of organizations—in terms of their functions in society—will vary as much within each type as between types. Thus, some schools, hospitals, banks, and steel companies may have more in common, because of their routine character, than routine and nonroutine schools, routine and non-routine hospitals, and so forth. To assume that you are holding constant the major variable by comparing several schools or several steel mills is unwarranted until one looks at the technologies employed by the various schools or steel mills. (p. 203)

While we may argue about Perrow's emphasis on technology as the key variable, his point is very important. It is organizational characteristics that should serve as the classificatory basis. The great danger in most classificatory schemes is oversimplification; they are based on a single characteristic. Typologies thus derived ". . . can be expanded indefinitely as some new factor is seized upon to indicate an additional class" (Katz and Kahn 1966, p. 111). Such problems with typologies are not limited just to the study of organizations. Burns (1967) notes that "the history of sociology, from Montesquieu through Spencer, Marx, and up to Weber himself, is littered with the debris of ruined typologies that serve only as the battleground for that academic street-fighting that so often passes for theoretical discussion (p. 119).

Typologies that end in debris did not stop at Weber's era. A generally accepted typology of organizations is nonexistent in spite of the general agreement that a good typology or set of typologies is desperately needed. While simple typologies can be used for limited analyses, such as comparing organizations in their turnover rates, growth rates, or rates of investment in research and development, classifications of this sort have only a limited usefulness. We end up knowing only one thing about organizations, not understanding them in their rich complexity.

The essence of the typological effort really lies in the determination of the critical variables for differentiating the phenomena under investigation. Since organizations are highly complex entities, classificatory schemes must represent this complexity. An adequate overall classification would have to take into account the array of external conditions, the total spectrum of actions and interactions within an organization, and the outcome of organizational behaviors. A review of some of the efforts made to classify organizations will indicate the diversity of variables that have been considered, the relative fruitlessness of the schemes, and some possible future directions for typological efforts.

Some Typologies

For the purposes of the present analysis, we will use the terms, *classification, typology, and taxonomy* interchangeably, although in a strict sense each term has a distinct meaning (Burns 1967, p. 119). The most common form of typology is what Warriner (1980) has labeled traditional, folk, or common sense typologies. Thus, organizations can be classified into profit or nonprofit categories. Rushing (1976) found differences between nonprofit and profit oriented hospitals in terms of their emphasis on coordination. Other research (Hall 1961) found no important differences between profit and nonprofit organizations in a more heterogeneous sample of organizations. The point here is not to debate the importance of a profit orientation. Indeed, a profit, or entrepreneurial, orientation might be an important consideration in a serious typological effort if it is remembered that many public organizations engage in entrepreneurial efforts as they seek funding and many so-called profit-oriented organizations in regulated industries are so protected from competition that the profit orientation would appear to be hardly a major consideration.

Another form of common sense typology would be to classify organizations by their societal "sector," such as educational, agricultural, health and medical, and so on. Like the profit-nonprofit distinction, such classifications tend to obscure more than they illuminate. Warriner (1980) notes that such typologies contain dimensions that overlap in unpredictable ways. They are also unscientific in that the categories are not related to each other in any systematic way. The major problem with such common sense typologies is that they simply do not classify. The State University of New York, for example, contains two-year colleges, four-year colleges, graduate university centers, medical colleges and their attendant hospitals, specialized colleges in ceramics and forestry, plus an enirely noncampus-based administrative headquarters with no students. In addition, there is a semiautonomous research foundation that does not conduct research but rather seeks funds—an entrepreneurial role—and administers grants and contracts—an administrative role. In a similar manner, General Motors and the United States Army maintain college-degree-granting facilities. The realization of these difficulties has led organizational analysis to develop other forms of classification. The first form to be discussed are "intentional" (Warriner 1980) or "special" classifications (McKelvey 1978) which have focused on a limited aspect of the organization.

This analysis will move from some relatively simple schemes to more elaborate formulations. Typical of the simple schemes is that of Parsons (1960, pp. 45–46), based on the type of function or goal served by the organization. In this analysis, Parsons is concerned with the linkages between organizations and the wider society. He distinguishes four types of organizations, according to what they contribute to the society.

The first type is the production organization, which makes things that are consumed by the society. The second type is that oriented toward political goals; it seeks to ensure that society attains its valued goals, and it generates and allocates power within the society. The third type is the integrative organization, whose purposes are settling conflicts, directing motivations toward the fulfillment of institutionalized expectations, and ensuring that the parts of society work together. The final form is the pattern-maintenance organization, which attempts to provide societal continuity through educational, cultural, and expressive activities.

While each of these functions is clearly important for society (other societal goals could be identified), this type of classificatory scheme does not really say much about the organizations involved. In the first place, some organizations can be placed in more than one category. A large corporation, such as General Motors, is clearly a production organization. But it is also important in the allocation of power. Through public relations, corporate contributions to foundations and colleges, and attempts at working with disadvantaged youths, the same corporation falls into the other categories. Its prime effort is undoubtedly production, but these subsidiary concerns make such a classificatory scheme less than totally useful. Even more important, such a typology does not differentiate among the characteristics of organizations themselves. As Perrow noted, there can be as much—or more—organizational variation within such categories as between them.

An elaboration of this type of approach is provided by Katz and Kahn (1966, 1978). After identifying *production* or *economic, maintenance, adaptive,* and *managerial* or *political* organizations, they then select four organizational characteristics thought to be important for differentiating organizations. The first is the nature of the "though-put" or what is being processed by the organization. Organizations can transform objects or people, with the important distinction here that people react to organizations, while objects do not. Hasenfeld (1972) has noted differences between organizations that merely process people and those that seek to change them, so that even the distinction between people and object processing organizations is complicated. Katz and Kahn then go on to note that organizational members' orientations vary, their structures differ, and the means by which they utilize energy or resources also vary. Katz and Kahn then suggest that the societal function categories interact with the organizational characteristics to form types of organizations, "each with its own logic" (1978, p. 183). Katz and Kahn recognize the difficulties inherent in categorizations such as theirs, but argue that their approach yields meaningful categories, which does not seem to be the case from my perspective, since there appears to be insufficient discrimination among organizations.

Etzioni and Blau and Scott

Another approach to developing intentional typologies is exemplified by the work of Etzioni (1961) and Blau and Scott (1962). Both attempt to classify organizations on the basis of a single principle.

Etzioni uses *compliance* as the basis for his system. Compliance is the manner in which lower participants in an organization respond to the authority system of the organization. Compliance is expressed through the nature of the lower participants' involvement in the organization. According to Etzioni, there are three bases of authority—coercion, remuneration, and normative. There are also three bases of compliance—alienative, instrumental or calculative, and moral. The resulting three-by-three classificatory scheme yields nine possible types of organizations, with most falling into "congruent" types. These are: *coercive-alienative, remunerative-calculative,* and *normative-moral.* Incongruent types, such as coercive-utilitarian would tend to move toward congruency.

Etzioni's approach has been criticized from several standpoints. Burns (1967) notes that the reasons for congruence or incongruence are not well explained. Hall, Haas, and Johnson (1967) found that it was difficult to place some organizations into Etzioni's categories. Public schools, for example, can yield alienative, calculative, and moral compliance on the part of various students. In addition, they found that the typology did not relate well to important structural characteristics such as complexity or formalization (see Weldon 1972 and Hall et al. 1972 for additional discussion of this). Clegg and Dunkerly (1980, pp. 142–54) further criticize the Etzioni scheme on the grounds of its logical consistency and its inattention to organizational environments.

Lest this discussion lead to the conclusion that Etzioni's work makes little contribution, it should be noted that Etzioni (1975) followed up his original work by compiling the results of some 60 studies which used his typology. He found that the compliance patterns which were predicted by the typology generally were found. The compliance typology thus does appear to differentiate organizations in terms of the compliance patterns of its members, but it is not an inclusive typology.

Blau and Scott's basis of classification is the question of who benefits or *cui bono*. The prime organizational beneficiary serves as the basis for their fourfold classification. The types are: *mutual benefit* organizations in which the members themselves are the prime beneficiary, *businesses* with owners as the beneficiaries, *service* organizations with clients as the beneficiaries, and *commonweal* organizations in which the public-at-large benefits.

Burns (1967) has also criticized this formulation. He notes that some business firms may be more tightly controlled by managers, benefiting them rather than stockholders; some hospitals may benefit their medical practitioner owners more than their clients. More fundamentally, Burns suggests that it is difficult to isolate an explict, stable, and coherent group served by any organization. The beneficiaries themselves have factions, disagree, and engage in power struggles.

Hall, Haas, and Johnson (1967) found placement into the Blau and Scott categories difficult here, as in the Etzioni formulation. Using schools again as the example, aspects of service and commonweal benefits can be easily identified. Mass media organizations such as newspapers or television stations benefit their owners and the public. Welfare organizations may serve clients, but also serve their members. Placement difficulties are not the only issue, of course, since the critical function of a typology is to "allow us to combine a number of variables into a single construct, and thus allow us to deal with extremely complex phenomena in a relatively simple fashion" (Mechanic 1953, p. 158). Hall, Haas, and Johnson (1967) also found that the Blau and Scott typology did not do an adequate job in ordering the organizations they studied in terms of important structural variables. Clegg and Dunkerly (1980) point out that this approach also does not deal with the critical issue of who actually controls the organization or of who does *not* benefit from its activities. Like the Etzioni typology, the Blau and Scott approach does serve to sensitize us to the issue of who benefits, but it also is not inclusive.

Mintzberg

As a final example of this form of building intentional typologies, we will turn to the work of Mintzberg (1979). This is a multifaceted approach, based largely on the ways in which organizations are structured to meet various contingencies which they face.

The first type is the *simple structure*, as exemplified by the brand-new government department, an automobile dealership with a flamboyant owner, a small college headed by an aggressive president, or a new government headed by an autocrat. Supervision is direct. The organizations are small and exist in dynamic environments. Their technologies are not sophisticated.

The second type is the *machine bureaucracy*, such as a postal system, a steel manufacturing firm, an airline, or a custodial prison. These share the characteristics of standardized work, large size, stable environments, and control by some external body.

The third type is the *professional bureaucracy*, such as a university, law firm, social welfare agency, craft production firm, or medical center. Work is standardized through professional or craft training, the environment is stable, but does not contain external controls on the organizations. The key factor here is the skills and knowledge of the operating workers who are professionals or highly skilled craft workers.

The fourth type is the *divisionalized form*, as exemplified by the large corporation, multicampus university, or socialist economy. Each division has its own structure, which may take one of the other forms already listed in this typology.

Finally, there is the *adhocracy*. This is a complex form and is exemplified by space agencies, new artistic organizations, and research and development laboratories at the frontiers of science. Their environment is dynamic and unknown and their structure can change rapidly as events demand adjustment.

Mintzberg has a complex scheme from which these types of organizations are developed. The utility of the types and the scheme from which they are developed will have to stand the test of time. What is of relevance here is the fact that the groupings shatter common sense notions of how and why organizations differ. Instead, Mintzberg is suggesting that we look at organizational characteristics themselves as the basis for our classification schemes. This is exactly what those who advocate empirical taxonomies propose.

Organizational Taxonomy

A very different approach to the classification issue is taken by those who have advocated and tried to develop organizational taxonomies (Haas, Hall, and Johnson 1966; Pugh, Hickson, and Hinings 1969; McKelvey 1975, 1978; Pinder and Moore 1979; Warriner 1980; Carper and Snizek 1980). The Haas, Hall, and Johnson effort was designed to be a taxonomy of organizations, similar to that used in zoology to differentiate vertebrata at the phyla level (amphibia, mammalia, aves, and reptilia), at the class level, and so on. Using data from 75 organizations and some 100 different organizational variables, this study was able to generate some nine major classes of organizations. Unfortunately, the bases for differentiation among the classes were seemingly trivial as organizational properties. The reason for the rather unusable findings may have been the type of measurement used or it may have been the fact that certain key variables were not included in the analysis. In any event, this initial effort at developing a classification scheme from empirically based characteristics did not produce usable classifications.

The Pugh, Hickson, and Hinings classification effort is an attempt to type organizations according to important structural characteristics. It is also empirically based and uses the following structural dimensions: (1)

the structuring of activities, or the degree of standardization of routines, formalization of procedures, specialization of roles, and stipulation of specific behavior by the organization; (2) the concentration of authority, or the centralization of authority at the upper levels of the hierarchy and in controlling units outside the organization; and (3) the line control of workflow, or the degree to which control is exercised by line personnel as opposed to control through impersonal procedures. Using a sample of 52 English organizations and the three bases of classification, Pugh, Hickson, and Hinings suggest the following types:

1. Full Bureaucracy: ". . . relatively high scores on both structuring of activities and concentration of authority, a high dependence score . . . , and a relatively low score on workflow integration of technology. . . . It has high scores on both standardization of procedures for selection and advancement, etc., and formalization of role definition. . . ."

2. Nascent Full Bureaucracy: Possesses the same characteristics, but not to such a pronounced degree.

3. Workflow Bureaucracy: "High scores on structuring of activities combined with relatively low scores on the remaining two structural factors. Their use of impersonal control mechanisms is shown by the high scores on formalization of recording of role performance as well as a high percentage of nonworkflow personnel and clerks . . . high scores of workflow integration."

4. Nascent Workflow Bureaucracy: ". . . show the same characteristics to a less pronounced degree, and are considerably smaller."

5. Preworkflow Bureaucracy: ". . . are considerably lower on scores of structuring of activities, but have the typical workflow—bureaucracy pattern of dispersed authority and impersonal line control."

6. Implicitly Structured Organizations: ". . . have low structuring of activities, dispersed authority, and high line control."

7. Personnel Bureaucracy: ". . . low scores on structuring and high scores on line control . . . high scores on concentration of authority." (pp. 121-23)

This scheme is graphically shown in Figure 2-1. The authors suggest that a developmental sequence occurs on two of their dimensions. More highly structured organizations develop as the organizations grow in size over time, and growth in size is in turn related to general economic development. The control dimension tends to move from line control— that is, control exercised by the workflow personnel themselves and their subordinates—to impersonal control. As technology develops, more and more of the control system is passed to procedures dictated by standardization and the new specialists who devise the procedures. No such developmental sequence is seen in the case of the concentration of authority; the patterns here are linked to historical factors and the auspices under which the organization operates. Like the other typologies discussed, this one has problems, such as how or why the shifts between types take place. Further, there is no indication of what the typology predicts; what are the consequences of an organization being of one type or the other?

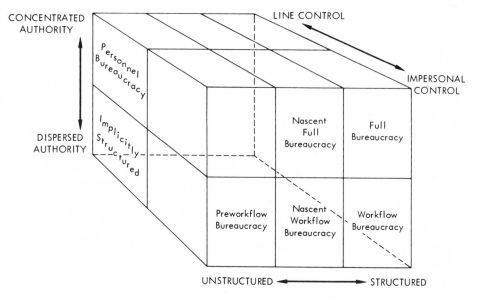

Figure 2-1 A three-dimensional typology

Source: D. S. Pugh, D. J. Hickson, and C. R. Hinings, "An Empirical Taxonomy of Work Organizations," *Administrative Science Quarterly*, 14, No. 1 (March 1969), *123*.

Advocates of the taxonomic approach (Warriner 1979, 1980; McKelvey 1978; Pinder and Moore 1979; Carper and Snizek 1981; Warriner, Hall, and McKelvey 1981) argue that a sound taxonomy is the only way in which theoretical advances in organizational analysis can be made. The argument is that unless there is an adequate taxonomy or classification system, both theorists and practitioners have little guide for action. The practitioner has no way of knowing if what works in one organization will work in another, since he or she has no basis for knowing if the organizations are of the same type. The theorist cannot theorize in the absence of an adequate system.

Despite the need for a taxonomy, it should be noted that a truly adequate one is probably in the distant future. Warriner (1979) has pinpointed the issues which must be confronted in taxonomic development. These include the number and kinds of characters or classifying dimensions to be used for describing organizations, identifying the unit to be classified, the range and number of cases required for taxonomic purposes, and the analyatical procedures to be used in sorting out the cases. This is a huge task, beyond the scope of a single investigator. At the same time, it is a necessary concern for anyone interested in organizations. An effort is currently underway (Warriner, Hall, and McKelvey 1981) to move in the direction of taxonomic development, so that there is some hope that such a usable classification scheme may be available in the future.

The Voluntary Organization

Most of the discussion and examples used thus far have focused on organizations with paid members or employees. Another set of organizations confuses typological and general theoretical concerns: these are the voluntary organizations. These organizations have unclear boundaries; a person can be in many such organizations without taking an active part in any of them. Involvement in such organizations can be zealous to the point of suicide or it can be totally passive. To make matters more complicated, many voluntary organizations, such as unions, political parties, religious organizations, and so on also have paid employees. The paid staff can be treated as any other organizaton, thus minimizing the issue, but the rather ephemeral nature of the volunteers makes their inclusion problematic. Unless otherwise noted, the analyses in this book will be oriented to organizations with paid members.

SUMMARY AND CONCLUSIONS

This chapter may have raised more issues than it resolved. After developing a rather inclusive definition, we then considered the thorny issues of the reality of organizations and the classification of organizations. Neither of the last two issues was resolved conclusively. It was stated that the present analysis will take the position that organizations are real and do act. This was stated not as a fact, but rather as the orientation of this book. It was also stated that an organizational taxonomy is the best way to classify organizations and that this is a needed development. Again, this is the orientation here and others certainly disagree.

By raising these issues and taking a stand on them, it has been my intent to help in the understanding of organizations. One could take an opposite position to that taken here and still analyze organizations. The important thing is to realize that a stand has been taken.

Now that organizations have been defined and issues regarding the types of organizations have been identified, we can turn to the actual analysis of organizations by beginning to examine organizational structure.

II

Organizational Structure

The topic of organizational structure dominated the field of organizational analysis during the 1960s and the first half of the 1970s. Interest in this topic has apparently declined, with attention now focused on the environments of organizations and other broad issues, such as the processes of growth and decline among organizations (Kimberly and Miles 1980). This shift in focus has been beneficial in that organizational analysts are now examining a broader range of phenomena than once was the case. The unfortunate aspect of this shift in focus is that it has deflected analyses away from the limited theoretical development that was emerging in regard to structure. The shift in focus has also led to a situation in which much of what is known about organizations and what is important to organizations is receiving little attention in the literature. Some contemporary writers, such as Perrow (1979), continue to emphasize the importance of structure, but others, such as Aldrich (1979), scarcely pay any attention to the issue at all.

The present analysis is intended to integrate the studies which have been concerned with different aspects of organizational structure. As the analysis proceeds, we will attempt to demonstrate the importance of structure for organizational participants, for the organization itself, and for those in contact with an organization.

What is structure? In the next chapter a formal definition will be given. Here, a few examples will be presented to begin to indicate the importance of the topic. The example will be drawn from my own

university, the State University of New York (SUNY). Readers in other
kinds of settings or who have had their educational experiences in
similar or different settings can make comparisons with the examples
based on their own experience.

SUNY is quite *complex*. It has units scattered throughout the State of
New York. It has a myriad of divisions and departments, both by
academic specialty and by administrative divisions. It has a tall
hierarchy, with a chancellor, vice chancellors, assistant vice chancellors,
and other ranks at the central office and presidents, vice presidents,
associate and assistant vice presidents, deans, associate and assistant
deans, faculty members of various ranks, and clerical and service
personnel arranged along an array of civil service rankings. By almost
any standard, it is a very complex organization. Very complex
organizations face difficult coordination and control considerations and
SUNY is no different. One way in which coordination and control can
be accomplished is through effective communications among units. This
can be partially accomplished through the use of computerized record
keeping and information transfer, which is part of what SUNY does.
This is not necessarily successful, of course, and the system can be
plagued with its right hand not being sure of what its left hand is doing.

SUNY is *formalized* to varying degrees. In some areas rules and
procedures are spelled out in minute detail, while in other areas low
formalization exists. As an example of high formalization at SUNY-
Albany, each department (both academic and administrative) is required
to prepare an annual update on its "three-year plan." This is a formal
document which is reviewed by at least three levels before it reaches the
President. The format of the plans is specified in advance, as is the
review procedure. At the low end of the formalization continuum is the
classroom. Individual faculty are almost totally free to select their texts
and their method of classroom presentation. Only in truly extreme cases
would the organization intervene into the classroom. For students, the
registration process is highly formalized, with specific dates and times to
register, steps to be taken in the process, and forms to be completed.
Again, the classroom is at the opposite extreme, except in the case of
laboratories, with no rules on attendance, method of taking notes, or
studying for exams.

Another aspect of structure, *centralization*, varies in a manner similar
to formalization in that there is both high and low centralization. Low
centralization is evidence by the fact that academic departments are
almost totally free to choose faculty members on the basis of their own
judgment. There is a minimal amount of power utilized at the campus
or central administrative levels. The potential for the exercise of power
is there, but it is seldom invoked. High centralization occurs when
decision-making power is retained at or near the top of the
organization. When new academic programs are developed, and
particularly when these involve scarce resources, the central
administration is heavily involved in the decision-making process. As a
general rule, it appears that the higher the quality of the higher

educational organization, the lower the level of centralization (Blau 1973), but that is not the issue here. The important conclusion is that complexity, formalization, and centralization can vary within a single organization. They are multidimensional phenomena.

Almost all of the research to be considered is comparative in the sense that data are collected from more than one organization (Heydebrand 1973). Some of the research is comparative in the sense that there is an attempt to compare organizations in different settings or societies. Comparative research has been emphasized in the belief that it permits generalizations beyond a single research setting. As the discussion of typologies suggests, of course, in the absence of a sound typology such generalizations are risky. Most analysts try to make their findings as widely usable as possible, but the problem of crossing "types" should continue to be recognized. Indeed, as will be evident in the discussion, some of the major research projects have included such a limited range of organizations that it does make generalization difficult.

There is an additional problem in the studies to be considered, and this involves measurement (Price 1972). Data can come from organizational documents and records, key organizational informants, samples of members from the whole organization, or government- or other-published data sets. (See Pennings 1973; Azumi and McMillan 1974; Dewar, Whetten, and Boje 1980; and Lincoln and Zeitz 1980 for more detailed discussions of some of the methodological issues.) The problem has been that measures of different types, which are designed to measure the same phenomena, such as formalization, do not correlate well together. It may be that the multidimensionality of the concept leads to the situation in which formalization measures are weakly or negatively correlated (Pennings 1973), or it may be that some measures are simply not measures of what they are purported to be.

The problems of typologies and measurement cannot be resolved here. The discussion of the problems is designed to indicate that the research findings on structure are not complete. At the same time, many of the findings make a great deal of sense. As in the case of all research, the materials to be presented should be understood as tentative.

3

The Nature
and Bases
of Organizational
Structure

The idea of structure is basically simple. Buildings have structures, in the form of beams, interior walls, passageways, roofs, and so on. The structure of a building is a major determinant of the movements and activities of the people within it. Buildings are supposed to have structures that fit the activities that go on within them. An office building is different from a factory. Factories where automobiles are made are different from those where computers are made. Architects design buildings to fit the needs of the activities that are to be carried out within them. They are designed to accommodate populations of various sizes—no architect would design a huge cathedral for a small congregation—and to withstand the environment in which they are located. Buildings in Minnesota are different from those in Arizona. While the size, the major activity or technology to be used, and the environment are all important in building design, so too is the element of choice—of decor, color, and so on.

The analogy of organizational structures to those of buildings is not perfect, since organizations are not built by architects but by the people within them. But the factors that affect or determine the structure of buildings do the same for organizations. This chapter will examine the interacting influences of size, technology, environment, and choice on organizational structures.

By organizational structure we mean "the distributions, along various lines, of people among social positions that influence the role relations among these people" (Blau 1974, p. 12). This simple definition requires amplification. One implication of the definition is the division of labor: people are given different tasks or jobs within organizations. Another implication is that organizations contain ranks, or a hierarchy: the positions that people fill have rules and regulations that specify, in varying degrees, how incumbents are to behave in these positions.

Ranson, Hinings, and Greenwood (1980) have a slightly different perspective on organizational structure. They conceive of structure as "a complex medium of control which is continually produced and recreated in interaction and yet shapes that interaction: structures are constituted and constitutive" (p. 3). This approach emphasizes that an organization's structure is not fixed for all time. Rather, it shapes what goes on in an organization and is shaped by what goes on in an organization. This point highlights the fact that organizations are by nature conservative. Their structure "constitutes" the interactions that take place within it. The structure does not yield total conformity, but it also prevents random behavior.

Meyer and Rowan (1977) and Kamens (1977) have a very different view of structure. They view structure as a myth, created by social demands. Kamens claims that colleges and universities, for example, create membership categories, such as college graduates, which legitimate the social rights and meanings attached to such groups. Organizational structure, according to Kamens, is an organizational self-definition of its advertised effect on students. Meyer and Rowan's approach is that structure is the practices and procedures defined by the prevailing rationalized concepts of organizational work which are institutionalized in society.

While these approaches sensitize us to the fact that the formal organizational structure may not be what actually goes on in an organization, they seem too far removed from the reality which people in and out of organizations confront. Certainly some structural requirements have an impact beyond their stated purpose. College and university graduation requirements do serve to sort people into categories, but they are also a reality which confront students, faculty, administrators, and others who must deal with the requirements. It would appear worthwhile not only to recognize that structure can serve to disguise certain unrecognized consequences, but also to deal directly with its presence. Thus, the Blau and Ranson et al. approaches discussed above will serve as the basis for the succeeding analysis.

Organizational structure serves three basic functions. First and foremost, structures are intended to produce organizational outputs and to achieve organizational goals. Second, structures are designed to minimize or at least regulate the influence of individual variations on the organization. Structures are imposed to ensure that individuals conform to requirements of organizations and not vice versa. Third, structures are the settings in which power is exercised (structures also set or determine which positions have power in the first place), in which decisions are made (the flow of information which goes into a decision is largely determined by structure), and in which organizations' activities are carried out.

Many discussions of structure do not take the individual into account. It was just noted that one function of structure is to regulate the influence of individual variations. This regulation can be severe or hardly noticeable.

In some cases every individual action is monitored, while in others the individual is encouraged to utilize the utmost discretion possible. It should be noted that when discretion is emphasized, the organization typically has exercised strong initial control in its processes of selecting the individuals (Blau and Schoenherr 1971).

Organizational structures have impacts on individuals above and beyond this determination of the amount of discretion exercised. For example, the position of an individual in an organization, such as clerk, supervisor, middle manager, or whatever, shapes that individual's reactions to the organization (Herman, Dunham, and Hulin 1975). Although such demographic factors as age or sex are also determinants, the position of the individual appears to be more important. Similarly, the satisfaction of the individual with work is related to organizational structure (Ivancevich and Donnelly 1975). Although the difficulties in classifying both individuals and organizations make the evidence inconclusive, it appears that some kinds of workers are more satisfied in one kind of organizational structure while others prefer a different kind. In the Ivancevich and Donnelly study, for example, the research subjects, salesmen, were found to be more satisfied and less anxious in "flat" organizational structures, ones with few hierarchical levels.

Structural characteristics and individual characteristics interact. Indeed, things that might appear to be a consequence of individual actions can turn out to have important structural linkages. For example, the capacity for innovation, generally thought to be crucial for organizational survival, would seemingly be based on the capabilities of the individuals in the organization. This may not be the case, however; Baldridge and Burnham (1975) found that structural factors, such as organizational size and complexity, together with environmental characteristics, were more related to organizational innovations than were individual factors, such as age, attitudes, and education. Once again, the point is not that individuals are unimportant, but rather that individual characteristics interact with organizational structural characteristics to produce the events within organizations.

In the discussion that follows, there is an unfortunate problem with much of the literature to be discussed: the overwhelming majority of studies of organizational structures wittingly or unwittingly make the assumption that there is *a* structure in an organization; but there is ample evidence that this is not the case (Litwak 1961). There are structural differences among work units, departments, and divisions. There are also structural differences according to the position on the hierarchy. For example, a hospital admissions unit has explicit rules and procedures so that all persons who are admitted are treated the same way and so that employees are guided by a clear set of organizationally prescribed expectations. The physical rehabilitation unit of the same hospital has many fewer specific guidelines concerning what it is to do. Similarly, the behavior of lower-level workers, such as orderlies and kitchen workers, is prescribed to a much higher degree than is that of nurses and physicians. There is intraorganizational variation, both across organizational units and up and down the hierarchy.

Organizational structures take many forms. A brief review of some important earlier work in the area will demonstrate the manner in which variations occur. The seminal work on structure is Weber's (1947) description of the ideal type of bureaucracy. He states that a bureaucracy has a hierarchy of authority, limited authority, division of labor, technically competent participants, procedures for work, rules for incumbents, and differential rewards. If all of these components are present to a high degree, it is the ideal type bureaucracy. The important implication, of course, is that organizations in practice will vary from this ideal type as has been demonstrated (Hall 1963). A bureaucratic organization is designed for efficiency and reliability (Hage 1980; Perrow 1979). As Hage notes, subsequent analysts have noted that a true bureaucracy contains the seeds of rigidity and ritualistic behavior. Hage also notes that Weber did not develop alternatives to bureaucracy, which suggests that bureaucracy was viewed as the single "best" organizational form, a point which has been widely challenged in recent years.

Burns and Stalker (1961) provided a major step forward in the analysis of multiple organizational forms in addition to developing yet another typology. They identified the "mechanical" form, which is very close to Weber's ideal type of bureaucracy, and the "organic" form, which is almost a logical opposite. Thus, instead of having hierarchical authority, organic organizations have a network structure of control; instead of task specialization, a continual adjustment and redefinition of tasks; instead of hierarchical supervision, a communication context involving information and advice; and so on. They see organizational form as being closely linked to the environment in which organizations are embedded, particularly in terms of the technology being employed by the organization. A point later emphasized by Lawrence and Lorsch (1967).

Hage (1965) has moved the analysis of organizational forms a step further. He first noted that structural characteristics, such as centralization, formalization, complexity, and stratification, vary in their presence from high to low. In a series of axiomatic hypotheses, he links these structural characteristics with each other and with a series of outcome variables, such as productivity, innovation, efficiency, and morale. He later (1980) attempts to develop a comprehensive organizational theory based around these core set of variables. For the moment, the theory is not the key issue; the analysis of structure as a set of variables is. In the present analysis we will consider complexity, formalization, and centralization as the critical structural characteristics. Before doing so, however, we will first examine a series of factors which are thought to be strongly associated with structure, beginning with organizational size.

The Size Factor

At first glance, size appears to be a simple variable—the number of people in an organization. The size issue is much more complicated than that, however. The discussion of organizational boundaries suggested that it sometimes is problematic who is in or out of an organization. In a penetrating article, Kimberly (1976) demonstrated that size actually has four components.

The first component of size is the physical capacity of the organizations. Hospitals have a fixed number of beds. Production organizations have a relatively fixed capacity, such as the number of assembly lines and their speed, to transform raw materials. Universities have capacities in terms of classroom or dormitory space.

The second aspect of size is the personnel available to the organization. This is the most commonly used measure and conceptualization of size, being used in 80 percent of the studies reviewed by Kimberly. The basic problem with using this aspect is that the meaning of the number of personnel is ambiguous. For some religious organizations and universities, size in this form is a goal of the organization. Larger size means an increased budget. For other organizations, the goal is to keep the size of the organization at a minimum, to reduce costs.

The third aspect of size is organizational inputs or outputs. This can involve such factors as the number of clients or students served, or the number of inmates housed in a prison, as inputs and sales volume as an output. Kimberly suggests that this measure is limited in its usage to comparisons between organizations of a similar type.

The final aspect of size is the discretionary resources available to an organization, in the form of wealth or net assets. This is conceptually distinct from the other aspects of size.

Kimberly suggests that these aspects of size may be highly intercorrelated in some instances, and indeed they are, but that the conceptual distinctions among them are so great that they should be treated separately. He also notes that structural characteristics may be a consequence, covariant, or determinant of size, making the waters even more muddy and turbulent in regard to the utility of the size variable. Martin's (1979) research has verified Kimberly's conceptualization of the four aspects of size.

Much of the work relating size to organizational structure was conducted prior to Kimberly's analysis. We will review some of that literature now, with the realization that these studies are based almost exclusively on the number of personnel available. These studies do indicate the directions that have been taken in research on size, with some authors arguing that size is *the* determinant of structure and others arguing the opposite.

The major proponents of the importance of size as a determinant of structure have been Peter M. Blau and his associates (see Blau, Heydebrand, and Stauffer 1966; Blau 1968, 1973; Blau and Schoenherr 1971, 1970; Meyer 1968a, 1968b, 1971; also Blau 1972; and Klatzky 1970). Their data were collected primarily from studies of government agencies, such as state employment services and municipal finance divisions, and of universities and department stores. The data reveal some fascinating anomalies about organizations and also some important considerations about the role of organizations in contemporary society. There are also some problems with the data, which will be discussed later in this section.

Blau's studies are concerned primarily with organizational size and differentiation. Differentiation is measured by the number of levels, departments, and job titles within an organization. The research findings indicate that increasing size is related to increasing differentiation. The rate of differentiation decreases, however, with increasing size. On the other hand, administrative overhead is lower in larger organizations, and the span of control for supervisors is greater. Since administrative overhead is inversely related to size, and the span of control is directly, or positively, related to size, larger organizations are able to achieve an economy of scale. It is here that the anomaly is demonstrated. Size is related to differentiation, and differentiation, bringing increased need for control and coordination, is related to increased requirements for administrative overhead. Size and differentiation thus work at cross purposes. Blau concludes that the size factor is more critical and that economy of scale still results from large size. Mileti, Gillespie, and Haas (1977) extend these findings with a different set of data.

The second major set of studies that find size to be the major determinant of organizational structure of those of the "Aston" group. (The Aston group refers to a series of researchers in the United Kingdom who were associated with each other at the University of Aston in Birmingham; see Pugh et al. 1963; Pugh et al. 1968; Hickson, Pugh, and Pheysey 1969; Inkson, Pugh, and Hickson 1970. These works represent the original Aston studies. More recent replications and extensions include Child and Mansfield 1972; Donaldson and Warner 1974; Hickson et al. 1974.) These studies have been carried out primarily in Great Britain, with some supporting evidence from international comparisons. The major conclusion of these studies is that increased size is related to increased structuring of organizational activities and decreased concentration of authority. Most of the data come from manufacturing organizations, but some are based on studies in government agencies and labor unions.

There is still other evidence in regard to the importance of size. Mahoney et al. (1972) report that managerial practices are related to the size of the unit being supervised. Flexibility in personnel assignments, the extent of delegation of authority, and an emphasis on results rather than procedures, are related to larger unit sizes.

There is another set of literature on organizational size and its relationship to the proportionate size of the administrative or supportive component in organizations. The notion is that the larger the relative size of the administrative or supportive component—that part of the organization not directly involved in production or service—the less efficient the organization will be. This line of research has basically led nowhere, since much of the research appears to have been based on the availability of data rather than on theoretical or practical concerns. Freeman's (1979) linkage of this issue to environmental pressures has the potential of developing interesting theoretical insights, but the bulk of the literature on this topic has yielded little and will not add to our understanding of the size issue.

Size and the Individual

Before turning to some problems with the relationships between size and structure, we will touch upon the impact of organizational size on the individual. For anyone who has any contact with an organization as an employee, client, or customer, its size has an immediate reality. A large organization confronts the individual with many unknowns, and size is probably the first thing that a person notices. There are sheer numbers of people doing things that are at first beyond comprehension. Unfortunately, the impact of organizational size on the individual has not been systematically investigated. A subjective impression is that the size factor has an immediate impact, which then diminishes the longer a person is in the organization or in contact with it.

This impression comes from two indirectly related sorts of studies. The first type of evidence is from investigations of the "informal work group," a phenomenon that has been universally found in all types of organizations and at all levels within them. It involves the interaction patterns that develop on the job among coworkers. These interaction patterns may or may not represent deviations from official expectations—for the present analysis this issue is unimportant. What is important is that members of organizations, large and small, are found in such groups. These groups become a meaningful part of the organization for their members. The impact of size is therefore probably strongly moderated by such groups. The person who is for whatever reason an isolate would not have the effect of size moderated and would probably face the impact continually (which in this case cannot be categorically considered either positive or negative for the mental health of the individual).

The second source of indirect evidence about the impact of size on the individual comes from studies in the community. Here the evidence suggests that, although in a large community an individual does not know or interact with the majority of those with whom he comes in contact, he still maintains primary relationships with many persons in and out of his own family (Nelson 1966). A smaller proportion of his relationships are warm and open, but the total number is probably not too different in a large community from that in a small one. This same point would appear to be true in organizations. Without the research that is needed for verification of these ideas, it seems clear that the immediate effects of size on the individual are moderated by the processes discussed. Studies of membership participation in voluntary organizations of varying sizes usually conclude that there is less participation in larger organizations.

Research evidence is inconclusive regarding the relationships between size and individual performance and reactions to the work situation. Meltzer and Salter (1962) report that among the physiological scientists they studied, no relationship was found between size of the employing organization and scientific productivity as measured by number of publications. On the other hand, there is a curvilinear relationship between size and job satisfaction. Satisfaction is greater in medium-sized (twenty-one to fifty employees) than in either larger or smaller organizations. Meltzer and Salter suggest that variables other than size are probably more important in accounting for morale and satisfaction. (See also Melcher 1975.)

In respect to the stress felt by the individual in the organization, the comprehensive research of Kahn et al. (1964) points to the same conclusion. They note:

> Americans are accustomed to thinking of growth as synonymous with organizational life, and of large size as a condition for maximum efficiency. Against these assertions must be placed the finding that stress and organi-

zational size are substantially related. The curve of stress begins to rise as we turn from tiny organizations to those of 50 or 100 persons, and the rising curve continues until we encounter the organizational giants. Only for organizations of more than 5,000 persons does the curve of stress level off— perhaps because an organization so large represents some kind of psychological infinity and further increases are unfelt. (p. 394)

The authors then suggest that stress cannot be eradicated by shrinking organizations to small size, since the economic consequences of such a move would be "tragic." They suggest that the reason for stress in large organizations is the need for coordination among the many members, and that the way to reduce stress is by reducing coordination requirements. This can be done, in their opinion, by giving subunits more autonomy.

The research findings discussed suggest that size is related to morale. Larger organizations do present their members with situations that lead to stress and lowered morale. The effects of size are undoubtedly different on different types of members. A subjective impression, for example, is that students who come to a large university from a small town with a small high school face a much more stressful situation than those from large urban schools. The same would appear to be true for other kinds of members in other kinds of organizations. The kinds of expectations and general background a person brings to the organization will be a major factor in determining how he reacts to the organization.

The issues being discussed here are obviously important in any broad conception of human values. Some of the unrest of the late 1960s can be attributed to the size of the organizations involved. Charges of depersonalization, of being treated like an IBM card, of regimented learning, and so on are essentially true. Large organizations necessitate that members to some degree be treated as members of categories rather than as separate individuals. At the same time, large organizations can and do vary in structure and performance. The negative effects of size can be minimized, if not eliminated, through such devices as granting more subunits autonomy and decentralization. Except for some attempts at communal living among those who choose to "drop out" of society, a return to the "good old days" of small, intimate organizations is impossible. It is impossible for two major reasons. The first is that contemporary technology for all kinds of organizations is such that it is probably impossible to keep an organization at a small size. (It is hardly conceivable that a moratorium would be called on technological development and that a society would be forced to go back to an earlier technological state.) The second reason is that human values themselves have undoubtedly shifted. Whether for better or worse, most members of the contemporary large organization are probably more satisfied there than they would be in a smaller, more intimate setting.

Size affects not only the people who work in organizations but also those who have contact with it as "outsiders." Even supposedly impersonal and professional people, such as accountants, apparently are awed by organizational size and give larger business firms more favorable audits than smaller ones. (Forbes 1973)

Size and Structure

This excursion into the impact of organizational size on the individual has taken us away from our major concern—that of the impact of size on structure. The evidence presented has emphasized the strong, positive relationship between size and structure. Other researchers question this emphasis. For one thing, both Blau and the Aston group utilize the official documents approach to measurement of structure. In a study that used a subjective approach, Hall and Tittle (1966) found only a modest relationship between size and perceived degree of bureaucratization. In another study, utilizing an approach similar to that of Blau and the Aston group, Hall, Haas, and Johnson (1967b) came up with mixed findings in regard to size and structure. Using data from a set of seventy-five organizations of highly varied types, they concluded:

> In general, the findings of this study in regard to size are similar to those of previous research which utilied size as a major variable; that is, the relationships between size and other structural components are inconsistent. . . . There is a slight tendency for larger organizations to be both more complex and more formalized, but only on a few variables does this relationship prove to be strong. On others, there is little, if any, established relationship.

> The complexity indicators related to size fall within three major categories. The first of these is spatial dispersion. This conclusion, in which both physical facilities and personnel are considered, is congruent with the suggestion of Anderson and Warkov that the relative size of the supportive component is also related to spatial dispersion. On a common-sense basis, such dispersion is possible only for sufficiently large organizations. A decision to add dispersed facilities may require a secondary decision to add more personnel, rather than the reverse. It also appears that a very large or extensive market is more easily or economically reached through physical dispersion. Thus, it could be argued that both size and complexity are dependent upon available economic "input," and to the extent to which such potential "input" is dispersed, large organizations will also be more complex in regard to physical dispersion.

> A second set of significant relationships is found in regard to the hierarchical differentiation. Although Woodward has noted differences in the "width" of the span of control according to the technological stages of industry, the generally accepted principle of limiting the number of subordinates supervised by one person seems to be operative here. More hierarchical levels are found in larger organizations.

> The third set of significant relationships is in the area of intradepartmental specialization or the specific division of labor. While the number of divisions is not related to size, this form of internal differentiation is. Performance of the major organizational activities plus such prerequisities as accounting and personnel management apparently are accomplished by departmentalization regardless of organizational size. Further specialization may take place within the existing departmental structure as the organization grows in size.

> In general, the relationships between size and the complexity indicators appear to be limited to a few factors. Even in those relationships found to

be statistically significant, enough deviant cases exist to cast serious doubts on the assumption that large organizations are necessarily more complex than small organizations.

The same general conclusion can be reached in regard to the formalization indicators. . . . Relatively strong relationships exist between size and the formalization of the authority structure, the stipulation of penalties for rule violation in writing, and the orientation and in-service training procedures. A general association does exist to the extent that larger organizations tend to be more formalized on the other indicators, even though the relationship is quite weak.

The most immediate implication of these findings is that neither complexity nor formalization can be implied from organizational size. A social scientist conducting research in a large organization would do well to question the frequent assumption that the organization under study is necessarily highly complex and formalized. If these two general factors are relevant to the focus of his research, he will need to examine empirically, for each organization, the level of complexity and formalization extant at that time. The ideal research procedure would be to have standardized measures of these phenomena to allow comparative research. At the minimum, the degrees to which these phenomena are present should be specified, at least nominally.

A second implication of these findings lies in the area of social control. Increased organizational formalization is a means of controlling the behavior of members of the organization by limiting individual discretion. At least one aspect of complexity, hierarchical differentiation, also is related to social control in that multiple organizational levels serve as a means of maintaining close supervision of subordinates. It seems rather clear, on the basis of this evidence, that a large organization does not necessarily have to rely upon impersonal, formalized control mechanisms. At the same time, the fact that an organization is small cannot be taken as evidence that a *gemeinschaft* sort of social system is operating. An organization need not turn to formalization if other control mechanisms are present. One such control mechanism is the level of professionalization as Hage and Blau et al. have suggested. The organizations with more professionalized staffs probably exhibit less formalization.

These findings suggest that size may be rather irrelevant as a factor in determining organizational structure. Blau et al. have indicated that structural differentiation is a *consequence* of expanding size. Our study suggests that it is relatively rare that the two factors are even associated and thus the temporal sequence or causality (expanding size produces greater differentiation) posited by Blau and colleagues is open to question. In these cases where size and complexity are associated, the sequence may well be the reverse. If a decision is made to enlarge the number of functions or activities carried out in an organization, it then becomes necessary to add more members to staff and new functional areas. (pp. 111–12)

These findings do not suggest that size is unimportant, but rather that factors other than size must be taken into account to understand structure.

Some of these additional factors will be discussed in the sections that follow.

Research on size has met with additional criticisms. Argyris (1972) has analyzed Blau's research and found it wanting in several regards. He first questions the reliance on official descriptions of organizational structures. Citing several studies that have found that organization charts are nonexistent or inaccurate, and that members of top management cannot always accurately describe their own organization, Argyris wonders if the approach that Blau has taken might not invalidate the results.

Moreover, Blau's results are open to interpretations other than Blau's. Much of the data come from civil service organizations in which there are budget limitations, distinct geographical limits or boundaries, and predetermined staff sizes. These organizations also would probably adhere most rigorously to traditional organizational forms:

> civil service organizations are designed directly from such organizational principles as task specialization, span of control, and unity of command, etc. As employees are hired they are, in accordance with unity of command and task specialization, grouped together into a functional unit. Given the notion of chain of command each unit has to have a boss. Given span of control each boss may supervise a certain number of subordinates. As the organization grows larger the number of units increases and so does the number of bosses increase, but given the span of control regulations, so does the need to coordinate the bosses. So we have super bosses. . . . Size *may be correlated with, but may not be said to generate or to cause, structural differentiation* [italics in original]. (Argyris, pp. 11–12)

The continuation of Argyris's argument is that factors other than size should be considered as determinants of organizational structure. Civil service organizations take the form that they do primarily because of civil service regulations. It also appears that the nature of the personnel in the organization affects its shape (Kasarda 1973). If the personnel are highly professionalized, for example, more administrators are needed for coordination than if the personnel are not so professionalized.

Another major criticism of viewing size as the determinant of structure comes from Aldrich (1972a). (See also Hilton 1972, Aldrich 1972b, and Heise 1972.) In a reanalysis of the Aston data, Aldrich suggests that size is actually a dependent variable: ". . . the more highly structured firms, with their greater degree of specialization, formalization, and monitoring of role performance, simply need to employ a larger work force than less structured firms" (Aldrich, p. 38). In Aldrich's reanalysis, technology emerges as the major determinant of structure.

The Technology Factor

The concept of technology in organizational analysis involves much more than the machinery or equipment used in production. Interest in technology as a major component of organizational analysis was sparked by the work of Woodward (1958, 1965), Thompson (1967), and Perrow (1967). (See also, Burns and Stalker 1961; Blauner 1964; Emery and Trist 1965; Lawrence and Lorsch 1967.) Woodward's work is particularly interesting because she stumbled on the importance of technology during the course of a research project in the United Kingdom. She found that several critical structural variables were directly linked to the nature of the technology of the industrial firms being studied. The organizations were categorized into three types: first, the small-batch or unit-production system, as exemplified by a ship-building or aircraft-manufacturing firm; second, the large-batch or mass-production organization; third, the organization that utilizes continuous production, as do chemical or petroleum manufacturers.

Woodward's findings show that the nature of the technology vitally affected the management structures of the firms studied. The number of levels in the management hierarchy, the span of control of first-line supervisors, and the ratio of managers and supervisors to other personnel were all affected by the technology employed. Not only was structure affected, but the success or effectiveness of the organizations was related to the "fit" between technology and structure. The successful firms of each type were those that had the appropriately structured technical systems. Zwerman (1970) replicated Woodward's findings in the United States.

Thompson (1967) attempts to go beyond Woodward by developing a technology typology that encompasses all organizations. Again, a threefold system is derived. The first type is the long-linked technology, involving "serial interdependence in the sense that act Z can only be performed after successful completion of act Y, which in turn rests upon act X, and so on" (pp. 15–16). The most obvious example is the assembly line, but many office procedures would involve the same serial interdependency. The second form of technology is the mediating technology. This links "clients or customers who are or wish to be interdependent" (p. 16). Telephone companies, banks, employment agencies, and post offices are examples here. The final type is the intensive technology in which "a variety of techniques is drawn upon in order to achieve a change in some specific object; but the selection, combination, and order of application are determined by feedback from the object itself" (p. 17). This form of technology is found in work with humans, as in hospitals or universities, in construction work, and in research.

Thompson does not explicitly link these types of technology with organizational structure in the sense that it has been discussed here. It is these technologies, however, upon which all of the organization's actions are based as the organization attempts to maximize its goal attainment. Thus, "under norms of rationality, organizations group positions to minimize coordination costs . . . , localizing and making conditionally autonomous, first . . . reciprocally interdependent positions, then . . . sequentially interdependent ones, and finally, . . . grouping positions homogeneously to facilitate standardization" (p. 17). Such groupings are also linked through hierarchical arrangements.

Perrow's (1967) approach to technology is based on the "raw material" that the organization manipulates. This raw material

> may be a living being, human or otherwise, a symbol or an inanimate object. People are raw materials in people-changing or people-processing organizations; symbols are materials in banks, advertising agencies and some research organizations; the interactions of people are raw materials to be manipulated by administrators in organizations; boards of directors, committees and councils are usually involved with the changing or processing of symbols and human interactions, and so on. (p. 195)

The nature of the raw material affects how the organization is structured and operated. According to Perrow, the critical factors in the nature of the raw material, and hence the nature of the technology employed to work on it, are the number of "exceptional cases encountered in the work" and the nature of the "search process" that is utilized when exceptional cases are found (pp. 195–96). Few exceptional cases are found when the raw material is some object or objects that do not vary in their consistency or malleability over time. Many exceptions are found in the obvious cases of human beings and their interactions, or the less obvious cases of many craft specialities or frontier areas within the physical sciences. Search processes range from those that are logical and analytical to those that must rely upon intuition, inspiration, chance, guesswork, or some other such unstandardized procedure. Examples of the first form of search would be the engineering process in many industries and computer programming in most instances. The second form of search would involve such diverse activities as advertising campaigns, some biomedical research, or many activities of the aerospace industry. The examples in both cases have been chosen to suggest the manner in which both the nature of the exceptions and the search process can vary across traditional organizational types.

Both the variables discussed take the form of continua along which organizations vary. These continua interact.

> On the one hand, increased knowledge of the nature of the material may lead to the perception of more varieties of possible outcomes or products, which in turn increases the need for more intimate knowledge of the nature of the material. Or the organization, with increased knowledge of one type of material, may begin to work with a variety of related materials about which more needs to be known, as when a social service agency or employment agency relaxes its admission criteria as it gains confidence, but in the process sets off more search behavior, or when a manufacturing organization starts producing new but unrelated products. On the other hand, if increased knowledge of the material is gained but no expansion of the variety of output occurs, this permits easier analysis of the sources of problems that may arise in the transformation process. It may also allow one to prevent the rise of such problems by the design of the production process. (Perrow 1967, p. 197)

Perrow's framework has been tested several times with mixed results. In a study of welfare organizations, Hage and Aiken (1969) found good support for relating routineness of the work with structure. Lawrence and Lorsch's (1967) study of effectiveness in the plastics, food, and container industries utilized the basic technological approach. Comstock and Scott (1977) found that technology was more important than size in determining structure at both the work unit and organizational levels. Their study was conducted in hospitals. On the other hand, among a series of health departments, Mohr (1971) found only a weak relationship between technological manageability and the participation of subordinates in decision making. Further, the original Aston studies did not find a strong relationship between technology and organizational structure.

The mixed results in regard to technology appear to be based on several factors. In the first place, there has been uncertainty as to the level at which technology is operative in the organization. The Aston group sheds some light on the subject. Hickson, Pugh, and Pheysey (1969) break down the general concept of technology into three components: operations technology—the techniques used in the workflow activities of the organization; materials technology—the materials used in the workflow (a highly sophisticated technique can conceivably be applied to relatively simple materials); and knowledge—the varying complexities in the knowledge system used in the workflow. In their own research, these authors have been concerned with operations technology.

In the English organizations they studied, operations technology had a secondary effect in relationship to size. They conclude:

> Structural variables will be associated with operations technology only where they are centered on the workflow. The smaller the organization, the more its structure will be pervaded by such technological effects; the larger the organization, the more these effects will be confined to variables such as job-counts of employees on activities linked with the workflow itself, and will not be detectable in variables of the more remote administrative and hierarchical structure [italics in original]. (pp. 394–95)

These findings mean that operations technology will intervene before the effects of size in these work organizations. They also imply that the administrative element in large organizations will be relatively unaffected by the operations technology. It is here that the form of the knowledge technology, which was not examined, becomes important. Meyer (1968a) has found that the introduction of automated procedures into the administrative structures of state and local departments of finance results in more levels of hierarchy, a wider span of control for first-line supervisors, fewer employees under the direction of higher supervisors, and fewer responsibilities—with more communications responsibilities—for members who are nominally in supervisory positions. In these particular organizations, the introduction of automation would be found in relatively simple knowledge technologies.

If the converse of the Meyer findings is considered, a very different picture emerges. If administrative and organizational procedures are highly nonroutine and are laden with problems and new issues, a less complex, less formalized system would be expected. It is thus very possible, as has been previously suggested, that each of the various segments of an organization can have a structure quite different from those of other segments. The operations of some units of an organization could be highly formalized and complex, while other units take an entirely different form. Analyses of intraorganizational structural variations empirically verify that different units of the same organizations have different structural forms (Hall 1962). Variations in knowledge technology would affect the administrative units of manufacturing organizations, just as operations technology affects the workflow in manufacturing. For organizations devoted wholly to administration, the knowledge technology would be of paramount importance.

Another basic problem with the studies on technology has been the kinds of organizations studied. The Aston group is most confident of its data when service and administrative units are removed from the sample. Child and Mansfield (1972) have noted that the type of industry and its technology are related—for example, the steel industry versus the computer industry—so that sampling differences between studies could increase or decrease the relationship between technology and structure.

The technology approach has also been criticized by Argyris (1972) on the ground that it is static, since change cannot be accounted for. Because organizations change, albeit slowly, there must be a reason for change. If technology is the sole source of structure, then technology must change before structure. If the technology is imported into the organization from outside, then someone or some set of individuals within the organization must decide to import the technological change. If the change is from within, again decisions have to be made. In addition, the technological approach does not include considerations of the role of individuals, separately or collectively, as they respond to or try to lead organizations.

The technology-structure issue has been approached in a diametrically different manner by Glisson (1978). He found that the structural attributes of division of labor and procedural specifications determined the degree of routinization and thus the nature of service delivery among a set of human service organizations. Glisson thus reverses the causal argument. The issue thus may be one of those chicken-versus-egg phenomena. Additional research, particularly longitudinal studies, are needed to begin to resolve this particular issue.

A good part of the literature on size and technology has been presented in an "either/or" fashion, with either technology *or* size being proposed as the key structural determinant. This is basically absurd. Some recent analyses are now combining these factors.

The Size-Technology Mix

Van de Ven, Delbecq, and Koenig (1976) examined task uncertainty, task interdependence (technological variables), and work unit size as they related to coordination mechanisms within a large state employment security agency. They found that as tasks increased in uncertainty, mutual work adjustments through horizontal communications channels and group meetings were used instead of hierarchical and impersonal forms of control. As task interdependence increased, impersonal coordination decreased, while more personalized and interactive modes of coordination, in the form of meetings, increased. Increasing size, on the other hand, was related to an increased use of impersonal modes of coordination, such as policies and procedures and predetermined work plans. Their study cannot answer the question of what happens if there is both large size and great task uncertainty and interdependence. They suggest that the technological factor is more important, but cannot demonstrate it. In a related study, Ouchi (1977) found that both size and homogeneous tasks were related to output controls on workers.

Blau and McKinley (1979) approached the issue somewhat differently. Their study of architectural firms revealed that structural complexity and task diversity were dependent upon size when there were uniform tasks, but that cognitive ideas and a professional orientation were more important with nonuniform tasks. Thus, size is important under one technological condition but not another.

The idea that size is important for certain structural variables, while technology is important for other aspects of structure receives additional support from the research of Marsh and Mannari (1981). Using data from Japanese factories, they found that structural differentiation and formalization were more a function of size than technology. On the other hand, labor inputs, cybernetic complexity, costs and wages, differentiation of management from ownership, span of control of the chief executive, and union recognition varied more with technology than with size.

Dewar and Hage (1978) found that size and technology were associated with complexity. They suggest that increases in size are related to the development of administrative specialties, while technological diversity is related to increased specialization among persons. Beyer and Trice (1979) reexamined the original Blau and Schoenherr (1971) and suggest that the earlier findings, with their strong emphasis on size, were probably a result of the type of organizations studied—state employment agencies which had very routine technologies. Beyer and Trice's own data shows that in nonroutine organizations, personnel specialization generates horizontal differentiation. They correctly suggest that a search for a single or primary cause of organizational complexity is doomed to failure. They also suggest that there should be a focus on the strategic choices that decision makers select, which may be an important step forward in the analysis of structure. We will consider this issue at a later point.

The final study to be considered in regard to the size-technology issue is that of Daft and Bradshaw (1980). In a study of universities, they found that a growth in administrative departments was related to large size, while growth in academic departments has more of a technological base. This is similar to the Dewar and Hage (1978) findings just discussed. Daft and Bradshaw go on to consider some additional explanations. They suggest that factors in an organization's environment, such as pressures from the community or government, contribute to differentiation among the academic departments. They also suggest that the decision-making process is critical and offer the interesting notion that there are two levels of decisions—the formal decision to add a department or program and an earlier decision by someone who senses a problem and becomes an "idea champion" who pushes for the formal decision. They are correct in this regard, of course, since the idea to make some kind of structural change has to begin somewhere. They do miss the fact that decisions in organizations are highly political (Pfeffer, 1978) and that many ideas that are developed never see the light of day in the sense that there is no formal action on them because they died in some committee. A final suggestion of Daft and Bradshaw's is that financial resources affect decisions about structural change. This is almost never considered by organizational analysts, economists aside, of course, but would appear to be of great importance.

These studies confirm the conclusion of Pfeffer (1978) that "there has been a pronounced tendency to examine the various determinants of structure one at a time, with one study examining technology, another the environment, and still another size" (p. 33). The possibility exists, however, that these various determinants affect structure in an interactive, rather than additive, fashion. This is very reasonable, but the presentation here will continue on a one-at-a-time basis, with our attention going next to the environment and then to the issue of choice and decision making. This is done with the understanding that these factors do interact.

The Environment Factor

In later chapters we will deal with organizational environments in detail; here the concern is simply to trace some of the implications of organizational environments for organizational structure. Of primary interest is the social environment of organizations, but the physical environment, such as climate or geography, can also be important, particularly for organizations that utilize or affect that physical environment.

Ranson, Hinings, and Greenwood (1980) suggest that environmental characteristics are constraints on organizations, affecting their scale of operations and their mode of technical production. They refer specifically to the socioeconomic infrastructure in which organizations are located. The demographic situation, including factors such as the racial and ethnic mixes present, constrains organizations as do the institutionalized values surrounding the organization. Thus, they suggest that as clergy revise their theology, the structural forms of religious organizations will be altered. Similarly, if teachers modify their pedagogical frames of reference, schools will change. The value changes are brought into the organization from outside. Organizational decision makers are faced with making the organizational structure congruent with the demands placed on it.

Ranson, Hinings, and Greenwood were concerned with the nature of the general socioeconomic situation in which organizations are embedded and the values that are related to such conditions. Other researchers have examined additional environmental elements. Khandwalla (1972) analyzed the impacts of "friendly" versus "hostile" environments on organizations. By friendly, he means that the environment is supportive, providing funds and value support. A hostile environment is a situation in which the very underpinnings of the organization are being threatened. The grave doubts raised about the nuclear energy industry in the wake of the Three Mile Island accident in Pennsylvania, plus other assorted problems with the industry, made the environment hostile for organizations in that industry. Colleges and universities had friendly environments during the 1960s and early 1970s. Money poured in for new facilities and personnel and there was a general belief that education was the key to social and international problems. Obviously, this situation has moved from one of friendliness to one of neutrality, if not hostility.

Khandwalla suggested that in a friendly environment, organizations will be structurally differentiated. The environment will be monitored by differentiated personnel who are then integrated by a series of mechanisms, such as committees and *ad hoc* coordinating groups. If the environment turns hostile, the organization will "tighten up" by centralizing and standardizing its operations.

In a slightly different approach to the same issue, Pfeffer and Leblebici (1973) analyzed the effects of competition on structure. They found that in more competitive situations, there is a greater demand for control and coordination. Reports are more frequent and there are more written communications and a greater specification of decision procedures. When competition is less intense, there are more frequent changes in product design, production processes, and number of products. Less competition provides some "slack" so that the organization can afford to do more than its routine competitive activities.

Competition is an interesting phenomenon. It occurs in the public and private sectors. It also has ramifications above and beyond economic factors. DuBick (1978), for example, studied a set of newspaper companies. He found that in a competitive environment—for example, where there was more than a single newspaper in a city—the structure of the newspaper reflected the complexity of the community. If there was not competition, the newspaper did not mirror the community as closely. Thus, in the competitive situation, attention would be paid to all components of the community, such as minority-group news. Without competition, these groups could be ignored.

Another study of competition among hospitals shows an additional side of the noneconomic aspects of competition (Fennell 1980). Fennell found that in competitive situations, hospital services increased. She attributes the increase in services to the competition rather than to service needs. Thus, competition here is counter to economic rationality, raising the costs of medical services as each hospital in a competitive situation adds more and more expensive equipment and services that are not actually needed.

Another approach to the analysis of environment on organizational structure is represented by those who have attempted to compare organizations in different social settings. Meyer and Brown (1977) made an historical analysis of government organizations in the United States. They found that the era of origin and subsequent environmental shifts were related to the degree of formalization, which is in turn related to multiple levels of hierarchy and the delegation of personnel decisions to lower levels in the organization. While the era of origin effects are pervasive, the environmental shifts force the organization to continually adjust to the context in which it is found.

Meyer and Brown studied organizations over time in one country. It is also possible to compare organizations across countries. Brown and Schneck (1979) compared Canadian and American firms. They were able to test the importance of foreign control on the structure of the organizations, with Canadian-owned firms in the United States and American-owned firms in Canada, as well as domestically owned firms in each country. They found the effects of foreign control to be problematic, with somewhat less innovation in the foreign-controlled firms, but with the rest of the relationships rather weak. Some earlier studies by the Aston group (McMillan et al. 1973; Hickson et al. 1974) reported the same basic findings in comparisons of organizations in the United Kingdom, Canada, and the United States. Tracy and Azumi (1976) found similar relationships among structural variables in Japanese firms as were found in British and American firms. They argue *against* too much emphasis on cultural differences.

Brown and Schneck (1979) did reach an important conclusion beyond the issue of foreign control. They suggest that government policy is very important for the organizations. National policies in areas such as health care or banking appear to have a direct impact on organizational structure, with clear differences here between Canada and the United States. Their call for an examination of national policies should be stressed and heeded, since it is a rather overlooked element of organizational environments. The importance of national policies and resultant funding can be seen in Freeman's (1979) findings in regard to the structure of schools. Federal money typically goes to schools for specific programs, usually in terms of specific professional services. Freeman found that federally supported programs tended to be maintained even as the rest of the local school district shifted as a result of other environmental factors. Enrollment declines could lead to a reduction in the number of teachers, but not of federally funded or mandated program personnel, such as teachers of the educationally handicapped or personnel required for the completion of federal reports.

The importance of the environment for organizations can be examined most clearly, perhaps, in cases of multinational organizations. The use of the multinational organization permits an examination of the effects of the country of origin versus the effects of the host country. Schollhammer (1971) suggested that the multinational firm is affected by its country of origin so that a Dutch-based firm would exhibit different characteristics from a Japanese-based firm in their American operations.

In an analysis of Japanese companies in the United States, Ouchi and

Jaeger (1978) and Ouichi and Johnson (1978) found the following general differences between Japanese and American firms:

American	*Japanese*
Short-term employment	Lifetime employment
Individual decision making	Consensual decision making
Individual responsibility	Collective responsibility
Rapid evaluation and promotion	Slow evaluation and promotion
Explicit, formalized control	Implicit, informal control
Specialized career path	Nonspecialized career path
Segmented concern	Holistic concern

For the sake of clarity, the notion of concern in the last difference refers to the nature of the supervisory practice, with the Japanese approach taking the whole person into account, including concern in regard to other family members. Ouichi and his associates present these differences in the form of an ideal type.

The Ouichi findings are that Japanese firms with operations in the United States resembled the Japanese model more than the American model, suggesting that the country of origin is of critical importance. Lincoln, Olson, and Hanada (1978) have approached the same issue somewhat differently. They found that the degree of presence of Japanese nationals or Japanese-Americans in a set of organizations located in the United States was related to the degree of specialization found, but not to centralization, formalization, and vertical differentiation. They suggest that their findings generally support those who say that the host country's characteristics are more important than those of the country of origin. At the same time, they note that Meyer and Rowan (1977) have developed the notion of organizational structure as a myth, so that the companies involved adopt the structure which conforms to prevailing ideologies and norms. They also imply that there may be some sort of technological imperative involved—that there are only so many ways to structure the manufacturing of electronic goods or automobile production. The argument regarding the relative importance of the origin or host country cannot yet be resolved. It would appear that both are important, with the host country characteristics modifying those of the country of origin. This would occur in interaction with technology and size.

Before concluding this section, the issue of the directionality of the relationship between environment and structure should be considered. We have already discussed the fact that organizations attempt to manipulate their environment. Neither can be viewed as determining the other in a one-direction causal link. Further, the nature of the environment is perceived by organizational decision makers and boundary spanners. The perception of the environment is then enacted in the organization through decision making. In an interesting examination of an aspect of this linkage, Leifer and Huber (1977) examined boundary-spanning behavior. They found that an organization's structure had a greater impact on the behavior of boundary spanners than did the nature of the environment that was perceived. The kind of boundary spanning activity they were concerned with was the frequency with which personnel dealt with groups and organizations outside of their own unit. They suggest that the activity of boundary spanning may affect structure, which in turn influences the nature of the perception of the environment. The environment is thus not something that is fixed "out there" beyond the organization's boundaries. Rather the environment is interpreted by individuals whose perceptions are in turn influenced by their position in the organizational structure. This in turn is reflected back into the organization and contributes to the "constituting" of the organizational structure (Ranson, Hinings, and Greenwood 1980).

The final factor to be considered in relationship to organizational structure is the issue of strategic choices made within the organization. Choices are critical in terms of the environmental factor. As Van de Ven and Ferry (1980) note, organizations in essence create their environment by choosing the domains in which they operate. Japanese firms *chose* to move some of their operations to the United States. At the same time, of course, other environmental conditions are imposed, as when laws are passed regarding the conduct of business in a host country.

The Strategic Choice Factor

The idea of strategic choice is not a new one. Chandler (1962) emphasized the importance of strategic choices for business firms such as Sears Roebuck and General Motors as they attempted to take advantage of perceived markets in their environment. The breakdown of General Motors into Chevrolet, Pontiac, and the other automotive divisions was a consequence of strategic choices.

Child (1972b) advanced this argument by noting that the internal politics of organizations determine the structural forms, the manipulation of environmental features, and the choice of relevant performance standards that are selected by organizations. The internal politics are themselves dependent upon the existing power arrangements in the organization. Again, structure begets structure.

Strategic choices are made on the basis of "bounded rationality" (Simon 1957). While the nature of rationality as a component of the decision-making process will be considered in detail in a later chapter, it is important here to note that the bounded-rationality idea means that the strategic choices are not necessarily the optimal choices. Rather, they are those that appear to be optimal as a consequence of decisions made through the political process within organizations. Katz and Kahn (1966), in their consideration of organizations as systems, utilize the concept of "equifinality," or the presence of several means available to reach a given end. Organizations are faced with both equifinality of means to ends and the presence of multiple ends. This is why the notion of choice is so important. An organization is faced with multiple environmental pressures and must choose one path among many options toward one of many objectives.

Approaching the issue from a somewhat different perspective, Miles, Snow, and Pfeffer (1972) noted that the size and technology approaches to structure have been found wanting. They suggest that organizations are faced with environments differing in their rates of change and degree of uncertainty. They also suggest that specific parts or organizations are affected by specific environmental elements. The legal department of an organization has different environmental interactions than the public relations department.

Pfeffer (1978) and Pfeffer and Salancik (1978) have emphasized the political context of the decision-making process and its relationship to structure. Pfeffer (1978, p. 48) suggests, for example, that persons carrying out nonroutine tasks are likely to have power because of their expertise; those doing routine tasks do not have this power source. The persons with expertise can claim and receive more discretion, or decentralization on a broader basis, as something won from a position of power, rather than something delegated from above.

The power perspective is also taken by Ranson, Hinings, and Greenwood (1980). They note that the power holders in organizations decide what are issues and what are not issues. Thus the decision whether to make a strategic choice or not is based on power arrangements. The term that is most commonly used to describe power arrangements in organizations is the "dominant coalition" (Thompson 1967). According to Pennings and Goodman (1977), the "dominant coalition comprises a direct and indirect 'representation' or cross-section of horizontal constituencies (that is, sub-units) and vertical constituencies (such as employees, management, owners, or stockholders) with different and possibly competing expectations" (p. 152).

This approach does not see the dominant coalition as representative democracy. Rather, the dominant coalition is the outcome of the power held by the various parties in the coalition. Thus, some units are more powerful among the horizontal constituencies and there is obvious power differentiation among the vertical constitutencies. The dominant coalition, then, is comprised of the power center in the organization. This power center or coalition is that which makes the strategic choices in regard to the organization and its structure.

Decision makers in the dominant coalition select those parts of the environment with which they will be concerned. This selection is done within a political framework in which membership in the dominant coalition can shift, as can the distribution of power within it. On the basis of selective perception of the environment, appropriate strategies can be selected for dealing with this environment. This decision making includes utilizing the appropriate technology for implementing the strategy. In the strategic choice, perspective technology is thus brought into the organization. The decisions also involve strategies for arranging roles and relationships to control and coordinate the technologies being employed. This is done to ensure continuity of the organization, its survival and growth (Chandler 1962). This is not done automatically or on a totally rational basis, as will be demonstrated.

In order to illustrate the strategic choice perspective, a partially hypothetical example will be used. Suppose that a city or cities has professional football and baseball teams. Various groups in the cities, as well as the teams themselves, have been considering the feasibility and desirability of building a domed stadium to protect both fans and teams from inclement weather and not, incidentally, to make more money. Once it is decided that such a venture is feasible and desirable, an organization is established to supervise the construction of the stadium. After initial power struggles to determine the composition of the dominant coalition, it is decided that a particular form of fund-raising technique will be used to support the construction of a particular type of stadium. Both of these are technologies; both require staffing of a particular size; both have to deal with a particular environment. Some of the environment is hostile to the idea of a stadium in the first place, while others are supportive. The construction wing of the organization must deal with a physical environment; the fund-raising wing must deal with the social environment. Both have to make choices of how they will proceed.

An organization's structure is thus not just an automatic response to size, technology, and environment. At the same time, the type of responses to size, technological, and environmental demands are limited in number. If we want to raise funds for a stadium, there are just a few ways to do it, just as there are only a few ways to produce television sets. The conclusion then must be that all four of the factors which have been discussed—size, technology, environment, and choice—are important and interactive. In some cases the environment might predominate, while in others there is a great deal of strategic choice (Hage 1980, p. 423). Organizational theory has not developed to the point where these can be combined into a predictive mathematical formula. We do know, however, that large size, coupled with routine technology, coupled with a hostile and competitive environment, coupled with a dominant coalition composed of traditional line executives will yield a structure with an intense division of labor, high formalization, and high centralization. These are structural elements that will be considered in the next chapters.

SUMMARY AND CONCLUSION

This chapter has defined organizational structure, noting that organizations actually have multiple structures because of intraorganizational variation. We have also examined those factors which have been analyzed as leading to particular structural configurations. Research regarding each factor has been presented and analyzed, with the conclusion that the most intelligent approach combines these structural determinants.

We are now ready to discuss the specific features of structure—complexity, formalization, and centralization.

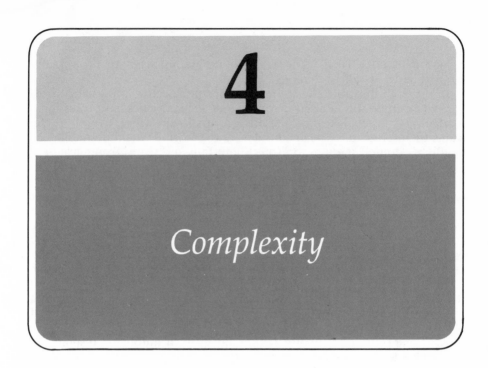

4

Complexity

The term "complex organizations" describes the subject matter of this entire book—and indeed is the title of several important works. In this chapter we will look carefully at the concept of complexity, noting what it is, and what are its sources and its consequences. From this examination it should become clear that the complexity of an organization has major effects on the behavior of its members, other structural conditions, processes within the organization, and relationships between the organization and its environment. The premise will again be that external conditions and internal processes are the dominant factors determining the form of an organization.

Like size, complexity is one of the first things that hits a person entering any organization beyond those of the simplest form: division of labor, job titles, multiple divisions, and hierarchical levels are usually immediately evident. Any familiarity with large corporations (and many small ones), the government, the military, or a school system verifies this. Organizations that seem very simple at first glance may exhibit interesting forms of complexity. Local voluntary organizations, such as the Rotary Club, labor union locals, and garden clubs usually have committees for programs, publicity, membership, community service, education, finance, and other matters, all with their attendant structure. These kinds of organizations must make provisions for the control and coordination of activities just as their more complex counterparts must.

The issue is itself made more complex by the fact that individual parts of an organization can vary in their degree of complexity. In a study of the regional office of a major oil company, for example, it was found that there were six divisions, as shown on the organization chart, Figure 4-1. The heads of the divisions had equal rank in the organization, and each was thought to be equally important to the overall success of the organization. When the divisions themselves were examined, it was found that they varied not only in size—from three to 100 members—but also in complexity. The largest division, distribution, had five separate hierarchical levels with three important subdivisions, each of which was further specialized by tasks performed by specific work groups. The smallest division, which performed legal services associated with land acquisition and other problems of service-station development, was composed of a lawyer and two secretaries.

Intraorganizational variations in complexity can also be seen in manufacturing firms with research and development departments. These departments are likely to be characterized by a shallower hierarchy than other divisions of the organization have. While there may be several levels above them, the research and development workers will be rather loosely supervised, with a wide span of control. In manufacturing departments, the span of control for each supervisor is shorter and the whole unit will look more like a pyramid. (See Figure 4-2.)

Figure 4-1   Regional office organization

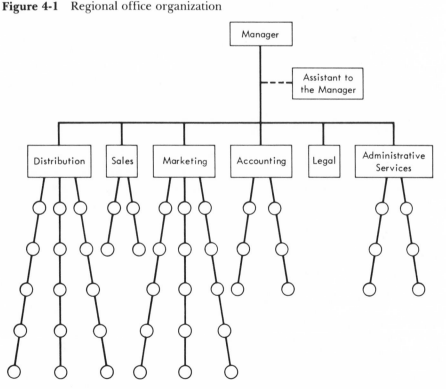

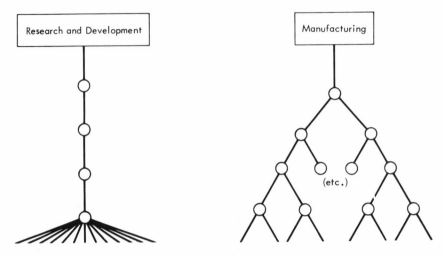

Figure 4-2 The shape of two departments in the same organization

These examples indicate the obvious—complexity is not a simple issue. The concept contains several components, which do not necessarily vary together. At the same time, the concept itself conveys a meaning in organizational literature: complex organizations contain many subparts requiring coordination and control, and the more complex an organization is, the more serious these issues become. Since organizations vary widely in their degree of complexity, regardless of the specific component of complexity used, and since wide variations are found within specific organizations, the issue is important for the overall understanding of organizations.

COMPLEXITY AS A VARIABLE

Before we can make sense out of the various research studies on complexity, we must examine the components of the concept. The three elements of complexity most commonly identified are: horizontal differentiation; vertical, or hierarchical, differentiation; and spatial dispersion.

Horizontal Differentiation

Horizontal differentiation applies to the subdivision of the tasks performed by the organization among its members. Unfortunately for conceptual clarity, there are two basic ways in which such tasks can be broken down and assigned. The first way is to give highly trained specialists a rather comprehensive range of activities to perform, and the second is to minutely subdivide the tasks so that nonspecialists can perform them. The first approach is exemplified by the professionals or craftpersons in the organizational setting who are solely responsible for complete operations. (For a discussion of craft-organized work, see Stinchcombe 1959. For a comprehensive discussion of the nature of professionally controlled work, see Vollmer and Mills 1966 and Hall 1975.) They are given the responsibility and the authority to carry out the task to its completion. The second form of horizontal differentiation is most plainly seen on the assembly line, where each worker performs only one or a few repetitive tasks. The nature of the task itself is important here, since it is the routine and uniform task that is most amenable to the second type of differentiation; nonroutine and quite varied tasks are more commonly subdivided according to the first type.

Several writers have developed specific definitions for these forms of horizontal complexity. Hage (1965), in his "axiomatic" theory, defines complexity as the "specialization in an organization . . . measured by the number of occupational specialties and the length of training required by each. The greater the number of occupations and the longer the period of training required, the more complex the organization" (p. 294). Hage's assumption is that the more training people have, the more they are differentiated from other people who might have similar amounts of training but in different specialties. This definition is almost identical in its implications to that of Price (1968), who states: "Complexity may be defined as the degree of knowledge required to produce the output of a system. The degree of complexity of an organization can be measured by the degree of education of its members. The higher the education, the higher the complexity" (p. 26).

In some later research, Hage and Aiken (1967a) develop this approach further:

> We interpret complexity to mean at least three things: the number of occupational specialties, the professional activity, and the professional training. Organizations vary in the number of occupational specialties that they utilize in achieving their goals. This variable was measured by asking respondents to report their major duties; each respondent was then classified according to the type of occupational specialty, e.g., psychiatrist, rehabilitation counselor, teacher, nurse, social worker, and so on. The variable, degree of professional activity, reflects the number of professional associations in which the respondents were involved, the number of meetings attended, and the number of offices held or number of papers given at professional meetings. The amount of professional training was based on the amount of college training as well as other professional training. (pp. 79–80)

Hage and Aiken's research was carried out in health and welfare organizations, where the emphasis on professional backgrounds was very appropriate. While this emphasis is not universally applicable in all types of organizations, the point regarding extent of training and depth of experience would hold across organizations.

This form of horizontal differentiation introduces additional complexities into the organization, in that a high level of specialization requires coordination of the specialists. In many cases, personnel specifically designated as coordinating personnel have to be assigned to ensure that the various efforts do not work at cross-purposes and that the overall organizational tasks are accomplished.

A different approach to horizontal differentiation can be seen in the work of Blau and Schoenherr (1971). Their definition is the "number of different positions and different subunits in the organization," and their emphasis is on the formal structure as defined by the organization (p. 16). An organization is more complex if it has more such positions and subunits. Organizations spread out horizontally as work is subdivided for task accomplishment. This definition is similar to the indicators of complexity used by Hall, Haas, and Johnson (1967b). They used the number of divisions within an organization and the number of specialties within the divisions as complexity indicators. Pugh, Hickson, Hinings, and Turner (1968) approach the issue in a closely related way, although they use the term "specialization" in their discussion of this phenomenon. They also introduce the concept of "configuration" as an overall indicator of the "shape" of the organization. This latter concept contains the vertical as well as the horizontal factor of work subdivision by task.

These two approaches to horizontal differentiation appear to have very similar roots, since both are concerned with the division of labor within the organization. The critical difference between these forms of horizontal differentiation appears to be the scope of the ultimate tasks of the organization (Dewar and Hage 1978). Organizations that attempt to carry out a wide variety of activities and that have clients or customers who require a variety of services would divide the labor into work performed by specialists. The more minute division of labor would occur when the organization's tasks are not so diffuse and when the organization has grown in size, since such a division of labor provides an economy of scale. These two forms of complexity are not alternative ways to organize for the same task. But the two forms are likely to occur within the same organization, since most organizations face uncertainty and must deal with the routine.

In the last chapter we discussed the various arguments that have been presented to explain horizontal differentiation. Much of the argument centered around the issue of routinization versus size in determining horizontal differentiation. Dewar and Hage (1978) emphasized the importance of the scope of the tasks of the organization, while Daft and Bradshaw (1980) emphasized the importance of external pressures on the organization. Beyer and Trice (1979) suggested that the technological factor was crucial, with personnel specialization or professionalization as the key to horizontal differentiation in nonroutine settings. Blau and McKinley (1979) also emphasized the importance of professional personnel. It may well be that some sort of "occupational principle" (Freidson 1973) of organization operates in highly professionalized settings, with the professional personnel having power through their expertise, which enables them to set the parameters of their work. Since autonomy is critically important for professionals (Hall 1968), the presence of a variety of types of professionals in an organization, as in the case of the Hage and Aiken (1967a) study, would lead to horizontal differentiation by occupational specialty. In situations in which there is not occupational power, it is to the organization's interests to subdivide the tasks more minutely. This argument involves technology and choice as the major determinants of horizontal differentiation, but the research of Blau and Schoenherr (1971) and the replicative study by Mileti, Gillespie, and Haas (1977) reaffirms the importance of the size factor. The Daft and Bradshaw (1980) research emphasizes the importance of the environment. Disentanglement is thus not possible, nor desirable, in terms of the sources of horizontal differentiation.

Vertical Differentiation

Vertical or hierarchical differentiation is a less complicated matter than horizontal differentiation. Research into this vertical dimension has used straightforward indicators of the depth of the hierarchy. Meyer (1968a) uses the "proliferation of supervisory levels" as his measures of the depth of an organization. Pugh, Hickson, Hinings, and Turner (1968) suggest that the vertical dimension can be measured by a "count of the number of job positions between the chief executive and the employees working on the output" (p. 78). Hall, Haas, and Johnson (1967) used the "number of levels in the deepest single division" and the "mean number of levels for the organization as a whole" (total number of levels in all divisions/ number of divisions) as their indicators (p. 906).

These direct indicators of vertical differentiation involve an important assumption that should be made explicit: authority is distributed in accordance with the level in the hierarchy; that is, the higher the level, the greater the authority. Although in the vast majority of cases this would be a valid assumption, the proliferation of levels can represent phenomena other than the distribution of authority. For example, in organizations that utilize professional personnel, arrangements may not have been made to allow advancement within the same job title. A physicist may be hired as a physicist, but if the organization's policies do not allow much of a salary range for that job title, the person in question may be "promoted" to a higher position without an actual change in his work. In this example, the organization would not be as deep as it appears. Many organizations facing this issue have removed salary restrictions for their professional personnel, allowing the person to retain his job title but providing a wider range of pay within a particular job title. Nevertheless, an essentially false hierarchy may be erroneously observed through the exclusive use of number of levels as defined by the organizations.

Another, similar difficulty is the question of whether authority is actually distributed throughout the hierarchy. This issue will be taken up in detail in a later chapter, but it should be noted here that a relatively deep hierarchy concentrates power at the top of the organization, with those in intermediate positions having little to do other than routine administrative work. Both these exceptions to the rule (that authority is distributed according to the rank in the hierarchy) require an extremely detailed knowledge of the organization before these conclusions may be drawn. In the great majority of cases, however, the simple measures of vertical differentiation that have been used are realistic indicators of the distribution of authority.

Most analyses of the sources of vertical differentiation focus on the familiar issues of size and technology, with size being consistently found to be related to vertical differentiation, usually at a decreasing rate. That is, as size increases, the number of levels in the hierarchy will increase, but at a slower rate than the increase in size. An interesting exception to this explanation is provided by Meyer and Brown (1977) in their analysis of city, county, and state financial agencies. They found that as formalized personnel (civil service) procedures were introduced into organizations, multitiered hierarchies developed. They develop a causal chain from environment to formalization to vertical differentiation. Again, the multiple sources of structure must continue to be taken into account.

Both horizontal and vertical differentiation present organizations with problems of control, communication, and coordination. Subunits along either axis (this would include both aspects of horizontal differentiation) are nuclei that are differentiated from adjacent units and the total organization according to horizontal or vertical factors. The greater the differentiation, the greater the potentiality for difficulties in control, coordination, and communication.

There is inconsistent evidence in regard to the relationship between horizontal and vertical differentiation. Blau and Schoenherr (1971) found that they did not vary together, while Mileti, Gillespie, and Haas (1977) found that they did covary. The answer to the different findings may lie in the issue of the types of organizations studied, as Mileti et al. suggest.

Spatial Dispersion

The final element in complexity, spatial dispersion, can actually be a form of horizontal or vertical differentiation. That is, activities and personnel can be dispersed in space, according to either horizontal or vertical functions, by the separation of power centers or tasks. An example of the former case are field offices of sales or welfare organizations, in which the tasks performed by the various field offices are essentially identical (low complexity on the horizontal axis) and the power in the organization is differentiated between the central office and the field offices. An example of the latter case are local plants of a manufacturing concern, each of which is specialized by product and technology.

Spatial dispersion becomes a separate element in the complexity concept when it is realized that an organization can perform the same functions with the same division of labor and hierarchical arrangements in multiple locations. A business firm, for example, can have a complex set of sales procedures requiring highly specialized salesmen in the field. These salesmen can be dispersed from a central office or through regional or state or local offices, with essentially the same hierarchical arrangements. Complexity is thus increased with the development of spatially dispersed activities, even if the horizontal and vertical differentiation remains the same across the spatially separated units.

The spatial-dispersion concept is relatively simple to operationalize. In a study of labor union locals, Raphael (1967) notes:

> The spatial dispersion of members refers to the number of spatially separated places in which the members of a local union are employed. This . . . is a continuous quantitative variable. At one extreme of the continuum, organizations have memberships concentrated in one-plant settings. At the opposite end of the continuum, the members are so extremely dispersed spatially that they even rotate continuously among numerous shops, jobs, and employers within a geographical space of at least several square miles. (p. 770)

Hall, Haas, and Johnson (1967b) used the following indicators in their study: (1) the degree to which physical facilities are spatially dispersed, (2) the location (distance from the organizational headquarters) of the spatially dispersed facilities, (3) the degree to which personnel are spatially dispersed, and (4) the location of spatially dispersed personnel (p. 906). These indicators are highly correlated.

VARIANCE OF COMPLEXITY ELEMENTS

The discussion thus far has suggested that the three major elements of complexity vary, often independently of each other. Before further discussing such independent variance, it should be stressed that these elements can obviously vary together. Organizations with little horizontal, vertical, or spatial complexity can easily be identified—the small business comes most readily to mind. The same phenomenon can occur, however, in large organizations. Crozier's (1964) analysis of two separate government organizations in France graphically demonstrates this. The first organization, a clerical agency, was characterized by a very simple division of labor: while tasks were highly routine and repetitious, there was little differentiation among them. Also, considering the size of the organization, there was a very shallow hierarchy. The organization was not complex on the horizontal and vertical axes.

The third axis of spatial dispersion is added when the French tobacco company (the "Industrial Monopoly") in Crozier's analysis is considered. Thirty spatially dispersed plants comprise the system. The plants are fairly large, with 350 to 400 employees on the average, but there are only six categories of workers in each plant. Production workers, who are paid equal wages throughout the system, comprise the bulk of the labor force, and there is little differentiation among their tasks. Maintenance workers are more specialized, with electricians, boilermakers, and metal workers in this group. The third group is the shop foremen, who hold supervisory positions in both plant and white-collar office operations. Even here, the tasks performed are quite similar. Administrative jobs, such as personnel, purchasing, or accounting, are few in number and minimally professionalized. There is one technical engineer per plant. The top position is that of the plant director, who usually has an assistant.

This relatively large dispersed organization is structurally very simple. The simplicity does not mean that it does not face severe problems—Crozier documents these in great detail—but that the problems are based on external and internal conditions that are not related to its structure. The imposition of civil service personnel regulations, the power of the maintenance personnel—who can actually control the output of the plants by the speed at which they maintain the equipment—and certain characteristics of the French society combine to make these organizations much less efficient and effective than they might be. It seems clear that increased complexity on the vertical and horizontal axes would do little to improve the performance of these plants. In both the tobacco monopoly and the clerical agency (which was also characterized by a poor performance record), the structural characteristics are based upon the tasks to be performed and the technology available, rather than being a simple function of size. These noncomplex organizations are massive systems designed to perform simple and unchanging tasks. It can be hypothesized that if the tasks and technology were altered to develop a more effective system, the organizations would become more complex.

In direct contrast to the simple organizations just described, the diversified industrial or government organization serves as an example of the organization that is complex on all three axes. Huge industrial concerns, such as Standard Oil of New Jersey or du Pont, are characterized by extreme complexity. The same would be true for operations of national, state, and some local governments, as well as such diverse organizations as the Catholic Church, the New York City school system, and the University of California.

These extreme cases serve as a reminder that organizations can be highly or minimally complex in all facets of the complexity concept. Other common sense examples suggest that such covariance is not the necessary pattern. A college, for example, usually has a low degree of vertical differentiation and usually no spatial dispersion, but a high degree of horizontal differentiation. Most manufacturing plants would have a greater division of labor along the horizontal axis than those studied by Crozier, although the hierarchical levels may be the same. The offensive unit of a football team is highly specialized but essentially has only two ranks. High vertical differentiation with little horizontal differentiation is exemplified by the army battalion.

In Chapter 3 we considered the factors associated with different structural characteristics. These are the sources of the various forms of complexity that have been discussed. If we know why organizations are differentially complex, we should then be able to specify some of the consequences of this complexity.

THE CONSEQUENCES OF COMPLEXITY

The first point to be considered is that of spatial complexity, a topic that has been overly neglected in research. Anderson and Warkow (1961), in their examination of the size of the administrative component of organizations, considered the spatial-dispersion factor. One of their major findings was that the "relative size of the administrative component increases as the number of places at which work is performed increases" (p. 27).

This finding was not upheld in Raphael's (1967) study of labor union locals. In this case, spatial dispersion was associated with a decrease in the size of the administrative component. Raphael attributes the difference in findings to the fact that labor unions are voluntary associations and that dispersed locals are semiautonomous from centralized control and operate on their own. She also points out that the dispersed locals tend to be less democratic than those that are centralized and have a larger administrative apparatus. In the centralized setting, according to this analysis, there is a greater likelihood that intensive communication networks will develop, thus enhancing the likelihood of democratic processes. The differences in the control mechanism of the voluntary association lead to a more oligarchic situation in the dispersed voluntary association, since a managerial clique can be formed containing elected leaders and selected members who perform many of the administrative functions. This lowers the size of the administrative component in the dispersed unions, but also decreases the opportunities for participation of the rank and file.

These findings reemphasize the fact that voluntary organizations are qualitatively different in many important attributes from nonvoluntary organizations. The differences in control and administrative mechanisms found by Raphael are only part of the picture. Such organizations obviously require a different form of attachment of members and consistent efforts to maintain member support (see Etzioni 1961, 1975, for an extended discussion of this point). These differences make generalizations comparing nonvoluntary to voluntary organizations extremely dangerous. It is fairly clear that they are not exact opposites in every characteristic, but the structure and processes in voluntary organizations clearly require careful analysis to determine where the two forms of organizations coincide and where they do not.

Another examination of spatial dispersion is contained in the research of Pugh, Hickson, Hinings, and Turner (1969). As in the case of size, they treat number of operating sites as a contextual variable rather than as an element of the organization's structure, but as was also the case with size, spatial dispersion can perhaps more legitimately be treated as a structural characteristic. The research setting, it will be remembered, is the English Midlands, and the organizations themselves do not represent the entire spectrum, being concentrated in engineering and the metallurgical industries. Nevertheless, the organizations did vary in dispersion, with service-oriented organizations having the greatest degree of dispersion.

The relationships with other structural characteristics further indicate the consequences of complexity in general. Spatial dispersion was inversely related to structuring of activities. Activities are structured when work roles are predefined; and in dispersed organizations, the workers have more discretion in how they carry on their day-to-day activities. Spatial dispersion was positively related to concentration of authority. Important organizational decisions were dispersed to multiple operating sites. Since the work is specialized and a taller hierarchy is found in such situations, the findings that authority is concentrated in these settings is consistent with the earlier findings. There was also a positive relationship between dispersion and line control of work flow, meaning, as was indicated earlier, that the actual work being performed is controlled by the workers in direct contact with the product, clients, or customers. When there is line control of work flow, there are centrally controlled personnel policies to ensure that the workers are selected for their ability to carry out the work, without a lot of variation among them. In the case of spatial dispersion, therefore, while the workers on the "line" do not have specific operating procedures spelled out for them and have a rather large degree of control over what they do on the job, the basic decisions regarding what they work on and who will be employed in the first place are retained by the organization. Dispersion is thus accompanied by the retention of certain kinds of control by the central organizations.

An assumption throughout this discussion is that most organizations are complex in one of the various configurations discussed. Another assumption, verifiable from a variety of forms of evidence, is that *there is a strong tendency for organizations to become more complex as their own activities and the environment around them become more complex.* Since organizations grow in size, and since size and complexity are related, this is a moderately well-supported assumption. Organizations that survive become more complex.

Increased complexity leads to greater problems of coordination and control. Now let us examine these problems in more detail.

COORDINATION AND CONTROL

In their significant study, *Organization and Environment*, Lawrence and Lorsch (1967) examined the sources and consequences of complexity. Their approach to complexity is through the term *differentiation*, by which they mean the division of organizations into parts to perform their activities (horizontal differentiation, in our terms), such as sales, production, or research. To this rather standard approach to differentiation, Lawrence and Lorsch add components that are implicit in the discussions of complexity presented here. They note that structural differentiation includes differences in attitude and behavior on the part of members of the differentiated departments. These include orientations toward the particular goals of the department, differing emphases on interpersonal skills, varied time perspectives, and the type and extent of formalization of the structure. Departments therefore vary not only in the specific tasks they perform, but also in the underlying behavior and outlooks of their members.

The data for the analysis of differentiation come from firms in three industries in the United States. The first set of industries was comprised of firms making and selling plastics in the form of powder, pellets, and sheets.

> Their products went to industrial customers of all sizes, from the large automobile, appliance, furniture, paint, textile, and paper companies to the smaller firms making toys, containers, and household items. The organizations studied emphasized specialty plastics tailored to specific uses rather than standardized commodity plastics. They all built their product-development work on the science of polymer chemistry. Production was continuous, with relatively few workers needed to monitor the automatic and semiautomatic processing equipment. (p. 24)

These organizations were in a highly competitive market situation. According to the executives interviewed, the major competitive issue was the development of new and revised products and processes. The life cycle of any product was likely to be short, since competitors were all engaged in intensive research and could make even a very successful product quickly obsolete. The executives noted that "the most hazardous aspect of the industrial environment revolved around the relevant scientific knowledge" (p. 25). These organizations were in a changing and "turbulent" environment, with both input—in the form of scientific knowledge—and the consumption of output—in the form of customer satisfaction from purchasing the product—highly uncertain. On the other hand, the production process itself was characterized by its certainty. Once the original technical specifications for a particular product were developed, the production process could proceed quite automatically, since the mix between such production variables as pressure, temperature, and chemical composition could be easily measured, and monitoring was part of the production process itself.

The six organizations studied within the plastics industry each had four basic functional departments—sales, production, applied research, and fundamental research—that differed in their own structures. The production departments were the most formalized, the fundamental research units the least. Sales department personnel were the most concerned with interpersonal relationships, and production departments were the least, with the two research units falling in between. The interesting dimension of the time perspective taken shows the departments falling into a predictable pattern—from shortest to longest time perspective, sales, production, applied research, and fundamental research. The members of the various departments were also differentiated in terms of personal goals, with sale personnel concerned with customer problems and the marketplace; production personnel with cost reduction and efficiency; and research personnel concerned with scientific matters, as well as the more immediate practical issues of process improvement and modification. The scientific personnel were not as concerned with purely scientific matters as the authors had anticipated, but they did have clearly different goals from those of the members of other departments.

Differentiation in these organizations thus clearly involves more than sheer differentiation by task. The members of the departments were differentiated according to organizationally important behaviors and attitudes. Equally or perhaps more important for the general discussion is the fact that these differences in task, behavior, and attitude are directly related to the kind of environment that the various departments must work with in their short- and long-run activities. *A high degree of differentiation (complexity) is therefore related to a highly complex and differentiated environment* (Burns and Stalker 1961). In this case the complexity refers to the competitive situation in which the organizations find themselves (this degree of competition is not limited to profit-making organizations) and to the rapidly changing and complicated technological world in which they must survive.

To provide contrasts for the plastics firms, Lawrence and Lorsch studied two other industries; the major factor in their selection was the rate of environmental change. The second chosen was the standardized container industry. The rate of sales increase in this industry was at about the level of the rate of population growth and the growth of the gross national product, so the organizations in the industry were approximately keeping even with the environment in these respects. More important for the purposes of their study, no significant new products had been introduced in two decades. The major competitive factors were "operational issues of maintaining customer service through prompt delivery and consistent product quality while minimizing operating costs" (p. 86). While these are not easy or simple tasks to perform, they are stable; and the problems and prospects for the future are much more certain than in the plastics field.

The third set of organizations studied was in the packaged foods industry. In terms of environmental conditions, these organizations were intermediate between the plastics and container firms. While they engaged heavily in innovations, the rate of new-product introduction and the growth of sales were less than in the plastics industry, but more than in the container field.

When the differentiation within the organizations in these three industries was examined, the findings were as predicted—the plastics firms were the most differentiated, followed by the food firms, and then by the container firms. From this evidence and that presented earlier, the role of the environment in shaping an organization becomes obvious. The specific form an organization takes is dependent upon the environmental conditions it faces. Added to this, of course, are the considerations of size, traditions within a particular organization or set of organizations, and the idiosyncrasies of individual organizations. These latter factors are "added on" after the environmental considerations, since the environment imposes the basic requirements for shaping the organization; the other considerations appear to be limited to variations on the central theme provided by the environment.

If this interpretation of the sources of complexity is taken as correct (and even if it is not), the major question remains: What does complexity do to an organization? Lawrence and Lorsch provide some important indications of the consequences in their further analysis of organizations in these three industries. They base their analysis on the concept of *integration*, which they define as "the quality of the state of collaboration that exists among departments that are required to achieve unity of effort by the demands of the environment" (p. 47). The authors are also concerned with the effectiveness of the organizations. Here they use rather standard and appropriate market and economic measures. Organizations are more effective when they meet environmental pressures and when they allow their members to achieve their individual goals.

The results of the analysis of integration and effectiveness are in some ways surprising. In the plastics industry, the most effective organizations are those with the greatest degree of differentiation, and these also face the most severe integration problems. Their effectiveness in the face of high differentiation is explained by their successful conflict resolution. It is not the idea of successful conflict resolution that is surprising; it is the fact that the effective organizations were characterized by a high degree of conflict in the first place—that they were not totally harmonious, with all personnel working as members of one happy team. From the data discussed earlier, it is apparent that the differentiation in terms of departmental and individual attitudes and behavior would lead inevitably to conflict. In these organizations, such conflict contributes to effectiveness.

Conflict per se, of course, would be detrimental to the organization if it were not resolved. So another important contribution of this research is its analysis of conflict resolution. The authors do not suggest that there is one best form of such resolution. Rather, they provide evidence that conflict-resolution processes vary according to the specific conflict situations in a particular form of organization. In the case of the highly differentiated plastics organizations, integration is achieved by departments or individuals who are in a position, and have the knowledge available, to work with the departments involved in conflict situations. In this case, the position is relatively low in the managerial hierarchy rather than at the top. This lower position is necessary because of the specific knowledge required to deal with the departments and issues involved. The highly differentiated and effective organization thus anticipates conflict and establishes integrating (conflict-resolving) departments and individuals whose primary purpose is to work with the departments in (inherent) conflict. Another important consideration is that the integrating departments or individuals are equidistant between the conflicting departments in terms of their time, goal, interpersonal, and structural orientations. This middle position leads to effective resolution not through simple compromise, but rather through direct confrontations between the conflicting parties. Conflict resolution in this setting thus becomes a process whereby the parties thrash out their differences in the open with the assistance of integrators who understand both their positions.

In the container corporations, with their lesser degree of differentiation, conflicts also arise, but not to the extent found in the plastics firms, owing to less differentiation. In the container industry, conflicts are resolved at the top of the organization, because those at the top have greater knowledge, made possible by the stable environment and the lack of differentiation between organizational segments. Lacking differentiation, knowledge is not as specialized, and a top executive can have a good grasp of what is going on in the major divisions. Lawrence and Lorsch suggest that in this case, and in others like it, decentralization of influence would be harmful. The food-processing firms generally fall between the plastics and the container firms in the extent of their differentiation and in the integration problems faced.

A major conclusion from this analysis is that *effectiveness is not achieved through following one organizational model.* While our concern here is with neither effectiveness nor organizational models, this conclusion is vitally important for understanding organizations. In other words, *there is no one best way to organize for the purpose of achieving the highly varied goals of organizations within a highly varied environment.* Particular combinations of goals and activities within particular kinds of environments do call for particular organizational structures if effectiveness is a major criterion for the organization. Organizational structure is thus not a random phenomenon, but is based on the factors that have been stressed throughout this analysis.

This conclusion is strengthened from consideration of Blau and Schoenherr's (1971) findings, which were based on research into government finance and public personnel agencies. They also find that increased complexity engenders problems of communication and coordination. Personnel in the managerial hierarchy spend more time in dealing with these problems than in direct supervision in a highly complex organization. There is also pressure in complex organizations to add personnel to handle the increased control and coordination activities, increasing the proportion of the total personnel devoted to such activities.

This fact introduces an interesting paradox into the analysis of organizations. While large organizations can experience savings through economies of large size, the complexity that is related to large size creates cross-pressures to add managerial personnel for control, coordination, and conflict-reduction. Decisions to physically disperse, add divisions, or add hierarchical levels may be made in the interests of economy. At the same time, the economies realized may be counterbalanced by the added burdens of keeping the organization together. Complex organizations are thus complex in more ways than just their structure. The processes within such organizations are also complex. The techniques that are effective and efficient within a simple structure just may not be effective or efficient in a more complex case.

SOME ADDITIONAL CORRELATES OF COMPLEXITY

Complexity is related to additional characteristics of organizations. Hage and Aiken's (1967b) analysis of program change in the sixteen welfare organizations they studied illustrates this point well. Program change in these agencies involves the adoption of new services and techniques— implicitly to increase the quality of the services rendered. Whether this is in fact the case is not specified, but it can be hypothesized that in a period of rapid change in the total social system and rapid developments in treatment technologies, program change would at least be related to efforts to upgrade the services performed.

The findings from this study suggest that complexity is related to the rate of program change. The more occupational specialties represented in an agency, the greater the likelihood of program change. However, the effect of this form of complexity is minimized when other organizational characteristics are examined. The function (or task) of the organization, as defined by the amount of time a client spends with the agency (the more time the client spends with the agency, the more complete its service), is highly correlated with the number of occupational specialties. When organizational size and auspices are controlled, the relationship between the number of occupational specialties and rate of program change disappears. This is explained by the sequence of the development of these characteristics. The function, size, and auspices affect the number of occupational specialties found in an organization, and this is in turn related to the rate of program change. Since function is the strongest of the predictors, the line of reasoning presented previously is again confirmed. What an organization does affects its structure, in terms of both size and occupational specialization.

Evidence from the same study in regard to vertical differentiation suggests that when authority is concentrated at the top of the organization, the rate of program change decreases. Although Hage and Aiken do not have direct information on the number of hierarchical levels, the implication from their data is that a low number of levels is negatively associated with this form of change. In this case, the lower-level organizational members—professionals—are not used in the decision-making process and are thus underutilized. Another finding in the same study bears directly on this: the rate of participation in decision making is strongly and positively related to high rates of program change. The effective utilization of professional personnel involves their being allowed to enter the decision-making process through some power in the hierarchy. If they are without power, their contributions are minimized. These findings and the derived interpretations are consistent with the general literature on professionals in organizations.

Both vertical and horizontal differentiation are related to higher rates of program change. This finding suggests that when such forms of differentiation are present, much information will be flowing in the system—information that will contain conflicting ideas and proposals. Organizations that are complex in this way face the problem of integrating the diverse occupations and ideas deriving from the different organizational members. Later studies confirm that such conflict is present and must be dealt with by the organization. The proper method of handling such conflict is *not* by suppression; we have seen that this would represent the exact opposite of the effective utilization of highly trained personnel. We will see later that such conflicts actually work to the organization's advantage.

Aiken and Hage (1968) continued their investigation of these sixteen agencies three years later, following up some of the leads from the previous research. The dependent variable in the most recent study was organizational interdependence, as indicated by the number of joint programs in which the agencies participate. The findings from this analysis are not surprising in light of the earlier findings and discussion. *"Organizations with many joint programs are more complex organizations, that is they are more highly professionalized and have more diverse occupational structure"* (p. 920). The interpretation given to these findings is that a decision to engage in joint programs leads to the importation of new specialties into the organization, since joint programs are likely to be highly specialized and the personnel in the agency would not have the skills necessary for participation.

These findings have interesting implications for organizations and for the society of which they are a part. Aiken and Hage state:

> Our assumptions help to explain the increasing frequency of organizational interdependency, especially that involving joint programs. As education level increases, the division of labor proceeds (stimulated by research and technology), and organizations become more complex. As they do, they also become more innovative. The search for resources needed to support such innovations requires interdependent relations with other organizations. At first, these interdependencies may be established with different goals and in areas that are more tangential to the organization. Over time, however, it may be that cooperation among organizations will multiply, involving interdependencies in more critical areas, and involve organizations having more similar goals. It is scarcity of resources that forces organizations to enter into more cooperative activities with other organizations, thus creating more integration of organizations into a community structure. The long-range consequence of this process will probably be a gradually heightened coordination in communities. (pp. 928–29)

If there is a tendency for organizations to become more complex because of internal and external pressures, the implication of these findings is that joint programs and other interorganizational relationships will continue to develop, probably at an increasing rate. In the long run this would lead to a society in which the web of interrelationships between organizations would become extremely intricate and the total society more organizationally "dense." This in turn implies a condition in which both individuals and the society as a whole are dependent upon fewer and more complex organizations. The nature of these organizations and their orientation toward the good of the few or of the many present the society with the dilemma of the source of control of the organizations. If this trend is realized, decisions regarding organizational futures become decisions about society.

The short-run implications of these findings would seem to be that the more complex an organization is, the more complex it will become, since the development of new programs and interorganizational relationships both lead to additional complexity. The Aiken–Hage approach to complexity has been organized around the utilization of professionals to accomplish and advance the tasks of the organizations studied. Since not all organizational members are professionalized, and since horizontal differentiation involves more than this variable, our focus will now shift to alternative modes of differentiation and their relationships with other variables.

Hage and Aiken's work on program change implies that how organizations change is related to their organizational characteristics. This implication is supported in later research by Baldridge and Burnham (1975). Their research compared the effects of structural characteristics (such as size and complexity), together with environmental conditions (changing or heterogeneous), with individual characteristics (age, attitudes, and education) in terms of their impact on organizational innovation. They found that the organizational characteristics were more strongly related to innovation in organizations. This does not negate the role of the individual, but suggests that factors such as complexity are crucial in understanding how and why processes such as innovation occur.

SUMMARY AND CONCLUSIONS

This chapter has dealt with a central variable in organizational analysis. The discussion has been based on research carried out in a wide variety of organizational settings. The emphasis has been on comparative research rather than on case studies, in the belief that, while case studies can generate interesting hypotheses, firm conclusions can be drawn only from a broader test of the hypotheses derived. Despite the soundness of the research cited in the discussion, it is still premature to accept the results without reservations. Additional research in a wider variety of settings, including the vast array of voluntary organizations, is necessary before definite conclusions are warranted. The disparity between formal specifications of relationships and the manner in which they are actually carried out must be determined. In spite of these reservations and problems, this chapter has revealed several important points about complexity and, more important, about organizations.

Complexity takes several forms: horizontal differentiation—through an intense division of labor or through the performance of tasks by specialists; vertical differentiation; and spatial dispersion. It was emphasized that organizations can vary internally in the the degree to which complexity on these various axes is present. In terms of structure, organizations with an intense subdivision of labor tend to have less vertical differentiation. Those with horizontal differentiation by specialists usually have rather tall hierarchies. These differences are largely attributable to the nature of the technology being employed in the organization.

Regardless of the form, high degrees of complexity introduce problems of coordination, control, and communication for the organization. The Lawrence and Lorsch research indicates that such problems are sources of conflict for the organization, but that such conflict is positively related to effectiveness if it is resolved in the appropriate manner. Indirectly, therefore, complexity is also related to effectiveness. This conclusion only holds, of course, when the technology and environment require complexity. In those cases where less internal differentiation is demanded, high levels of complexity would not contribute to organizational effectiveness.

The evidence presented strengthens the theme of the entire analysis. Environmental and technological factors, together with the related consideration of the nature of the personnel, traditions, decision making, and other internal conditions, determine the form of an organization at any particular point in time. As these factors change, the form of the organization will also change, as will its outcomes in terms of innovations or interactions with other organizations.

5

Formalization

We have already alluded to formalization several times. In this chapter the exact nature of this important aspect of organizational structure will be explicitly defined. The antecedents and consequences of formalization will also be spelled out. In addition, the reactions of individuals to the degree of formalization will be analyzed. In many ways, formalization is the key structural variable for the individual because a person's behavior is vitally affected by the degree of such formalization. The amount of individual discretion is inversely related to the amount of preprogramming of behavior by the organization.

Before examining the nature of formalization it should be noted that formalization is not a neutral concept. Indeed, the degree to which an organization is formalized is an indication of the perspectives of its decision makers in regard to organizational members. If the members are thought to be capable of exercising excellent judgment and self control, formalization will be low; if they are viewed as incapable of making their own decisions and requiring a large number of rules to guide their behavior, formalization will be high. Formalization involves control over the individual (Clegg and Dunkerley 1980) and thus has an ethical and political meaning in addition to being a structural component.

The introduction of the individual does not mean a shift away from the organizational level of analysis. Formalization has important consequences for the organization and its subunits in terms of such processes as communications and innovation.

Some of the essence of formalization has already been discussed under the subject of the Weberian model of bureaucracy. The rules and procedures designed to handle contingencies faced by the organization are part of what is called formalization. The extent of rules and procedures varies. The simple matter of what time a person gets to work can differ widely among and within organizations in regard to the degree to which this act is formally specified. At the high end of the formalization continuum are organizations that specify that people must be at their desk or work spot at 8 A.M. or they will be "docked" a half-hour's pay. Close to the other end there are no rules about being in the office or shop at a particular time, just as long as the work gets done. This is typified by many academic institutions. There may well be informal norms operative in this area that are quite strong. For example, I once worked in a situation where, for a period of time, the informal expectation was that Saturday mornings were to be spent at the office, even if this meant only a token appearance. For the moment, however, the informal aspect of rules, procedures, and so on will be ignored. The variation in the extent of such rules is not a matter of the professionalization of the labor force, as might be assumed. Many law firms, for example, require their members to register with their secretaries exactly where they will be going when they leave the office and how long they will be gone.

Maximal Formalization   Rules, therefore, can vary from highly stringent to extremely lax. These variations exist on the whole range of behaviors covered by organizational rules. The same kinds of variations exist in terms of *procedures*. A simple example of highly formalized procedures is the assembly line, where a piece of material is always passed in the same direction, with the same work being performed on it, or, in an office setting, where letters requesting a certain type of information are always processed in the same way, with the same type of information returned to the requester. The extreme examples of this, of course, are the computer-prepared responses to inquiries about such things as under- or overpayments of credit-card bills. This is one example of a highly formalized procedure in which the organization has been able to preprogram its responses to a wide variety of contingencies. Much of the frustration that people feel when they receive a computer printout rather than a personal letter is due to their feeling that their request was apparently just like everyone else's—that they are not unusual cases and therefore can be treated in a highly formalized way. The real frustration comes, of course, when it is in fact an unusual case and the computer procedures are inappropriate to the request. Despite the personal exasperation that this can develop, the fact remains that a large proportion of the communications that come into an organization can be handled by such formalized procedures.

Minimal Formalization   At the other end of the formalization-of-procedures continuum would be cases that are unique and for which no procedures have been developed. In these cases, members of the organization must use their own discretion in deciding what to do. At the extreme would come the cases Perrow (1967) has said call for intuition, and even perhaps inspiration, in solving—unique situations with no preprogrammed answers. In terms of our concern with organizational structures, such uniqueness must be a regular part of the organization's (or subunit's) activities. That is, a unique situation becomes routine if it is repeated over time, and formalized procedures can then be developed to handle this once-unique situation. Thus, nonformalized organizations are those that deal constantly with new situations for which precedents do not exist—such as, for example, organizations engaging in frontier areas of scientific research of which the forthcoming results are not known. Organizations dealing with human problems, such as mental health clinics, would be in a similar situation.

At this point it should be noted that it usually doesn't matter whether the procedures or rules are formalized in writing. Unwritten norms and standards can frequently be just as binding as written ones. Nevertheless, most research utilizes the written system as the basis for assessment and analysis.

Hage (1965) makes essentially the same point when he states:

> Organizations learn from past experiences and employ rules as a repository of that experience. Some organizations carefully codify each job, describing the specific details, and then ensure conformity to the job prescription. Other organizations have loosely defined jobs and do not carefully control work behavior. *Formalization*, or standardization, is measured by the proportion of codified jobs and the range of variation that is tolerated within the rules defining the jobs. The higher the proportion of codified jobs and the less the range of variation allowed, the more formalized the organization. (p. 295)

In their later research, Hage and Aiken (1967a) follow essentially the same definition of formalization:

> Formalization represents the use of rules in an organization. Job codification is a measure of how many rules define what the occupants of positions are to do, while rule observation is a measure of whether or not the rules are employed. In other words, the variable of job codification represents the degree to which the job descriptions are specified, and the variable, rule observation, refers to the degree to which job occupants are supervised in conforming to the standards established by job codification. Job codification represents the degree of work standardization while rule observation is a measure of the latitude of behavior that is tolerated from standards. (p. 79)

These variables are operationalized by asking the members of organizations to respond to a series of questions bearing directly on these issues. Measures of their perceptions of their own organization are thus used to determine the extent to which the organizations are formalized.

A similar definitional perspective is found in the work of Pugh, Hickson, Hinings, and Turner (1968). They define formalization as "the extent to which rules, procedures, instructions, and communications are written" (p. 75). They also include "standardization" (the extent to which "there are rules or definitions that purport to cover all circumstances and that apply invariable") as one of their basic dimensions of organizational structure (p. 74). These variables are operationalized by using official records and documents from the organization to determine such matters as the number of procedures of various kinds and the proportion of employees who have handbooks describing their tasks. An analysis of the data from the English firms studied reveals that standardizaton and formalization combine with specialization when the component scales are factor analyzed. The authors call this the "structuring of activities" (p. 84). They note that this brings the issue of role specificity to the forefront as an important organizational consideration. In highly formalized, standardized, and specialized situations, the behavior of role occupants is highly specified, leaving them few options that they can exercise in carrying out their jobs.

The similarities between these definitions point up the general consensus about the meaning of formalization. Even when quite different measures of this variable are used in research, the same meaning is utilized, an all too rare occurrence in organizational analysis. The methodological differences deserve some comment at this point. Formalization has been approached from two basic perspectives. The utilization of members' perceptions, as exemplified by the Hage and Aiken work, relies upon the average or median score on responses to a question or set of questions to determine the degree of formalization for the organization (or subunit) as a whole. The alternative approach, as followed by Pugh, Hickson, Hinings, and Turner, is the utilization of official records and information from key informants about the organization. This also yields a formalization score for the organization. Unfortunately, despite the similar conceptualizations, these methods apparently yield somewhat different results (Pennings 1973).

There are several possible reasons for these differences. In the perceptual approach, members of the organizations may not be giving their actual perceptions, possibly because of some fear of reprisal by the organization even though the researchers assure the anonymity of the respondent. While this undoubtedly occurs in some cases, it does not seem to be a major factor; other research using the same approach has demonstrated that the scores from the perceptual scales are quite valid when other indicators are used as validity checks (Hall 1963). In a reanalysis of the Hage and Aiken data, along with some new data, Dewar, Whetten, and Boje (1980) found rather low degrees of convergent and discriminant validity. They attribute this to the fact that the Hage-Aiken formalization scales probably tap some aspects of formalization, but cannot be considered to measure the total degree of formalization.

The use of perceptual measures has the advantage of recognizing the existence of informal procedures. These have long been noted in organizational research. These deviations from the official descriptions and prescriptions cannot be detected with the use of official records only (Argyris 1972).

Scores on perceptual scales may thus represent an accurate portrayal of an organization's degree of formalization or other structural features. This would imply that the use of offical records or statements is of no use. This is not the case. The official system sets the parameters for any deviance that does occur. A prescribed degree of formalization is the starting point from which actual behavior begins. As a general rule, organizations that are more formalized on paper are more formalized in practice. Both methods can be used in ranking a set of organizations on their degree of formalization, even though the exact scores for each organization are not the same. The ideal method, of course, would be to measure rates of behavior to determine any aspect of organizational life; but the costs involved would be so tremendous that little more than a case study would be possible. The more economical measures described are used in order to obtain data that, although somewhat less accurate, do allow comparisons across organizations.

Another interesting point here is that deviations from the officially prescribed patterns are undoubtedly not random. That is, in some organizations, the deviance will be more pronounced and widespread than in others. Although the factors associated with these varying patterns of deviance in organizations are yet to be determined, the cruciality of the norms and the strength with which they are enforced appear to be decisive here. The extent to which the members *believe* in the norms would also be important. Policies are carried out by individuals. At the same time, the establishment of procedures and policies by an organization essentially sets its course for future activities. The organization and its members perform in accordance with the established policies.

FORMALIZATION AND OTHER ORGANIZATIONAL PROPERTIES

Centralization of Power

Power is an important component in any social system. As we shall see in detail in the next chapter, the distribution of power has major consequences for the performance of an organization and the behavior of its members. In their study of social welfare agencies, Hage and Aiken (1967a) found that formalization was rather weakly associated with a centralized decision-making system. Organizations in which the decisions were made by only a few people at the top relied on rules and close supervision as a means of ensuring consistent performance by the workers. These organizations were also characterized by a less professionalized staff. Thus, the presence of a well-trained staff is related to a reduced need for extensive rules and policies.

This interpretation is supported in Blau's (1970) analysis of public personnel agencies. In organizations with highly formalized personnel procedures and rigid conformity to these procedures, Blau found a decentralization of authority. At first glance this is contradictory, since the evidence seems to say that formalization and decentralization are related. A closer examination reveals strong compatibility with the Hage and Aiken findings. In this case, adherence to merit-based personnel procedures ensures the presence of highly qualified personnel at the local (decentralized) level. These people are then entrusted with more power than are personnel with fewer qualifications. Formalization in one area of operations is thus associated with flexibility in another.

On this point Blau states:

> Rigidity in some respects may breed flexibility in others. Not all aspects of bureaucratization are concomitant. The bureaucratic elaboration of formalized personnel procedures and rigid conformity with these personnel standards do not necessarily occur together, and neither aspect of bureaucratization of procedures gives rise to a more rigid authority structure, at least not in employment security agencies. Indeed, both strict conformity with civil service standards and the elaboration of these formalized standards have the opposite effect of fostering decentralization, which permits greater flexibility. (p. 160)

This rather simple set of findings reinforces a notion expressed earlier—complex organizations are complex. Formalization in one area brings pressures to bear to decrease formalization in another area. Organizations are thus constantly in conflict, not only between individuals or subunits, but also between and within the processes and structures that make up the organization. Formalization is not just a matter of internal adjustment. Meyer and Brown's (1977) study of environmental influences on organizations found that increases in formalization, which led to multitier hierarchies, was based on environmental shifts.

It is important to note that the research of Hage and Aiken and of Blau deals with relatively professionalized work forces. One of the hallmarks of professionalization is the ability and willingness to make decisions based upon professional training and experience. It is not surprising to find lower levels of formalization in such situations. When the work force under consideration does not or is assumed not to have this decision-making capacity, the implications of the Blau findings have to be reexamined. In that case, formalized personnel procedures would probably be associated with a more centralized decision-making system, with the formalization level probably more consistent in all phases of the operation. It must be noted that the organization retains control over the individual in both cases. By selecting highly qualified or indoctrinated individuals, it assures itself that the individuals will act according to organizational demands (Blau and Schoenherr 1971, pp. 347–67).

Program Change

Further research by Hage and Aiken (1967b) into the rate of program change in the agencies reveals that formalization is also related to the number of new programs added in the organizations. In this case, formalization is negatively associated with the adoption of new programs. The reduction of individual initiative in the more formalized setting is suggested as the major reason for this relationship. In organizations that establish highly specific routines for the members to follow, there is likely to be little time, support, or reward for involvement in new ideas and new programs.

In their analysis of organizational interdependence, Aiken and Hage (1968) found that formalization was not very important in explaining the number of joint programs in which the agencies under investigation were engaged. Apparently, factors other than formalization come to be important for this type of linkage. This is somewhat inconsistent with the idea expressed earlier that formalization would tend to impede the innovativeness that joint programs would seem to require. Aiken and Hage suggest that the development of joint programs has increased suddenly, so that organizational procedures might be in a state of flux. They also believe that the diversity of occupations (complexity) is by far the dominant influence here, actually overriding other considerations.

Technology

In their continuing research in these sixteen agencies, Hage and Aiken then looked at the relationship between technology and facets of organizational structure. They follow the suggestions of Perrow (1967) and Litwak (1961) and divide the organizations into "routine" and "nonroutine" categories on the basis of scores derived from members' responses to a series of questions. Even though these are all social agencies, there is a marked difference in the degree of routineness.

The highest on routineness is a family agency in which the case-workers use a standard client interview that takes less than fifteen minutes. The purpose of the interview is to ascertain the eligibility of clients for county, federal, or state medical aid. An interviewee said: ". . . somewhat routine—even though each patient is individual, the type of thing you do with them is the same. . . ." The organization at the other extreme is an elite psychiatric family agency in which each member is an experienced therapist and allowed to work with no supervision at all. (Hage and Aiken 1969, p. 369)

The relationship between routinization and formalization is in the expected direction. "*Organizations with routine work are more likely to have greater formalization of organizational roles*" (Hage and Aiken 1969, p. 371; italics in original). Since these organizations tend to be on the nonroutine end of an overall continuum of routineness, the findings are even more striking: had organizations more toward the routine end of the continuum been included, the differences observed would probably have been greater. These findings, of course, strengthen the general argument that has been made throughout this book.

Hage and Aiken's research, one of the most thorough and systematic pieces of ongoing research available in the literature, is based on data from a limited number of organizations of relatively similar characteristics. The limitations inherent in using this type of data base are difficult to avoid, given the intrinsic difficulties in organizational research. But despite these limitations, their findings are generally consistent with those of Pugh's research team, which proceeded independently and with very different measures.

It will be remembered that the Pugh research was carried out on a sample of English work organizations. These researchers were interested in obtaining "hard" indicators of the organizations and the contexts in which they operated. Their major indicator of technology was work flow integration.

> Among organizations scoring high, with very integrated, automated, and rather rigid technologies, were an automobile factory, a food manufacturer, and a swimming baths department. Among those scoring low, with diverse, nonautomated, flexible technologies, were retail stores, an education department, and a building firm. (Pugh, Hickson, Hinings, and Turner 1969, p. 103)

While they contain more diversity than those in the Aiken and Hage study, these organizations are clustered toward the routine end of the routine-nonroutine continuum. As would be expected from the previous discussion, technology emerges as an important predictor of the degree to which activities are structured in these organizations. It is not as closely associated with structuring as is the size factor, but as Chapter 3 pointed out, size is misleading as a predictor in these circumstances.

In a later examination of the same data, Hickson, Pugh, and Pheysey (1969) subdivide the technology concept into three components. "Operations technology," the techniques used in work flow activities, ranging from automated equipment to pens and pencils, includes the ideas of the degree of automation of equipment, the rigidity of the sequence of operations, and the specificity of the evaluation of the operations. The second component, "materials technology," concerns the materials processed in the work flow. Perrow has pointed out the importance of the perceived uniformity and stability of the materials, and Rushing (1968) has shown that the "hardness' of materials makes an important difference in the division of labor in organizations. The third component, "knowledge technology," refers to the characteristics of the knowledge used in the work flow. Perrow's approach is again used, with the primary indicators the number of exceptional cases encountered and the degree of logical analysis used in solving problems.

This appears to be a useful set of distinctions for the technology concept. Unfortunately, the British researchers have data on only the operations technology phase. Nevertheless, their findings and interpretations are vital additions to the understanding of what leads to important organizational structural characteristics. The primary conclusion from this analysis is that technology is not the major "cause" of structure. Using only the operations-technology component, the finding remains that size predominates as a predictor of structure. Hickson, Pugh, and Pheysey conclude that:

> variables of operations technology will be related only to those structural variables that are centered on the workflow. The smaller the organization, the wider the structural effects of technology; the larger the organization, the more such effects are confined to particular variables, and size and dependence and similar factors make the greater overall impact. In the smaller organizations, everyone is closer to the "shop-floor," and structural responses to the problems of size (for example) have not begun to show. In larger organizations, managers and administrators are buffered from the technology itself by the specialist departments, standards procedures, and formalized paperwork that size brings with it. (p. 395)

These conclusions seem extremely reasonable, given all the arguments that have preceded these findings. While the role of technology is discounted from the evidence at hand, it appears quite logical that the material and knowledge phases of the technological concept would come into play among those organizational units "buffered" from the operations technology.

Another study which examined the technology-formalization linkage found strong evidence in favor of the routinization-high formalization conclusion. Dornbusch and Scott (1975) studied an electronics assembly line, a physics research team, a university faculty, a major teaching hospital, a football team, schools, a student newspaper, and a Roman Catholic archdiocese. Their evidence, from this diverse set of organizations, is consistent with the technological argument that has been presented.

Lest it appear that the relationship between technology and formalization is settled because of the weight of the evidence presented, it should be noted that Glisson (1978) essentially reverses the causal ordering. He finds that procedural specifications (formalization) determine the degree of routinization in service delivery. This finding reinforces the interpretation presented in Chapter 3 in which the interactions of size, technology, the environment, and choice were seen as essential for organizational structure. In the case of the Glisson study, a decision made in regard to how to structure the organization led to the utilization of a particular service delivery technology. While the high correlation between routinization and formalization remains, the reason for the correlation is reversed in this case.

Tradition

One additional component should be added to these considerations. Organizations emerge in different historical eras (Meyer and Brown 1977), face varying contingencies, and develop different traditions. These differences in turn influence how such factors as size and technology affect the degree of formalization and other such characteristics. For example, if for some reason—such as the belief system of an important early top executive—an organization became highly formalized in its codification of job descriptions in writing, it would probably continue to be more formalized over time than other factors would predict.

Organizations cannot be viewed as solely subject to the pressures of size, technology, environment, and so on. They develop characteristics that are embedded in the formal and informal systems of the organization. These traditional factors have largely been ignored by organizational analysts, perhaps because they are so difficult to codify. At the common-sense level, they are important and deserve more attention than they have received.

We have seen from the total discussion that formalization is related to several important organizational characteristics. By its very nature, formalization is central to the life of and in organizations. The specification of rules, procedures, penalties, and so on predetermines much of what goes on in an organization. Indeed, formalization is a major defining characteristic of organizations, since behavior is not random and is directed by some degree of formalization toward a goal.

We have examined the relationships between formalization and other organizational properties. The focus will now shift to the individual in the organization. Like formalization, individuals, too, must be treated as variables, since they bring different abilities and habits and other behaviors with them into the organization. Formalization is designed to be a control mechanism over individuals (Clegg and Dunkerley 1980). People react to rules and procedures in a variety of ways (Goffman 1959). They "move" within the structure of rules (Burrell and Morgan 1979). Silverman (1971) proposed an "action" frame of reference for organizational analysis. This approach emphasizes the meanings that people attach to their work environment and the individual meanings and actions that derive from the interpretations that people attach to their organizational roles. (See also Benson, 1977.) The emphasis on the analysis here is not on individual psychological or phenomenological interpretations of their organizational roles, but rather on the relationships among social phenomena. This is not to downplay more individualistic approaches, but rather to maintain the emphasis on organizational phenomena.

Formalization and the Individual Members

An extreme example of formalization can be found in Crozier's (1964) analysis of the two French organizations. He notes: "Impersonal rules delimit, in great detail, all the functions of every individual within the organization. They prescribe the behavior to be followed in all possible events. Equally impersonal rules determine who shall be chosen for each job and the career patterns that can be followed" (pp. 187–88). This extremely high degree of formalization, plus several other characteristics of the organizations, create a "vicious circle" in which the workers follow the rules for the sake of the rules themselves, since this is the basis on which they are evaluated. The rules become more important than the goals they were designed to help accomplish. The organization becomes very rigid and has difficulties dealing with customers and other aspects of the environment. Since the rules prescribe the kinds of decisions to be made, those in decision-making positions tend to create more rules when situations arise for which there are no precedents. Rules become security for the employees. There is no drive for greater autonomy, since that would be threatening. There is a strong desire to build safeguards through increased rigidity. The personnel in such a system become decreasingly free to operate on their own initiative and, in fact, seek to reduce the amount of freedom to which they are subject. To one who values individual freedom, this is a tragedy. It would be presumptuous to say that it is such for the individuals involved, even though the argument could be made that the long-run consequences for them and for the total social system may indeed be tragic from several moral and ethical perspectives. For the organization, the consequences are clear: it becomes maladaptive to changes of any sort.

The personal and organizational dysfunctions were recognized in Robert Merton's (1957) seminal discussion of the "bureaucratic personality." Merton notes that a trained incapacity can develop in the kind of situation under discussion. Actions and decisions based on past training and experience may be very inappropriate under different conditions. Merton suggests that the process whereby these conditions develop is part of the system itself.

> The bureaucrat's official life is planned for him in terms of a graded career, through the organization devices of promotion by seniority, pensions, incremental salaries, etc., all of which are designed to provide incentives for disciplined action and conformity to the official regulations. The official is tacitly expected to and largely does adapt his thoughts, feelings, and actions to the prospect of this career. But *these very devices* which increase the probability of conformance also lead to an over-concern with strict adherence to regulations which induces timidity, conservatism, and technicism. Displacement of sentiments from goals onto means is fostered by the tremendous symbolic significance of the means (rules) [italics in original]. (pp. 200–01)

Organizations are primarily concerned with the work behavior of their members. They also can extend their control into the other areas of life. Quinn (1977) has demonstrated the manner in which organizations attempt to control romance in organizations. While not claiming that organizations are a hotbed of romance, Quinn documents the obvious point that it does occur. When such romance does occur, actions are taken to terminate the relationship, since it is typically seen as disruptive for the organization. Punitive actions, such as dismissals, are one course of action, a course which is much more likely to happen to the women involved rather than the men. Less drastic measures, such as transfers, reprimands, or simple efforts to persuade people to stop the romance were also found. The point is that even in areas of intimacy, organizations attempt to control behavior.

At a more collective level, factors such as worker turnover are also related to formalization. Price (1977) concludes that where there is high turnover, organizations will tend to move toward greater levels of formalization. On the other side of the coin, Walton (1980) reports that, when there is a high level of commitment to the organization, there will be less formalization.

Nonmembers

This strict and even excessive adherence to the rules can also have negative consequences for persons not in the organization itself. Clients who have regular contact with the organization, such as welfare recipients or students in registration lines at colleges and universities, are constantly dismayed and angered by the impersonal and rule-bound treatment they all too often receive. The individual feels like a number, or a "hole in an IBM card."

Reactions to Formalization

The rather dismal view of life in a highly formalized organization is extended by Thompson's (1961) description of "bureaupathic" and "bureautic" behavior. Thompson suggests that the kinds of behavior discussed by Merton are caused by feelings of insecurity. Bureaupathic behavior "starts with a need on the part of the person in an authority position to control those subordinate to himself." Superordinates themselves, except at the very top of the organization, are subordinate to someone else, and so this control can tend to be the too-rigid adherence to rules that has been discussed, since this protects the individual from making possibly erroneous decisions and actions on his own. According to Thompson, the most significant source of insecurity in modern organization is

> the growing gap between the rights of authority (to review, to veto, to affirm) and the specialized ability or skill required to solve most organizational problems. The intellectual, problem-solving content of executive offices is being increasingly diverted to specialists, leaving hierarchical rights (and duties) as the principal components of executive posts. Persons in hierarchical positions are therefore increasingly dependent upon subordinate and non-subordinate specialists for the achievement of organizational (or unit) goals. The superior tends to be caught between the two horns of a dilemma. He must satisfy the nonexplicit and nonoperational demands of a superior through the agency of specialized subordinates and nonsubordinates whose skills he only dimly understands. And yet, to be counted a success he must accept this dilemma and live with its increasing viciousness throughout his life. He must live with increasing insecurity and anxiety. (pp. 156–57)

Thompson suggests that these pressures lead to a "drift" toward the introduction of more and more rules to protect the incumbents of offices, exaggerated aloofness, resistance to change, and an overinsistence on the rights of office. These reactions are organizationally and personally damaging.

The second form of behavior—bureautic—is also personally and organizationally dysfunctional. This type of reaction involves striking out at the system, personalizing every encounter, and taking every rule as one designed to lead to one's own personal frustration.

> The bureautic employee is not likely to get into the hierarchy, and so may come to be regarded as a failure. Because of his inability to enter intelligently into abstract, complex, cooperative relationships, he tends to be pushed to one side, unless he has some unusual skill that the organization badly needs. He is often regarded as "queer." All of these facts add to his bitterness and increase his suspiciousness. He projects his failure onto the organization and the impersonal "others" who are his enemies. He feels he is surrounded by stupidity and maliciousness. He feels powerless and alienated from the system. (p. 176)

While some would argue with the psychological mechanisms that Thompson uses in his development of these reactions to the organization, the reactions themselves do exist.

From the discussion thus far, it seems that life in an organization almost inevitably leads to some form of personal and organizational malfunctioning. But these negative reactions are not inevitable and universal. There are critics of the total system who suggest that it is too corrupt and corrupting and should be abolished. A more reasoned approach is to ask under what circumstances and with what consequences such conditions exist.

Some clues to the answers can be found in the literature on professionals in organizations. There is strong interest in this topic since increasing numbers of professionals of all sorts are working in organizations, and many occupations are attempting to professionalize. Analyses of the relationships between professionals and their employing organizations formerly proceeded from the premise that there are built-in strains between professional and organizational principles and values (see, for example, Kornhauser 1963; Blau and Scott 1962). Recent research has looked at this relationship more closely, attempting to discover the conditions under which strain is felt, since it assumes that there can be situations in which the professional is able to carry out his work with a minimum amount of interference from the organization, while the organization is able to integrate the work of the professionals for its own benefit.

This approach is followed in Miller's (1967) analysis of the degree of alienation experienced by scientists and engineers employed in a large corporation in the aerospace industry. These professionals reported that they felt more alienation when their supervisor used directive, rather than participative or laissez-faire, supervisory practices, and less alienation in situations in which they themselves had some control over the decisions affecting their work. The same general pattern was found in regard to other incentives that the organization provided professionals. There was less alienation when the scientists and engineers had some part in deciding the nature of their own research efforts, when the company provided opportunities and a climate for the pursuit of their own professional careers, and when the company encouraged purely professional activities, such as the publication of papers or pursuit of additional training.

Miller also found that the length of professional training was associated with the extent of alienation felt. The more training a person has, the more he is likely to feel alienation under those conditions that produce it for the group of professionals as a whole. That is, for a Ph.D. scientist, the absence of encouragement of professional activities is more likely to produce alienation than it is for an M.A. scientist. Some differences were also found between the scientists and engineers, but this is not of importance in the present discussion. Utilizing the idea of intraorganizational variations in structure, Miller examined the extent of alienation felt by the professionals when the specific work location was controlled. Some of the professionals worked in a basic-research laboratory in the company, but most were employed in research and development in one of the major production units. As might be expected, the personnel in the basic-research laboratory experienced much less alienation than those in the production-oriented unit.

The organizational structure in which these professionals worked was related to their degree of alienation from work. Professionals were chosen to be examined because they bring to the organization a set of externally (professionally) derived standards by which they can guide their own behavior. The presence of organizational guidelines (formalization) is thus a duplication and probably perceived as less valid than are the norms of the profession involved. For professionals, therefore, the greater the degree of formalization in the organization, the greater the likelihood of alienation from work.

This point is supported further when two additional research reports are considered. Part of the research of Aiken and Hage (1966) has been concerned with the degree of alienation felt by the professionals in the sixteen social welfare agencies they examined. They too, were concerned with alienation from work—although their measurement of this variable was quite different from that used by Miller—but they also looked at alienation from expressive relations. This was measured by responses to questions asking the degree of satisfaction felt about superiors and coworkers. The less satisfaction felt, the more the individual is alienated from expressive relations.

As would be expected from the direction of this discussion, the greater the degree of job codification of the organization, the more alienated were the workers in both areas of alienation. Alienation was much more strongly felt in terms of the job itself. "This means that there is great dissatisfaction with work in those organizations in which jobs are rigidly structured; rigidity may lead to strong feelings of work dissatisfaction but does not appear to have such a deleterious impact on social relations in the organization (p. 504). Strict enforcement of rules was strongly related to both forms of alienation; social relations are also disturbed when rules are strictly enforced. It was also found that both forms of alienation were high when authority in the organizations was centralized and the members had little opportunity to participate in decision making. Hage (1980) later reports similar findings from a longitudinal continuation of the original study and from a study in Japan. This relationship is thus not culture bound.

A different approach was taken in my analysis of the relationships between professionalization and bureaucratization (Hall 1968). Bureaucratization is a broader concept than formalization, but it contains many of the same implications, as indicated in earlier discussions of the topic. I attempted to demonstrate that professionalization, like formalization, is a continuous variable, with some occupations being more professionalized than others. The study included physicians, nurses, accountants, teachers, lawyers, social workers, stockbrokers, librarians, engineers, personnel managers, and advertising account executives. After the occupations were ranked according to their attitudes toward several professional values, the average scores for each occupation were matched with the scores on bureaucratization measures for the organizational units in which these people worked. The results of the rank-order correlational analysis are shown in Table 5-1.

These results indicate that, in general, bureaucratization is inversely related to professionalization. This is consistent with the argument in this section. Examined more closely, these findings reveal some interesting patterns. There is a relatively weak inverse relationship between the hierarchy-of-authority dimension and the professional attitudes. The presence of a relatively rigid hierarchy may not adversely affect the work of professionals if the hierarchy is recognized as legitimate. This is similar to the findings of Blau (1968), who suggests that the presence of a hierarchy may facilitate communications from the professionals to the top

Table 5-1 Rank-Order Correlation Coefficients Between Professionalism Scales and Bureaucracy Scales

	Professional Organization Reference	Belief in Service to Public	Belief in Self-Regulation	Sense of Calling to Field	Feeling of Autonomy
Hierarchy of Authority	−.029	−.262	−.149	−1.48	−.767**
Division of Labor	−.236	−.260	−.234	−.115	−.575**
Rules	−.144	−.121	−.107	.113	−.554
Procedures	−.360**	−.212	−.096	.000	−.603**
Impersonality	−.256	−.099	−.018	−.343*	−.489**
Technical Competence	.593**	.332*	.420**	.440**	.121

* = $p < .05$.
** = $p < .01$.

Source: Richard H. Hall, "Professionalism and Bureaucratization," *American Sociological Review,* 33, No. 1 (February 1968), 102.

of the organization. If the hierarchy of authority is legitimate and does facilitate communications, it apparently does not matter whether or not decisions are made in a prestructured way—and particularly if the work of the professionals can be carried out without extensive interference by the organization.

A stronger negative relationship is found on the division-of-labor dimension. This means that the presence of professionals impedes minute specialization of tasks within the organization. A weaker relationship is found on the presence-of-rules dimension. The kinds of rules the organizations develop in these cases apparently do not interfere with the work of the professional. There is a stronger negative relationship on the procedural-specifications dimension. As more procedures are specified by the organization, the burden on the professionals apparently is stronger. In this case, the professionals are likely to want to utilize procedures that they themselves develop on the job or through their professional training. The inverse relationship between degree of professionalization and the organizational emphasis on impersonality is indicative of the fact that the professional personnel are inclined to deal face-to-face with fellow professionals and develop strong colleague ties. These strong ties are the exact opposite of organizationally desired impersonality, which implies an absence of affective relationships within the organization. The strong positive relationship between the professional variables and the organizations' utilization of technical competence as the basis for their personnel procedures is not surprising. The professions themselves verbalize and practice the idea that a person should be judged by his performance and other rational criteria. This is clearly compatible with organizational usage of the same idea.

Viewing these findings from another perspective, the strong negative relationships between the "feeling of autonomy" professional variable and the first five bureaucratic dimensions is an important indicator of the relationship between bureaucratization and professionalization. This finding indicates that:

> increased bureaucratization threatens professional autonomy. It is in these relationships that a potential source of conflict between the professional and the organization can be found. The strong drive for autonomy on the part of a professional may come into direct conflict with organizationally based job requirements. At the same time, the organization may be threatened by strong professional desires on the part of at least some of its members. (Hall 1968, pp. 102–03)

Formalization and Professionalization

All the studies that have been discussed have concluded that professionalization and formalization are incompatible. The more professionalized the work force, the more likely that formalization will lead to conflict and alienation. A major implication of these findings is that formalization and professionalization are actually designed to do the same thing—organize and regularize the behavior of the members of the organization. Formalization is a process in which the organization sets the rules and procedures and the means of ensuring that they are followed. Professionalization, on the other hand, is a nonorganizationally based means of doing the same thing. From the organization's point of view, either technique would be appropriate, as long as the work gets done.

It is exactly at this point that the organization faces a major internal dilemma. If it allows too little freedom for its members, they are likely to feel oppressed, alienated, and "bureaucratic," and to engage in rule following for its own sake. If, on the other hand, it allows more freedom, behavior is apt to become erratic and organizationally irrelevant. A basic factor here appears to be the kind of guidelines for behavior that the individuals themselves brings to the organization. The more work standards they bring with them the less the need for organizationally based standards.

It is difficult, of course, for the organization to know what kind of standards people bring with them. Even the use of a relatively common criterion, such as membership in a recognized profession, is not a perfect predictor, since not all members of a profession act in accordance with its standards. And when the organization moves into other personnel areas, away from the professions or established crafts, the availability of such external criteria may disappear. Because even well-developed external criteria, such as professionalization, may at times be organizationally irrelevant, the organization has to develop its own system of rules and procedures to accomplish what it is attempting to do.

A basic problem here is that the organization may have uncertain and inaccurate knowledge about its personnel. It may, for example, assume that its female workers are interested only in finding a husband and getting married, and may thereby rigidly structure the positions involved. This could make the work so unenjoyable that marriage would look like an attractive alternative to the women involved.

Here one point should be mentioned that is obvious but often ignored. There is nothing inherently more moral or excellent in professional or craft standards than in organizational norms. Many analyses of the relationships between professionals and their employing organizations seem to imply that the professional standards are somehow better than those of the organizations. Unless there are available specific criteria of what the organization and the professionals are trying to accomplish, such an assumption is unwarranted.

Before moving to additional implications of formalization for the individual and the organization, we must draw another conclusion from the analysis of professionals in organizations. The emphasis in much of the research in this area is on conflict between the professional and his employing organization. Evidence from the Hall research suggests that such conflict is not inevitable and should not be assumed without demonstration. This research found, for example, that the legal departments of large organizations are not necessarily more bureaucratized than law firms of comparable size. The lawyer working in the trust department of a bank may actually be working in an organizational environment similar, and perhaps even identical, to the one he or she would find in a law firm. This suggests that it is very possible to find organizational structures that are compatible with the degree of professionalization of their members.

The finding that legal or other professional departments in organizations may not be more bureaucratized or formalized than autonomous law firms raises another issue. The legal department of a bank is clearly less formalized than the division in charge of handling, sorting, and verifying checks. As is true of complexity, degrees of formalization vary within the organization. This can be most easily seen between departments, but it also occurs between levels in the organization. In general, the higher the level, the less the formalization (Hall 1962; Child 1973).

At the beginning of this chapter it was noted that formalization involves assumptions about the nature of the men and women in organizations. Without delving very far into the realm of psychology, it should be noted that the evidence is unclear in regard to exactly what people are like in their interactions with organizations. Some writers, such as Argyris (1973), believe that people move toward "adulthood," in which they seek autonomy, independence, control over their world and to develop their abilities to the utmost. Others are not so sure (see Lorsch and Morse 1974; Parke and Tausky 1975). Some people may simply not have any desire for autonomy or for self-actualization of any sort. While this is deplorable on humanistic grounds, it is nevertheless a fact. Thus, while some people are highly frustrated in a highly formalized setting, others would not be. By the same token, a low degree of formalization would be a satisfying condition to some, but not to others.

SUMMARY AND CONCLUSIONS

This chapter began with the premise that an organization's degree of formalization significantly affects how the organization and its members perform. While none of the studies discussed attributed causal primacy to structural factors, it is clear from the analysis that structural characteristics have important relationships with other major organizational features, such as rate of change, the distribution of power within the organization, and relationships with the environment. We have also seen that the degree of formalization has important consequences for individuals. They can overreact, becoming slaves to the rules or fighting them for the sake of fighting. The individual can be dulled by an overspecification of how he or she is to perform in the organization. At the same time, if inappropriately guided by the organization by either too much or too little specification, the behavior of individuals can have extremely negative consequences for the organization.

The entire discussion has been guided by evidence suggesting strongly that organizational structure is formed by influences from outside and inside the organization. A major external influence is certainly the technological environment in which the organization operates. This would include the material, operations, and knowledge facets of the technology concept. While technology appears to be the key environmental variable, others would include relationships with other such general environmental factors.

Internally, the role of the professional was stressed, largely owing to the amount of evidence that has been amassed regarding the professional in the organization. Since they probably constitute the most conspicuous occupational group in organizations—with the possible exception of some of the crafts, which, for the purposes of this discussion, would have similar characteristics—and since more and more occupations are attempting to professionalize and more and more professionals are working in organizations, it is understandable that the work of professionals would be so highly emphasized.

Although the evidence discussed comes largely from the realm of the professions, the major point made was that individuals bring guidelines for their behavior with them. It is the degree of congruence between these individual guidelines and those that the organization needs for the fulfillment of its tasks that is critical in determining the appropriate degree of formalization. These personal guidelines can obviously vary in terms of their strength, saliency, and content within any occupational grouping in the organization. Whether people are professionals or not, their amount of previous training and experience is probably a major factor in determining how self-guiding they can be.

Another obviously important source of the degree of formalization is the decision-making process within organizations. People in decision-making positions determine whether or not the organization should "tighten up" its procedures. They also develop images about the people in the organization as being capable or incapable of self-direction.

Formalization is necessary in organizations. The degree of formalization is the variable that should be kept under constant scrutiny as an important practical matter. For the organizational analyst, the degree of formalization is a major variable for understanding both the organization and the performance and thoughts of its members.

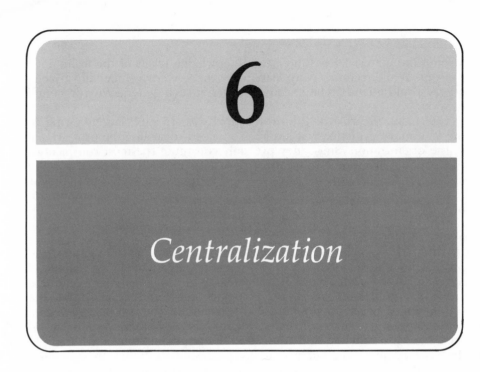

6

Centralization

This is the last chapter on structural characteristics of organizations. Centralization refers to the distribution of power within organizations. Centralization is thus one of the best ways to summarize the whole notion of structure. As noted earlier. Ranson, Hinings, and Greenwood (1980) deal with structure as constituted and constitutive. In the case of centralization, a given distribution of power is constitutive in that it generates other actions—people comply with organizational rules and decisions. Centralization is also constituted in that power distributions are subject to change, as groups and individuals gain or lose power over time. Power itself will be considered in the next chapter. Here we will consider the nature and correlates of the structural aspect of power in organizations.

Centralization has been defined in several ways, with the emphasis always on the distribution of power. Hage (1980) defines centralization as "the level and variety of participation in strategic decisions by groups relative to the number of groups in the organization" (p. 65). The greater the level of participation by a greater number of groups in an organization, the *less* the centralization. Hage's approach emphasizes the fact that power is exercised in a variety of ways and in a variety of locations in an organization. For example, at my university—and at most good universities (see Blau 1973)—the decision of *who* to hire for a faculty position lies with the hiring department. The decision here is decentralized. The decision of whether a particular department will be able to hire someone is centralized, however. The central administration reviews faculty vacancies and determines whether or not there needs to be a redistribution of vacancies, with departments with declining enrollments and weaker programs likely to lose positions to departments with high enrollment demands and strong programs. This is a centralized decision.

Van de Ven and Ferry (1980) define centralization as "the locus of decision making authority within an organization. When most decisions are made hierarchically, an organizational unit is considered to be centralized; a decentralized unit generally implies that the major source of decision making has been delegated by line managers to subordinate personnel" (p. 399). Van de Ven and Ferry go on to note that the substance of the decisions is an important consideration. In a highly professionalized organization, for example, decisions in regard to areas of professional competence are left to the professionals involved. Areas that are considered to be outside the limits of professional competence are likely to be more centralized.

WHAT IS CENTRALIZED OR DECENTRALIZED?

Of the several aspects of centralization, the most obvious is the right to make decisions. This can be very specifically spelled out in terms of who or what has the right to make which kinds of decisions and when. If most decision making occurs at the top, the organization is centralized. The matter is not that simple, however, since the organization can have predetermined policies regarding even these decisions. Table 6-1 illustrates the intermixing of decision-making rights and organizational policies.

In the table it can be seen that in the "bureaucracy/centralized" cell (no. 12), operating personnel can make decisions, but they are limited by the policies of the organization. Because the extent to which situations are covered by policies can vary widely, however, centralization is not a simple matter of who makes decisions. If personnel at lower levels in the organization are making many decisions, but the decisions are "programmed" by organizational policies, a high degree of centralization remains.

Another element of centralization is how activities are evaluated (Dornbusch and Scott 1975, p. 82). The evaluation process involves the determination of whether work was done properly, well, or promptly. If evaluation is carried out by people at the top of the organization, there is centralization, regardless of the level at which decisions are made. A situation in which there is centralized evaluation would probably—but not necessarily always—also be one in which policies are centralized.

Like formalization, the degree of centralization of an organization indicates its view of its personnel. In a highly centralized situation, the personnel are not trusted to make decisions or evaluate themselves. Less centralized situations indicate a greater willingness to permit the personnel to carry out their activities in a more autonomous way.

It is not just the organization's definition of the qualities of its personnel that determines centralization, however. Research evidence strongly indicates that the familiar factors of size, technology, environment, and, of course, choice are also critical matters.

Table 6-1 Forms of Centralization

Level for Referring Decisions Not Covered by Policies	Policies, Procedures, and Rules	
	Few Policies/Broadly Defined	Many Policies/Narrowly Defined
TOP—Headquarters personnel	11 *Autocracy*/Highly Centralized. Few decisions are made by lower-level personnel, and these are governed by broad policies. Most decisions must be referred to higher-level management.	12 *Bureaucracy*/Centralized. Decisions are made by operating personnel within the framework of restrictive policies, procedures, and rules; problems not covered must be referred to higher levels for decisions or policy clarification.
BOTTOM— Operating personnel	21 *Collegial*/Highly Decentralized. Most decisions are made at lower levels without policy restrictions; other decisions made at lower levels within the framework of policies.	22 *Bureaucracy*/Decentralized. Most decisions are made at lower levels within the framework of the policies; personnel have discretion on problems *not* covered by policies.

Source: Arlyn L. Melcher, *Structure and Process of Organizations: A Systems Approach* (Englewood Cliffs, N.J.: Prentice-Hall, Inc., 1975), p. 150.

Size

Research evidence in regard to the relationships between size and centralization is paradoxical. From their study of state employment security offices, Blau and Schoenherr (1971) conclude that "the large size of an agency produces conflicting pressures on top management, as it heightens the importance of managerial decisions, which discourages delegating them, and simultaneously expands the volume of managerial responsibilities, which exerts pressure to delegate some of them" (p. 130). The net result of increasing size is increased delegation or decentralization. The risk of delegation is lessened if personnel have expert qualifications. A centralized policy in regard to employee qualifications thus appears to contribute to delegated power.

One problem with this line of reasoning (a variation of the chicken-egg debate) should be noted: it is impossible to determine if increased size leads to pressures to delegate and thus to utilize experts, or if the hiring of experts leads to pressures to delegate, with size not really being a factor.

The question cannot be answered with the kinds of data now available, but probably a combination of the two types of answers is most appropriate.

Blau's (1973) further research on colleges and universities revealed basically the same findings. Large universities were more decentralized than smaller ones. Academic institutions and government agencies show a major difference in the qualifications of their personnel. In the government agencies, qualified personnel were utilized to carry out the organization's policies; in the academic organizations, the highly qualified personnel were able to gain power for themselves and to exercise a great deal of power over educational policies. In this case, size is clearly in interaction with a technological factor in its contribution to decentralization. (See also Holdaway et al. 1975.)

In a study using the Aston data and their measures on a second set of data, Mansfield (1973) reaches conclusions essentially the same as those of the Blau research. Mansfield found that increasing size is related to the increasing use of rules. This leads to the decentralization of decision making but not to loss of control for the organization. In smaller organizations, specialists report directly to the top of the organization, while in larger ones, problems are handled at a decentralized level, but under the guidance of organizationally based rules.

It is only common sense that it is impossible to control large organization from the top: because much more is happening than an individual or set of individuals can comprehend, there is inevitable delegation. As in the case of other structural characteristics, however, size is not the only answer.

Technology

The technological factor has already been implied in the discussion. Some work is delegated, with the control remaining at the top of the organization by the use of rules governing the work. Other work is delegated to specialists who make their own decisions at lower levels in the organizations. Work that is delegated with controls is routine in terms of its technology (Child 1973). In a bank, for example, each teller can handle thousands of dollars if the transactions are routine in the form of series of small cash deposits and withdrawals, But if an individual presents a check for $2000 and asks for cash, it is a different matter. In this case, handling thousands of dollars is not delegated, but rather the decision moves back up the organization.

Dornbush and Scott (1975) contribute to the analysis of technology and centralization by noting that organizations deal with a variety of tasks that vary in their clarity, predictability, and efficacy. These are rather familiar distinctions in the literature on technology, with the possible exception of efficacy, which refers to "the means which have been developed for achieving desired outcomes" (p. 82). Dornbusch and Scott point out that the variety of tasks performed in an organization means in essence that it has multiple technologies and thus must structure itself differently according to the task. This is in keeping with our earlier comments on intraorganizational structural variations. These variations are linked to these different tasks with their varied technologies.

Dornbusch and Scott utilize the concepts of "directive," guidance by rules, and "delegation," the actual decentralization of power to lower-level personnel. They conclude:

> Generally, in the interests of organizational effectiveness and efficiency, we would expect tasks which are high on clarity, predictability, and efficacy to be allocated by directive, tasks low on these three dimensions we would expect to be allocated by delegation. In its simplest terms, the argument is that, given high clarity as to the objectives to be obtained, high predictability of the resistance to be encountered, and established procedures for successfully handling this resistance, it is efficient to develop standardized, routine procedures which performers are directed to follow. High clarity contributes specific success criteria for use in designing sequences of activities. When the resistance confronted is predictable, it is possible to specify in advance the appropriate task activities to perform. When highly efficacious sequences of activities have been developed, performers will be expected to follow these set routines. (pp. 82–83)

These ideas were proven to be accurate by tests in a diverse set of organizations. It is thus critical to know what the task is before assuming a given degree of centralization will be found or before making a decision in regard to the appropriate degree of decentralization. The complex task will be delegated to a specialist, who uses his or her knowledge in handling the issue. As Blau's work suggests, organizations retain control through their hiring of specialists, but the control is not as tight as that which derives from organizational directives.

Dornbusch and Scott's findings receive corroboration from a variety of other studies. Hage and Aiken (1969), Comstock and Scott (1977), and Ouichi (1977) all report the same basic pattern. Ouichi notes that organizations can monitor peoples' behavior or their work outputs. He finds that a combination of large size and homogeneous tasks contributes to the utilization of output controls, such as monitoring the number of units produced, sales transacted, or cards punched.

Another aspect of technology adds some slight confusion to the discussion. Participative management, which means that subordinates are consulted in regard to decisions that affect them, was analyzed by Taylor (1971), who found that it was more likely to be successful in situations involving advanced technology. Advanced technology here refers specifically to that concentrated at the workflow level; thus, participative management is most effective in the more automated kinds of situations. Participative management can occur in situations that are otherwise highly centralized, if the final authority is still retained by the superior in the situation.

Hage and Aiken's (1967a) work has shown that participation in decision making—a different aspect of centralization—is related to the absence of rules, thus suggesting that centralization by rules and centralization by nonparticipative decision making tend to operate together. Hage and Aiken's work, it should be remembered, is based on reports from organizational members themselves rather than on official records such as the Aston and Blau researchers use. In this instance, the findings in regard to centralization appear to be equivalent. In routine situations, rules govern the actions of the organizational members and there is likely to be little in the way of delegation of power through participation. In less routine situations, where there is task uncertainty, phenomena such as group meetings are likely to be held to attempt to come up with problem resolutions (Van de Ven, Delbecq, and Koenig 1976).

The issue of routinization and uncertainty and their relationship to centralization is closely linked to the level of professionalization of the personnel in the organization. Lincoln and Zeitz (1980) report that individual professionals desire and achieve participation in decision making. They also find that the overall level of professionalization of an organization results in all employees experiencing an increase in influence.

Hage (1980) offers an additional insight into the relationship between professionalization and centralization. He finds that a concentration of specialists (professionals) generally leads to decentralization. If, however, the people involved are trained as generalists, there is likely to be greater centralization. Hage uses the example of the military, where officers are trained as generalists through varied tours of duty. Here there is a high degree of centralization.

There are two cautions that should be noted in regard to participation in decision making. First, the fact that there is participation by organizational members may *not* mean that power is delegated. If the final decision still rests in the hands of the superiors in the organization, little power is actually delegated and participation is advisory at best. Although participation *may* help in the implementation of a decision, there is no decentralization or delegation of power unless it contributes to the actual decision.

The other caution regards a phenomenon that is too seldom considered by sociologists and other organizational researchers—budgetary controls, such as internal audits. Although Hofstede (1972) and Ouichi and Maguire (1975) have dealt with this issue, it has tended not to be considered, which is a loss for organizational theory. Budgetary controls have the potential of retaining a great deal of control at the top of the organization. The studies which have been cited here have not included budgetary control mechanisms. It would certainly appear that budgetary matters could be centralized in different ways than the allocation of tasks or decision making on other issues.

Environmental Factors

The relationships among size, technology, and centralization have not been straightforward. The same is true in the case of environmental conditions. Research in this area has come to rather contradictory conclusions, although the contradictions can probably be resolved.

The contradiction is based largely on how much competition an organization faces in the environment. From their study of thirty business firms in India, Negandhi and Reimann (1972) suggest that competitive market conditions make decentralization more important for organizational success than do less competitive situations. This study was a successful replication of the Lawrence and Lorsch (1967) contingency theory previously discussed. Further analysis of their data indicated that the degree of dependence on other organizations was actually more strongly associated with decentralization than were the factors of size, technology, and market competitiveness (Negandhi and Reimann, 1973a). Negandhi and Reimann (1973a, b) indicate, as has been done in the present analysis, that the perceptions of the organizational decision makers are a critical mediating variable between the organization and the environment. It is they who make the strategic choices about the environment and about how the organization will respond to it. In this set of findings, the competitiveness of the environment affects the degree of decentralization.

A very different conclusion is reached in a study of thirty-eight small manufacturing firms in the United States (Pfeffer and Leblebici 1973). In this study it was found that a more competitive environment led to a greater demand for control and coordination. There was a greater frequency of reporting, more emphasis on written communications, and a greater specification of decision-making procedures—in short, a much greater degree of centralization. It was also found that in less competitive environments there were more changes in product design, production processes, and number of products.

The contradictory findings seem to offer few conclusions about the effects of competition on centralization. A good part of the difficulty may lie in the fact that the more general characteristics of the organizational environments were not specified. For example, in an expanding economy in which the competing organizations are all gaining, decentralization may occur. If the economy is one of scarcity, in which one organization's gain is the others' loss, the tightening up and centralization that Pfeffer and Leblebici found would occur (Khandwalla, 1973).

Another aspect of organizational environments is their degree of stability. Whetten (1980) notes that research on this topic also reaches contradictory findings. Authors such as Burns and Stalker (1961) and Aldrich (1979) have argued that decentralization is more appropriate for conditions of turbulence or nonstability in the environment, while others (Hawley and Rogers 1974; Yarmonlinsky 1975; Rubin 1979) have argued in favor of centralization in such situations. Again, a resolution of the differences in these findings may be possible if it were possible to determine if the environment was expanding or contracting, as was suggested in the case of competition. In a situation of growth, decentralization might be the most appropriate response to turbulence, while centralization might be necessary in periods of contraction.

Closely related to centralization is the notion of "loose coupling" (Weick 1976; Aldrich 1979). This idea was developed to describe situations in which organizational units have low levels of interdependence. Whetten

(1980) concludes that there is agreement that loosely coupled organizations tend to be more flexible and responsive to environmental pressures. Loose coupling is not the same as decentralization, since the degree of coupling refers to the level of interdependence among units rather than to the distribution of power. In general, a loosely coupled organization would also be decentralized. An example of a loosely coupled organization is the business conglomerate. If the consumer products division is having a difficult time due to high interest rates, this would not affect the heavy machinery division whose market is growing. Such an organization would be loosely coupled. Each division may be more or less centralized in such a situation.

Aldrich (1979, pp. 83–84) describes seven characteristics of loosely coupled organizations. First, loose coupling permits organizational units to persist and evolve independent of other units. Since environments are complex, it is unlikely that all organizational units will be equally successful in their environmental adaptation. As Aldrich notes, of course, loose coupling permits archaic or anachronistic organizational elements to be maintained, as well as those which are more efficient or effective.

A second characteristic of loosely coupled organizations is that it is sensitive to environmental shifts. At the same time, it may be overly sensitive, according to Aldrich, and follow transitory fads or foibles. Thirdly, loose coupling permits adaptation to local conditions. This would be particularly important in geographically dispersed organizations. A disadvantage is that a successful local adaptation might not be spread throughout the system. The fourth characteristic is related to this. Weick (1976) noted that novel solutions to problems can emerge in loosely coupled systems. These novel solutions may not be used throughout the organization but are available as alternatives in times of stress.

A fifth characteristic is the fact that loose coupling has the capability of limiting failure in one part of an organization to just that part. The rest of the organization is insulated from a unit's failure. At the same time, of course, loose coupling may prevent other organizational units from helping prevent failure. Aldrich does not note another problem in this regard. Loose coupling would also insulate a unit's success from the rest of the organization. It would appear that loose coupling would be maladaptive in this regard if the total organization did not benefit from the success of one of its units.

A sixth characteristic proposed by Aldrich is that loose coupling permits greater individual self-determination and involvement in the organization since individuals are directly confronting the environment. There is no empirical evidence in this regard, however, and the point seems to be stretched quite a bit. Finally, Aldrich suggests that loosely coupled systems are less expensive to operate, since coordination costs are lower. The coordination could lead to a situation of units engaging in activities that are not desired by the central administration, of course, which would raise costs.

Aldrich suggests that the idea of loose coupling is useful as a "sensitizing device" (p. 84) and that the degree of coupling is a matter of observer judgment. This certainly appears to be the case. My university appears to be very loosely coupled from the perspective of a faculty member. The success of the Sociology Department is independent of the success of the Physics Department. The failure of a department has little in the way of repercussions beyond that department. When viewed from another perspective, however, the university is extremely tightly coupled. When I served as an acting vice president, it was evident to me that a decision or event in one area was directly linked to events in other areas. Decisions, for example, in regard to personnel reductions were made on the basis of extremely tight coupling, with a cut in one area weighed against its impact on every other area.

The point of this discussion of loose coupling is to illustrate that what may appear to be an attractive idea may not actually contribute as much as its advocates claim. While the idea is currently popular, the concept of centralization-decentralization appears to be more usable in research and practice. The idea of centralization, when approached from the standpoint that there are multiple levels of decision making and power that can be distributed, seems to have more relevance than the coupling imagery.

Centralization is concerned with power. Since organizations are a major means by which power is exercised in society, an examination of the political systems in which organizations are located indicates that this aspect of organizational environments is important for centralization.

Centralization and Macropolitical Considerations

The overriding importance of organizations for the social order is underscored by considering some examples of their use for political purposes. Organizations can be shaped to be part of the process of political change and development. China has used its organizations as a means of continuing political indoctrination and involvement. Yugoslavian socialism has developed a program of "self-management" in which the workers in an enterprise elect a workers' council that in turn elects the management of the enterprise. This is not participative management of the sort discussed above, but rather management by participation. Enterprises in the Israeli kibbutz system (composed of small organizations) have a socialist ideology that is promoted by a system of rotation of all people through all positions.

These ideological purposes are not always met. In Yugoslavia, participation is lower and alienation is higher than the ideology indicates or political leaders desire (see Rus 1972). In Israel, nonkibbutz organizations are more like their Western counterparts than they are like the kibbutz.

A major study of differing patterns of centralization in five countries has been conducted by Tannenbaum et al. (1974). This research was carried out in manufacturing plants in Austria, Italy, Israel, Yugoslavia, and the United States. Austria and Italy are basically capitalist, like the United States, and Israeli kibbutzim and the Yugoslav economy are socialist. Israel and the United States contained the plants that were most successful—as defined by the standards used in the country in question, but included such universal factors as efficiency and morale. The kibbutz plants are highly decentralized, with the effects of hierarchy virtually eliminated. In the United States, hierarchy is present, but its effects are mitigated by several factors. There is a limited potential for upward worker mobility in the American plants, but it is greater than in the Italian plants. There is also greater participativeness in the American plants. Workers are consulted and treated more as equals, even though they are not equal in power, and the rewards are higher.

Nevertheless, in the American plants there is no attempt to reduce inequality. This is a political stance, even though it may be unrecognized as such. The tendency toward participativeness in the American plants is viewed by some as manipulation. For example, the Tannenbaum researchers conclude:

A position to which some of us subscribe, for example, argues that the approach to hierarchy described above supports techniques of "human relations" that maintain rather than eliminate substantial gradients of power and reward. It therefore covers over and diverts attention from the exploitation and injustice suffered by workers. Workers in the American plants, for example, do not *feel* as alienated as workers elsewhere but in fact they *are* powerless with respect to basic policy issues. Because of "human relations" a discrepancy exists between the subjective and objective experience of alienation. The Italian workers are more realistic and better adjusted in this sense. Jobs are frustrating to them, opportunities for self fulfillment or for achievement are sparse, and workers feel dissatisfied and poorly motivated. Italian workers *know* they are without power and quite realistically, they *feel* alienated. This realism is a symptom of good adjustment, not bad, although in terms of our conventional measures the Italian worker looks poorly adjusted. American workers, on the other hand, appear well adjusted and they report high levels of opportunity and satisfaction. Some actually feel a sense of responsibility in their plant—at least more than do workers in other places. But this is only because the "human relations" approach is so effective in its manipulation. The approach no doubt works in mitigating some of the psychological effects of hierarchy, but it does so without making any basic changes in hierarchy and, in the view of some of us, it is therefore subject to question from a moral standpoint. (p. 220)

This Marxist approach gets at the very heart of the political issue involved in centralization. Management by participation, as in the case of Israel and Yugoslavia, is a direct attempt to alter traditional power arrangements within a society. The Chinese approach, which is not participative but rather is designed to strengthen the power of the current regime, emphasizes political indoctrination and loyalty. It is highly centralized. The American approach, which increasingly features participation of some degree in decision making, does not attempt to redistribute power. It does, however, minimize the perceptible effects of power differences. Those of the Tannenbaum et al. researchers who judge this as immoral and misleading miss an important consideration. Even if it is agreed that workers are exploited to even a small degree, the end result remains in question: What is the more likely—a situation such as that in Italy, where the exploitation is definitely felt, or a situation such as that in the United States, where it is more moderately felt? It could be, for example, that at some time in the future, American workers, having experienced at least symbolic participation, would press very hard for actual participation. Those who had never experienced participation might not necessarily want to move in this direction.

This whole discussion is made somewhat moot by two considerations. First, participation schemes in Israel, Yugoslavia, and elsewhere are typically most successful in situations of relatively simple technology and in organizations that are relatively small and not complex. It is very questionable whether participative management would work in situations of technological sophistication or in large organizations of high complexity. Rank and file workers would be unable to comprehend all of the operations of such organizations, and probably would not desire to do so. They would yield to technical experts and those trained for management of large-scale organizations. This, of course, is basically what happens now in the United States and elsewhere.

The final consideration, developed by the Dutch sociologist Lammers (1975), is that participative management involves taking *part* in decision making, while both management by participation and self-management involve workers taking *over* organizational management. The former is a functional form of decentralization that leads to greater efficiency and effectiveness, while the latter two forms are structural decentralization that lead to power equalization. Both forms of democratization are unlikely to occur together.

True power equalization in organizations is extremely unlikely. The very nature of organizations requires some form of hierarchy, once organizations move beyond very small size, simple technologies, and low levels of complexity. As in the wider society, power differences are ubiquitous. The effects of such power differences can perhaps be minimized by making them less abrasive through participative schemes. As Child (1976) notes, however, demands for greater participation face situations of greater bureaucratization and centralization.

Centralization and Micropolitical Considerations

Organizations are part of the political system. They also contain their own internal political system and this is an important consideration for centralization. Heydebrand (1977) has noted the contradiction between traditional control structures and new forms of organizing, as along the lines of professional organizations. As noted earlier, the presence of professionals increases the level of participation in the organization. The increased participation is not accomplished benignly. Instead, it is fought for and over, since those who had decision-making power are not likely to give it up easily to the professionals coming into the organization.

Some authors view the internal politics of an organization as a reflection of the external political system. Marglin (1974) suggests that the technology employed in many factories is there not so much for technical efficiency, but rather as a means by which maximal control over labor can be achieved. Whether or not this was a conscious capitalist decision cannot be ascertained, since the original participants in industrialization are long dead. We do know that there are ongoing labor-management negotiations and battles over the prerogatives of management and workers. Bacharach and Lawler (1980) have pointed out that power can be delegated to lower participants and that power can be *taken* by these same lower participants. Universities in the late 1960s and early 1970s exemplified the give and take of power as students gained in power and thus had the right to make decisions that previously had been made by faculty or administrators. This was a reflection of the larger political context.

The exercise of power within organizations will be considered in the next chapter. In terms of centralization, it is critical to note that the micropolitics of organizations (Pfeffer 1978) involves the continuing power struggles that occur within organizations, whether among departments, hierarchical levels, or individuals. While the micropolitical approach emphasizes power struggles, the fact that power is distributed at one point in time (the degree a nature of centralization) will have a crucial impact on the distribution of power at succeeding points in time.

The Consequences of Centralization

The centralization in organizations says a great deal about the society in which they are found. A society in which the majority of organizations are highly centralized is one in which the workers have little say about their work. The same would probably be true in terms of their participation in the society. The degree of centralization of organizations also is an indication of what the organization assumes about its members: high centralization implies an assumption that the members need tight control, of whatever form; low formalization suggests that the members can govern themselves. In both cases, it should be remembered, the control is in behalf of the organization (Blau and Schoenherr 1971). Professionals and other expert personnel in organizations do not work in behalf of their professions. Their expertise is in behalf of the organization.

A major consequence of varying degrees of centralization is for the organization itself. As shown in Table 6-2, the consequences of a high degree of centralization can be positive or negative for the organization, depending on the situation. Once again, the appropriate degree or form or organizational structure depends on the situation at hand. Thus a major problem is that it is not always possible to adjust the degree of centralization to fit a changing situation.

SUMMARY AND CONCLUSIONS

Centralization is the power distribution in an organization that is determined in advance by the organization. Like the other structural properties that have been examined, it is related to the factors of size, technology,

Table 6-2 Consequences of Centralization on Organizational Processes

Organizational Processes	Consequences	
	Advantages	Disadvantages
Coordination	Greater coordination through central direction and uniform policies	Uniform policies apply regardless of the degree to which local conditions vary
Decision making: perspective	Company as a whole is considered in decisions when made by top management and staff personnel and where lower-level managers make decisions within the parameters of policy statements issued by headquarters	The company perspective is likely to ignore the special features/problems of divisions, departments, and work units
Decision making: speed	In emergencies, central staff and management can moblilze the information and make decisive decisions without delay	The normal decision process results in delays; flow of information up and flow of orders/ policies down take time; central personnel are often overloaded so decisions are further delayed.

Source: Arlyn L. Melcher, *Structure and Process of Organizations: A Systems Approach* (Englewood Cliffs, N.J.: Prentice-Hall, Inc., 1975), p. 157.

environment, and choices made within the organization. Forms of centralization have important implications for both individuals and the wider society.

Like all structural characteristics, centralization is a given condition of organizations at any point in time. This does not mean that it never changes in degree. Indeed, the most severe power struggles in organizations can involve the issue of centralization. Strikes and rebellions have to do with power.

Organizations change, sometimes slowly and sometimes dramatically. Whenever they change, a new structure is formed. This new structure serves as the basis for both organizational actions and actions in response to the organization. Organizational change results from structure and leads to structure. In the chapters that follow, we will consider successively the processes of power, conflict, leadership, decision making, communications, and change.

III

Organizational Processes

Our examination of organizational structure has indicated that organizations have a framework in which actions take place. In considering organizational processes we are considering organizational actions. Processes are the dynamics of organizations. The subjects of this section—power, conflict, leadership, decision making, communications, and change—result from structure and lead to it. These processes also contribute to the output of organizations in terms of their effectiveness. As will be seen in the later discussion of effectiveness, this involves organizational outputs, impacts on members, and impacts on society.

Each process is a critical component for understanding organizations. Leadership, for example, has been so talked about, written about, researched—and occasionally practiced—that many people believe that it is the key to organizational success or failure. We will examine leadership in conjunction with the rest of what we know about organizations to see just how important it really is. The approach in this section is to treat each topic in relation to other processing and structural characteristics. We will see how they operate in organizations and what the impact of their operation is.

The concern of this section is with issues that are important to members of any organization. For example, what individual(s) or group has power in an organization and why? The answer is more complex than the simple matter of rank in a hierarchy. The use of power has products more complex than simple compliance. Are power differences based on interpersonal relationships, or are there some power differences between organizational units as well? We know that conflict occurs within organizations, but we are less sure about its implications. Is conflict ever good for an organization? Decisions are constantly being made in organizations, but is there any hope that they are rational? Furthermore, for whom are they rational? Is the answer to almost every organizational problem more and better communications? What leads to change and innovation in organizations?

Questions like these will occupy our attention for the next several chapters. The answers will not be perfectly clear. The issues are complex and often contradictory. Furthermore, the study of process is more difficult than the study of structure, so that research in the area is both less plentiful and less rigorous. It is rather hard, for example, to study organizational conflict, since the participants are quite unlikely to want a sociologist intruding into the heat of conflict with an eighteen-page questionnaire or other data-collection instrument. Furthermore, much of the writing in the area is in the form of advocacy or in terms of how to be a better leader, communicator, or conflict resolver. The concern will continue to be the organization, with less interest in the individuals involved. As will be seen, however, individual variations have a tremendous effect on processes in the organization.

7

Power
and Conflict

The issue of power in organizations has become a dominant interest in organizational analyses. Every social relationship involves power. When a superior asks or orders a subordinate to do something or a professor makes a reading assignment, power is being exercised. The whole issue of centralization involves the distribution of power. One result of power is conflict, and even though this is not the only result, conflict will be considered in this chapter along with power. Conflict is not the inevitable result of power. Indeed, the outcome of most power acts is compliance, with conflict being the exception rather than the rule. At the same time, conflict is crucial for organizations since it affects both the individuals involved and the total organization. It is from conflict that many important changes develop.

Power and conflict have been approached from a variety of perspectives. Burrell and Morgan (1979) have summarized these perspectives as indicated in Tables 7-1 and 7-2. Their "unitary view" reflects an older managerial viewpoint which has limited relevance today. The "pluralist view" is the one which will be followed primarily in the present analysis. The "radical view" sees organizations as elements within the political structure of society. They are viewed as a reflection and extension of the power structure. We will consider this radical view at appropriate points in the analysis. In the discussion here, the components of Tables 7-1 and 7-2 will be elucidated as each topic is considered.

Bacharach and Lawler (1980) provide another overview of power in organizations. They see organizations as political bargaining systems.

Organizations are composed of work groups, people who work in a common unit or at the same level of the organization; interest groups, people who are aware of the commonality of their goals of their fate; and coalitions, groupings of interest groups with a common goal. They then focus on intracoalition and intercoalition activities. Membership in coalitions can shift and coalitions can join with other coalitions to form stronger coalitions. When viewed in this way, organizations can be seen as dynamic arenas of action, with intracoalition and intercoalition bargaining and conflict "inextricably intertwined" (p. 138). Power and conflict are thus at the core of understanding organizations. (See also Pfeffer 1981.) We turn now to the specific consideration of the nature of power in organizations.

Table 7-1   The Unitary and Pluralist Views of Interests, Conflict and Power

	The Unitary View	*The Pluralist View*
Interests	Places emphasis upon the achievement of common objectives. The organization is viewed as being united under the umbrella of common goals, and striving toward their achievement in the manner of a well-integrated team.	Places emphasis upon the diversity of individual and group interests. The organization is regarded as a loose coalition which has but a remote interest in the formal goals of the organization.
Conflict	Regards conflict as a rare and transient phenomenon which can be removed through appropriate managerial action. Where it does arise it is usually attributed to the activities of deviants and troublemakers.	Regards conflict as an inherent and ineradicable characteristic of organizational affairs and stresses its potentially positive or functional aspects.
Power	Largely ignores the role of power in organizational life. Concepts such as authority, leadership and control tend to be preferred means of describing the managerial prerogative of guiding the organization toward the achievement of common interests.	Regards power as a variable crucial to the understanding of the activities of an organization. Power is the medium through which conflicts of interest are alleviated and resolved. The organization is viewed as a plurality of power holders drawing their power from a plurality of sources.

Source: Burrell and Morgan, 1979, p. 204.

Table 7-2 The Radical Weberian View of Interests, Conflict and Power

	The Radical View
Interests	Places emphasis upon the dichotomous nature and mutual opposition of interests in terms of broad socioeconomic divisions of the "class" type within social formations as a whole, which are also reflected in organizations in the middle range of analysis.
Conflict	Regards conflict as a ubiquitous and disruptive motor force propelling changes in society in general and organizations in particular. It is recognized that conflict may be a suppressed feature of a social system, not always evident at the level of empirical a "reality".
Power	Regards power as an integral, unequally distributed, zero-sum phenomenon, associated with a general process of social control. Society in general and organizations in particular are seen as being under the control of ruling interest groups which exercise their power through various forms of ideological manipulation, as well as the more visible forms of authority relations.

Source: Burrell and Morgan, 1979, p. 388.

THE NATURE OF POWER IN ORGANIZATIONS

Power can usually be rather simply defined. Most of the many treatises dealing with the concept are in general agreement that it has to do with relationships between two or more actors in which the behavior of one is affected by the other. The political scientist Dahl (1957) defines power thus: "*A* has power over *B* to the extent that he can get *B* to do something *B* would not otherwise do" (pp. 202–03). (For other general discussions of power see Bierstedt 1950; Blau 1964; Kaplan 1964; and Weber 1947, pp. 152–93.) This simple definition is the essence of the power concept. It also implies an important point that is often neglected: the power variable is a relational one; power is meaningless unless it is exercised. A person or group cannot have power in isolation; it has to be in relationship to some other person or collectivity.

Power Relationships

The relational aspect of power is specifically developed in Emerson's (1962) comments on the importance of dependency relationships in the total power constellation. He suggests that power resides "implicitly in the other's dependency"; in other words, that the parties in a power relationship are tied to each other by mutual dependency.

Social relations commonly entail ties of mutual dependence between the parties. A depends upon B if he aspires to goals or gratifications whose

131

achievement is facilitated by appropriate actions on B's part. By virtue of mutual dependency, it is more or less imperative to each party that he be able to control or influence the other's conduct. At the same time, these ties of mutual dependence imply that each party is in a position, to some degree, to grant or deny, facilitate or hinder, the other's gratification. Thus, it would appear that the power to control or influence the other resides in control over the things he values, which may range all the way from oil resources to ego-support, depending on the relation in question. (p. 32)

Dependency is particularly easy to see in organizations, which by their very nature require interdependence of personnel and subunits (see Bacharach and Lawler 1980). The existence of power relationships is also generally easy to see. Wamsley notes (1970) that in highly bureaucratized organizations, "power or authority would tend to be hierarchic: each level would have just that amount of power necessary to carry out its responsibilities; ascendant levels in the hierarchy would have increasing power based on broader knowledge about the organization and/or greater task expertise" (p. 53). The design of these types of organizations rests largely on the power variable, with the intent of ensuring that each level in the organization has sufficient power. When an issue arises that is out of the purview of an office at a particular level, it is passed up the organization until it reaches the level where the decision can appropriately be made. Of course, few organizations approximate this ideal type, because the power arrangements are affected by informal patterns worked out over time and by personal differences in the exercise of the power available in an office. Nevertheless, in many organizations, power relationships are tightly prescribed and followed, and they are highly visible to all who enter the organization.

While in such settings power is very easily seen and experienced, in others it is more obscure. In some situations it is extremely hard to isolate. Bucher tells the following anecdote as an example of this (1970):

According to the students' statements, the dean asserted that "nobody in the university has the authority to negotiate with the students. . . ." "Obviously somebody in the university makes policy decisions," the statement said, "and until an official body comes forward, we consider the present situation a refusal to negotiate our demands." (p. 3)

The anecdote is based on an incident during the student movement of the 1960s. In the situation described, neither the students nor the university administration in question could locate an office or individual who had the power to negotiate with students. The students' perception that this constitutes a refusal to negotiate is only partially accurate. This type of matter had not arisen before, and there was undoubtedly no established way to handle such situations because the power relationship was yet to be determined. Wamsley (1970) notes that in such situations, power is "variable; situationally or issue specific; surrounded by checks and balances; an interdependent relationship, often employing negotiation and persuasion and often found in changing coalitions" (p. 53).

Power is as much a fact of university life as of corporate life, even if it takes a different form and is expressed in different ways. In campus situations such as student-administration confrontations, issues and relationships are being explored that had not really been part of the preexisting power system. (It is interesting that it is usually the administration that is involved in such confrontations, when the issues the students are most concerned about generally have their origins in faculty actions or inactions.) Because more power is thus introduced into the system as arrangements are made to handle such incidents in the future, we see that there is no fixed amount of power (zero-sum game) in the system for all time; the amount of power can contract or expand.

In the discussion of the relative clarity of power relationships in organizations, it is implicit that power must be viewed as more than merely interpersonal. The subunits in an organization also have varying amounts of power. Perrow (1970a), for example, in a study of industrial firms, found that the sales departments were overwhelmingly regarded as the most powerful units in the organizations involved. The members of the other departments regarded them that way and apparently behaved accordingly. Ignoring interdepartmental power relationships by looking only at interpersonal power obscures an important facet of organizational power.

Two additional aspects of power should be noted. First, power is an act; it is something that is used or exercised. Too frequently the act of power is ignored in analyses of power, which tend to focus on the results of a power act. These results can be of several forms, including compliance or conflict, but the exertion of power is what is of interest to us here. The second point is that the recipient of power is crucial in determining if a power act has occurred. If the recipient interprets an act as a power act, he or she will respond on that basis, whether or not the power wielder intended to utilize power.

Types of Power

The discussion thus far has treated power as a unitary concept, but there is a long history of distinguishing *types* of power. Probably the best known and most widely used classification system is that of Weber (1947). Weber makes a basic distinction between power and *authority*. Power involves force or coercion and would not be an important factor as an internal process in organizations except in cases such as slave-labor camps, some prisons, some schools, and so on. Authority, on the other hand, is a form of power that does not imply force. Rather, it involves a "suspension of judgment" on the part of its recipients. Directives or orders are followed because it is believed that they ought to be followed. Compliance is voluntary. This requires a common value system among organizational members, as Scott (1964) notes, and this condition is usually met.

It is useful at this point to distinguish between authority and influence

(Bacharach and Lawler 1980). Authority involves an acceptance of the power system as one enters the organization, while influence is a power situation in which the decision is made, consciously or unconsciously, at the particular moment the power appeal is sent from the power holder. When a persuader becomes institutionalized, in the sense of being always accepted and thus legitimated by the recipient, this becomes authority.

Many social controversies revolve around the authority issue. When members of a system do not accept the values of the system, as in the case of the radical movement, authority as expressed by the police, courts, or organizational rules becomes nonlegitimate for the people involved. A whole new frame of reference is brought into play, as are other forms of power, such as coercion and persuasion. The fact that such situations are noteworthy is indirect evidence of the overwhelming dominance of authority as the form of power in organizations.

Weber (1947) further distinguishes between types of authority, developing his well-known typology of traditional, charismatic, and legal authority. *Legal* authority is the type of most power relationships in modern organizations; it is based on a belief in the right of those in higher offices to have power over subordinates. *Charismatic* authority stems from devotion to a particular power holder and is based on his or her personal characteristics. This type is certainly found in modern organizations, to which it can be either a threat or a benefit. If a person in an authority position can extend legal powers through the exercise of charismatic authority, there is more power over subordinates than that prescribed by the organization. If the performance of the subordinates is enhanced (assuming for the moment that their performance enhancement is also beneficial to the actors themselves), such an addition is beneficial. If, on the other hand, charismatic authority is present in persons outside the formal authority system, distortions in that system will be evident. As we will see later, it is unlikely that people with legal authority will be able to extend their power through the exercise of charisma. The third form, *traditional* authority, is based on belief in the established traditional order and is best exemplified by operating monarchies. Vestiges of this form can be found in organizations in which the founder or a dominant figure is still present, when terms such as "the old man wants it that way" are verbalized and the wishes of the "old man" are followed.

Dornbusch and Scott (1976) have added an important contribution to our understanding of authority. They found that control in organizations was based on the process of evaluation. The individual who evaluates one's work has authority. Control through evaluation is most effective when the individuals being evaluated believe the evaluations are important, central to their work, and capable of being influenced by their own efforts. If the evaluations are believed to be soundly based, they will be more controlled by the evaluation process. Dornbusch and Scott also note that authority is granted from above as well as from below. In a multilevel hierarchy, people in a position to evaluate others are legitimated from subordinates and also from their own superiors.

Power Bases

Since Weber's time, there have been several attempts to classify the power concept into still more useful categories. One of the approaches that has attracted a good deal of attention is that of French and Raven (1968). Their concern is primarily with the bases of interpersonal power, but their conclusions can easily be extended to the organizational level. Their typology is based on the nature of the relationship between the power holder and the power recipient. *Reward* power, or "power whose basis is the ability to reward," is limited to those situations in which the reward is meaningful for the power recipient. The second power basis is *coercive* power, based on the recipient's perceptions of the ability of the power holder to distribute punishments. French and Raven note that the same social relationship could be viewed as one of reward power in one instance and coercive power in a second. If a worker obeys a foreman's order through fear of punishment, it is coercive power; if another worker obeys in anticipation of a future reward, it is reward power.

The third form of power is very close to the implication of the Weberian distinction between power and authority. This type is called *legitimate* power. The recipient acknowledges that the power holder has the right to influence him and he has an obligation to follow the directions of the influence. *Referent* power is present when a power recipient identifies with a power holder and tries to behave like him. In this case, the power holder may be unaware that he is in fact a power holder. The final form, *expert* power, is based on the special knowledge attributed to the power holder by the recipient. The power recipient behaves in a particular way because he believes that the information possessed by the holder is relevant and that he himself does not have that sort of information available. The simplest example here, of course, is in the professional-client relationship, when the client follows the "doctor's orders."

Bacharach and Lawler (1980, p. 34) add an additional power base. This is *access to knowledge*. Individuals or groups can control unique information and thus have a power base when it is time to make a decision. Thus, coercion, rewards, expertise, legitimacy, referent, and information bases of power have been identified.

Power bases are what individuals or groups control that enables them to manipulate the behavior of others. Bacharach and Lawler (1980) go on to make an additional distinction. They note that there are four *sources* of power in organizations. They use the term sources to refer to the manner in which parties come to control the power bases. The sources are: 1) office or structural position; 2) personal characteristics, such as charisma; 3) expertise, which is treated as a source and a basis of power, since individuals bring expertise with them to the organization through such mechanisms as professional training, which is then converted into a power basis at a specific point in time; and 4) opportunity or the combination of factors which give parties the chance to utilize their power bases.

These sources of power are used in the power situations of authority and influence, which in turn utilize the bases of power which have been distinguished. Thus, an individual or unit in an organization has a power source, such as an official position in which power in the form of authority or influence is exercised. As the power is exercised, the power holder utilizes the power bases that are available. In this formulation, the bases cannot be used unless the power holder first of all has the appropriate power source. The distinctions among sources, bases, and types have little meaning unless we consider the outcomes of power acts for the organization and its participants.

SOME CONSEQUENCES OF POWER RELATIONSHIPS

Compliance and Involvement

The most frequent consequence of a power act is compliance. This is frequently overlooked in analyses of power, since it is the resistance to a power act—conflict—that is more dramatic and exciting. The fact of the matter is that it is the less dramatic phenomenon of compliance that is much more frequent.

Etzioni (1961, 1975) made compliance the heart of his typology and conceptualization of organizations. It will be remembered from the discussion of typologies that Etzioni identified alienative, calculative, and moral involvement on the part of lower participants as they comply with the various forms of power used. Etzioni recognizes that in many cases there are mixed reasons for compliance. Thus, school children generally believe that their teachers are to be admired (normative power), but there is always the potential for punishment (coercive power). Etzioni's classification of power is different, of course, from that developed earlier in this chapter, but his types of power are quite compatible with the power bases which have been discussed here.

The findings associated with the Etzioni scheme suggest that when organizations are able to develop moral involvement on the part of their members, their commitment to the *organization is higher*. This is particularly the case for voluntary organizations.

Wood (1975) examined churches as voluntary organizations. He was interested in the ways in which church leaders could pursue interests, such as social justice, which church members did not necessarily embrace. He found that commitment or moral involvement contributed to members going along with church leaders' positions. In some churches, more formal commitment through submission to hierarchical authority also contributed to members' compliance with leaders' wishes. In some later research, Hougland, Shepard, and Wood (1979) and Hougland and Wood (1980) found that the amount of control exercised in church organizations was related to members' commitment to the organizations. Members who were committed to and satisfied with the organization reported that they also exerted more control in their organizations. Commitment thus increases moral involvement, but at the same time raises the level of control or power which the lower participants experience. In an examination of another set of voluntary organizations Styskal (1980) found that while lower participants did not participate in decision making to the extent that they wanted to, the fact that they did participate to some degree appeared to be sufficient to maintain their level of commitment to the organization. This research was carried out in educational change organizations and the lower participants were community members.

Compliance and involvement are interrelated phenomena. Voluntary organizations rely on moral involvement. Moral involvement is apparently increased when members are encouraged to participate and do participate. Participation thus contributes to compliance through the process of involvement.

Conformity

A different approach to the issue of compliance was taken by Warren (1968). He studied the ways in which a sample of school teachers conformed to the exercise of power. He distinguished between simple *behavioral* conformity, in which the power recipient complies without internalization of the norms involved and *attitudinal* conformity in which there is both compliance and internalization. Using the French and Raven (1968) power bases, Warren found that attitudinal conformity was strongly related to the exercise of expert, legitimate, and referent power, while coercive and reward power bases were more strongly related to behavioral conformity. Warren also found that the level of professionalization of school staffs interacted with the power bases. Greater attitudinal conformity was reported when expert, legitimate, and referent power bases were present. Coercive and reward power have less relevance among professionalized teachers.

There are two important implications from the Warren findings. First, multiple power bases are utilized in a single organization. Power is a variable within the system, both in terms of the types involved and the amount of power involved. Second, the type of power base used will have an impact on the outcome of the exercise of power. This is in keeping with Etzioni's interpretations.

It should be noted that none of the power bases is inherently better or more moral. In Nazi Germany the power bases were referent and legitimate for the non-Jewish population and obviously coercive for the Jewish population. There is no inherent goodness or badness in any of the power forms discussed.

Perceptions of Authority

Power is a relational phenomenon. An important aspect of the relationship is the manner in which the power recipient perceives the exercise of power. In an analysis of a social welfare agency, a police department, and an elementary school, Peabody (1962) found that authority was perceived in four different ways. Some authority was seen as legitimate or residing in legal codes or organizational rules. Authority was also perceived to be based on a superior's position, with the simple fact of a higher position accepted as the basis for authority. A third basis for authority which was perceived was personal competence, while the fourth base was perceived as involving the personal attributes of the power holder.

Peabody's four types of perceived authority are very close to the French and Raven power bases that have been used earlier. The key point here is that power recipients perceive power acts differently. The same power act by a superior could be perceived as authority on the basis of legitimacy, position, competence, or personal attributes. In one sense, this does not matter at all, since the perception of authority in this case led to compliance. In another sense, this differential perception of authority matters a great deal. Differential perception means that authority, or more generally power, might not be perceived at all. If a power holder attempts to exercise power and the recipient does not perceive the activity as a power situation, power won't be exercised. An exception here, of course, is the case of physical coercion. This point on perception of power is a major reason why organizations utilize power symbols, such as uniforms, insignia, or offices to predesignate the fact that a person has authority. The use of such power symbols is designed to prevent misperceptions of the power relationship.

Power and Participation

Our analysis of power in the form of authority has not yet taken into account the potential of participation by power recipients in the power relationship. In the last chapter, the impact of participation on centralization was discussed. Here we are concerned with the simple question of the extent to which participation in decision making affects the power of the individuals in power positions. There appears to be very little effect—although participation can sometimes increase the power of the power holder. Rosner et al. (1973) found that greater worker participation did not reduce the influence of the manager. Workers felt that they had more personal influence, trust, and responsibility, but the actual influence of the manager was unaffected. In a related study, Mulder and Wilke (1970) found that participation actually increases the power of the power holder. This occurs when neither the power holders nor recipients have expertise in the issue at hand. If the power recipients gain in expertise before the participation, their power relative to that of the power holder will increase.

Power and Communications

So far, we have focused principally on the manner in which individuals are controlled within various power systems. But power systems involve more than the control of individuals. A study by Julian (1966) indicates that the communication system within an organization is also affected by the power arrangements. Using data from five hospitals, Julian found that the hospital power systems differed largely according to the nature of the hospitals. In voluntary general hospitals, the power system tended to be normative, while in a tuberculosis sanatorium and a veteran's hospital, coercive patterns were a more evident part of the power relationship. Julian obtained his information about the power relationships from the patients in the hospital. Obviously, patients are only one of several groups in hospitals subject to the power system. The "semi-professional" staff (including nurses and technicians) and the nonprofessional staff (orderlies and kitchen help) also are subject to the established power system. Data are not available to determine if the power relationships with patients are the same as those with the paid staff. They are probably not exactly equivalent, especially since remuneration enters the picture with regard to the staff personnel. This indicates again the probability that multiple power relationships characterize most organizations. This would particularly be the case when the organization contains such members as clients or students.

Julian supplies some insights into the nature of normative and coercive power as applied through sanctions on the patients. Normative sanctions include "explaining the situation to the patients again in more detail," and "asking relatives or friends to talk to the patient." The explanations and talks are designed to make the patient comply with the hospital's (doctor's) wishes. Coercive sanctions include "putting a patient under sedation to keep him quiet and restricting the patient's activity" (p. 385).

When the communication patterns between hospital staff members and the patients are analyzed, it is found that there are more communication blockages under the more coercive system. These communication blockages are actually functional for the organizations. Julian states:

> Within the framework of this study, normative-coercive hospitals, which control and block patient activities to a greater extent than normative hospitals, restrict communication for coordinative purposes. In a more general way, normative-coercive organizations have more communication blocks because they are more effective for realizing the goal of control or coordination. (p. 386)

Another important finding of the Julian study is that the hospitals varied not only the *type* of control utilized but also in the *amount*. In the largest general hospital more coercive sanctions were employed than in the other general hospitals, and the overall amount of control exercised was also higher. At any point in time, the amount of power is undoubtedly fixed, but over time and across organizations the amount varies.

In our discussion thus far, we have been concerned with the power relationships between upper and lower participants in organizations—the vertical dimension of power. As indicated earlier, these relationships can occur at any point in the vertical structure of an organization. That is, vertical power can be found between a president and the vice presidents of a university, as well as between faculty and students. Much of this relationship involves the way in which a superior interacts with his subordinates. The behavior and attitudes of both parties in a vertical relationship have been a primary focus of studies of "leadership" or management "styles," and will be dealt with in the next chapter.

HORIZONTAL POWER RELATIONSHIPS

The vertical dimension is only one part of power relationships in organizations. But power relationships between individuals and units horizontal to each other are a less systematically studied component of total power systems. Interdepartmental, staff-line, and professional-organizational relationships are all familiar loci of the horizontal dimension.

Before we look at some of the research in this area, an apparent contradiction must be clarified. The term "horizontal power relationships" seems to represent an inconceivable situation. If the parties in the relationship have exactly equal amounts of power, then as soon as one gains power at the expense of the other, a vertical element is introduced. But the concern here is with relationships among units and persons who have positions relative to each other that are basically lateral. In these lateral relationships, the power variable can become a major part of the total relationship. It is conceivable that power will not enter the relationship if the parties have no reason to attempt to influence each other's behavior. However, the power variable would almost inevitably enter such relationships when issues such as budgetary allocations, output quotas, priorities for personnel, and other such matters come into the picture.

Staff-Line Relationships

Horizontal or lateral power relationships have been carefully analyzed by Dalton (1959). Perhaps his best known contribution is the analysis of staff-line conflict. Dalton found that these personnel were in rather constant conflict in several areas. The staff personnel tend to be younger, have more formal education, be more concerned with proper dress and manners, and be more theoretically oriented than the line managers in the organizations studied. This is a basis for conflict, but it is also part of the power relationship. The power aspect, aside from its importance in actual conflict situations, comes in when the staff attempts to get some of its ideas implemented (expert power).

Power is also exerted in terms of the personal ambitions of the people involved. Dalton assumes that both sets of managers seek income, promotions, power in the organization, and so on. In the organizations studied, the line personnel held the power in controlling the promotion process; but at the same time, they feared that the staff might come up with ideas that would put the line's modes of operations under serious scrutiny as being outmoded or unimaginative. In this instance we have an example of two different forms of power as a part of one power relationship. The outcome is a series of conflicts between line and staff that, viewed from outside the organization, are costly to it. There is a fairly high turnover among staff personnel, who apparently feel that they are not getting anywhere in the organization. The staff resents the line, and vice versa.

In order to accomplish anything, the staff must secure some cooperation from the line. This requires giving in to the line by moderating proposals, overlooking practices that do not correspond to rigid technical standards, and in general playing a rather subservient role in dealing with the line. If this is not done, the staff's suggestions would probably go unheeded. This in turn would make their output zero for the time period, and their general relevance for the organization would then be questioned. This, of course, is not a unique situation. The exact extent of such conflicts and conditions under which they occur are unfortunately not clear, since Dalton had a small sample, composed only of manufacturing organizations. But that this sort of phenomenon is a major component of traditional manufacturing firms, and that variations of the patterns described are found in every organization, seem to be generally accepted.

Professional-Organizational Relationships

The analysis of staff-line relationships has been largely replaced in recent years by a concern with professional-organizational relationships. These are usually expressed in terms of conflict. The power components of this type of relationship are similar in many ways to the staff-line conflicts discussed by Dalton. A major difference would appear to be that the organizational members with whom the professionals interact, while nót professionals in the traditional sense, are usually not poorly educated people who have come up through the ranks. The modern executive is also well educated and is likely to show the same kinds of interest in general social values as the professional.

It is commonly noted in discussions of professionals in organizations that the "reward" power system for them is more complicated than for other organization members. (For extended discussions of these points, see Kornhauser 1963; *Administrative Science Quarterly*, June 1965, entire issue; Vollmer and Mills 1966). Professionals typically desire the same kinds of rewards as other people, in terms of money and other extrinsic factors, but they are also likely to want recognition from fellow professionals as good lawyers, scientists, or whatever. In addition, evaluation of their work, which is difficult for someone not in that profession, is likely to be made by just such personnel. This is true in many cases even if the evaluator, in an administrative position, is a member of the same profession. For example, a research scientist in an organization is likely to be under the supervision of another scientist who has been promoted to research administration. The very fact that the latter is now working in administration prevents him or her from keeping up with developments in that scientific discipline; since they occur rapidly it is difficult even for the practicing scientist to keep abreast of what is occurring.

Since the organization must in some way control all its members, the issue becomes very difficult with respect to the professional. If it tries to exert legitimate control through the hierarchy, the professional is apt to resist it. If it turns over the control of the professional to other professionals, the organization not only loses control, but is uncertain as to whether the professionals involved are contributing to the organization exactly what the organization thinks they should. This dilemma is frequently resolved by allowing the professionals to control themselves, with a fellow professional (for example, the research administrator) held accountable for the work of that unit as a collectivity. This allows the professional to work in a situation of less direct scrutiny but provides the organization with a system of accountability.

The reward system in these situations is also frequently altered. Instead of promoting professionals by moving them higher in the administrative system, organizations are developing "dual ladders" for their promotion system, whereby professionals can advance either by being promoted in the traditional way or by staying in their professional unit and with their work, but at increasingly higher salaries. (For a criticism of this technique, see Argyris 1969.) Additional rewards for professionals can come through publication and participation in the affairs of their profession. Organizations can also provide these kinds of incentives. As the professional becomes better known in the field, his or her own power increases. At the same time, the organization continues to have power, by providing the reward system as a whole.

This discussion has involved ways in which the power issue may be resolved. But obviously, in many cases the issues are not resolved, and professionals are in conflict with the rest of the organization. They may feel that the organization is intruding into their work through unnecessary rules and regulations or that their contributions are receiving insufficient attention and reward. The members of the organization in contact with the professionals, on the other hand, may view them as hopelessly impractical and out of touch with what is really important for the organization. These lateral power relationships will probably increase, because professionals and professionalizing occupations are becoming increasingly important to organizations of every variety.

Another form of lateral power relationship that would often involve professionals is in the area of expertise. Since there is no one universal organizational or societal truth system, experts can take differing views on what is good, rational, legal or effective for the organization. When the perspectives of accountants, lawyers, research scientists, management consultants, and executives are combined, it is extremely unlikely that a common viewpoint will emerge even after serious discussions. As the level of training and expertise increases in organizations, differences in perspective will be magnified, and the power of expertise may well become a greater source of conflict for organizations. Professionals in organizations will continue to seek more power (Hage 1980).

Cliques and Coalitions   In his study of industrial organizations, Dalton (1959) found that cliques were an important component of the power system. Dalton showed that personal self-interest took the form of clique formation across organizational lines. Cliques were formed to defend the members in the face of real or imagined threats to their security by automation or reorganization. Aggressive cliques were formed to accomplish some purpose, such as to halt the expansion of a department perceived as usurping some of the power of clique members. Dalton's analysis shows that organizations are constantly filled with interpersonal power situations as events and conditions shift over time. These cliques need not, and in fact usually do not, follow the established organizational hierarchical or horizontal system.

Cliques can also be based on the sheer fact of differentiation within organizations. Mintzberg (1979) concludes that people in different parts of organizations deal with qualitatively different information. The sales representative, sales manager, and marketing vice president are in the same functional area, but deal with information with different time frames and referents. The sales representatives would be differentiated from other managerial personnel at the same level in the organization and would undoubtedly form cliques on this basis.

Some recent analyses of power in organizations have focused on coalitions (Bacharach and Lawler 1980; Pfeffer 1981). Coalitions are formed as parties seek to advance their own interests. Coalitions seek to exert power over other coalitions and advance their own interests. Analyses of coalitions suggest that organizations are highly political, with shifting alliances and power arrangements. Pfeffer (1981, p. 37) suggests that factors such as age, position in the organization in terms of department, educational background, length of time in the organization, and personal values all may influence coalition formation. These factors also may lead the individual into different coalitions, depending on the issue.

The analysis of cliques and coalitions can lead one to view organizations as a "bewildering mosaic of swiftly changing and conflicting cliques, which cut across departmental and traditional loyalties" (Mouzelis 1967, p. 159). While this view is warranted as a check on an overstructured view of organizations, it is an overreaction. Cliques and coalitions would not form if there were not a common basis for interaction or if there were not already interaction among members. Rather than being random, clique and coalition formation obviously begins from the established organizational order and then becomes variations from that order. The fact that these cliques and coalitions can form vertically and horizontally and represent personal and subunit interests reflects the constant interplay of the power variables within the organization.

Uncertainty, Dependency, and Interdepartmental Power Crozier's (1964) analysis of the French organizations gives another view of power along the horizontal dimension. Departments in the tobacco firms were in a constant power struggle, with the maintenance men holding the most power because of their knowledge in repairing the equipment necessary to the production process. Production workers and their supervisors were essentially helpless unless the maintenance personnel performed their work. This, of course, gave the maintenance men a great deal of power in the organization. Crozier states:

> With machine stoppages, a general uncertainty about what will happen next develops in a world totally dominated by the value of security. It is not surprising, therefore, that the behavior of the maintenance man—the man who alone can handle the situation, and who by preventing these unpleasant consequences gives workers the necessary security—has a tremendous im-

portance for production workers, and that they try to please him and he to influence them. (p. 109)

In analyzing this situation, Mouzelis notes:

The strategy consists in the manipulation of rules as means of enhancing group prerogatives and independence from every direct and arbitrary interference from those higher up. But as rules can never regulate everything and eliminate all arbitrariness, areas of uncertainty always emerge which constitute the focal structural points around which collective conflicts become acute and instances of direct dominance and subordination re-emerge. In such cases the group which by its position in the occupational structure can control the unregulated area has a great strategic advantage which is naturally used in order to improve its power position and ensure a greater share of the organizational rewards. (p. 160)

This is a vivid example of the dependence relationship inherent in a power situation. If it were not for the essential expertise of the maintenance men in this situation, the production workers would not be so dependent. Although the Crozier study is perhaps an extreme case, it does illustrate how lateral relationships can become built around the power of the parties involved.

Additional insights into this kind of power relationship are provided by Perrow (1970a) in a study directly concerned with the power of different departments in organizations. Using data from twelve industrial firms based on answers to the question, "Which group has the most power?" Perrow found that the firms were overwhelmingly dominated by their sales departments. This domination is shown in Figure 7-1. Although he does not have direct evidence, Perrow believes that this would be the case in most industrial firms in the United States.

Since manufacturing firms must sell their products, and since customers (institutional or individual) "determine the cost, quality, and type of goods that will be produced and distributed" (p. 65), the customer determines organizational success. While all departments in the organization contribute to customer satisfaction, it is sales that has the most direct contact with this important group:

Sales is the main gate between the organization and the customer. As gatekeeper, it determines how important will be prompt delivery, quality, product-improvement, or new products, and the cost at which goods can be sold. Sales determines the relative importance of these variables for the other groups and indicates the values which these variables will take. It has the ability, in addition, of changing the values of these variables, since it sets pricing (and in most firms adjusts it temporarily to meet changes in opportunity and competition), determines which markets will be utilized, the

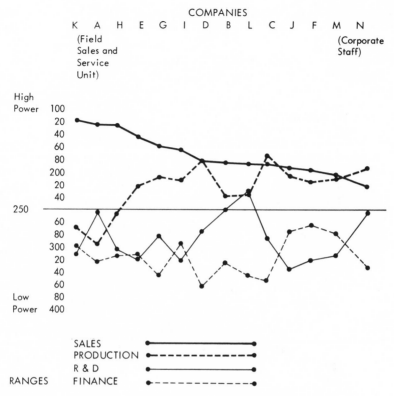

Figure 7-1 Overall power of departments in industrial firms (means of departmental means)

Source: Perrow 1970, p. 64.

services that will be provided, and the changes in products that must be made. As the link between the customer and producer, it absorbs most of the uncertainty about the diffuse and changing environment of customers. (p. 65)

Perrow then generalizes that the most critical function in an organization tends to have the most power, linking his analysis to Crozier's. He notes that in the one firm that was production-dominated, the production department was able to get control of the computer and inventory and purchasing. It was in a position to tell the sales department what could or could not be done under existing conditions. These same functions could be handled in the finance department, as was the case in another firm, with finance passing the information along to sales, thus giving sales power over production. The combination of critical function and dependence gives sales its power position in these organizations.

A PERSPECTIVE ON POWER IN ORGANIZATIONS

The discussion thus far has been largely descriptive, dealing with various studies of vertical and horizontal power relationships. In this section, we will try to bring some of these considerations together in an overview of power in organizations.

Amount of Power

The first point to be made here is a quantitative one, concerning the amount of power in an organization. This would appear to be a rather simple issue, since someone in a management position has a specified amount of power over a person beneath him or her. The matter is not that simple, however, when multiple bases of power are present. Lammers (1967) deals with this issue when he states: "To sum up, managers and managed in organizations at the same time come to influence each other more effectively and thereby generate joint power as the outcome of a better command by the organization over its technological, economic, and human resources in the service of certain objectives" (p. 204). Lammers assumes that the members are seeking the same basic goals. This joint influence is actually a condition of more power in the organization than was the case before mutual influence entered the picture. If the French and Raven classification of power bases is utilized, it is obvious that the amount of power in an organization, as well as in a single interpersonal situation, is a variable. The amount of power in an organization changes over time.

In summarizing a series of studies on the amount of power in organizations, Tannenbaum (1968) notes that the expansion of power

> may occur under either of two classes of conditions. The first is that of an external expansion of power into the organizations's environment. The second concerns a number of internal conditions that subsume: (1) structural conditions expediting interaction and influence among members, and (2) motivational conditions implying increased interest by members in exercising control and a greater amenability by members to being controlled. These conditions may sometimes be related. For example, extending control by the organization into its environment may bring more decisions within the purview of the organization that are subject to the control of its members, thus increasing the possibility of a greater total amount of control. At the same time such increased opportunities to exercise control within the organization may increase the members' involvement in and identification with the organization and hence increase their interest in exercising control and their amenability to being controlled. Members, then, as possible control agents, engage in more frequent influence attempts, and as possible objects of control, provide new opportunities to one another to exercise control. Thus external developments may affect social and psychological processes within the organization conducive to a high level of internal control, just as conditions of a high level of involvement by members and of a high level of

control within the organization may contribute to the strength of the organization and hence to its power in the environment. (pp. 14–15)

This view that the amount of power varies in organizations has to be approached with some caution. First, the amount does not vary dramatically from situation to situation. Factors leading to an increase or decrease would typically not be rapid or sudden in their impact—with the exception of something like a disaster, in which case the amount of power in the organization could change very dramatically. Generally, however, changes in the amount of power will be gradual. A second caution is that at any one point in time the amount of power in an organization is fixed—a zero-sum game. If one person or group gains in power, another loses. Power acts are carried out within a fixed-amount framework. It is the framework that is altered over time.

Factors Affecting the Distribution of Power

When the focus is shifted from the amount of power to the reasons why power is distributed as it is, several points stand out. The ability to cope with uncertainty has been analyzed as contributing to power differentials (Hickson, Pugh, and Pheysey 1969). Coping with uncertainty means that an organizational unit is able to deal with some issue of concern to the organization. If the concern is financial, for example, the unit able to attract resources will gain in power (Salancik and Pfeffer 1974). In the perspective of the Aston group, coping with uncertainty is coupled with both the centrality of the organizational unit to the total organization and its nonsubstitutability. Units that cope well with uncertainty and are irreplaceable and central to the work flow of the organization will have increased power.

An empirical examination of this theoretical approach revealed that this process did in fact operate, but with a minor modification (Hickson, et al. 1974). The modification is the fact that some organizational units are delegated important tasks in the first place. They can increase their power by effective coping. In other instances, power can be developed in situations in which organizational units enter new and important areas of uncertainty, cope well, and develop more power.

This approach implies that power is constantly shifting within organizations, as units gain or lose power according to how well they cope with uncertainty. While it is true that power is a component of any situation, the imagery of constantly shifting power seems to be a mistake for two reasons. First, the importance of the established hierarchy and degree of centralization is ignored. While the coping with uncertainty approach is concerned with horizontal power relationships, the more vertical ones cannot just be ignored. Second, once an organizational unit gains power by its success in coping, it would try very hard to maintain its power. Earlier success gives a unit an immediate advantage over other units because it already has more power. Before considering this issue further, it should also be noted that the Hickson et al. approach has been criticized for its heavy managerial bias. Lower-level personnel in units in power struggles are seldom aware of or involved in such struggles (Clegg and Dunkerly 1980, pp. 440–41).

Returning to the consideration of the effects of successful coping with uncertainty, we can see the importance of a unit's original power position in two studies of university budget allocation decisions. Pfeffer and Salancik (1974) found that the more powerful units received more resources—the rich get richer and the poor get poorer. Hills and Mahoney (1978) found this pattern to be particularly evident in times of financial adversity.

As Michels (1962) reminds us, power has a self-perpetuating aspect. Thus, those in power in an organization tend to remain in power. They have resources, and the power recipients do not. The very fact that legitimacy is such an important consideration in organizational power arrangements sets the stage for the perpetuation of existing power distributions.

Most of the discussion of power in organizations has been concerned with the manner in which an individual or unit is able to control the behavior of others in the organization. The emphasis has been on the idea that power is not a static phenomenon, even with the same personnel involved. But the issue becomes more complicated if problems of succession of personnel at all levels are considered. Studies by Gouldner (1954), Guest (1962), and Grusky (1961) have indicated that changes in the top management can have important repercussions for the total organization, particularly when the new leader tries to utilize a different power basis than did his predecessor. The turnover of personnel also contributes to the instability of power relationships.

The distribution of power in organizations has ramifications beyond those already discussed. The distribution of resources within an organization, including rewards, budget items, and personnel, is affected by the power system (Zald 1970c; Pondy 1970). Since the allocation system is affected by the existing power system, it tends to perpetuate the existing system. Zald points out that the accounting and information systems within organizations are important agents of power; they determine the emphasis given to particular kinds of activities and the information that is available to various number of the organization. Zald also notes that the nature of the incentive system within the organization is an important power consideration, since it provides the basis, both in nature and extent, on which rewards are distributed.

As will be discussed in a later chapter, decision making is a critical organizational process. Power is obviously important in decision making as will be seen. Here we will simply note that power holders shape and decide what are issues and what are nonissues (Ranson, Hinings, and Greenwood 1980; Clegg and Dunkerley 1980). If an organizational member believes that something is a burning issue, it will only become one in the organization if power holders also define it as such.

External Factors

The focus of our discussion has been primarily on factors internal to the organization. Zald points out that external considerations also play an important role in the power system of the organization. Here factors such as associations of similar organizations (trade associations or baseball leagues), relationships with suppliers and users of the organization's output, regulatory agencies, and other indirectly involved parties affect the amount and distribution of power within the organization. An example of this is provided by Peterson (1970), who notes that the National Labor Relations Board, after its establishment in the 1930s, facilitated the growth in power of labor unions. At the same time, the increasing complexity of labor laws and regulations led to the development of specialists in labor relations, and these personnel also gained in power in the organization, largely as a consequence of these external factors. External economic conditions also affect the power system in organizations as markets for labor and putputs shift, the source of "raw materials" is altered, and the nature of the organization's clientele varies.

In an analysis of United Fund agencies, Pfeffer and Long (1977) found that community organizations that themselves were successful in raising funds received greater allocations from the United Funds. These community organizations were less dependent upon the United Fund, while the United Fund had the fear that the community organizations might strike out on their own fund-raising efforts. The external world thus invades the power structure of these organizations. These analyses emphasize the importance of external relationships for the power distribution and exercise within organizations. External relationships also are important to the extent that they provide access to wealth and power for the organization (Aldrich 1979), a topic which will be discussed in more detail later. Power, like other organizational phenomena, does not occur in the vacuum of just the organization itself.

POWER IN VOLUNTARY ORGANIZATIONS

This analysis appears to be applicable to all organizations. But before we conclude this section, a brief consideration of power in voluntary organizations is in order. Voluntary organizations have all the characteristics of other organizations in regard to the nature and importance of power as an internal process. They are somewhat different, however, because of the apparent need for membership participation in order for the organization to remain viable. Most analyses point to the cruciality of the democratic process for voluntary organizations, since this form of power determination tends to assure continued participation. Craig and Gross (1970) suggest that, in addition, voluntary organizations must remain permeable to new ideas and interests if democracy is to be maintained. This permeability assures continued participation by maintaining membership interest in issues that are new and around which power can cluster,

149

thus preventing the tendency toward oligarchy. Maintaining membership involvement is crucial for such organization. From most of the evidence, it is apparent that this involves distributing some form of power among all the organizational participants, regardless of the power form and other considerations, as the earlier discussion of commitment suggested.

LOWER PARTICIPANTS

We have focused on vertical and horizontal components of power relationships in organizations. Before attempting to bring together the findings of the studies examined and developing an overview of power, a final form of the power relationship should be examined. This type is rare in organizations, but anyone who has had any contact with an organization has confronted it from time to time. The power of "lower participants" in organizations can be a source of both frustration and wonder; secretaries are capable of causing extreme frustration and embarrassment, among other things, for their bosses, and hospital attendants can in some cases make physicians dependent upon them (Scheff 1961).

Mechanic (1962) has identified some of the sources of power of lower participants. As we shall see, these are not too different from the general sources of power that have been discussed in the earlier sections. What is different is that the lower members of organizations are able to amass the resources that a purely structural analysis would suggest should not be theirs. The first source of power is expertise coupled with the difficulty of replacing the person in question. The maintenance men in Crozier's study had this form of power over the managers in the tobacco industry. Another example is a person in a clerical position who gains power by being the only one in an organization who knows how to perform a particular operation. This person thus becomes indispensable, with all work having to go through his or her hands. In some cases, patterns of personal likes and dislikes can "make or break" another person in the organization who ostensibly has a higher position; for example, requests for information can be conveniently "lost."

A second source of power is the amount of effort and interest expressed on the job. Mechanic notes the example of university departmental secretaries who can have "power to make decisions about the purchase and allocation of supplies, the allocation of their services, the scheduling of classes, and, at times, the disposition of student complaints. Such control may in some instances lead to sanctions against a professor by polite reluctance to furnish supplies, ignoring his preferences for the scheduling of classes, and giving others preference in the allocation of services" (p. 359). Removal of this power from secretaries itself involves the expenditure of time and effort. A departmental chairman is unlikely to come down hard on a trusted secretary, whereas he might with younger or disfavored faculty.

Several other factors are associated with lower participants' power. One is the attractiveness of the individual involved; personal or physical attractiveness can lead to relationships that are outside the organization's (or individual's) intent. Physical location and position within an organization can make one person more critical than another; a major information processor can have strong control over those who are dependent on him for accurate information. Coalitions among lower participants can also increase their power. Rules themselves can provide a source of power, in that strict adherence to a highly formalized rules system can hold up operations in the organization. A supervisor cannot really criticize his subordinates if they point out to him that they are following the letter of the law.

THE CONSEQUENCES OF POWER

The discussion thus far has alluded to the consequences of the exertion of power. The dominant consequence is to some observers the least interesting: people or units comply. This is most typically the case when power is well legitimated. Compliance, and even willing compliance, is extremely frequent. People come to work on time, do what their bosses desire, and produce their goods or deliver their services. Organizational units generally also comply or obey.

This is not the only response, however. As Blau (1964) has pointed out, the power recipient can withdraw from the situation or attempt to circumvent or go around the power holder. Another possible response is conflict with the power holder. It is to conflict that we now turn.

CONFLICT IN ORGANIZATIONS

Many of the major forms of conflict within organizations are already well known to anyone concerned with organizations or the society in general. Labor-management conflict is a prominent part of our social heritage, as well as of organizational life. The existence of professional-organizational and staff-line conflicts has already been amply discussed. Many of the power relationships described in the previous section are also conflict situations.

In this section, the bases, forms, and consequences of conflict in organizations will be analyzed. (The analysis will focus on conflict *within* organizations; conflict between organizations and between organizations and the wider society, will be handled later.) The focus will be on the analysis rather than on providing detailed examples. Most such examples are well known, and can be extrapolated from the discussions of power. As in the case of power, relatively few empirical studies of conflict are more than ex post facto case studies.

Conflict in organizations involves more than simple interpersonal conflict. (Not that interpersonal conflict is necessarily simple, given the complexities of the human personality, but for our purposes it is only part of the picture.) The psychologist Sanford (1964) makes this point in an historical perspective when he states: "Twenty years ago, it seemed easy to account for organizational conflict by blaming the problem behavior of individuals. But the simple formula, 'trouble is due to trouble-makers,' is unfortunately inadequate in the light of our present knowledge of the social process (p. 95). The inadequacy of the individualized approach to conflict is based on the fact that organizational considerations and the very nature of organizations themselves contribute to conflict situations.

Bases of Conflict

Another psychologist, Katz (1964), has identified three organizational bases of conflict. The first is "functional conflict induced by various sub-systems within the organizations." This form of conflict involves the fact that

> every subsystem of an organization with its distinctive functions develops its own norms and values and is characterized by its own dynamics. People in the maintenance subsystem have the problem of maintaining the role system and preserving the character of the organization through selection of appropriate personnel, indoctrinating and training them, devising checks for ensuring standard role performance, and so on. These people face inward in the organization and are concerned with maintaining the status quo. People in the procurement and disposal subsystems, however, face outward on the world and develop a different psychological orientation. These differing orientations are one built-in source of conflict. Put in another way, the systems of maintenance, production, and adaptive development each develop their own distinctive norms and frames of reference which contain their own elements of potential conflict. (pp. 105–06)

Although the focus is on the psychological states of the members of the organizations, the point is important, since different subunits in organizations perform tasks that come into conflict because they are basically incompatible.

The second source of conflict is the fact that units have similar functions. Conflict here can take the form of "hostile rivalry or good-natured competition" (p. 106). Such competition can be beneficial, but it can also be destructive. Aldrich (1979) notes that conflicts develop when there is mutual task dependence. In this situation, coordination is another alternative. Aldrich also notes a conflict potential when there is asymmetric, or unbalanced, dependence among units in regard to a task. Katz's final form of organizationally based conflict is "hierarchical conflict stemming from interest-group struggles over the organizational rewards of status, prestige, and monetary reward" (p. 106). Since less than total satisfaction with the reward structure is common, and since subgroups develop their own communication systems and norms, it is normal that lower-level personnel "try" to improve their lot by joining forces as an interest group against the more privileged members of the organization" (p. 106). Although one typically thinks of blue-collar workers and unions in this regard, the process would operate with white-collar workers and subgroups in the management hierarchy.

Robbins (1974) approaches the bases of conflict in a different manner. He suggests that conflict can result from imperfect communications. Communications can be distorted, semantic difficulties can exist, knowledge itself contains intrinsic ambiguities, and communications channels can be imperfectly used. Structural conditions also lead to conflict; large size, the heterogeneity of the staff, styles of supervision, and extent of participation, the reward system, and the form of power used are among such conditions. Robbins also notes that personal-behavior variables are important in the areas of personality dimensions and interactions, role satisfactions, and individual goals. In addition, conflict can emerge from differences between total occupational groups, such as different professions, or between groups with different power in the organizations, such as in labor-management conflict (see Dahrendorf 1959; Hage and Aiken 1970; Silverman 1971; Hage 1980). Furthermore, just as we cannot assume that the organization will always act rationally, there can be no assumption that individuals will not "depart from rational, reality-based behavior in their individual struggles against one another or in their participation in group struggles" (Katz 1964, pp. 105–06).

These bases of conflict are an inherent element of organizations and thus conflict itself must be viewed as inherent. At the same time, the fact that these antecedents or bases of conflict are present does not mean that conflict will take place. Before conflict can ensue, the parties involved must perceive that they are in a position to interfere with the other party (Kochan, Huber, and Cummings 1975; Schmidt and Kochan 1972). A decision must be made to engage in conflict. Whether the decision is based on rational calculation or fervid emotion, or is individual or collective, it does not occur automatically.

The Conflict Situation

We have been looking at the bases of conflict situations and the parties engaged in them. A more complete view adds to these components the conflict process itself and the aftermath. Boulding (1964) has provided a framework for a composite view of the total conflict situation. He suggests that there are four components in the process. First are the parties involved. Conflict must involve at least two parties—individuals, groups, or organizations. Hypothetically, therefore, there can be nine types of conflict—person-person, person-group, and so on. Boulding suggests that there is a tendency toward symmetry in these relationships, in that person- or group-organizational conflict tends to move toward organizational-organizational conflict. This is based on the power differentials that are likely to exist between these different levels in the organization.

As the next component in his framework, Boulding identifies the "field of conflict," defined as "the whole set of relevant possible states of the social system. (Any state of the social system which either of the parties to a conflict considers relevant is, of course, a relevant state.)" (p. 138). What Boulding is referring to here are the alternative conditions toward which a conflict could move. If the parties in a conflict have a particular power relationship with one another, with one having more power than the other, the field of conflict involves a continuation of the present state, plus all the alternative conditions. These alternatives include both parties' gaining or losing power or one's gaining at the expense of the other. This concept is indicative of the process nature of conflict, in that the parties in the situation will seldom retain the same position in relation to one another after the conflict is resolved or continued. The field of conflict includes the directions of the movement as the process occurs.

The third component is the dynamics of the conflict situation. That is, each party in a conflict will adjust its own position to one that it feels is congruent with that of its opponent. If one of the parties becomes more militant, the other will probably do the same. This assumes of course that the power available to the two parties is at least moderately comparable. A nonorganizational example of the dynamics can be found in international relations, where nations will intensify their own conflict efforts in anticipation of or reaction to their opponents' moves. This can escalate into all-out war and eventual total destruction, or can stabilize at some point along the way. The same phenomenon occurs in organizations, with the equivalent of all-out war in the case of labor-management conflicts that end in the dissolution of the company involved. The dynamic nature of conflict can be seen in the fact that there is an increase and decrease in the intensity of a conflict during its course. While the field of conflict may remain the same, the energies devoted to it vary over time.

The final element in the Boulding model is the management, control, or resolution of conflict (p. 142). The terms used suggest that conflict situations are generally not discrete situations with a clear beginning and end. They obviously emerge out of preexisting situations and do not end forever with a strike settlement or lowering of the intensity of the conflict. Boulding notes that organizations attempt to prevent conflict from becoming "pathological" and thus destructive of the parties involved and the larger system. One form of conflict resolution is a unilateral move; according to Boulding, a good deal of conflict is resolved through the relatively simple mechanism of the "peaceableness" of one of the participants. While it relates primarily to interpersonal conflict, this idea can be utilized in the organizational setting. Peaceableness simply involves one of the parties' backing off from the conflict. The other party reacts to this in most cases by also backing off, even if he would prefer to continue, and the conflict is at least temporarily resolved. This kind of resolution is seen in labor-management disputes when one of the parties finally decides to concede on some points that were formerly "nonnegotiable."

Reliance upon peaceableness is potentially dangerous, however, because the parties just may not exhibit this kind of behavior. For the peaceable party itself, this strategy is hazardous if the opponent is operating pathologically or irrationally to any degree. For this reason, organizations develop mechanisms to resolve or control conflict. One technique here is to placate the parties involved by offering them both some form of "side

payment" as an inducement to stop the conflict—for example, in professional-organizational conflict the professionals may be given concessions
in the form of relaxing some organizational rules they feel to be excessively
burdensome.

Unfortunately, research in this area has not indicated what are the
reactions of the rest of the organization to conflicts with professional units.
It is possible that such conflicts are resolved simply by concessions to the
professionals, and a realistic view would suggest that something has to be
done for the other members of the organization also, since they often
resent the greater freedom given to the professionals. Even though the
professionals are sometimes physically separated from the rest of the
organization in an attempt to minimize comparisons and distinctions
between the groups involved, it would seem that increasing benefits for
the professional group would lead to a demand from the nonprofessionals
for comparable concessions. These could take the form of increases in the
rewards offered or greater likelihood of moving up in the organizational
hierarchy.

Conflicts in organizations can also be resolved through the offices of a
third party. The third party might be a larger organization that simply
orders the conflict behavior to cease under the threat of penalties (as when
the government prohibits strikes and lockouts in a labor dispute that
threatens the national interest) or might be a mediator. Since intraorganizational conflict takes place within a larger context, the organization can
simply prohibit the conflicting behavior. This does not resolve the issues
involved, but it reduces the intensity of the conflict behavior. Mediation
can do the same, and can even lead to a complete resolution of the conflict
by presenting new methods of solution that might not have occurred to
the parties involved, or by presenting a solution that would not be
acceptable unless it were presented by a third party.

The resolution of a conflict leads to a stage that Pondy (1967, 1969)
calls the aftermath. This is a useful concept because conflict resolution
does not lead to a condition of total settlement. If the basic issues are not
resolved, the potentiality for future, and perhaps more serious, conflicts
is part of the aftermath. If the conflict resolution leads to more open
communications and cooperation among the participants, this, too, is part
of the aftermath (see Coser 1956, 1967). Since an organization does not
operate in a vacuum, any successful conflict resolution in which the former
combatants are now close allies is not guaranteed to last forever. Changes
in the environment and altered conditions in the organization can lead to
new conflict situations among the same parties or with others.

Conflict is not inherently good or bad for the participants, the organization, or the wider society. Power and conflict are major shapers of the
state of an organization. A given organizational state sets the stage for the
continuing power and conflict processes, thus continually reshaping the
organization. In this way, conflict plays an important role in the development of variations between organizations. This may contribute to or
detract from their survival (Aldrich 1979).

SUMMARY AND CONCLUSIONS

This chapter has attempted to identify and trace the consequences of power and conflict in organizations. Common sense suggests that these are important to the operations of any organization and that the lives and behavior of organizational members are vitally affected by their relative power positions. The discussion concluded that power is a reciprocal relational phenomenon between the parties involved and that each party is dependent on the other. The power relationships can be rigidly specified in advance or can develop as the relationship itself develops. This point reemphasizes the close connection between organizational structure and processes, since it is the structure that sets the original limits on the relationship.

Although power relationships are typically thought to be interpersonal, power differentials between organizational units are also important. Interunit power relationships usually take place along the lateral or horizontal axis in the organization. Vertical or hierarchical arrangements by definition involve a power component. Also on the vertical dimension, but not in an organizationally planned way, are the power bases developed by lower participants that allow them to exert power over those farther up the organizational hierarchy.

In addition to this directional aspect of power, we discussed the forms of power inside and outside organizations. There is agreement that power in organizations does not take just one form—legitimate authority—and that extraorganizational considerations are important in power relationships. The empirical research reviewed provided additional insights into these relationships. From the outset it became apparent that most power relationships involve the use of more than one form of power. Because individuals and organizational units develop relationships over time, additional elements will almost surely be added to prestructured power arrangements.

The nature of the power system used in the organization has important consequences for the manner in which individuals attach themselves to the organization and for the more general issue of organizational effectiveness. If inappropriate power forms are used, the organization is likely to be less effective than it might otherwise be. Studies of power in organizations reiterate the dominant theme of this book—that organizational structure and processes are in constant and reciprocal interaction. Power relationships develop out of and then alter existing structural arrangements.

In a broader look at power, it was emphasized that power is not a fixed sum in organizations. The amount of power in the system can increase or decrease. Although a power system is often established by the organization, the considerations discussed above regarding multiple forms of power and the reciprocity involved in the power relationship make a general growth in power almost inevitable.

It was also pointed out in this section that the power variable is vital in determining internal resource allocations. This fact leads to the conclusion that power relationships in organizations tend to be stable, since the original allocation of resources will be an important determinant of future power relationships. The fact that external considerations affect the power distribution and relationships within an organization is a reaffirmation of the general approach that has been taken throughout. Organizational structure and processes are in interaction with the environment and organizational outputs affect the environment, which then in turn becomes a potentially altered form of input.

The discussion of conflict in organizations was somewhat truncated because of the close relationship between this process and power, power being an important, even decisive, element in conflict. The identification of the various forms, stages, conditions, and consequences of conflict point up its endemic nature in organizations. To view organizations as entities in which conflict upsets the equilibrium is to misunderstand reality. Conflict is part of the normal state of an organization. The consequences of conflict are also normal, in that they are both organizationally and individually positive and negative.

In the next chapter, an issue related to power will be discussed. Leadership involves one or more of the forms of power discussed, since it can be exerted from a position of legitimate authority or expertise, or can develop as a form of referent power. We will analyze alternative forms of leadership and their consequences for the organization.

8

Leadership and Decision Making

Probably more has been written and spoken about leadership than about any other topic considered in this book. Whether the organization be the local school district, a labor union, an athletic team, or the nation, there seems to be a constant assumption that new leadership will turn it, the organization, around. In every election at every level of government, the call for leadership goes out. Anyone who follows sports is aware of the air of expectation surrounding the appointment of a new coach or manager. A new school superintendent or university president is selected by a blue-ribbon committee with extensive inputs from all of the parties likely to be involved. Elections in labor unions and other voluntary organizations always contain the assumption that continuation of the old or the election of the new leaders will make an important difference in the continuing operation of the organization. As this is being written (January 1981), there is great anticipation in regard to the change in national leadership in the United States. In short, leadership would seem to be the crucial thing to understand about organizations.

The view presented in this chapter is exactly the opposite. In the research and theory to be examined, it will be found that leadership is heavily constrained by many of the factors discussed in previous chapters— organizational structure, power coalitions, and environmental conditions. It will also be argued that, for most organizations in most circumstances, changing leadership is little more than a cosmetic treatment. The same basic approach will be taken in discussing constraints on the decision-making process. These constraints limit the practical usefulness of formal sophisticated decision-making models.

LEADERSHIP

Why is leadership the subject of such belief and sentiment? Leadership seems to be an extremely easy solution to whatever problems are ailing an organization. Looking to new leadership can mask such issues as inappropriate structural arrangements, power distributions that block effective actions, lack of resources, archaic procedures, and other, more basic organizational problems.

With all this, one might wonder, then, why study leadership, and why have there been so many studies in the past? The fact is that in certain situations leadership is important, even critical. The situations, however, are much more infrequent and much more constrained than most treatises on leadership consider.

What is leadership? Leadership is a special form of power, closely related to the "referent" form discussed in the previous chapter, since it involves, in Etzioni's (1965) words, "the ability, based on the personal qualities of the leader, to elicit the followers' voluntary compliance in a broad range of matters. Leadership is distinguished from the concept of power in that it entails influence, i.e., change of preferences, while power implies only that subjects' preferences are held in abeyance" (pp. 690–91).

For our purposes, Etzioni's general definition, if not the specific distinction made, is extremely useful. That followers do in fact alter their preferences to coincide with those of the leader is an important consideration. The followers want to go along with the wishes of the leader. Gouldner (1950) takes essentially the same position when he states that the leader is "any individual whose behavior stimulates patterning of the behavior in some group" (p. 17). The leader therefore is an influence on what the members of the group do and think. Katz and Kahn (1978) follow this line of reasoning when they note: "We consider the essence of organizational leadership to the influential increment over and above mechanical compliance with the routine directions of the organization" (p. 528). Thus, leadership is closely related to power, but involves more than simply the power allocated to a position in the organization or claimed by a member or members of organizations.

Functions of Leadership

The differences between leadership and power are still insufficiently developed, however, since leadership can occur in any group at any level within the organization. Selznick (1957) provides the needed distinction when he notes that leadership involves critical decisions (p. 29). It is more than group maintenance. According to Selznick, the critical tasks of leadership fall into four categories. The first involves the definition of the institutional (organizational) mission and role. This is obviously vital in a rapidly changing world and must be viewed as a dynamic process. The second task is the "institutional embodiment of purpose," which involves building the policy into the structure or deciding upon the means to achieve the ends desired. The third task is to defend the organization's integrity. Here values and public relations intermix: the leaders represent their organizations to the public and to their own members as they try to persuade them to follow their decisions. The final leadership task is the ordering of internal conflict (pp. 62–63). In a monumental review of some 3000 studies of leadership, Stogdill (1974) identified essentially the same set of functions.

Leadership can occur at *all* organizational levels. The impact on the organization varies according to the level at which leadership is exercised. Figure 8-1 shows Katz and Kahn's (1978) approach to this issue. Their approach emphasizes the cognitive and affective abilities and skills which are part of the leadership process. We will consider the mix of these skills at a later point.

Most analyses of leadership recognize the fact that leadership occurs at different levels in organizations. There is a critical omission in most leadership analyses, however. This is the fact that most studies of leadership have been concerned with lower-level leadership, such as that exerted by the first-line supervisor. Stogdill's (1974) review of leadership studies does not consider the levels issue. It appears crucial to remember that what

Figure 8-1   Leadership patterns, their locus in the organization, and their skill requirements

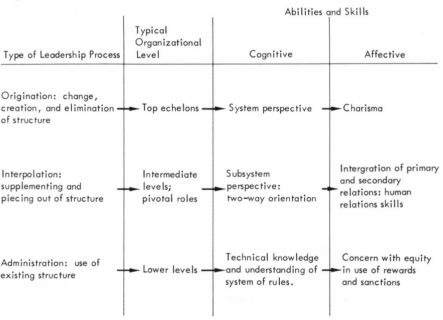

		Abilities and Skills	
Type of Leadership Process	Typical Organizational Level	Cognitive	Affective
Origination: change, creation, and elimination of structure	Top echelons	System perspective	Charisma
Interpolation: supplementing and piecing out of structure	Intermediate levels; pivotal roles	Subsystem perspective: two-way orientation	Intergration of primary and secondary relations: human relations skills
Administration: use of existing structure	Lower levels	Technical knowledge and understanding of system of rules.	Concern with equity in use of rewards and sanctions

Source: Katz and Kahn, 1978, p. 539.

might contribute to leadership at one level might be totally inappropriate at another level. Leadership at the top level in the organization has the greatest impact on the organization.

One further set of distinctions should be made before we proceed with an analysis of leadership. Studies carried out in small-group laboratories have consistently found that leadership is actually a differentiated process, with *task* or *instrumental* activities rather clearly separated from *socioemotional* or *expressive* activities. (See, for example, Bales 1953; Bales and Slater 1955.) Drawing on the work of Bales and his associates, Etzioni (1965) develops a "dual leadership" approach to organizations, suggesting that in most cases leadership rests in the hands of more than one person and that the demands of the two forms may conflict. Organizational demands will determine which form will be successful, with socioemotional more effective in normative organizations and task in instrumental organizations. Etzioni concludes that, at least for first-line supervisors, attempts to improve socioemotional leadership qualities are doomed to failure, since these efforts will run headlong into the existing socioemotional leader, who has risen to the position in the interactions of the work group. This type of interpretation, of course, is counter to the ideas and ideals of the "human relations" school of management, which stresses the utility of socioemotional interactions in the leadership process. There appears to be growing agreement that the use of human relations in leadership positions is no guarantee that any form of behavioral change by members of the organization will take place (Perrow 1979, pp. 132–38). The use of human relations skills has also been the subject of criticism in terms of the manner in which subordinates are actually manipulated without their knowing it, as was noted in the last chapter. The type of behavior that will lead to behavioral change is contingent upon the situation, as will be seen below.

It is critical to note again that leadership at the top of an organization is vastly different from leadership at the first-line supervisory level. Because most studies of leadership have been carried out with first-line people, a good part of the development of leadership theory is confused.

Components of Leadership

Every organization has an individual or set of individuals at the top decision-making level who can exercise power simply by giving orders and making decisions. This is simple power of position and does not involve leadership as we will approach it here. Our view of leadership involves what a person does above and beyond the basic requirements of his position. *It is the persuasion of individuals and innovativeness in ideas and decision making that differentiates leadership from the sheer possession of power.* A mechanical reliance on organizational position would bring about a situation in which the characteristics of the individuals filling top positions would make no difference whatsoever. The organization would be totally constrained by precedent and its own structure.

The ideas expressed thus far have implied strongly that individual characteristics are crucial for the leadership role. Although this appears to be the case, extreme care must be taken to put it in the proper perspective. There is a very real danger in assuming that because individual characteristics are crucial for the leadership function, there is a set of *traits* that leaders possess. The literature regarding leadership took this approach at one time, with a major goal of the research being identification of the key leadership traits. This approach didn't get very far, for two reasons. The basic one was that common leadership traits could not be identified. No set of characteristics is possessed by leaders and not by followers. This realization led to the second contributing factor in the downfall of the trait approach. Attention increasingly turned to the *situation* in which leadership was exhibited (Gouldner 1950).

The situational approach takes the position that the set of conditions of the moment—the situation—defines by whom and in what manner leadership will be expressed. In one situation, one individual will emerge as the leader; in another situation, another individual. This approach has largely dominated the sociological approach to leadership, especially in small-group studies, but in recent years it has come under fire for its inattention to the characteristics of those who rise into leadership positions. The emergent position is that while different situations demand different forms of leadership and thus generally different individuals, particular skills and behaviors will be called for in each different situation. This is a blending of the trait and situational approaches to avoid the serious pitfalls of each (see Yukl 1981 for an extended discussion of these points).

This combination approach is used by Hollander and Julian (1969). They reject the trait and situational approaches per se, noting that both tell us something about leadership, but not the whole story. To the ideas that have already been stated, they add the important element of inter-action between leader and followers. The leader influences followers in the interaction process, and their reactions, of course, have an impact on the leader's own behavior.

From the perspective taken here, organizational leadership is a com-bination of factors. The most obvious is the high position in the organi-zation. This gives the leader the power base and leads followers to the expectations that there is a legitimate right to that position and that the leader will in fact engage in the leadership process by shaping their own thoughts and actions and performing the leadership functions for the organization as a whole. These expectations can be seen even in periods of dissidence within the organization, when there is leadership succession and the followers express the hope that the new person will provide what the old one did not.

In addition to the position held, the leadership role demands that the individual behave in such a way that the expectations of the followers are fulfilled. Here the interrelationships between the characteristics of the individual and the position filled become crucial. Rather than suggesting that there is one set of leadership "traits," the evidence indicates that the particular characteristics giving rise to leadership behavior vary with the situation. According to Stogdill (1974):

Individuals who continue to rise in the hierarchy tend to identify themselves with top leadership and with the organization. Job satisfaction tends to increase as level in the organization increases. High-level leaders tend to value job challenge and autonomy, while lower-level leaders tend to value security and stability. Followers value the leader who has influence with his superiors, is identified with the organization, and demonstrates effectiveness in working for their welfare and comfort. Studies of leadership behavior indicate that leaders described high in both initiating structure (letting followers know what to expect) and consideration (looking out for the welfare of followers) tend to promote high degrees of follower satisfaction and, in some cases, group performance. Persuasiveness emerges as the most pervasive characteristic when leader behavior is described in terms of a wide variety of items. Other behavioral items highly weighted on a general factor are concerned with the reconciliation of conflicting demands, structuring expectations, retention of the leadership role, consideration of follower welfare, and pressure for goal attainment. (p. 412)

An individual would be able to "transfer" into another leadership role only if the situation and the followers were comparable to the previous leadership situation. The approach allows a rapprochement between the emphasis on individual traits and the emphasis on the situation.

Now let us move to the central issue: What do leaders do for or to an organization, and how do they do it?

THE IMPACT OF LEADERSHIP ON THE ORGANIZATION

There is little direct evidence regarding the effect that top leaders have on organizations, simply because there has been very little research on top organizational leadership. Organizational researchers have not gotten access to top business and government leaders. Nor have they been concerned with the role of leadership in terms of its broad organizational consequences. In order to study leadership, we will extrapolate from the large number of studies of supervision and the smaller number of studies of top leadership succession.

Studies of leadership in organizations are confusing, if not downright chaotic, even to those who are well versed in the literature (Cartwright, 1965, p. 3). A major factor in the confusion, aside from the ideological biases evident in some investigations, is the large number of dependent variables used in leadership analyses. If variations in the amount or style of leadership are taken as the independent variable, then a whole series of variables has been treated as the dependent ones. These run the gamut from hard measures of productivity to the more elusive factors of morale and satisfaction.

Leadership Styles

Research regarding leadership has come to focus around two constrasting styles or approaches to the leadership role. These are the authoritarian (task) and supportive (socioemotional) approaches. The biases alluded to earlier are evident and understandable when these two terms are brought into the discussion (who would want to support authoritarianism?). The supportive leader is "characterized by . . . employee oriented, democratic behavior, uses general supervision, and is considerate of his subordinates" (Filley and House 1969, p. 399). The authoritarian leader, on the other hand, is much more likely to rely on the power of his or her position and to be more punishment-centered. A very evident problem for the discussion here is that the authoritarian form actually may not be leadership in the way we have defined it.[1]

The supportive leader utilizes socioemotional appeals to his subordinates. This involves:

Consideration for Subordinates. The leader considers the needs and preferences of his subordinates, whom he treats with dignity and kindness, and is not punitive in his dealings with them. Such a leader is frequently referred to as "employee-centered" as opposed to "work centered" or "task-centered."

Consultative Decision Making. The leader asks his subordinates for their opinions before he makes decisions. Such a leader is consultative, participative, or democratic (as opposed to unilateral, autocratic, or arbitrary) in his decision making.

General Supervision. The leader supervises in a general rather than a close manner, delegates authority to his subordinates, and permits them freedom to exercise discretion in their work rather than imposing tight controls and close (frequently overbearing) supervision. (pp. 399–400)

In their excellent review of the research in the leadership area, Filley and House find that supportive leadership, as opposed to autocratic leadership, is quite consistently related to several indicators of subordinate satisfaction and productivity:

1. There is less intragroup stress and more cooperation.
2. Turnover and grievance rates are lower.
3. The leader himself is viewed as more desirable.
4. There is frequently greater productivity.

The evidence here is confounded, unfortunately, by the possibility that the workers themselves may contribute to their greater satisfaction and productivity by their own attitudes and behavior, independent of that of the leader. They might just be high-producing, positively oriented employees who "do not require close, autocratic supervision, and therefore it is possible for the supervisor of such employees to be more human-

---

[1] A series of studies at The Ohio State University used the terms "initiating and consideration" to mean essentially the same things, while another series of studies at the University of Michigan used the terms "production orientation and employee orientation" with little difference in meanings.

relations oriented" (p. 462). Despite this possibility, the weight of the evidence is that supportive leadership does lead to more positive attitudinal responses, particularly on the part of subordinates. This pattern seems to hold even in organizations which are thought to favor more authoritarian leadership styles. In a study of police units, Jermier and Berkes (1979) found that satisfaction and commitment to the organization were related to more supportive leadership.

The productivity issue is not as clear as the attitudinal one. While some evidence does suggest that greater productivity is associated with supportive supervision, other studies report no difference, or that there is actually more output when autocratic styles are used (Dubin 1965). Even more confusion is brought into the picture when Lawler and Porter's (1967) conclusions are brought into the picture. They suggest that the causal ordering between satisfaction and productivity might be reversed. It is typically thought that satisfaction leads to productivity, but Lawler and Porter suggest that productivity might lead to satisfaction. For the analysis of leadership, increasing satisfaction to increase productivity might be totally futile.

An obvious question here is, What does the organization want? If satisfied employees are desired, then the supportive approach has clearly been shown to be more effective. Short-run output gains, on the other hand, may be more easily achieved under an autocratic system. There is also evidence to suggest that when workers expect to be supervised in an autocratic style, supportive supervision can be counterproductive and satisfaction threatening.

In summarizing these leadership studies, Filley and House conclude that supportive leadership behavior is most effective when:

1. Decisions are not routine in nature.
2. The information required for effective decision making cannot be standardized or centralized.
3. Decisions need not be made rapidly, allowing time to involve subordinates in a participative decision-making process.

and when subordinates:

4. Feel a strong need for independence.
5. Regard their participation in decision making as legitimate.
6. See themselves as able to contribute to the decision-making process.
7. Are confident of their ability to work without the reassurance of close supervision. (pp. 404–05)

This particular kind of organization is similar to some that have already been described in the section on organizational structure: the less formalized organizations that must rely on the inputs of their own members if they are to be effective. Their technology is such that there is a constant search for new ideas and solutions to problems. The obvious corollary of the findings as to the kind of organization in which supportive leadership styles are likely to be effective is that in the opposite kind of organization, such forms of leadership are least likely to be effective. That is, in organizations in which decisions are routine, information is standardized, and so on, effective leadership is more likely to take the autocratic form, because inputs from the individual members of the organization are not so important and there is not the same need for time spent in the decision-making process. In addition, it can be postulated that there are organizational members who either are threatened by the decision-making process or have no wish to participate in it, and for whom the provision of ready-made answers in the form of formal procedures or decisions made for them is a satisfying or at least nonthreatening situation.

These interpretations are strongly buttressed by the findings emerging from Fiedler's (1967, 1972) continuing studies of the leadership process. Fiedler finds that in stable, structured situations, a more strict, autocratic form of leadership is most likely to be successful, while in a situation of change, external threat, and ambiguity, the more lenient, participative form of supervision would work better. Of course, in some organizations conditions will change in one direction or another, suggesting that an effective leader in one situation may not be such in another. Thus, another contingency approach is evident.

Factors Affecting Leadership Impact

Several aspects of the research discussed thus far ought to be made distinct before the present analysis proceeds. As indicated earlier, most of the studies have been performed with personnel from relatively lower echelons in the organization. Regardless of the level within the organization, it is clear that the situation being faced and the personnel being led are important determinants as to which form of leadership is likely to be most effective. It can be argued that it would be good, from an individual or societal perspective, if all personnel were self-motivating and desirous of participating in the decision making, and that the organization as a whole would be healthier if it were constantly innovating and engaging in continual interactions with its environment; but the facts suggest that neither condition necessarily exists in practice. This then leads to the conclusion that a revamping of leadership styles in organizations is no panacea to be applied to all organizations and all members therein.

The important aspect of the research for our purposes is the demonstrated fact that leadership at this level does make a difference in terms of objective performance indicators and the attitudes of the personnel involved. The question is not one of style but of impact. If production can be increased or the acceptance of a new mode of organization quickened, leadership does come to be an important process. The extrapolation from this conclusion to top leadership is relatively easy, if unsupported by existing research. The range of behavior affected by first- or second-line supervisors is actually quite small. If the jump is made to the range of behavior that can be affected by those at the top of the organization, the potential for a real impact of leadership can be readily seen. Even in terms of performance and attitudes, the high-level subordinates of high administrators can be affected, and their performance in turn has an impact right down the organization.

An additional point is that leadership and the total managerial function are apparently vitally affected by one of the major considerations throughout this analysis—the technology of the organization involved. The research of Woodward (1958, 1965) and of Lawrence and Lorsch (1967) lends support for this conclusion, as does the research of Burack (1967). These findings systematically document the interplay between the organization's structure, as affected by the technology, and the management structure. Technological factors set limits on the amount and kinds of variations that can be introduced into the system, thus limiting certain aspects of what a leader can do.

Now that we have formed some conclusions about the impact of leadership at both top and lower levels, let us examine the available evidence concerning changes in personnel at the top of the organization.

Leadership Succession

Analyses of managerial succession have been largely limited to case studies, with the exception of some concern about organizational size and the rate of managerial succession. These latter studies will be discussed later; for the moment, we shall look at some of the implications from the case studies.

Probably the best known of these is Gouldner's *Patterns of Industrial Bureaucracy* (1954), an analysis of a gypsum plant and mine that underwent a major and dramatic change in top personnel. The former manager had engaged in loose, almost indulgent practices in regard to rule observance and other standards. The parent organization, concerned about the production record of the plant, replaced the old manager with a new man who had the specific mandate of increasing production. The new man knew he would be judged by his record of production, so his alternatives were to continue the established pattern—a procedure that probably would not have worked in any event, since he did not have the personal ties of his predecessor—or to enforce the already-existing rules of conduct and performance. He chose the latter course, and as a result the total system became "punishment-centered." This lead to a severe increase in internal tension and stress.

This example is in direct contrast to a case described by Guest (1962). Guest's study was made from observations in a large automobile factory. He states:

Both studies [his and Gouldner's] examine the process by which organizational tensions are exacerbated or reduced following the succession of a new leader at the top of the hierarchy. Succession in Gouldner's case resulted in a sharp increase in tension and stress and, by inference, a lowering of overall performance. The succession of a new manager had the opposite results in the present case. Plant Y, as we chose to call it, was one of six identical plants of a large corporation. At one period in time the plant was poorest in virtually all indexes of performance—direct and indirect labor costs, quality of output, absenteeism and turnover, ability to meet schedule changes, labor grievances and in several other measures. Interpersonal relationships were marked by sharp antagonisms within and between all levels.

Three years later, following the succession of a new manager, and with no changes in the formal organizational structure, in the product, in the personnel, or in its basic technology, not only was there a substantial reduction of interpersonal conflict, but Plant Y became the outstanding performer among all of the plants. (p. 48)

The dramatic differences between these two cases might lead one to some sort of "great man" theory of leadership, with Gouldner's successor a nongreat man and Guest's the opposite. Guest correctly rejects this approach and instead attributes the differences to the actions each man took when confronted with an existing social structure. A major aspect of this social structure was the expectations of higher management in the organizations involved. While both new managers were expected to improve the situation, the new man at the gypsum plant felt that he was expected to get rid of the personnel who were not performing properly. He felt that he was—and probably actually was—under more severe pressure to turn the organization around in a short period of time.

There were some other important differences in the organizations. The tradition in the gypsum plant was that the new top man came from "inside," and in this case he did not. In addition, the former manager had been active in the community surrounding the plant. The successor thus came into a situation in which there were negative feelings from the outset. The former manager also had a cadre of subordinates tied to him through personal loyalty. The successor had little recourse but to use the more formal bureaucratic mechanisms of control. At the automobile factory, on the other hand, the total social setting was different. The factory was in a large metropolitan area in which the previous managers had not become involved. The history of top management succession was one of relatively rapid turnover (three to five years), with the new man coming from outside the plant itself. Thus, unlike the gypsum plant personnel, the auto plant personnel were used to the kind of succession they experienced.

Another, more subtle difference that Gouldner describes is the fact that in the gypsum plant, the indulgency pattern and the developed social structure among the personnel were such that there was no orientation toward cutting costs and improving productivity. The previous system was a comfortable one in which rewards, both intrinsic and extrinsic, came without such an orientation.

The predecessor at the auto plant had attempted to use his formal powers in increasing productivity. Like his successor, he was under great pressure to improve the operation, but he chose to attempt this by close and punitive supervision. The successor decided to move in a different path by using more informal contacts with his subordinates and bringing them into the decision-making process. Also, this man worked through the existing organizational hierarchy, whereas the new man at the gypsum plant, after some failures with the established subordinates, brought in some of his own men, thus setting up a formal hierarchy that was in a sense superimposed on the existing social structure.

Rational choice from a range of possible alternative courses of action is probably uncharacteristic of most decisions that are made; but alternative approaches to problems can still be selected, whether unconsciously, by default, or by some form of conscious decision making. In the first case under discussion, the gypsum plant manager chose to try to raise the organization's performance by enforcing rules to the letter of the law—dismissing men, for example, for offenses that had previously been largely ignored. The auto plant man, on the other hand, "relegated rule enforcement to a second level of importance."

Guest moves beyond his data and draws a conclusion from the comparison between his and Gouldner's cases. He suggests that the success of the auto plant manager was due in large part to gaining the consent of the governed, or democratization of the leadership process. Gouldner, in a comment regarding Guest's research, notes that the total situations in which the successions occurred were different. The gypsum plant event occurred during a period of recession, with labor relatively plentiful, but with the pressures for improvement probably more intense. The implication here is that when the total situation is viewed, it is incorrect to conclude that one or another approach to the leadership process is always the correct one, even though in both of these cases the autocratic approach was less successful.

From the evidence presented in these two studies, it should be clear that top management has the potential for really drastic impacts on the organization, although it cannot yet be stated what proportion of the variance of organizational performance can be accounted for by this leadership role. Indeed, it would appear that this would vary according to the situation, since the range of alternatives even formally allowed would vary widely. Nevertheless, leadership can be seen as having a major impact on what happens to and within the organization.

Some indications of the factors associated with leadership's potentiality for major impact emerge from additional studies of managerial succession. There have been several attempts to specify the relationship between organizational size and the rate of succession. Grusky (1961) examined the largest and smallest deciles of the 500 largest companies in the United States (in terms of sales volume), and Kriesberg (1962) looked at state and local mental health agencies and public health departments. Both came to the conclusion that size and rate of succession are related. That is, the larger the organization, the higher the rate of succession. Gordon and Becker (1969), noting some contradictions between these findings and some others, reexamined the Grusky data and supplemented it with additional information from a sample of the next 500 largest business organizations. They found an inverse relationship between size and rate of succession, with the smaller companies having a slightly higher turnover rate among top management. In commenting on this finding, Kriesberg (1964) notes that the rate of succession is undoubtedly affected by more than the size factor, with the typical career lines within the organization a major consideration. If the organization builds in the expectation of rapid executive turnover, they will obviously increase the rate.

An additional important factor noted by Kriesberg is the likelihood of interindustry differences. An industry-by-industry analysis would be more definitive than a simple lumping together of all organizations. In keeping with the general theme of this analysis, an adequate typology of organizations should allow some prediction of the kinds of organizations in which succession rates will be high. Without such a typology, the technology factor, implied by Kriesberg, would appear to be important. *What the organization does and the environment in which it works have an impact on how rapidly top leadership changes are made and the extent to which such leadership can actually affect the organization.*

But one point in regard to organizational size is clear: other things being equal, the larger the organization, the less the impact of succession would be. Large organizations are apt to be more complex and formalized, and thus more resistant to change. It would therefore be likely that top leadership would be unable to "turn the organization around" in either direction in a short period of time, unless it were a totally autocratic system. Referring back to the discussion of rationality in organizations, it would appear that the impact of top leadership on the organization would be a matter of rather small differences when compared with past administrations. This assumes, of course, that the past or present groups do not operate on the basis of total irrationality.

An indication of the extent of the difference that leadership can make on the organization can be found in some rather offbeat research regarding baseball managers and football coaches. Baseball managers stand in an unusual organizational position. In relation to the total baseball organization, their role is similar to that of the foreman; but in relation to the playing team only, their role is similar to that of the top executive. Baseball teams are convenient units for analysis since they "ideally, were identical in official goals, size, and authority structure" (Grusky, 1963, p. 21). Grusky was concerned with the relationship between managerial succession and organizational effectiveness. Here again, baseball teams are ideal because effectiveness is reflected directly in the won-lost statistics; how you play the game is not a crucial variable in professional sports.

The findings from the analysis were that the teams with the poorest records had the highest rates of succession. In interpreting these findings, Grusky rejects the commonsense notion built around succession as the dependent variable—that low effectiveness leads to a vote of confidence from the owner, then a firing. Instead, he develops a more complicated analysis, which is in keeping with the previous discussion:

> If a team is ineffective, clientele support and profitability decline. Accordingly, strong external pressures for managerial change are set in motion and, concomitantly, the magnitude of managerial role strain increases. A

managerial change may be viewed in some quarters as attractive in that it can function to demonstrate publicly that the owners are taking concrete action to remedy an undesirable situation. The public nature of team performance and the close identification of community pride with team behavior combine to establish a strong basis for clientele control over the functioning of the team. These external influences tend to increase the felt discrepancy between managerial responsibility and actual authority. Since the rewards of popularity are controlled externally, individual rather than team performance may be encouraged. Similarly, the availability of objective performance standards decreases managerial control and thereby contributes to role strain. The greater the managerial role strain, the higher the rates of succession. Moreover, the higher the rates of succession, the stronger the expectations of replacement when team performance declines. Frequent managerial change can produce important dysfunctional consequences within the team by affecting style of supervision and disturbing the informal network of interpersonal relationships. New policies and new personnel create the necessity for restructuring primary relationships. The resulting low primary-group stability produces low morale and may thereby contribute to team ineffectiveness. Declining clientele support may encourage a greater decline in team morale and performance. The consequent continued drop in profitability induces pressures for further managerial changes. Such changes, in turn, produce additional disruptive effects on the organization, and the vicious circle continues. (p. 30)

This rather complicated explanation is challenged by Gamson and Scotch (1964). Based on a different approach to baseball teams' won-lost records, Gamson and Scotch advance a "ritual scapegoating no-way casualty theory." This theory essentially suggests that the manager doesn't make any difference:

In the long run, the policies of the general manager and other front-office personnel are far more important. While judicious trades are helpful (here the field manager may be consulted but does not have the main responsibility), the production of talent through a well-organized scouting and farm system is the most important long-run determinant. The field manager, who is concerned with day-to-day tactical decisions, has minimal responsibility for such management functions. (p. 70)

Gamson and Scotch note that the players are a critical factor, suggesting that at one point in baseball history, regardless of who was manager, "the Yankees would have done as well and the Mets would have (or more accurately, could have) done no worse. When the team is doing poorly, the firing of the field manager is ritual scapegoating. "It is a convenient, anxiety-reducing act which the participants of the ceremony regard as a way of improving performance, even though (as some participants may themselves admit in less stressful moments) real improvements can come only through long-range organizational decisions" (pp. 70–71). Gamson and Scotch add that there does seem to be at least a short-run improvement in team performance in cases where the manager is changed in midseason. They suggest that this might be attributable to the ritual itself. Grusky (1964), in a reply to the Gamson–Scotch criticism, further analyzes the data regarding midseason changes. Adding the variable of whether the new manager came from inside or outside the organization, he finds that the inside manager is more successful. He takes this as partial evidence that his more complicated theory is more reasonable, since the inside man is likely to be aware of the interpersonal arrangements and the performance of his predecessor and thus more likely not to make the same mistakes again.

Sports teams provide a unique opportunity for analyzing leadership effects. Eitzen and Yetman (1972) studied college basketball teams and Allen, Panian, and Lotz (1979) reexamined major league baseball teams. These studies conclude that succession doesn't really change things—poor performance in the past leads to poor performance after succession. Brown (1981) continued this line of research with a study of coach succession in the National Football League. The findings in regard to the football teams is consistent with that of the other sports teams. Brown concludes that succession is cosmetic, which is consistent with the scapegoating approach. The head coach is fired and replaced by a successor with little opportunity to change policies, procedures, or personnel in the short run.

This may seem at first glance a lot of words spilled over a relatively minor matter in the larger scheme of things, but the points that these authors are addressing are very relevant for the present analysis. While Gamson and Scotch follow the line of reasoning taken here, that those of the very top of the organization have a greater impact than those further down the hierarchy, Grusky and Brown's argument that external and internal pressures for success affect performance is directly in line with the evidence presented by Gouldner and Guest. The kinds of personnel available are modified by the social system of which they are a part. It is within this framework that leadership behavior takes place. Although the important question of just how much leadership behavior actually contributes to the organization is left unanswered, the sports studies do suggest that both positive and negative results ensue with managerial succession. Few cases of neutral effects are found in the analyses. Impressionistic evidence that the conclusions of these sports studies are relevant for other organizations can be seen in Bauer's (1981) analysis of the firings occurring among top executives in the United States. In this journalistic account, many of the factors identified in the sports studies are also reported.

Additional research findings on rates of executive succession should be noted. In an analysis of a business firm and a military installation, Grusky (1970) came to the conclusion that rapid rates of succession are associated with limitations on executive control. In the military, which is characterized by a high degree of formalization, thereby limiting the discretion of any one individual, there is an intentional high turnover among all ranks. Pfeffer and Moore (1980) examined the length of tenure of academic department heads or chairs. They found that an important consideration was the "paradigm development" of the various disciplines. This refers to the extent to which there is agreement on and use of a common theoretical basis. With higher paradigm development, the tenure of the head was longer. Larger size operated against long tenure. The effects of both size and paradigm development were found to be more pronounced in periods of environmental scarcity. This is in line with Meyer's (1975b) conclusion that the situation in which leadership is imbedded needs study. In periods of uncertainty, both in terms of the environment and the nature of the organization itself (low-paradigm-development departments) there is likely to be a greater rate of succession. In this sense, executive succession is the easy answer to organizational problems. Like most easy answers, it appears not to make as much difference as people hope.

Our implication here is that in organizations with relatively loose structures and where the leadership is expected to have a great deal to do with what goes on in the organization, leadership behavior will have a large impact. Since most organizations are in fact relatively highly structured, either in terms of the formal system or the more informal interpersonal system, there are finite limits on what the leader can accomplish. Succession in the United States presidency, which is accompanied by pomp, circumstance, and lavish ceremonies, tends not to make as much difference as the partisan supporters of the new incumbent would hope. Indeed, there is evidence that the total system serves to frustrate the implementation of new policies. The suggestion has been made, for example, that each new administration of the United States government be allowed to replace civil servants with their own appointees (assuming that the appointees can qualify by civil service criteria), so that program implementation can be achieved.

The argument thus far has been that organizational structural conditions affect how much impact leadership can have. There are several other important considerations. As noted above, Grusky believes that whether the successor is an insider or outsider (to the organization) makes a difference, suggesting that, for baseball teams at least, the insider is more successful. In terms of overall change in the organization, however, it appears that the person brought in from the outside will be more able to institute greater changes. Helmich and Brown (1972) suggest that the outsider is able to replace subordinates with selected lieutenants of his or her own choice. The constellation of immediate personnel around the outsider can be changed more easily than the insider's could be. The decision to move to an insider or outsider is not always available, of course. Political considerations within an organization, its financial situation, and a dearth of outsiders may force an organization to go with insiders, thus limiting the amount of change possible. (In many cases, of course, change is not necessary or seen as desirable, so that the question of insider versus outsider is not a critical one.)

Any person coming into a top leadership position is, in a very real sense, a captive of the organization. Galbraith (1974), for example, has noted that, for many substantive decisions involving pricing, investment, merchandising, and new products, the chief executive of an organization is actually the "victim" or "captive" of the organization. He notes, however, that the chief executive does have powers of appointment to critical positions and can initiate studies that later bring about major changes.

Another set of constraints on what the top leadership of an organization can do consists of the external *environment* of the organization. This is dramatically seen in an analysis of 167 major U.S. corporations by Lieberson and O'Connor (1972). They were concerned with the sales, earnings, and profit margins of these corporations over a twenty-year period. Their ingenious research considered the issue of executive succession and its impact on these performance criteria. The effects of succession were also lagged over one-, two-, and three-year periods to permit the maximum impact of leadership change to demonstrate itself. They also considered the economic behavior of the industry (for example, steel versus air transportation), the position of the corporation within the industry, and the state of the economy as a whole. Their findings are startling to those who really believe in leadership: "All three performance variables are affected by forces beyond a leader's immediate control" (p. 124).

For sales and net earnings, the general economic conditions, the industry, and the corporation's position within it were more important than leadership. Leadership was important for profit margins, but still heavily constrained by the environmental conditions. These findings were replicated (with slight modification) by Weiner (1977) and Salancik and Pfeffer (1977). Salancik and Pfeffer looked at the impact of change in mayors on city budgets.

Lieberson and O'Connor do not claim that leadership is unimportant; nor is the claim made here. Leadership is clearly important in changing organizational directions, developing new activities, considering mergers or acquisitions, and setting long-run policies and objectives. At the same time, from all of the evidence that has been presented, it must be realized that the organizational and environmental constraints drastically limit the likelihood of major change on the basis of leadership alone. The implications of such findings are crucial for organizational analysis and for understanding a total society. In established organizations or nations, the impact of leadership is heavily constrained, and leadership change (whether to a new organizational or national leader) will not make too much of a difference. For the new organization or nation, leadership is obviously more important. Leadership is also crucially important in times of organizational crisis.

This discussion of leadership has ignored an important consideration—the motivations of the leaders. More than two generations ago, Berle and Means (1932) had argued that corporate executives have become technical managers, separated from the concerns of capitalist owners. More recently, Zeitlin (1974) and others have argued that corporate leadership is the modern capitalist class with phenomenal power and wealth in their organizations and in society as a whole (see also Allen 1976; Zeitlin 1976). From this perspective, organizational decisions are made on the basis of continued acquisition of power and wealth. James and Soref (1981) report that corporate presidents are fired on the basis of poor profit performance, thus disconfirming the Berle and Means hypothesis on the separation of ownership and management. We have already noted that such changes in top leadership may be little more than cosmetic. For the analysis of organizations, however, it does not matter if the top leaders are interested in their own power or wealth, if they are really controlled by owners, or if they are simply technocratic managers, since their organizational roles and impacts would not differ. The question of the organization's impact on society remains a major one, however, since what is good for the organization may not be good for society. This is true whether the organizations are corporations, school systems, or churches.

LEADERSHIP IN THE VOLUNTARY ORGANIZATION

The discussion thus far has concerned the work organization, in which the leader is appointed on the basis of criteria set up in advance. The situation is somewhat different in the voluntary organization, in which the leader is elected to office. Without getting into the questions of what kinds of persons are likely to be elected and how they perform their duties, some interesting issues should be mentioned. It has long been noted that in voluntary organizations there is a tendency toward oligarchy, in that the group in power wants to stay there and will endeavor to ensure its continuation in office (Michels 1962). In looking at union leadership, Tannenbaum (1965) notes that leaders have higher incomes than the rank and file they represent. In fact, they are more likely to live like their adversaries in management than like their own union members.

> In addition to its clear financial superiority, the leader's job places him in a world of variety, excitement, and broadened horizons which is qualitatively richer and psychologically more stimulating than his old job in the plant. There are also many tensions and frustrations in the leadership role, and long hours are often required. But these are part of the deep involvement which leaders have in their work. By and large, a return to the worker role would represent an intolerable loss to most leaders. (p. 752)

This personal desire to stay in the leadership position is coupled with several other factors that can lead to oligarchy. The leaders may be able to develop a monopoly on the kinds of skills required for leadership, such as verbal ability, persuasive techniques, and so on. They obtain political power within the organization through patronage and other favors. Given their position, it is relatively easy to groom their successors. Since the nature of unions involves a time cycle in regard to contract negotiations, the leaders can provide the membership with continual reminders of what they have achieved and what they are going to try to achieve the next time. The skills developed in this phase of the union's operation are unlikely to be part of the rank and file's repertoire.

The tendency toward oligarchy is apparently found in most voluntary organizations where there is a wide gap between members and leaders in the rewards (intrinsic and extrinsic) received. Where the gap is not so great, there is a greater tendency toward democracy. Lipset, Trow, and Coleman's (1956) analysis of the International Typographical Union demonstrates this point. This union is one in which the members enjoy relatively high pay and a strong sense of community with their fellow members and leaders alike, and it is quite democratic.

Voluntary organizations can also be differentiated from work organizations on the basis of the strong likelihood of a form of "dual leadership." Analyses of political parties have indicated the existence of both public and associational leadership. The public leaders are those who run for and hold public office, while the associational leaders operate behind the scenes. An exception would be the British parliamentary system, where the two forms of leadership tend to coincide. While unofficial power arrangements certainly exist in work organizations, they appear to be more fully developed in the voluntary organization, since the latter is characterized by much looser structural arrangements. And this looser structuring would appear to be related to another important consideration: in voluntary organizations, the leader is more likely to have a strong impact than in more structured organizations, because there are more possibilities for variation in the voluntary setting.

DECISION MAKING

One of the most critical activities of leaders is to engage in the decision-making process. Their decisions are made about the major functions that leadership is expected to perform—setting goals, deciding upon the means to ends, defending the organization from attacks from the outside, and resolving internal conflict.

In the abstract, decision making involves the immediate pressures on the decision maker, the analysis of the type of problem and its basic dimensions, the search for alternative solutions, and the consideration of the consequences of alternative solutions, including the anticipation of various types of postdecisional conflict and the final choice (Katz and Kahn 1978, p. 487). In actual practice, the situation is much more complicated. In the first place, there are important limits on the rationality brought to bear on decisions, as will be discussed shortly. In addition, not all decisions are of equal importance. Some are strategic, with high risks, while others are tactical, with low risks (Hage 1980, pp. 92–121). The implications of this can be seen in Figure 8-2. The high-risk decisions involve a much more complex system of trajectories or routes prior to the actual decision. In addition, Hage notes that administrators will try to avoid the high-risk decisions (p. 114). Fox and Staw (1979), in an experiment, found that administrators who experienced job insecurity and internal resistance to criticism tended to solidify their position and become more rigid. Hage also notes that most analyses of decision making tend to ignore instances of failure or bad decisions. In order to develop more

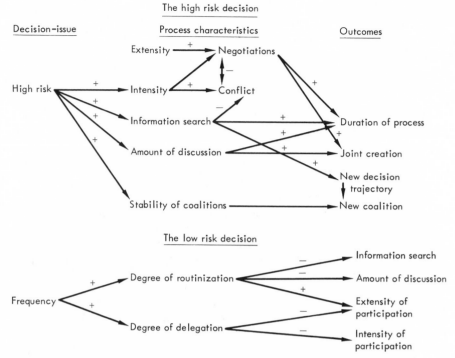

Figure 8-2 Decision characteristics and decision trajectory

Source: Hage 1980, p. 121.

understanding of the decision-making process in organizations, we will
now consider some of the variables and constraints that go into the process.

Variables and Constraints

A useful approach to the kinds of decisions that have strategic importance for the organization is provided by Thompson (1967). Thompson
notes that "decision issues always involve two major dimensions: (1) beliefs
about cause/effect relationships and (2) preferences regarding possible
outcomes" (p. 134). These basic variables in the decision-making process
can operate at the conscious or the unconscious level. As an aid in
understanding the process, Thompson suggests that each variable can be
(artificially) dichotomized as indicated in Figure 8-3.

In the cell with certainty on both variables, a "computational" strategy
can be used. In this case the decision is obvious and can be performed by
a computer with great simplicity. An example here would be simple
inventorying, in which, when the supply of a particular item reaches a
particular level, it is automatically reordered. Obviously, this is in no way
a strategic situation and will not be of concern to us here. The other cells
present more problems and are thus more crucial for the organization.

Preferences Regarding Possible Outcomes

		Certainty	Uncertainty
Beliefs About Cause/Effect Relations	Certain		
	Uncertain		

Figure 8-3 Decision processes

Source: Thompson 1967, p. 134.

When outcome preferences are clear, but cause/effect relationships are uncertain, we will refer to the judgmental strategy for decision making. Where the situation is reversed and there is certainty regarding cause/effect but uncertainty regarding outcome preferences, the issue can be regarded as calling for a compromise strategy for decision making. Finally, where there is uncertainty on both dimensions, we will speak of the inspirational strategy for decision making, if indeed any decision is forthcoming. (pp. 134–35)

The obvious critical factor in this framework is information. The amount and kind of information determine the certainty in the decision-making process. The implication is that the more certain that knowledge, the easier and better the decision making. Unfortunately, information does not flow automatically into an organization. Whatever is happening inside or outside an organization is subject to the perceptions and interpretations of the decision makers (Duncan 1972). Miles, Snow, and Pfeffer (1974) suggest that decision makers can take four stances in their perceptions. They can be "domain defenders," who attempt to allow little change to occur; "reluctant reactors," who simply react to pressures; "anxious analyzers," who perceive change but wait for competing organizations to develop responses and then adapt to them; or "enthusiastic prospectors," who perceive opportunities for change and want to create change and to experiment. These different perceptual bases are developed through the individual decision maker's experiences in the organization. Thus, the same external or internal conditions can be viewed differently, depending upon who is doing the perceiving.

Examples are easy to observe. Many organizational decision makers are now dealing with women employees who are no longer satisfied to work in just clerical positions or accept unequal pay for equal work. This can be viewed enthusiastically as an opportunity to bring more and more qualified personnel into the organization or as a threat to the domain of the "old boys," to be defended by ignoring the demands of women. In this regard, Miller, Labowitz, and Fry (1975) found that women who do advance in organizations tend to lose friendships and respect as well as influence and access to information. They call this a situation of *compartmentalized rationality* when technically qualified personnel are excluded from decision-making positions. Kanter's (1977) analysis of women in corporations also emphasizes that men in organizations tend to exclude women from informal interaction patterns. Whether the example is women, minority group members, young people, old people, or whatever, the exclusion of qualified personnel diminishes the likelihood that decisions will be in the best interest of the organization.

Information does not move automatically to those in decision-making positions. It is part of the communications process within organizations. As will be seen in the next chapter, the communications process itself is almost guaranteed to withhold, expand, or distort information. In addition, organizations scan different environments in different fashions. For example, although they usually use as much information as they can from outside the organization, they apparently cease to do this when they develop bases in other countries as multinational corporations have (Keegan 1974). In these cases, the information-scanning process turns inside the organization, with the potential that much will be missed on the outside.

Although information is a critical component of decision making, equally important are beliefs about cause and effect. In some areas of knowledge, certainty about cause and effect is quite well developed, while in others the knowledge is probabilistic at best. Since all organizations are social units interacting with society, any involvement of humans in either the cause or the effect part of the equation introduces an element of uncertainty. Complete knowledge is undoubtedly rare in the kinds of decisions with which we are concerned. In discussing the effects of the incompleteness of knowledge and information, Thompson notes that in organizations working at the frontiers of new knowledge—such as those in the aerospace industry and in medical research—the presence of imperfections and gaps in knowledge lead to the use of the judgmental strategy, even though all the variables that are known to be relevant are controlled as far as possible. Knowledge about cause and effect is further weakened when some elements of the process are beyond the organization's control. Welfare programs, for example, are affected by the people being served and the wider community that supports or rejects the total program. Still another situation in which the cause-and-effect relationship becomes unclear is when the organization is in competition with another organization over which it cannot exercise control. In this case the judgmental strategy is also used, since the organization cannot decide for sure exactly what will happen as a result of its own efforts.

In addition to changes in the nature of the cause-effect knowledge system that occur as new knowledge becomes available—as in the case of new medical discoveries that alter the approach of hospitals to their patients—another important component of the system should be specified. The nature of cause and effect is actually really certain in only a few cases. Cause-and-effect "knowledge" is vitally affected by the belief or truth system that is prevalent in the organization. The importance of this can be seen clearly in the case of welfare systems that have two major alternative truth systems, which can lead to different interpretations of the same knowledge inputs. The organizations can believe, on the one hand, that those on some form of welfare assistance are in that condition through their own fault or, on the other hand, that the condition exists because of societal inperfections. While there would seldom be a complete acceptance of either extreme position, the dominant truth system would serve as the mechanism by which information coming into the system is interpreted on a cause-and-effect basis, leading to different kinds of decisions being made. Similar examples can be noted concerning the strategies adopted in regard to supervisory practices, international relations, and most other organizational decisions. From the cause-effect standpoint, then, while information is a key factor, interpretation of it remains a variable that, while usually constant in most organizations, still affects the outcomes of the decisions that are made. The adoption of a different truth system could lead to entirely different decisions, based on the same information.

The outcome-preference side of the Thompson paradigm contains even more ambiguities for the organization than the cause-effect side. Goals in organizations are central here, since it is the decisions that are made about goals that become the outcome preferences. In the operations of an organization, the decisions that are made are obviously among several possible outcomes for the organization. Here the same concerns about knowledge and truth systems are extremely important, since they will help determine exactly what the leadership in the organization will decide about a particular issue.

Outcome preferences are also affected by several other factors. Thompson (1967) notes that when human beings are the objects of the organizations' efforts, conflicting desired outcomes can be derived from the subjects themselves. Here again the example of welfare clients can be used. Similarly, in a prison "with therapeutic objectives, some compromise seems inevitable, for conflicting outcome preferences of prisoners force the prison to add custody as an outcome preference" (p. 137). The organization may also be constrained in its choices among outcome preferences by shortages of inputs. If a university would like to develop a national reputation in some field, its preferred outcome may have to be modified if it is unable to secure the kinds of faculty and students to assist it in this endeavor. The case would be similar in the production process if the materials needed were in short or low-quality supply.

Rationality

To these constraints, which are outside the control of the organization and the decision makers, must be added the critical constraint of the limited amount of rationality available in the decision-making process. As Simon (1957) has so ably pointed out, decisions are made on the basis of "bounded rationality." The reasons for the limits on rationality are linked to the inability of the system as a whole to provide maximum or even adequate information for decision making and to the inability of the decision maker to intellectually handle even the inadequate information that is available. Leaving the issue of information aside for the moment, it is clear that the more important a decision is for the organization, the greater the number of factors contributing to the condition of the organization at the moment that the decision has to be made, and the more far-reaching the consequences of the decision. The intellectual ability to handle these multitudinous factors is just not available among current and past organizational leaders to the degree that they and those affected by the decisions would desire. This approach, by the way, contributed to Simon's Nobel Prize in Economics.

This line of reasoning is extended by Cohen, March, and Olsen (1972) in their "garbage can" model of decision making, in which it essentially is argued that organizations have a repertoire of responses to problems (located in the garbage can). If a proposed solution to a problem appears to be satisfactory or be appropriate, it is applied to the problem. Interestingly, this model also suggests that the garbage can also contains the problem. What this means is that organizational decision makers do not perceive that something is occurring about which a decision has to be made until the problem matches one with which they have already had some experience. The "garbage can" imagery has elements of both truth and cuteness. Too quick acceptance of the imagery can miss an important consideration in decision making. Garbage cans of organizations, as well as those of individuals do not contain random responses, problems, or other debris. Instead, garbage cans reveal a great deal about the life styles and interests of organizations and individuals. Thus, organizations turn to previous decisions that have been discarded or put aside. This means that little in the way of new decisions will enter the decision-making situation.

There are still other limits on rationality. Hage (1980) and Bacharach and Lawler (1980) emphasize the fact that decisions are made by coalitions of interest groups. Interest-group interests may or may not coincide with the best interests of the organization. They certainly will not coincide with the interests of those groups not in power. Hills and Mahoney (1978) found that in times of adversity, decisions were shaped by power considerations rather than by more bureaucratic considerations, such as workload. In periods of affluence, the more bureaucratic approach was used. This is similar to the findings of Pfeffer, Salancik, and Leblibici (1978), who found that social influence and social familiarity were used more in decision making during periods of adversity.

In another examination of rationality in decision making, Alexander (1979) concluded that the choices which determine outcomes in organizational context are made informally and intuitively, before the evaluation of the consequences of the decisions are made. The suggestion here is that top decision makers make their decisions and then develop the rational-sounding reasons for the decisions after the fact. As to rationality, then, we can conclude that there are severe limitations on the extent to which it can be found in organizations.

Another element of decision making that we will touch upon briefly is participation in the process itself. As we have seen previously, participation by subordinates has mixed consequences for the organization and the participants. The same is true of decision making. Alutto and Belasco

(1972) indicate that greater participation can be dysfunctional if the participants already feel satisfied or even saturated with their role in decision making. If they feel deprived, bringing them into the decision-making process will increase their involvement in and acceptance of the decision that is made. A useful insight on participation in decision making is provided by Heller (1973): if a decision is important for the organization, a nonparticipative style is likely to be used; if the decisions are important for the subordinates in terms of their own work, a more participative approach would be taken. If the organizational decision makers believe that the subordinates have something to contribute to the decision or its implementation, then participation is more likely. Again, this is done on the basis of limited or bounded rationality.

The entire decision-making process can be viewed as a dialectical process (Alexander 1974). The "thesis" is the condition in which the organization grows over time in a relatively stable environment. The organization attempts to limit its risks, and decisions are made in a discrete sequence. Unanticipated, sudden changes in the environment provide the impetus for the "antithesis," in which the previous operations no longer work. Older modes of decision making are inappropriate. New decision-making modes, however rational, are established, forming the new "synthesis." This in turn becomes standardized and the sequence is repeated.

It would be possible to list at length organizational decisions that have been spectacular successes and failures. On the failure side, one need only look at the Edsel, the Vietnam war, or Watergate and its cover-up. On the success side, we could examine the Mustang, other wars, or the election of President Nixon after Watergate (a temporary success, to be sure). The same organizations make successful and unsuccessful decisions. Organizational leaders do attempt to be rational, as they define it. Their sources of information, their belief systems, environmental constraints, organizational constraints, their own intelligence, and luck all contribute to the success or failure of a particular decision. Decision makers dip into their garbage cans or repertoires of decisions that have been successful in the past. The success and impact of the decisions are determined by the same set of constraints that surrounds the leadership role. Thus, decision making, like leadership, must be viewed as being *contingent* upon the internal and external constraints on all aspects of organizations.

SUMMARY AND CONCLUSIONS

In this chapter, the attempt was made to place a human factor, leadership behavior, within the larger framework of analysis. We began with the empirical conclusion that leadership behavior affects followers. To this was added the idea that since our concern was with top organizational leadership, the impact on the followers and the organization should therefore be greater. Since there is not as much information about this form of individual input into the organization as is desirable, the topic had to be approached somewhat indirectly.

It was first noted that the current conceptualization of leadership involves a combination of factors. *The position in the organization itself, the specific situations confronted, the characteristics of the individuals involved, and the nature of the relationships with subordinates all affect leadership behavior and the impact of that behavior.* Since all of these except the position itself are variable, it is exceedingly difficult to develop single standards or prescriptions for leadership. From the many studies of leadership effectiveness at lower levels in the organization, the conclusion was reached that there is no one style of leadership that is successful at all times. The total situation must be viewed if leadership is to be understood.

The important question of whether or not leadership makes any kind of difference in the organization was of necessity also approached indirectly. Since it has been found that leadership behavior affects both behavior and attitudes at lower levels in the organizations, the extrapolation was made that it is important at the top. The studies of top management succession led to the same conclusion, tempered by the many other factors that also determine what happens to the organization. It is unfortunate that we do not know exactly in what ways and under what conditions such impacts occur. From the perspective of the total analysis, it is clear that top leadership is important for the organization as a whole. But we cannot specify how much more or less important, or under what conditions, it is of importance when compared with some of the other factors considered, such as the existing organizational structure, informally derived power relationships, pressures from the environment, relations with other organizations, and so on. We can state, however, that it *is* important, and hope that future research will begin to assess the relative strengths of these factors under various conditions.

Since a large element of the leadership process involves making critical decisions, the nature of decision making was then considered. The importance of information and the nature of the belief systems of those involved was stressed. The complexity of the conditions under which decisions are made and the difficulties in predicting outcomes were also discussed. Like the rest of organizational life, decision making takes place in a situation of many cross- and conflicting pressures, so that a movement in one direction is likely to trigger countermovements in others. At the same time, it is critical for the organization as new contingencies are continually faced.

Since information is central to decision making, and since communications allow information to flow, we will now examine this process in organizations.

9

Communications

The communications process in organizations contains elements that are strongly organizational and strongly individual. At the individual level, consider the simple example of classroom examinations. If there were not individual differences in cognition and interpretation, everyone would give the same answer to an essay question. This obviously does not take place, as every student and faculty member knows. The organizational input into the communication process comes from the structured communication channels and the positions which people occupy. For example, the year I spent as acting vice president for research and dean of graduate studies at my university led me to interpret information from that position. Information of a particular sort had a different meaning than when I returned to the position of professor of sociology. In this chapter, those factors that affect the sending, receiving, perception, and interpretation of communications will be examined.

THE IMPORTANCE OF COMMUNICATIONS

Organizational structures, with their varying sizes, technological sophistication, and degrees of complexity and formalization, are designed to be or evolve into information-handling systems. The very establishment of an organizational structure structure is a sign that communications are supposed to follow a particular path. The fact that the officially designated structure is not the operative one indicates only that communications do not always follow the neatly prescribed lines. Power, leadership, and decision making rely upon the communication process, either explicitly or implicitly, since these processes would be meaningless in the absence of information.

Organizational analysts have ascribed varying degrees of importance to the communication process. Barnard (1938), for example, states: "In an exhaustive theory of organization, communication would occupy a central place, because the structure, extensiveness, and scope of the organization are almost entirely determined by communication techniques" (p. 91). This approach essentially places communications at the heart of the organization. Katz and Kahn (1978) state: "Communications—the exchange of information and the transmission of meaning—is the very essence of a social system or an organization" (p. 428). Other theorists, on the other hand, pay scant attention to the topic (for example, see Aldrich 1979; Clegg and Dunkerley 1980). Instead of declaring that communications is at the heart or the periphery of organizational analysis, a more reasonable view is that communications varies in importance according to *where* one is looking in an organization and *what kind* of organization is being studied.

Katz and Kahn (1978) note the varying importance of communication when they say:

> When one walks from a factory to the adjoining head-house or office, the contrast is conspicuous. One goes from noise to quiet, from heavy electrical cables and steam pipes to slim telephone lines, from a machine-dominated to a people-dominated environment. One goes, in short, from a sector of the organization in which energic exchange is primary and information exchange secondary, to a sector where the priorities are reversed. The closer one gets to the organizational center of control and decision making, the more pronounced is the emphasis on information exchange. (p. 428).

These intraorganizational differences are important. Equally vital are interorganizational differences. Wilensky (1967) suggests that four factors determine the importance of communications or intelligence for the organization:

> (1) the degree of conflict or competition with the external environment— typically related to the extent of involvement with and dependence on government; (2) the degree of dependence on internal support and unity; (3) the degree to which internal operations and external environment are believed to be rationalized, that is, characterized by predictable uniformities and therefore subject to planned influence; and affecting all of these, (4) the size and structure of the organization, its heterogeneity of membership and diversity of goals, its centrality of authority. (p. 10)

Communication is most important, therefore, in organizations and organizational segments that must deal with uncertainty, that are complex, and that have a technology that does not permit easy routinization. Both external and internal characteristics affect the centrality of communication. The more an organization is people and idea oriented, the more important communication becomes. Even in a highly mechanized system, of course, communications underlie the development and use of machines. Workers are instructed on usage, orders are delivered, and so on. At the same time, the routineness of such operations leads to a lack of variability in the communication process. Once procedures are set, few additional communications are required. While communications occur rather continuously in such settings, their organizational importance is limited unless they lead to severe distortions in the operations. The same point can be made in regard to many persons in the communications process itself. The long-distance telephone operator is vital to modern organizations as they attempt to communicate rapidly over wide geographical areas. What is desired of the operator, however, is unvarying performance; the operator's ideas and personality are irrelevant to the communication process. The current phasing out of the operator is indicative of the actual unimportance of this role. The important people—and machines—are those that can, as a matter of design or fact, provide an input into the communications system.

The process of communication is by definition a relational one; one party is the sender and the other the receiver at a particular point in time. (As we will see in more detail later, the relational aspect of communication affects the process.) The social relations occurring in the communication process involve the sender and receiver and their reciprocal effects on each other as they are communicating. If a sender is intimidated by his receiver during the process of sending a message, the message itself and the interpretation of it will be affected. Intimidation is just one of a myriad of factors with the potential for interrupting the simple sender-receiver relationship. Status differences, different perceptual models, sex appeal, and so on can enter the picture and lead to distortions of what is being sent and received.

These sources of distortion and their consequences will occupy a good deal of attention in the subsequent discussion. Ignorance of the potentiality for distortion has been responsible for the failure of many organizational attempts to improve operations simply by utilizing more communications. Katz and Kahn (1978, p. 430) point out that, once the importance of communications was recognized, many organizations jumped on a communications bandwagon, believing that if sufficient communications were available to all members of the organization, everyone would know and understand what was going on and most organizational problems would disappear. Unfortunately, organizational life, like that in the outside world, is not that simple, and mere reliance on more communications cannot bring about major, positive changes in the organization itself.

Before we turn to a more comprehensive examination of communications problems and their consequences in organizations, a simple view of optimal communications should be presented. The view is simple because it is complementary to the discussion of rationality and decision making. Communications in organizations should provide accurate information with the appropriate emotional overtones to all members who need the communications content. This assumes that neither too much nor too little information is in the system and that it is clear from the outset who can utilize what is available. It should be evident that this is an impossible condition to achieve in a complex organization.

In the sections that follow, the factors leading to this impossibility will be examined, from those that are apparently inherent (through learning) in any social grouping to those that are peculiarly organizational.

THE BASES OF COMMUNICATIONS SYSTEMS

Communications in organizations take many forms. Some are totally interpersonal, others concern matters internal to the organization, while still others are concerned with linkages between organizations and their environments. Tables 9-1 and 9-2 indicate the parameters of these forms of communications and some of the major variables to be considered for each form.

The focus of the present discussion will be primarily on communications within the organization. In the following chapters, the external communications will be considered. The discussion will generally follow the categorization of variables presented in Tables 9-1 and 9-2. We will be concerned with horizontal communications to a greater extent than is suggested in these tables.

Table 9-1 Communication Context, Types of Communication, and Primary Influences on Information Transmission

Context for Communication	Type of Communication (Level-of-Analysis)	Primary Influences on Information Transmission
Independent of the organization	a. Interpersonal	a. Cognitive phenomena and social roles and norms
Within the organization	a. Interpersonal	a. Organizational roles and norms plus applicable social norms
	b. Interunit	b. Interdepartmental relations, aggregate effects of information exchanged
External to the individual organization	a. Interorganizational	a. Relations among organizations
	b. Organizational-environmental	b. Environmental components

Source: Roberts et al. 1974, p. 515.

Table 9-2 Communication: Individual, Organizational, and Environmental Variables Related Within Each Level of Analysis

Context (1)	Level of Analysis (2)	Variables			
		Communication (3)	Individual (4)	Organizational (5)	Environmental (6)
Independent of the organization	Interpersonal	Message characteristics Feedback Information overload Source credibility Information processing Nonverbal	Personality variables Perceptions Needs Social roles and norms Social goals Attitudes		Culture Spatial arrangements
Within the organization	Interpersonal	Message characteristics Feedback Overload Information processing Source credibility Modality choice Gatekeeping Distortion Speed Directionality	Organizational rules, norms, goals Status-authority Influence Expectations Mobility Satisfaction	Hierarchy —number of levels —line/staff Size —total organization —subunit Structure —tall-flat —centralized/ decentralized Performance criteria	

		Liaison roles	Reward structure Technology/work flow Formalization
Interunit	Coding Network alignment Activity level Accuracy		Interdepartmental relations Departmental status Work group relations
	Aggregate effects of information by organizational members on the above variables		Interorganizational relations —dependency —status and influence
Interorganizational	Aggregated information Processing Sensing mechanism Uncertainity absorption —rules —cycles		Climate —satisfaction —leadership style Structure Hierarchy Technology Performance criteria Organizational maturity
Organizational-environmental			Rate of change —technology —market Perceived equivocality of the environment
External to the organization			

Source: Roberts et al. 1974, pp. 516–17.

INDIVIDUAL FACTORS

Since communication involves something being sent to a receiver, what the receiver does with or to the communicated message is perhaps the most vital part of the whole system. Therefore, the perceptual process becomes a key element in our understanding of communications in organizations.

The perceptual process is subject to many factors, which may lead to important differences in the way any two people perceive the same person or message. Zalkind and Costello (1962) have summarized much of the literature on perception in the organizational setting and have noted that even physical objects can be perceived differently. The perceiver may respond to cues he or she is not aware of, be influenced by emotional factors, use irrelevant cues, weigh evidence in an unbalanced way, or fail to identify all the factors on which his or her judgments are based. People's personal needs, values, and interests enter the perceptual process. Most communications take place in interaction with others, and how one person perceives the "other" in the interaction process vitally affects how a person will perceive the communication, since other people are more emotion inducing than physical objects. For example, research has shown that one person's interactions, and thus perceptions, are affected by even the expectations of what the other person will look like.

These factors are common to all perceptual situations. For the analysis of perceptions in organizations, they must be taken as basic conditions in the communication process. So it is obvious that perfect perception, that is, perception uniform across all information recipients, is impossible in any social situation. The addition of organizational factors makes the whole situation just that much more complex.

Communications in organizations are basically transactions between individuals. Even when written or broadcast form is used, the communicator is identified as an individual. The impression that the communication receiver has of the communicator is crucial to how the communication is interpreted. Impressions in these instances are not created de novo; the receiver utilizes his or her own learned response set to the individual and the situation. The individual's motives and values enter the situation. In addition, the setting or surroundings of the act of communication affect the impression. A neat, orderly, and luxuriously furnished office contributes to a reaction different from the one given by an office that looks as though a tornado just struck a paper mill. Since the perceptual process itself requires putting ideas and people into categories, the interaction between communicators is also subject to "instant categorization"; that is, you cannot understand another person unless he is placed in some relevant part of your learned perceptual repertoire. Zalkind and Costello point out that this is often done on the basis of a very limited amount of evidence— or even wrong evidence, as when the receiver notes cues that are wrong or irrelevant to the situation in question (p. 221).

The role that the individual plays in the organization affects how communications are perceived or sent (Wager 1972; Roberts, Hulin, and

190

Rousseau 1978). In almost all organizations, people can be superordinates in one situation and subordinates in another. The assistant superintendent of a school system is superordinate to a set of principals, but subordinate to the superintendent and the school board. Communications behavior differs according to the particular role being played. If the individual is in a role in which he or she is or has been, or feels, discriminated against, communications are affected. Athanassiades (1974) found that women who had suffered discrimination in their roles had a lower feeling of autonomy than others in the same role. This in turn was related to distortions in the information which they communicated upward in the organization.

All these factors are further complicated by the well-known phenomenon of stereotyping. This predisposition to judge can occur before any interaction at all has taken place. It can involve labels such as "labor" or "management" or any other such group membership. The characteristics of the individual involved are thus assumed to be like those of the group of which he is a member—and in probably the vast majority of cases, the characteristics attributed to the group as a whole are also great distortions of the actual world. In the sense being used here, stereotyping involves the imposition of negative characteristics on the members of the communications system. The reverse situation—attributing socially approved characteristics—can also occur, of course, with an equally strong potential for damage to the communication process.

Other factors that enter the communication process in somewhat the same manner are the use of the "halo effect," or the use of only one or a few indicators to generalize about a total situation; "projection," or a person's assuming that the other member of a communications system has the same characteristics as his or her own; and "perceptual defense," or altering inconsistent information to put it in line with the conceptual framework already developed. All the factors that have been mentioned here are taken note of in the general literature on perception and must be assumed to be present in any communications systems. They are not peculiar to organizations.

The literature has also indicated that the characteristics of the perceived person affect what is perceived. Zalkind and Costello cite four conclusions from research regarding the perceiver:

1. Knowing oneself makes it easier to see others accurately.
2. One's own characteristics affect the characteristics that are likely to be seen in others.
3. The person who is self-accepting is more likely to be able to see favorable aspects of other people.
4. Accuracy in perceiving others is not a single skill. (pp. 227–29)

These findings are linked back to the more general considerations—tendencies to stereotype, project, and so on. It is when the characteristics of the perceived are brought into the discussion that organizational conditions become important. Factors such as status differences and departmental memberships affect how a person is perceived. The person may be labeled a sales manager (accurately or not) by a production worker, and the entire communications system is affected until additional information is permitted into the system. The situation in which the communication takes place also has a major impact on what is perceived. This is particularly vital in organizations, since in most cases the situation is easily labeled and identified by the physical location.

ORGANIZATIONAL FACTORS

The rather general conclusions from the literature on perception are directly relevant for the understanding of communications in an organization. All the factors discussed are part of the general characteristics of communications. In the organization, two additional major components of the communications system must be examined: vertical and horizontal considerations greatly affect the communication process.

Vertical Communications

Patterns of vertical communications have received a good deal of attention, primarily because they are seen as vital in organizational operations. From the lengthy discussions of organizational structure, power, and leadership it should be evident that the vertical element is a crucial organizational fact of life. Since communications are also crucial, the vertical element intersects in a most important way. Vertical communications in organizations involve both downward and upward flows.

Downward Communications   Katz and Kahn (1978, pp. 440–43) identify five elements of downward communication. The first is the simple and common *job instruction*, in which a subordinate is told what to do either through direct orders, training sessions, job descriptions, or other such mechanisms. The intent of such instructions is to ensure reliable job performance. The more complex and uncertain the task, the more generalized such instructions. As a rule, the more highly trained the subordinates, the less specific such instructions are, because it is assumed that they will bring with them an internalized knowledge of how to do the job, along with other job-related knowledge and attitudes.

The second element is more subtle and less often stressed. It involves the *rationale* for the task and its relationships to the rest of the organization. It is here that different philosophies of life affect how much this sort of information is communicated. If the philosophy is to keep the organizational members dumb and happy, little such information will be communicated. The organization may feel either that the subordinates are unable to comprehend the information or that they would misuse it by introducing variations into their performance based on their own best judgment of how the task should be accomplished. Aside from the philosophy-of-life issue, this is a delicate matter. All organizations, even those most interested in the human qualities of their members, have hidden agendas of some sort at some point in time. If the total rational for all actions were known to all members, the potential for chaos would be high, since not all members would be able to understand and accept the information at the cognitive or emotional levels. This danger of too much communication is matched by opposite danger of the too little, which also has strong potential for organizational malfunctioning. If the members are given too little information, and do not and cannot know how their work is related to any larger whole, there is a strong possibility of alienation from the work and the organization. Obviously, the selection of the best path between these extremes is important in the establishment of communications.

The third element of downward communications is *information* regarding procedures and practices within the organization. This is similar to the first element, in that it is relatively straightforward and noncontroversial. Here again, whether or not this is linked to the second element is problematic.

Feedback to individuals regarding their performance is the fourth part of the communications system. This is almost by definition a sticky issue. particularly when the feedback has a negative tone to it. If the superior has attempted at all to utilize socioemotional ties to his or her subordinates, the issue becomes even more difficult. And it becomes almost impossible when the work roles are so thoroughly set in advance by the organization that the worker had no discretion on the job at all. In these cases, only a totally conscious deviation would result in feedback. In the absence of deviation, there will probably be no feedback other than the paycheck and other routine rewards. Where discretion is part of the picture, the problem of assessment deepens, because feedback is more difficult to accomplish if there are no clear criteria on which to base it. Despite these evident problems, feedback is a consistent part of downward communications.

The final element of this type of communication involves attempts to *indoctrinate* subordinates into accepting and believing in the organization's (or subunit's) goals. The intent here, of course, is to get the personnel emotionally involved in their work and add this to the motivational system.

In relation to the first-line supervisor-worker relationship, these elements seem simple; they become more complex when the focus is shifted to a top executive-vice president situation. While the same elements are present, the kinds of information and range of ideas covered are likely to be much greater in the latter example. Parsons (1960, pp. 63–69) provides a way of understanding these differences, when he categorizes organizations by institutional, managerial, and technical levels. The institutional level is concerned with relating the organization to its external world by ensuring that the organization continues to receive support from its constituency and other organizations in contact. Common examples here are boards of directors or trustees whose primary function is often to maintain this sort of support. It has been suggested that the college or university president has had a predominantly institutional role in recent history. Fund raising and legislative relationships occupied a great deal of his or her time. As student and faculty dissidence grew in the 1960s and 1970s, the college president was put into the position of attempting to solve internal problems while at the same time playing the institutional role. The incompatibility of these demands was readily observed through the exceedingly high turnover rate in this position. The managerial level deals with the internal administration of the organization. Once strategic decisions are made, they must be administered, and the managerial level is concerned with how the organization will carry out these decisions. The technical level is involved with the translation of this information into specific job descriptions and direction.

The existence of these three levels requires that communications be translated as they cross levels. While it can be assumed that all levels speak the same language and indeed that each may understand completely what the others are doing, the fact remains that the tasks are different and the content and intent of communications are also different.

Dysfunctions of Hierarchy The very presence of hierarchies in organizations introduces still more complications into the communications than those already discussed. The form of interaction itself is apparently affected by level in the hierarchy. Brinkerhoff (1972) has found that at higher levels in organizations, communications tend to take the form of staff conferences, while at the first-line supervisor level the communications are more often in the form of spontaneous communicative contacts. Even when new contingencies were faced by the higher levels, the spontaneous form did not occur. This does not mean that the spontaneous form is necessarily more appropriate, but rather that there is an apparent use of established protocol even in the face of new situations.

Information content is also related to hierarchy. O'Reilly and Roberts (1974) found that favorable information is passed upward, while unfavorable information, as well as more complete, more important information, tends to be passed laterally, rather than up or down the hierarchy. They also suggest that trust between superior and subordinate lessens the impact of hierarchy.

Blau and Scott (1962, pp. 121–24) have pointed out several specific dysfunctions of hierarchy for the communications process. In the first place, such differences inhibit communications. Citing experimental and field evidence, Blau and Scott note the common tendency for people at the same status level to interact more with one another than with those at different levels. There is a tendency for those in lower-status positions to look up to and direct friendship overtures toward those in higher-status positions. This increases the flow of socioemotional communications upward, but at the same time leaves those at the bottom of the hierarchy in the position of receiving little of this type of input. This situation is further complicated by the fact that those in higher-status positions also direct such communications upward rather than reciprocating to their subordinates, thus reducing the amount of satisfaction derived for all parties.

A second dysfunctional consequence is the fact that approval is sought from superiors rather than peers in such situations. Nonperformance criteria enter the communications system, in that respect from peers, which can be earned on the basis of performance, can become secondary to approval-gaining devices that may not be central to the tasks at hand. The plethora of terms ranging from "apple-polishing" to more profane expressions is indicative of this.

The third dysfunction identified by Blau and Scott has to do with the error-correcting function of normal social interaction. It is commonly found that interaction among peers tends to sort out errors and at least enter a common denominator through the interaction process. This is much less likely to happen in downward communication. The subordinate is unlikely to tell the superior that he or she thinks an order or an explanation is wrong, for fear of his or her own status. Criticism of one's superior is not the most popular of communications in organizations.

Another aspect of the hierarchical pattern that can present problems in organizations is the very nature of the hierarchy itself. If the superior is chosen on the basis of ability, it is likely that he or she is more able than the subordinates. If this is the case and the ability takes the form of intellectual superiority, a communications gap can exist because of the different levels of thought on which the superior and subordinates operate. The same type of situation occurs when the subordinates are all experts and the superior becomes a generalist because of his or her administrative duties. Examples here can be found within organizations employing professionals. When the superior communicates downward, it must be as a nonexpert, and this lack of expertise may limit his or her credibility to the subordinates.

These problems associated with downward communication in organizations are compounded by the previously discussed factors affecting perception. Since rank in an organization is a structural fact, it carries with it a strong tendency for stereotyping. The very terms "management," "worker," "enlisted man," and so on, are indicative of the value loadings associated with rank. As will be seen shortly, these status differences do have their positive side; but the negative connotations attached to many of the sterotypes, and the likelihood that communications will be distorted because of real or assumed differences between statuses, builds in difficulties for organizational communications.

In keeping with the earlier discussion in which it was noted that complex organizations contain characteristics that work in opposition to each other, there are also beneficial aspects to hierarchical patterns for the communication process. The studies by Blau and his associates (1966, 1968), cited earlier, are a case in point. It will be recalled that, in organizations with highly trained or professionalized personnel, these studies found that a tall or deep hierarchy was associated with effectiveness. The explanation was that the hierarchy provided a continuous source of error detection and correction. The presence of experts in an organization also increases the extent of horizontal communications (Hage, Aiken, and Marrett 1971). These can take the form of scheduled or unscheduled committee meetings or more spontaneous interactions. Communications are a vital source of coordination when organizations are staffed with a diverse set of personnel offering different forms of expertise (Brewer 1971). If a tall hierarchy is found in an organization with a low level of differentiation in terms of expertise, it is apparently due to the need for extensive downward communications. When a hierarchy is composed of people of equal or higher ability than the subordinates, their function in this regard is clear. They can make suggestions and offer alternatives that might not be apparent to subordinates. This assumes, of course, that some of the more dysfunctional elements of hierarchical arrangements are minimized. Furthermore, unless one assumes that people always rise to a level just above that of their competence, the superiors may in fact be superior (Peter and Hull 1969). That is, they may actually have more ability than their subordinates. If this is recognized and legitimated by the subordinates, some of the hierarchical problems are again minimized.

The most obvious contribution of a hierarchy is coordination (Hage 1980). If one accepts the common model of communications spreading out in more detail as they move down the hierarchy, then the role of the hierarchy becomes clear. It is up to the superior to decide who gets what kind of communications and when. He or she becomes the distribution and filtering center. Given the vast amount of information that is potentially available for the total organization, this role is crucial. In a later section, we will discuss the nature of hierarchical arrangements and how they can be optimally utilized. For the moment, it is sufficient to note that status differences are obviously important for and endemic to downward communications.

Upward Communications   Contrary to the law of gravity, communications in organizations must also go up, even when nothing is going down. According to Katz and Kahn (1978): "Communication up the line takes many forms. It can be reduced, however, to what people say (1) about themselves, their performance, and their problems, (2) about others and their problems, (3) about organizational practices and policies, and (4) about what needs to be done and how it can be done" (p. 446). The content of these messages can obviously range from the most personal gripe to the most high-minded suggestion for the improvement of the organization and the world; and they can have positive or negative consequences, from a promotion or bonus to dismissal. (A case in point is that of a civilian official in the U.S. Department of Defense who attempted to rectify excessively costly procurement procedures and lost his job.) The most obvious problems in upward communications is again the fact of hierarchy. The tendencies we noted regarding downward communications can be equally impediments to upward communications.

The situation is even more complex, in some ways, because the person communicating upward can realistically feel threats either to himself or to his work if certain kinds of information are made available to the superiors in the system. A person is unlikely to pass information up if it will be harmful to himself or his peers. Thus, the amount and kind of information that is likely to be passed upward is affected by the fact of hierarchy. Anyone who has been in any kind of organization knows that discussions with the boss, chairman, president, foreman, or other superior are, at least initially, filled with something approaching terror, regardless of the source of the superior's power in the organization.

Another facet of upward communications is important: whereas communications downward become more detailed and specific, those going up the hierarchy must become condensed and summarized. Indeed, a major function of those in the middle of a hierarchy is the filtering and editing of information. Only crucial pieces of information are supposed to reach the top. This can be seen in clear relief at the national level, where the president of the United States receives capsule accounts of the huge number of issues with which he is concerned. Regardless of the party in power, the filtering and editing process is vital in the hierarchy, since the basis on which things are "edited out" can have enormous repercussions by the time the information reaches the top. Here as well as in downward communications, the perceptual limitations we noted earlier are in operation, so there is a very real potential for distorted communications and, more important, for decisions different from those that would have been made if a different editing process were in force (Wilensky 1967; Halberstam 1972).

Communications in Flat Hierarchies   The discussion thus far has been built around the typical hierarchical arrangements, with multiple levels in a step-by-step progression up the line. When organizations are flatter, different considerations enter the picture. In the first place, more nonfiltered communications come to the superior in the system. Hypothetically, at least, all persons in a flat structure have equal access to the superior. On the basis of experimental evidence, Carzo and Yanouzas (1969) found that while communications took somewhat more time in a taller structure, conflict resolution and coordination were slower in the flat structure. In the flat structure also, superiors must be able to communicate with all their subordinates, so they must be able to understand what they are doing. Since the flat structure is more likely to be found when the subordinates are experts of one kind or another, this is quite unlikely in practice. In these cases, then, upward communications are inhibited by the strong potential for inability to communicate.

Communications with "Outsiders"   An additional form of vertical communications is too frequently omitted in the organizational literature. Organizations deal with customers and clients. These groups do not necessarily form a vertical relationship, to be sure, since the relationship can actually be in any direction—up, down, or sideways. In the case of clients, the direction is usually downward, in that the client, as a welfare recipient, patient, or student, is typically viewed in this light. Customers can be courted (upward), expected (horizontal), or merely accepted (downward). These are not fixed relationships, as we can see from revolts by students, welfare recipients, and consumers. Nevertheless, in most cases the direction seems to be downward.

The nature of the communications to these "outsiders" is affected by their relationships with the organization, in terms of the power they hold vis-à-vis the organization. Julian (1966) has shown that the structure of the organization itself also makes a difference in the communications system to clients. Using data from a set of hospitals, Julian related the nature of the compliance patterns in the hospital to the communications system. The hospitals were categorized according to the Etzioni formulation into normative (general hospital) and normative-coercive (sanatorium and veteran's hospital) types. Julian found more communications blockages in the more coercive hospitals; these blockages were used as a means of client control. In the normative hospitals, on the other hand, more open communications were related to greater effectiveness. Here the appeal was to the patients' beliefs that what the hospital was doing for them was the correct thing. The nature of the relationship to the clients in this case was related to the openness of the communications system.

In a somewhat related study, Rosengren (1964) found that in mental hospitals that move to the "therapeutic milieu" approach, the hierarchical tendencies are minimized, and the patient becomes much more a part of the communications system. As organizations dealing with clients redefine their relationships with the clients, such alterations in the communications system are inevitable. As clients and paraprofessionals are brought more and more into the decision-making process, previously existing hierarchical arrangements interfere with effective communications.

At this point, a major dilemma must be noted. The introduction of clients and paraprofessionals into the communications system of a welfare, medical, or school system increases the range of inputs into the communication and decision-making processes. This helps correct some of the misconceptions and blocked perceptions that can characterize the way in which some professionals and some organizations deal with clients. At the same time, however, if the nonprofessionals for one reason or another begin to dominate the communications and decision-making systems, then the very reason for the presence of the professionals is nullified. This is part of the constant interplay between expertise and the desire for participation. It is a major consideration in understanding the problems associated with vertical communications in organizations.

Horizontal Communications

Communications in organizations go in more directions than up and down. Despite the obvious fact of horizontal communications, organizational analysts for a long time have concentrated more on the vertical aspect. According to Simpson (1969), the major reason for this skewed perspective has been that the classical writers on organizations themselves focused on the vertical, leading to this type of focus by their successors. But whatever the reason, the horizontal component has received less attention, even though a greater proportion of the communications in an organization appear to be of this type. Simpson's study of a textile factory indicates that the lower the level in the hierarchy, the greater the proportion of horizontal communications. This is not surprising; if for no other reason, in most organizations there are simply more people at each descending level. This fact and the already-noted tendency for communications to be affected by hierarchical differences make it natural for people to communicate with those at about the same level in the organization. And those at the same level are more apt to share common characteristics, making communication even more likely.

It is important to distinguish between communications *within* an organizational subunit and those *between* subunits. In later sections, the latter will be examined more closely. For the moment our attention will be turned to communications within subunits.

This type of communication is "critical for effective system functioning" (Katz and Kahn 1978, p. 444). In most cases, it is impossible for an organization to work out in advance every conceivable facet of every task assigned throughout the organization. At some point there will have to be coordination and discussion among a set of peers as the work proceeds. The interplay between individuals is vital in the coordination process, since the supervisor and the organization cannot anticipate every possible contingency. This is a rather sterile analysis, of course, since people desire—and the communications process contains—much more than task-related information. The long history of research in industrial psychology and sociology has indicated the importance of peer interactions in at least partially meeting the socioemotional desires of the participants. The fact that the socioemotional side is brought in to the leadership role (or at least the attempt is made) indicates the recognition of its importance. In peer interactions there is the greatest likelihood of such experiences in the organization. Katz and Kahn state:

> The mutual understanding of colleagues is one reason for the power of the peer group. Experimental findings are clear and convincing about the importance of socio-emotional support for people in both organized and unorganized groups. Psychological forces always push people toward communication with peers: people in the same boat share the same problems. *Hence, if there are no problems of task coordination left to a group of peers, the content of their communication can take forms which are irrelevant to or destructive of organizational functioning* [italics in original]. (p. 445)

The implication here is clear. It is probably beneficial to leave some task-oriented communications to work groups at every level of the organization so that the potentially counterproductive communications do not arise to fill the void. This implication must be modified, however, by a reference back to the general model that is being followed here. It will be remembered that organizational, interpersonal, and individual factors are all part of the way people behave in organizations. If the organizational arrangements are such that horizontal communications are next to impossible, then there is little likelihood of any communication. Work in extremely noisy circumstances or in isolated work locales would preclude much interaction. (These situations, of course, contain their own problems for the individual and the organization.) On the other side of the coin, too much coordination and communications responsibility left to those who, through lack of training or ability, are unable to come to a reasonable joint decision about some matter would also be individually and organizationally disruptive.

While it is relatively easy, in abstract terms, to describe the optimal mix between vertical and horizontal communications in the sense that they are being described here, another element to communication among peers should be noted. Since the communications among peers tend to be based on common understandings, and since continued communications build up the solidarity of the group, work groups develop a collective response to the world around them. This is true for communications on the vertical axis as well as for other aspects of the work situation. This collective response is likely to be accompanied by a collective perception of communications passed to or through the work group. This collective perception can be a collective distortion. It is clear that work groups (as well as other interest groups) can perceive communications in a totally different light from what was intended. A relatively simple communique, such as the likelihood of reorganization, can be interpreted to mean that an entire work force will be eliminated. While this type of response can occur individually, the nature of peer relationships also makes it possible as a collective phenomenon.

Interaction among peers is only one form of horizontal communication. The other major form, obviously vital for the overall coordination of the operations, occurs between members of organizational subunits. While the former has been the subject of some attention, the research concerning the latter has been minimal (for an exception, see Hage 1980). The principal reason seems to be that such communications are not supposed to occur. In almost every conceivable form of organization, they are supposed to go through the hierarchy until they reach the "appropriate" office, at the point where the hierarchies of the two units involved come together. That is, the communications are designed to flow through the office that is above the two departments involved, so that the hierarchy is familiar with the intent and content of the communications. In a simple example, problems between production and sales are supposed to be coordinated through either the office or the individual in charge of both activities.

Obviously, such a procedure occurs in only a minority of such lateral communications. There is a great deal more face-to-face and memo-to-memo communication throughout the ranks of the subunits involved. A major reason for this form of deviation is that it would totally clog the communications system if all information regarding subunit interaction had to flow all the way up one of the subunits and then all the way back down another. The clogging of the system would result in either painfully slow communications or none at all.

Therefore, the parties involved generally communicate directly with each other. This saves time and can often mean a very reasonable solution worked out at a lower level with good cooperation. It may also mean that those further up the hierarchy are unaware of what has happened, however, and this can be harmful in the long run. A solution to this problem is to record and pass along the information about what has been done; but this may be neglected, and even if it is not neglected it may not be noticed.

   While the emphasis in this discussion has been on coordination between subunits, it should be clear that much of the communication of this sort is actually based on conflict. The earlier discussions of the relationships between professionals and their employing organizations can be brought in at this point. When professionals or experts make up divisions of an organization, their areas of expertise are likely to lead them to different conclusions about the same matter (Hage 1974, pp. 101–24). For example, in a petroleum company it is quite conceivable that the geological, engineering, legal, and public relations divisions could all come to different conclusions about the desirability of starting new oil-well drilling in various locations. Each would be correct in its own area of expertise, and the coordination of top officials would obviously be required when a final decision had to be made. During the period of planning or development, however, communications between these divisions would probably be characterized as nonproductive, since the specialists involved would be talking their own language, one that is unfamiliar to those not in the same profession. From the evidence at hand, each division would also be correct in its assessments of the situation and would view the other divisions as not understanding the "true" meanings of the situation.
   This type of communications problem is not limited to professionalized divisions. Whenever a subunit has an area of expertise, it will move beyond other divisions in its conceptualization of a problem. Communications between such subunits inevitably contain elements of conflict. The conflict will be greater if the units involved invest values in their understanding and conceptualizations. Horizontal communications across organizational lines thus contain both the seeds and the flower of conflict. Such conflict, by definition, will contribute to distortion of communications in one form or another. At the same time, passing each message up the line to eliminate such distortion through coordination at the top has the dangers of diluting the message in attempts to avoid conflict and of taking so much time that the message can become meaningless. Here again, the endemic complexities of an organization preclude a totally rational operation.
   Communications Networks Before turning to a more systematic examination of the consequences of all these communications problems in organizations, a final bit of evidence should be noted regarding the manner in which communications evolve. The communication process can be studied in laboratory situations; among organizational characteristics, it is perhaps the most amenable to such experimentation. There has been a long history (Bavelas 1950; Leavitt 1951) of attempting to isolate the communications system that is most efficient under a variety of circumstances. These laboratory studies are applicable to both the vertical and horizontal aspects of communications, since the manner in which the communications tasks are coordinated is the major focus. Three primary communications networks between members of work groups have been studied. The "wheel" pattern is one in which persons at the periphery of the wheel all send their communications to the hub. This is an imposed hierarchy, since those at the periphery cannot send messages to each other; it is the task of the hub to do the coordinating. The "circle" pattern

permits each member of the group to talk to those on either side, with no priorities. The "all-channel" system allows everyone to communicate with everyone else.

Using success in arriving at a correct solution as the criterion of efficiency, repeated investigations have found the wheel pattern to be superior. The other patterns can become equally efficient if they develop a hierarchy over time, but this of course takes time, and meanwhile efficiency is reduced. Katz and Kahn (1978, pp. 437–38) and Blau and Scott (1962, pp. 126–27) note that the more complex the task, the more time is required for the communications network to become structured. The importance of these findings for our purposes is that whether the communications are vertical or horizontal, hierarchical patterns emerge. In the vertical situation, the hierarchy is already there, although the formal hierarchy can be modified through the power considerations of expertise or personal attraction. In the horizontal situation, a hierarchy will emerge. In addition, it must be noted that the task being performed, based on the technology involved, will in part determine where the coordination will occur. It is not a random phenomenon, nor is it necessarily one based on formal position. There is another critical aspect of this for our overall analysis: most organizations have a preestablished structure, and it is this that is critical to the success of the communications that take place within it.

Now let us examine in more detail the consequences of the communications patterns we have discussed.

COMMUNICATIONS PROBLEMS

From all that has been said above, it should be clear that communications in organizations are not perfect. The basic consequence of existing communications systems is that messages are transformed or altered as they pass through the system. The fact that they are transformed means that the ultimate recipient of the message receives something different from what was originally sent, thus destroying the intent of the communication process.

Omission

Guetzkow (1965, p. 551) suggests that there are two major forms of transformation—omission and distortion. Omission involves the "deletion of aspects of messages," and it occurs because the recipient may not be able to grasp the entire content of the message and only receives or passes on what he or she is able to grasp. Communications overload, which will be discussed in more detail later, can also lead to the omission of materials as some messages are not handled because of the overload. Omission may be intentional, as when certain classes of information are deleted from the information passed through particular segments of the organization. Omission is most evident in upward communications, since more messages are generated by the large number of people lower in the hierarchy. As the communications are filtered on the way up, the omissions occur. As was indicated earlier, when omissions are intentional, it is vital to know the criteria for decisions to omit some kinds of information and not others. It should be noted that omission can occur simply as a removal of details, with the heart of the message still transmitted upward. This is the ideal, of course, but is not usually achieved, since part of the content of the message is usually omitted also.

Distortion

Distortion refers to altered meanings of messages as they pass through the organization. From the earlier discussion of perceptions, it is clear that people are selective, intentionally or unintentionally, about what they receive as messages. Guetzkow states that:

> because different persons man different points of initiation and reception of messages, there is much assimilation of meanings to the context within which transmission occurs. Frames of reference at a multitude of nodes differ because of variety in personal and occupational background, as well as because of difference in viewpoint induced by the communicator's position in the organization. (p. 555)

Distortion is as likely to occur in horizontal communications as in vertical, given the differences between organizational units in objectives and values. Selective omission and distortion, or "coding" in Katz and Kahn's terms, are not unique properties of organizations. They occur in all communications systems, from the family to the total society. They are crucial for organizations, however, since organizations depend upon accurate communications as a basis for approaching rationality.

Overload

A communications problem that is perhaps more characteristic of organizations than other social entities is communications overload. Overload, of course, leads to omission and contributes to distortion. It also leads to other coping and adjustment mechanisms on the part of the organization. Katz and Kahn (1978, pp. 449–55) note that there are adaptive and maladaptive adjustments to the overload situation. Omission and distortion are maladaptive. They are also normal.

Another device used when overload occurs is queuing. This technique lines up the messages by time of receipt or some other such criterion. Queuing can have positive or negative consequences. If the wrong priority system is used, less important messages may be acted upon before those that are really crucial reach the recipient. At the same time, queuing does allow the recipient to act on the messages as they come in without putting him in a state of inaction because of total overload. An example of this is an anecdote from a disaster following a major earthquake. Organizations dealing with the earthquake were besieged with messages. Those to which the victims could come and plead for help on a face-to-face basis, crowding into an office and all talking at once, quickly brought the organizations involved to a halt. The overload was so great that the communications could not be filtered in any way. Another organization received its messages by telephone, a device providing an arbitrary queuing mechanism based on an operating phone and the luck of finding an open line. This organization was able to keep functioning, because the messages came in one at a time. In a queuing situation, of course, there are no real criteria concerning which messages get through and which do not, other than time phasing and luck in getting a phone line.

A useful modification of queuing is the filtering process previously mentioned, which involves setting priorities for messages. The critical factor here is the nature of the priorities.

All the communications problems discussed derive from the fact that communications in organizations require interpretation. If there is a case of extreme overload, the interpretive process becomes inundated with so much material that it becomes inoperative. Queuing and filtering are techniques designed to sort messages into priorities. Any priority system established in advance means that an interpretation of messages has already been made, with some deemed more important than others. Decisions made in this regard determine which messages enter the organization and which do not. Thus, interpretation occurs regardless of whether or not priorities are set in advance or simply as messages are received.

Possible Solutions

With all the problems, potential and real, in the communication process, it is obvious that a "perfect" communications system is unlikely. But although perfection, like rationality, will not be achieved, organizations do have mechanisms by which they attempt to keep the communications system as clear as they can. Downs (1967) suggests several devices that are available to reduce the distortions and other complications in the communication process. Redundancy, or the duplication of reports for verification, while adding to the flow of paper and other communications media in an organization, allows more people to see or hear a particular piece of information and respond to it. This is a correction device. Several means are suggested to bring redundancy about, including the use of information sources external to the situation—such as reports that are generated outside the organization itself—thus ensuring that reporting units and individuals coordinate their communications. This coordination can lead to collusion and thus more distortion, but it can be controlled through other monitoring devices.

Downs also suggests that communications recipients should be aware of the biases of the message senders and develop their own counterbiases as a protection device—a process that, of course, can be carried too far and be overdone, but that is the "grain of salt" that is part of all communications. But there is no guarantee that the recipient knows what the sender's biases are. Another method Downs advises is that in vertical communications the superior should often bypass intermediate subordinates and go directly to the source of the communications. While this can help eliminate some distortion, it can also lower morale in those bypassed.

Downs' final suggestion involves the development of distortion-proof messages (pp. 126–27). All organizations use this approach, but it becomes dangerous as soon as the communications begin to deal with areas about which there are uncertainties. Overquantification can be a real danger, and the same is true of present categories that do not fit new or emerging situations. Nevertheless, for many routine events, such a communications device is highly rational.

Hage (1974, p. 241) has suggested that adding communications or coordination and control specialists is another possible answer to communications problems. These would facilitate feedback in the communications process and also enhance the socialization of organization members. Hage also suggests that communications with the external environment are crucial and that the "boundary-spanning" role is crucial to the overall communications viability of the organization. These external relations are the subject of the final two chapters of this book, but it should be obvious that communications must extend outside the organization as well as within.

The nature, problems, and suggested solutions of communications all point to the centrality of this process for much of what happens in an organization. But it is evident that the communications system is vitally affected by other structural and process factors. Communications do not exist outside the total organizational framework. They cannot be over- or underemphasized. More and more accurate communications do not lead inevitably to greater effectiveness for the organization. The key to the communication process in organizations is to ensure that the correct people get the correct information (in amount and quality) at the correct time. All these factors can be anticipated somewhat in advance. If organizations, their members, and their environments were all in a steady state, the communications tasks would be easier. Since obviously they are not, the communication process must be viewed as a dynamic one, with new actors, new media, and new definitions constantly entering the scene.

SUMMARY AND CONCLUSIONS

The communications process in organizations is a complicated one—complicated by the fact that we as individuals have our idiosyncracies, biases, and abilities and complicated by organizational characteristics such as hierarchy or specialization. Nonetheless, communications within organizations are central for the other processes of power, leadership, and decision making. Communications are shaped by organizational structure and continue to reshape structure.

The "perfect" communications system is yet to be devised and probably will never be. The advent of computers in their various forms has contributed to the processing of information, but the issues and problems considered in this chapter are not erased by advanced technology; in fact, in some instances they are exacerbated.

Less than perfect communications systems and the search for improvements contribute to both changes and innovations in organizations. Change and innovation are related to more than communications, however, and it is to this topic that we now turn.

10

Change and Innovation

The analyses of power, leadership, decision making, and communications have stressed the dynamic aspect of organizations. In this chapter, we will analyze the ways in which organizations change. The analysis will consider change per se and then examine innovation in organizations as a less inclusive phenomenon than change in the organization itself. At times change is virtually forced on an unwilling organization, while at other times change is openly embraced and sought. Change can be beneficial or detrimental to organizations. Change can bring growth or decline or an alteration in form.

The Nature of Organizational Change

Organizational change has been approached from a variety of perspectives. Kimberly and Miles (1980) have examined the "life cycle" of organizations. The use of this biological metaphor, which they note is imperfect, sensitizes us to the fact that organizations do not go along in the same state for eternity. While most organizational "deaths" occur among small and new organizations, they also occur among huge and powerful organizations, such as the Penn-Central Railroad. As this is being written, the Chrysler Corporation may be about to receive its last rites and there is a strong indication that the U.S. Department of Education may be dismantled. Kimberly and Miles note: "Organizations are born, grow, and decline. Sometimes they reawaken, and sometimes they disappear" (p. ix).

This fact, of course, is well recognized in the private sector, as investors try to determine which organizations are in a growth phase and which are in the decline phase. While organizational analysts are now turning to an analysis of phenomena such as the organizational life cycle, we have not yet developed the tools by which we can diagnose exactly where an organization is in the cycle at a particular point in time. If we could, of course, we should probably stop being academic organizational analysts and become full-time stock market investors. That consideration aside, growth and decline are important components of organizational change.

There is another important aspect of organizational change not contained in life-cycle analyses. Organizations change in form irrespective of the life cycle. Hage (1980) defines organizational change as "the alteration and transformation of the form so as to survive better in the environment" (p. 262). This is a good definition of organizational change, with a major exception. The exception is that Hage does not consider organizational goals in this formulation of change. As will be argued in detail at a later point, analyses of organizations which do not include the goals of the organization are shortsighted, since organizations engage in many activities and make many decisions which are not related to survival in the environment.

Organizational survival, or the avoidance of death, is, of course, the ultimate test of an organization, but at any point in time, unless death is really imminent, what goes on in an organization is based on both environmental pressures and goals. Changes are made to make more profit or to secure more members. These have both an environmental and goal relationship. While change is frequently discussed, it is also well recognized that organizations are strongly resistant to change.

Resistance to Change

One of the premier analysts of organizational change has been Herbert Kaufman. Kaufman (1971) states: "In short, I am not saying that organizational change is invariably good or bad, progressive or conservative, beneficial or injurious. It may run either way in any given instance. But it is always confronted by strong forces holding it in check and sharply circumscribing the capacity of organizations to react to new conditions— sometimes with grave results" (p. 8).

Kaufman then goes on to describe the factors within organizations that resist change. These include the "collective benefits of stability" or familiarity with existing patterns, "calculated opposition to change" by groups within the organization who may have altruistic or selfish motivations, and a simple "inability to change" (pp. 8–23). The last point refers to the fact that organizations develop "mental blinders" which preclude change capability. These occur as personnel are selected and trained to do what was done in the past in the manner in which it was done. Some people attribute the difficulties of American automobile manufacturers to just this point. People have been hired and trained into executive positions from just one mold and changes were not made at an appropriate point.

Katz and Kahn (1978) approach resistance to change from a slightly different perspective. They suggest that there are six factors that contribute to change resistance:

1. Organizations are "overdetermined." This means that there are multiple mechanisms to ensure stability. Personnel selection, training, and the reward system are designed to lead to stability.
2. Organizations commit the error of assuming local determinism, or believing that a change in one location won't have organization-wide impacts. In addition, a change in local operations can be nullified by the larger organization.
3. There is individual and group inertia. The force of habit is very hard to overcome.
4. Organizational change can threaten occupational groups within organizations. Some specialties can foresee that they will no longer be needed if certain changes are implemented.
5. Organizational change can threaten the established power system. Management, for example, might foresee some of its power going to other groups.
6. Organizational change can threaten those who profit from the present allocation of rewards and resources. This can occur horizontally, between organizational units, as well as on the vertical axis. (pp. 414–15)

The basic point is that organizations by their very nature are conservative. Even organizations that try to have a radical impact on society demonstrate this conservatism. The history of the Christian religion or the Communist party is one of conservatism, with deviants subject to inquisitions, purges, or Siberia.

There are additional factors which contribute to resistance to change. Kaufman (1971, pp. 23–39) calls these "systemic obstacles" to change. These are obstacles within the overall system in which organizations operate. They include such factors as "sunk costs," or investments in the status quo; the accumulation of official constraints on behavior, such as laws and regulations; unofficial and unplanned constraints on behavior in the form of informal customs; and interorganizational agreements, such as labor-management contracts.

Another systemic obstacle to change has to do with resources. Organizations may not have the financial or personnel capabilities to engage in change efforts even if the need is identified. Despite all of these obstacles, of course, organizations do change.

The Change Process

Kaufman concludes that change takes place through personnel turnover. Despite selection and training, differences in people emerge. Kaufman also suggests that change occurs as the obstacles to change are overcome. Recognition of the obstacles contributes to their diminished importance.

A major approach to change has been through the "human relations" approach. This approach has a long tradition, which is well documented by Katz and Kahn (1978) and Perrow (1979). The emphasis in this approach is on changing individuals and groups. The current conclusion is that attempts to create organizational change in this manner is doomed to failure, unless basic changes in the organization itself are accomplished. Katz and Kahn conclude that successful changes involve organizational structure, several methods of change in combination, and inclusion of extrinsic rewards as a potential area of change (pp. 747–49). These changes are also organization-wide or plant-wide in scope and involve changes in technology as well as adaptations to it. What Katz and Kahn mean is that the factors which have been at the heart of the analysis in this book, including structure and technology, are crucial to the change process. Their mention of extrinsic rewards refers to the fact that the human relations approach to change made no mention of factors such as wages and salaries in the attempt to change or motivate people. Katz and Kahn emphasize the fact that organizational change efforts have to be comprehensive and include all aspects of the organization.

There is an additional aspect of organizational change which cannot be overlooked. At times change is forced on an organization. Affirmative action personnel practices have altered many organizations, as have pollution control regulations. Meyer and Rowan (1977) have argued that organizations are sometimes driven to incorporate policies and practices which are a part of the prevailing ethos in the society in which they are embedded. The environment has institutionalized concepts of how organizations should operate and has forced organizations to incorporate the institutionalized practices. For example, some colleges and universities experimented with systems in which no grades were given to students. These experiments have virtually disappeared, as the environment has forced the experimenting institutions back into the traditional grading system. In this case, the environment consists of employers, graduate and professional schools, and significant others, such as parents.

Once a change is implemented, it is not simply put into place. Biggart (1977) has documented the enormous power struggles which took place within the U.S. Postal Service in 1970–1971. She concludes: "The reorganization of the U.S. Postal Service unleashed incredible forces both in and out of the organization; the forces were aimed at protecting or consolidating the power of interest groups" (p. 423). This conclusion is in line with Hage's (1980) emphasis on the importance of interest groups within organizations. These interest groups can be based around occupational specialties or hierarchical position.

We have not adequately addressed the issue of what exactly contributes to overcoming the obstacles to change. This has been hard to analyze at the organizational change level, since most studies of overall change have been case studies that have not lent themselves to generalization. We can get strong clues to the overall change process, however, when we look at findings on innovation in organizations.

Innovation in Organizations

Innovations are departures from the existing practices or technologies. (See Downs and Mohr 1976 for an extensive discussion of the nature of innovation.) Most analyses of innovation have focused on the technological side of the coin, with studies of the patterns by which hospitals adapt new medical techniques or examinations of the patterns of utilization of computers. Other forms of innovation involve organizational practices. Such organizational practices as management by objectives, or MBO (Drucker 1973; Odione 1965), and organizational development, or OD (French 1969), are prime examples. These organizational practices have been largely management tools designed to improve organizational functioning.

Innovations can take a variety of forms. They can vary in their degree of radicalness (Hage 1980, p. 191). A radical innovation is a significant departure from previous practices. Innovations can develop within an organization or be imported from outside. Innovations can also be things that are totally new and never tried before or they can be things that are only new to a particular organization.

Innovations within an organization are not random; innovation occurs in relation to the past and present conditions of the organization. Zaltman, Duncan, and Holbek (1973) suggest that there are three forms of innovation, or change, that can take place in organizations. The first is the programmed innovation that is planned through product or service research and development. Nonprogrammed innovations occur when there is "slack" in the organization in the form of more resources available than are presently needed. These are then used for innovative purposes. They are nonprogrammed because the organization cannot really anticipate when such extra resources will be available. Innovation is distressed when it is forced on the organization through failure and the perceived need to do something about it. Innovations can develop within the organization or be imposed upon it by government agencies or other forces in the environment. As will be seen in the following chapters, these contacts with the environment are of critical importance.

The characteristics of the innovation itself are of critical importance in determining whether or not it will be adapted. Zaltman, Duncan, and Holbek note that the following characteristics of an innovation make them more or less attractive and thus more or less likely to be utilized by an organization:

1. Cost. Cost factors involve two elements, the economic and the social. Economic costs include the initial cost of adapting an innovation or new program and the continuing costs of keeping it in operation. Social costs involve changed status arrangements within the organization as individuals and groups gain or lose power because of the new developments. Either type of cost is likely to be viewed as exorbitant by opponents and minimized by proponents of a proposed change.

211

2. Return on Investment. It is obvious that innovations will be selected which will yield high returns on investments. The situation is much more difficult, when an innovation or technological policy is in the nonbusiness sector.

3. Efficiency. The more efficient innovation will be selected over a less efficient status quo situation or alternative innovation.

4. Risk and Uncertainty. The less the risk and uncertainty, the greater the likelihood of adapting an innovation.

5. Communicability. The clarity of the results is associated with likelihood of innovation.

6. Compatibility. The more compatible the innovation is with the existing system, the more likely it is to be adapted. This, of course, implies that organizations are likely to be conservative in their innovations or technological policies, since what is compatible is unlikely to be radical.

7. Complexity. More complex innovations are less likely to be adapted. Again, this is a strain toward conservativism.

8. Scientific Status. If an innovation is perceived to have sound scientific status, it is more likely to be adapted.

9. Perceived Relative Advantage. The greater the advantage, the more likely that adaption will occur.

10. Point of Origin. Innovations are more likely to be adopted if they originate within the organization. This is based at least partially on the perceived credibility of the source of the innovation.

11. Terminality. This involves the timing of the innovation. In some cases, an innovation is only worthwhile if it is adopted at a particular time or in a particular sequence in the organization's operations.

12. Status Quo Ante. This factor refers to the question of whether or not the decision to innovate is reversible. Can there be a return to the previous state of the organization, or is the decision irreversible? Related to this is the question of whether or not the innovation or technological policy is divisible. Can a little bit at a time be tried, or does a total package have to be adopted?

13. Commitment. This involves behaviors and attitudes toward the innovation. Participation in the decision to innovate tends to raise the commitment of organizational members toward the innovation. A higher level of commitment is associated with more successful innovation.

14. Interpersonal Relations. If an innovation or technological policy is likely to be disruptive to interpersonal relationships, it is less likely to be adopted.

15. Publicness versus Privateness. If an innovation is likely to affect a large part of the public, it will typically involve a larger decision-making body than an innovation that is limited to a private party. The larger decision-making body will tend to impede adoption.

16. Gatekeepers. This refers to the issue of whether or not an innovation must pass through several steps of approval or only one or two. The greater the number of gatekeepers, the more likely that an innovation will be turned down.

17. Susceptibility to Successive Modification. If an innovation itself can be modified as conditions or the technology itself changes, it stands more chance of adoption. This is related to the idea of reversibility, since the organization is not "locked" into a path that might begin to move away from the original objective.
18. Gateway Capacity. The adoption of one innovation or the development of a technological policy is likely to lead to the capacity to involve the organization in additional such actions.
19. Gateway Innovations. This refers to the fact that some innovations, even small changes in an organization's structure, can have the effect of paving the way for additional innovations. (pp. 33–45)

What these characteristics suggest, of course, is that innovations that are less radical are the ones that are most likely to be adopted. Innovations just do not arrive at an organization's doorstep with adaptation automatic. Instead, innovation characteristics interact with organizational characteristics, with both innovation characteristics and organizational conditions embedded in an environmental situation.

Organizational Characteristics

The characteristics of the innovation interact with the characteristics of the innovating organization. Hage and Aiken have found that the following organizational characteristics are related to high levels of innovation (1970):

1. High complexity in the professional training of organizational members.
2. High decentralization of power.
3. Low formalization.
4. Low stratification in the differential distribution of rewards (if high stratification is present, those with high rewards are likely to resist change).
5. A low emphasis on volume (as opposed to quality) of production.
6. A low emphasis on efficiency in the cost of production or service.
7. A high level of job satisfaction on the part of organizational members. (pp. 30–61)

Hage (1980, pp. 205–06) continues this line of reasoning. He argues that more radical innovations will occur when there is a high concentration of cosmopolitan professionals or specialists. Hage also concludes that the values of the dominant coalition are critical. If these values are prochange, then innovation is more likely.

Moch (1976) and Moch and Morse (1977) essentially confirm the directions taken by Hage and Aiken. They find that adaption of innovations is related to organizational size, specialization, differentiation, and decentralization. They also consider the role of values, but focus on the values of lower-level decision makers, whose perspectives and interests must be compatible with the innovation.

There is some controversy regarding the relative importance of organizational characteristics versus the perspectives of organizational members. Baldridge and Burnham (1975), for example, have argued that organizational characteristics are more important to the innovation process than the attitudes of the members of the organization. Hage and Dewar (1973) argue the opposite, that the values of the elites in organizations are more important than structural characteristics. This is another example of the chicken-egg situation, since the interaction of elite values and organizational characteristics is undoubtedly what leads to high or low rates of change. For example, a highly specialized organization headed by a dominant coalition that favors change is much more likely to change than a nonspecialized organization headed by a coalition that values stability. Other combinations of organizational characteristics and elite values would yield different rates of change.

The role of elite values can perhaps be seen more clearly if the process of change and innovation is viewed as a political process within the organization. In a study of the Teacher Corps, a federal program of the 1960s, Corwin (1973) found that the training programs were affected by the political economy of the colleges and universities involved. The economic conditions and the internal politics of the organizations involved affected how the innovation was adopted. Organizations are characterized by power struggles. The outcome of these struggles, together with organizational characteristics, determines whether or not a particular change will be made.

Another important element in the innovation process, ignored thus far, is the environment in which the innovation and the organization are found. In a study done during a period of growth, Daft and Becker (1978) found that innovation increases as incentives for innovation increase, the efficiency of organizational mechanisms for developing innovative alternatives increases, and the presence of organizational characteristics enabling innovation increases. This was a study of schools during a period of relative affluence, with schools being encouraged by federal policies and funds to try new programs. In essence, in this case, success in innovation led to more innovation.

Another study examined innovation in periods of adversity. Manns and March (1978) looked at university departments and found that under adversity, departments tended to increase the variety of course offerings, provide more attractive packaging, make courses more accessible, and increase course benefits, through such mechanisms as credits and grades. A key finding of this study was that strong departments responded to adversity with fewer innovations than the weaker ones. The point here is that in adversity the less successful programs had to innovate more, while the stronger programs were insulated from adversity. The stronger programs had access to alternative sources of resources, such as federal grants.

As noted earlier, innovation can essentially be forced on an organization by other organizations. McNeil and Minihan (1977) document this in a study of hospitals and medical-device manufacturers. Because of the growth of performance standards for hospitals, largely based on federal regulations, there is a growing dependence of the hospitals on the medical-device manufacturers. This dependence is due to the fact that the quality and reliability of the devices is in the hands of the manufacturers and not the hospitals. The adoption of devices, such as body scanners, are forced on hospitals, rather than the hospitals making adoption decisions on their own.

There is an additional environmental influence on innovation. Governmental policies can encourage or discourage innovation (Hall 1981). It has been rather clearly demonstrated (Holden 1980, pp. 751–54) that Japanese governmental policies—including tax, trade, tariff, and regulatory policies—are better coordinated and more conducive to innovation than are those of the United States. The result has been rapid and intense innovation by Japanese business firms.

We have now identified organizational characteristics, elite or dominant coalition values, and environmental conditions as critical factors in the adoption of innovations and in change itself. This has been largely a structural approach to change and innovation.

An alternative approach to these issues is provided by Weick (1979). He views organizations as constantly changing or "enacting" entities. He recognizes the importance of factors such as size and technology, but places much greater emphasis on individual perception and interpretation than has been the case in this analysis. In Weick's approach, constantly shifting constructions of reality within the organization mean that the organization is fluid as the environment is interpreted and enacted. I view organizations as much less fluid, with both structural factors and power arrangements playing key roles in the inhibition of change and innovation.

The innovation process itself is not a simple matter. Zaltman, Duncan, and Holbeck (1973) identified two stages in the innovation process—initiation and implementation. Hage (1980 pp. 209–10) expands the process to four stages—evaluation, initiation, implementation, and routinization. Regardless of the number of stages, there is agreement that successful innovation requires different organizational arrangements for each stage. Thus, decentralization might be most desirable in the initiation stage, while a more centralized approach might be more appropriate for the implementation stage.

SUMMARY AND CONCLUSIONS

This chapter has analyzed both change and innovation from the perspective that there are organizational characteristics which resist and facilitate such processes. From the research findings in regard to innovation we concluded that organizational characteristics, the values of elites and environmental pressures all contribute to change and innovation. Thus far in the book we have been focusing on organizational characteristics, including the interplay between power, leadership, and decision making with elite or dominant coalition values. In the next section we will turn to a specific focus on the environment.

In regard to innovation and change, we can conclude that these are critical processes for organizations. They contribute to growth and survival and death. The purpose here is not to do a life-cycle analysis, but rather to try to demonstrate that these are not trivial processes for organizations. Again, if we could identify exactly what leads to growth or which changes or innovations are going to be successful, we would have the key to understanding and control of organizations. We do not have the key. We do have at least partial answers, however, which, it is hoped, have been identified in the analysis thus far. Bringing in the environment will strengthen our understanding.

IV

Organizational Environments

The critical importance of organizational environments has been suggested throughout this analysis. In this section we will deal specifically with the nature and impact of organizational environments. By environment we mean *"all phenomena that are external to and potentially or actually influence the population under study"* (Hawley 1968, p. 330, italics added). The population under study here, of course, is organizations.

We will deal with the environment in two ways. We will first look at the environment in a rather general way. In this analysis, we will present some research findings and conclusions on the impact of environments on organizations. In the second chapter in this section, we will focus on interorganizational relationships. While almost all organizational environmental phenomena take some kind of organizational form, the focus on interorganizational relationships is designed to indicate that this particular form of social relationship has characteristics that are themselves worthy of study.

Before turning to the materials themselves, one additional comment must be added. The focus of the entire analysis in this book is on organizations. Organizations are the population or unit of analysis. We thus are making the assumption that environments are important to individuals in organizations through the organization itself.

11

The Environment

The conclusion of this chapter should be evident to anyone who has followed the analysis thus far: The environments of organizations are critical factors in understanding what goes on in and about organizations. Said in another way, no organization is an island unto itself. As we will see, some analysts view the environment as the *only* factor necessary for the understanding of organizations. In my view, this is too extreme a position.

The environment appears to have been rediscovered in recent years. The title of books reflects this. Lawrence and Lorsch's *Organization and Environment* (1967), Meyer and Associates' *Environments and Organizations* (1978), Pfeffer and Salancik's *The External Control of Organizations* (1978), and Aldrich's *Organizations and Environments* (1979) are symptomatic of the movement to embrace the importance of the environment.

In reality an emphasis on the environment is not new. Certainly Max Weber's (1947) classical analysis of the rise of capitalist organizations suggests that environmental conditions were no less important in the period following the Protestant Reformation than they are today. As Perrow (1979) points out, some of the more recent "classics," such as Selznick's (1949) *TVA and the Grass Roots* and (1952) *The Organizational Weapon: A Study of Bolshevik Strategy and Tactics* were based on an environmental emphasis. Other important contributions, such as Clark's (1956) analysis for adult education, Gusfield's (1955) study of the Women's Christian Temperance Union, and Janowitz's (1960) conclusions regarding civilian control of the military, all specifically dealt with environmental impacts on the organizations studied.

Why, then, is the environment now being reemphasized? There are many reasons. On the intellectual side there was the realization that the structural analyses of the 1960s and 1970s were not explaining enough of the variance in organizational outputs of all sorts. Research funding was increasingly concerned with factors such as human service delivery, which meant a concern with interorganizational phenomena. Political considerations led many analysts to be concerned with sources of organizational control. A concern with the outcome of organizational actions from a moral point of view led others to examine and question the legitimacy of organizational actions and hence an examination of the environment into which organizational outputs were distributed. There was probably also an element of opportunism among some organizational analysts as they saw the field shifting to a concern with the environment and, they quickly jumped on that bandwagon.

In Chapter 1 we examined the impact of organizations on their environments; here the order is reversed. We will examine the impact of environments on organizations. We will begin by examining some studies that have pinpointed the environmental impact. These studies are mostly recent and will illustrate how the environment is currently being viewed. We will then turn to a more systematic analysis of how the environment affects the growth and development of organizations. We will then attempt to place the environment in usable categories so that it can be more easily understood. Finally, we will look at the manner in which the environment is perceived and reexamine some material on the impact of the environment on the organization. In the final Part of the book we will attempt to merge the environmental factor with other important considerations as we come to grips with organizational effectiveness and organizational theory.

SOME RESEARCH FINDINGS ON THE ENVIRONMENT

In this section a series of research findings will be discussed. There will be no particular order in the presentation. The point is to demonstrate the importance of the environment for organizations. The research studies selected will demonstrate the practical importance of the environment for organizations. We will also see that the relationships analyzed have importance above and beyond organizational analysis.

Hospital costs have increased markedly and alarmingly in the past decade. Part of the reason for the increased costs is increased service. Fennell (1980) found that hospitals expanded their services not because of needs within their patient population but rather because they believed that they would not be judged as fit themselves if they could not offer everything that other hospitals in their area provided. Fennell claims that hospitals are status, rather than market or price, oriented. For our purposes, the environment that is important to such hospitals is other hospitals and those people or groups in the community that are perceived to have budgetary and decision-making power about the hospitals.

Earlier we noted Dubick's (1978) analysis of newspapers in which the absence of competition was found to be related to a lack of coverage of all groups in the community. In this case, competition with other organizations contributes to the good of the community, which is beside the point. The point is that interactions with the environment impinge upon the operations of the newspapers.

In a study of school districts, Freeman (1979) found that "rational" decisions could not be made during a period of decline. When budgets and enrollments drop, rational decisions could be made in regard to programs and personnel which might be terminated. Freeman found that this was not the case. Because of the demands of categorical programs from the federal government, some cuts could not be made in programs with little demand. Interest groups were able to maintain highly specialized programs through their abilities to convince federal program officers to maintain the programs. The cuts in the local school districts reflected external, environmental pressures, rather than the decisions that the school organizations might have made themselves.

Turning to another kind of organization, Whetten (1978) found that the directors of manpower agencies were subject to role conflicts based on environmental pressures. They had to cope with their own staffs, relevant community leaders, and regional and state administrators. In dealing with community leaders, they had to engage in behavior that made them visible to community leaders. Whetten notes that such behavior may or may not be related to organizational tasks. Here Whetten is hinting at the importance of organizational goals, a point that we will stress in subsequent chapters.

Environmental effects are not just a part of the service type organizations which have been discussed. Pearson (1978) found that uranium mines did not make expenditures for remedial technology to combat injuries and disease until there was governmental (environmental) pressure. In addition to governmental pressures, the uranium mines were also subject to economic pressures such as lower demand, higher compensation claims, and an industry shift away from small mines. This particular study raises the interesting question of the role of government in the protection of workers, but for our purposes it offers yet another example of the ways in which organizational environments impinge upon operations.

Organizational responses to environmental pressures are not automatic nor necessarily rational. McNeil and Miller (1980) have documented the manner in which United States automobile manufacturers have not responded organizationally to the pressure of foreign imports. The United States firms use a short-term accounting system, with a heavy emphasis on cost control. The emphasis is on immediate financial return on sales, service, and warranty work. According to McNeil and Miller, the continued adherence to this particular sort of accounting system may "blind the industry to the long-term ramifications of the coming era" (p. 426). There is an irony here in that the short-term accounting system was itself a response to earlier crises of the 1920's.

We have noted that organizations can engage in illegal acts. Staw and Szwajkowski (1975) have found that activities such as unfair market practices and restraint of trade are related to environmental conditions. When resources in the environment are scarce, there is a greater tendency for illegal acts to occur.

There is another line of research that throws additional light on the environment-organization relationship. At an earlier point we noted that national cultures appear to have an impact on organizational form. Ouichi and Johnson (1978) found different control structures in a comparison of Japanese and American firms. Even though McMillan, et al. (1973); Hickson, et al. (1974); Tracy and Azumi (1976); and Lincoln Olson, and Hanada (1978) report that cultural effects do not affect the relationships among structural variables in a statistical sense, there are cultural differences that show up in the particular configurations of structure in these two societies. Maurice, Sellier, and Silvestre (1980) have demonstrated that differences in social class relationships between France and Germany are reflected in the hierarchical patterns in organizations in those countries. Meyer and Rowan's (1977) notion that organizational structures are a "myth" based on the prevalent values in a society is potentially relevant here. It seems inappropriate to label the fact of structure as a myth, but the point that structures will conform to prevailing values is not a myth.

These research findings provide a solid basis for concluding that the environment of organizations has a critical impact on the organizations themselves. The manner in which the environment affects organizations can be further understood when some analyses of the development of organizations are considered.

The Environment and the Development of Organizations

Arthur Stinchcombe (1969) has examined the interface between organizations and the social structure. In a discussion of organizational development and historical conditions, Stinchcombe maintains that

> it seems that in some societies the rate at which special purpose organizations take over various social functions (economic production, policing, education, political action, military action, etc.) is higher than in other societies, and that within societies some population groups are more likely to found new types of organizations to replace or supplement multiple-purpose groups such as families or geographical communities for certain purposes. (p. 143)

According to this approach, in order to develop a new organization a population must be *aware* of alternative techniques for accomplishing some task or set of tasks in the society. This means that the traditional approaches are at least being questioned, the population concerned is in contact with other ideas, and there are some possibilities for change within the society. The alternative of developing a new form of organization must be viewed as *attractive* in terms of a cost-benefit analysis; that is, the social and economic costs associated with starting a new organization must be less than the benefits it is expected to yield. Stinchcombe also points out that the benefits are expected to go to those engaged in organizational development rather than to other groups in the society. Another important condition is that the people involved have to have sufficient *resources*—such as wealth, power, legitimacy, and strength of numbers—to get the new organization off the ground. (Kimberly, 1975)

> In societies where most of the land passes through inheritance and is not freely alienable outside the family, where labor's obedience is to its traditional lord rather than to the highest bidder, where wealth stays in bags in the lord's warehouse to be used to support retainers rather than for investment, the rate of organization formation is low. (Stinchcombe, 147)

The final condition is that those seeking to establish the new organization must have the *power* to defeat those interested in maintaining the older system.

These conditions necessary for the start of a new organization have not been distributed randomly throughout history, but they are present in sufficient degrees to allow many new organizations and new organizational forms to develop at many points in time. Stinchcombe notes that new organizations are more likely to survive over time than are new organizational forms. Similarly, new organizations, and more particularly new organizational forms, have a higher organizational death rate than old organizations or old organizational forms. This "liability of newness" is indicative of the inherently conservative nature of society.

The reasons for the liability of newness are found in the social relations that are part of the larger society and in the behaviors of the members of the new organizations and organizational forms. In the first place, new *roles* have to be learned in new settings. These cannot be the traditional passing on of skills and behaviors; the new organization must rely on general skills possessed by the population. This again means that the nature of the population surrounding the organization is vital for its development and form. If not enough people have the requisite general skills, the new organizations will have extreme difficulties in accomplishing their tasks and thus will probably not survive.

The fact that new roles have to be learned leads to other organizational problems. There is likely to be little of the semiautomatic communication and interaction that characterize mature organizations. In a totally new organization, where the new roles are not yet part of the repertoire of the personnel, the whole system is apt to be barely operative *until the roles and role relationships are learned.* This can be accomplished by the imposition of the organizational structure, but this, too, must be learned and must also coincide in some degree with the behaviors and expectations of the organization members. Stinchcombe notes that if the people coming into the organization have skills and values that are relevant for the organization, the task of developing the organization is simpler. The liability of newness is reduced when there is a "disciplined and responsible work force" (Stinchcombe, 149).

Another characteristic of new organizations is that they involve *social relations among strangers*, without the trust that is generated by long years of association. Here again, the state of the society makes a difference. If the general social relations are characterized by universalistic religious and legal codes that make oaths sacred and laws binding, and by achievement norms that are stronger than kinship ties, the liability of newness will be reduced. Social relations in these situations will be built around the current situation, rather than on past experiences and expectations. Strangers can interact with more trust, allowing the organization to get off the ground more easily.

New organizations suffer another drawback in that *they do not have established ties with the larger society*. There are no steady customers or clients. If the social system is one in which the use of alternative organizations for common tasks is an accepted thing, new organizations will have an easier time establishing themselves. It will not be as unusual for customers and clients to try alternative organizations for supplying their products and services.

This analysis makes it clear that the conditions under which organizations and organizational forms are likely to develop are not constant for all times and places. While the points made are clearest in a cross-cultural and historical perspective, it should also be apparent that within one society and in a relatively short period of time, conditions can change sufficiently to produce intrasocietal differences in the rates of organizational development.

Other Environmental Conditions   The conditions just discussed do not exist independently of other environmental characteristics. They are in fact intermediate variables between some basic environmental characteristics and the rate of organizational development. One major societal determinant of the other variables of organizational development is the general literacy and specialized advanced schooling of the population. The presence of literacy raises the likelihood that each of the intermediate variables will be sufficiently present for organizational development to occur. Stinchcombe states that

> literacy and schooling raise practically every variable which encourages the formation of organizations and increases the staying power of new organizations. It enables more alternatives to be posed to more people. It facilitates learning new roles with no nearby role model. It encourages impersonal contact with customers. It allows money and resources to be distributed more easily to strangers and over distances. It provides records of transactions so that they can be enforced later, making the future more predictable. It increases the predictability of the future environment of an organization by increasing the available information and by making possible a uniform body of law over a large area. (pp. 150–51)

In addition to the key variable of education and literacy, several other factors are crucial for the conditions permitting organizational formation.

Urbanization is a second factor identified by Stinchcombe in this regard. He notes that the rate of urbanization should be slow enough to allow the rural migrants to learn and develop routines of urban living. At the same time, the development of urban life is associated with greater heterogeneity of lifestyle, thus providing more alternative working and living arrangements. The urban scene is one of dealing with strangers, and this too assists organizational development, since ascriptive role relationships are likely to be minimized. Impersonal laws are necessary in urban areas just as they are in organizations. Urbanization, like education, increases the organizational capacity of populations, although not to the same degree, according to Stinchcombe.

Another important condition, and one that has long been identified, is the presence of a *money economy*. This sort of economy

liberates resources so that they can be more easily recruited by new organizations, facilitates the formation of free markets so that customers can transfer loyalties, depersonalizes economic social relations, simplifies the calculation of the advantages of alternative ways of doing things, and allows more precise anticipation of the consequences of future conditions on the organization. (Stinchcombe, p. 152)

The *political base* of a society is also important. For the creation of a new organization, political revolutions are held to be important because of their rearranging of vested interest groups and power systems. Resources are allocated on bases different from those in the past.

The final societal condition identified by Stinchcombe is the existing level of *organizational density*. The greater the density and the greater the range of organizational alternatives already available, the greater the likelihood that people will have had experience in organizations. This suggests that there is likely to be an exponential growth curve for organizations in a society—assuming, of course, that the other conditions are also present.

Stinchcombe's discussion is concerned with the conditions of the society that are important for the development of new organizations and new organizational forms. These conditions are components of those discussed earlier in this chapter—the contemporary environmental conditions that are important for the life of an organization. While the picture is drawn in broader relief with historical data, the factors identified remain important for analyses at any particular point in time.

Technology and Organizational Form   Stinchcombe's article contains an additional set of ideas that is relevant for our purposes. He maintains that the technological conditions available at the time of the formation of an organization set the limits for the form the organization can take.

Organizations which have purposes that can be efficiently reached with the socially possible organizational forms tend to be founded during the period in which they become possible. Then, both because they can function effectively with those organizational forms and because the forms tend to become institutionalized, the basic structure of the organization tends to remain relatively stable. (p. 153)

The emphasis on technology is consistent with the argument here, with the addition that if the newly introduced organizational form is compatible with the technology of the times, it tends to persist over time regardless of gradual changes in technology.

Pennings (1980a, pp. 144–60) approaches the development of new organizations from a slightly different perspective than Stinchcombe's. Pennings' focus is on urban environments in which organizations develop. He suggests four factors as the determinants of organizational "births." First is the *urban level* which involves urban size and differentiation. Second is the *population level*. Here Pennings is referring to the population of organizations in terms of existing organizations and their size and stage of development. Lincoln (1979) pursued this line of reasoning and found that the density of organizations contributed to organizational differentiation through competition. Pennings next suggests that *economic resources* must be considered. Savings and venture capital, governmental tax support, and governmental regulations and programs are included here. Finally, *social resources* must be present. These include an entrepreneurial climate, the presence of colleges and universities and other innovation producing organizations, the educational level of the population, the centrality of the urban area in regard to its region or nation, and the general quality of life.

Pennings' approach is one of environmental determinism. This extreme emphasis on the importance of the environment is countered somewhat by Kimberly's (1980) analysis of the creation of a new medical school. Kimberly places heavy weight on the importance of individual entrepreneurship in the success of the organization that he studied. While the earlier analysis here warns against too great a reliance on "the leader," at the time of the emergence of an organization such an individual would appear to be of critical importance as Kimberly's analysis demonstrates.

Marrett's (1980) study of the emergence of new organizations takes us an additional step in understanding the environment and the emergence of organizations. In her study of women's medical societies she found that it was the presence of similar organizations and not the overall level of organizational activity that was critical for the emergence of the medical organizations. The presence of other similar organizations permits people to develop skills and social ties which aid in the development of new organizations.

The emphasis in the analyses which have been discussed in this section has been on the development of new organizations and new organizational forms. The implication is that the environment at the time of organizational formation is critical for the form that the organization takes and that this form persists over time. According to Meyer and Brown (1977), this is overly simplified. They demonstrate that the conditions surrounding the origins of an organization do persist in their impact on the organization, but that these conditions are constantly being confronted with ongoing environmental conditions. Thus, the organizational—environmental relationship is dynamic.

Thus far we have treated the environment in a rather undifferentiated manner. In the next section we will consider two ways in which the environment can be viewed along various dimensions.

ENVIRONMENTAL DIMENSIONS

In this section we will identify environmental dimensions in two ways. First, we will examine the environment in terms of its content, including technological and economic considerations. Then we will consider the environment from a more analytical perspective in terms of factors such as the stability or turbulence of the environment.

Technological Conditions

Probably the easiest place to begin the discussion of the general environment is with *technology*. Since this topic and the research surrounding it have already been the subject of much attention, it can set the stage for the less systematically researched topics that follow.

It will be remembered, following the works of Perrow, Lawrence and Lorsch, and others, that organizations operating in an uncertain and dynamic technological environment exhibit structures and internal processes different from those operating in a rather certain and unchanging technological situation. While we need not at this point review the direction of the relationships and the supporting evidence, it is important to recognize that the organization responds to this aspect of its environment. In fact, in the business firms Lawrence and Lorsch studied, special organizational divisions were established (research and development) to keep the organization current. In other organizations, departments such as industrial engineering, management analysis, and so on, are so designated.

Beyond their empirical evidence that technology is salient in the operation of organizations, these findings have implications vital to our understanding of organizational–environmental transactions. In the first place, technology and other environmental characteristics are something "out there." The organization does not exist in a vacuum. A technological development in any sphere of activity will eventually get to the organizations related to it. New ideas come into circulation and become part of the environment as soon as they cease being the private property of any one individual or organization. Since the sciences have a norm of distributing knowledge, scientific developments become part of the public domain as a matter of course. A development that can be patented is a different matter, but if it is thought to be significant, other organizations will seek to copy it or further extend the previous development. In either case, an organization must keep up with such developments in any activity crucial to its continued success.

More subtle forms of the technological environment are found outside the hard sciences and engineering. In management and administration, new ideas are introduced through research, serendipity, or practice. In service-oriented organizations, such as schools, social-work agencies, and hospitals, the same types of technological shifts can be seen. Through one mechanism or another, the organization in any sphere of activity is made aware of technological developments that are or can be part of its own activities. An important mechanism appears to be the introduction of new personnel or clients who have had contact with alternative technologies and advocate their use in the organization in question. This, of course, can be a source of conflict in the organization, as can the technology-development and monitoring departments.

Organizations do not respond to technological change through absorption. Instead, the organization's political process operates through the advocacy of change or stability. Organizations of every kind contain their own internal "radicals" and "reactionaries" in terms of their responses to technological and other environmental conditions. Since the rate of technological and other environmental changes is not constant for all organizations, the degree to which they must develop response mechanisms varies. For all, however, technology remains an important consideration.

Legal Conditions

An environmental consideration often overlooked but potentially critical is the *legal conditions* that are part of the organization's surroundings. Most organizations that operate outside the law respond to the legal system by their attempts to evade the law and remain underground. Organizations such as voluntary associations with a strictly local base may be relatively unaffected by legal considerations until laws are passed that affect their operations, or until they become developed to the point that they must register with one or another government agency. Airlines, for instance, must comply with safety, rate, alcoholic beverage, and a host of other laws and regulations. Since almost all organizations are affected directly or indirectly by the legal system, this fact must be introduced into the analysis. (For a moment, we will ignore the fact that regulated industries appear to have a great deal of control over their respective regulatory agencies.)

Many, probably most, organizations must live with federal, state, and local laws as constants in their environments. At the very least, they set many of the operating conditions of many organizations, ranging from specific prohibitions of certain kinds of behavior to regulations requiring reporting of income and staffing at periodic times of the year. The importance of laws is shown by the staffs of legal and other experts who form an important part of many organizations and who are specifically charged with interpreting and protecting the organizations' positions.

While the body of laws as a constant is an interesting analytical point, the dynamic aspect of the legal system points up the importance of laws for organizations. When a new law is passed or an interpretation modified, organizations must make some important changes if the law has relevance for them. Here again, relatively mundane matters such as tax and employment regulations are important. More striking are the cases of major shifts that affect organizations in the public and private sectors. For example, U.S. Supreme Court decisions regarding school desegregation have had tremendous impacts on the school organizations involved. The recent concern with the environment has resulted in laws and regulations concerning pollution that have affected many organizations as they utilize their resources in fighting or complying with the new statutes. Laws are thus important external constraints on organizations.

Political Conditions

Laws are not passed without pressure for their enactment. The *political situation* that brings about new laws also has its effects on organizations. To use the pollution example again, the political pressures brought by various conservation groups concerned about potential pollution has contributed in part to a real shortage of electrical power. The strong political pressures to reduce military and aerospace spending have led to crises of one sort or another for organizations in those areas. Police departments are buffeted back and forth between support for "law and order" and condemnation of "police brutality." School systems have drastically altered parts or all of their curricula in the face of threats from groups concerned with such topics as sex education or "left-wing" text-books. Some organizations are directly affected by the political process because their hierarchy can be drastically changed by election results. All government units face this possibility after every election as top officials are changed at the discretion of a new administration.

Organizations in the private sector are less directly affected than public ones, but they must still be attuned to the political climate. Since lobbying for legislation that will be favorable in terms of tax advantages or international trade agreements is an accepted part of the legislative and administrative system of the United States, organizations must devote resources to the lobbying process. The widespread illegal corporate contributions to domestic and foreign political parties and individuals is further evidence of the importance of the political factor for organizations. "Institutional advertising" is designed to generate some form of public support for the organization involved, as exemplified by the large amounts of money spent by oil companies during petroleum crises. This evidence points up the importance of the political process in the wider society for the organizations contained in it.

Economic Conditions

A societal condition that is more obvious, but again strangely neglected by most sociologists, is the state of the *economy* in which the organization is operating. To most business leaders, this is the crucial variable. In universities and in government work, experience also shows the importance of economic conditions when budgets are being prepared, defended, and appropriated in nonindustrial areas. Changing economic conditions serve as important constraints on any organization. Much of the earlier discussion of organizational size was based on the assumption that an organization has the economic capability to increase in size. In periods of economic growth, organizations, in general, also grow—and vice versa.

The economy is important for organizations in more than its relationship to gross size. Changing economic conditions do not affect all parts of an organization equally. In periods of economic distress, an organization is likely to cut back or eliminate those programs it feels are least important to its overall goals, except, of course, for those instances in which external political pressures preclude such "rational" decisions (Freeman 1979). Economic affluence permits government agencies to engage in a wider range of programs. Klatzky (1970) found that state employment agencies in wealthier states provided unemployment insurance to a greater proportion of the unemployed than did the agencies in the poorer states. Since these agencies were paying out more, they also received a disproportionately larger share of federal funds than their less affluent peers in other states. The rich agencies get rich as the poor agencies get poor. This might well change as there is a movement to an economy of no growth, in which abundance is replaced by scarcity. Economic shifts of this sort will have a clear impact on organizational behavior and values (Scott 1974).

Changing economic conditions are, in fact, excellent indicators of the priorities of organizations. That organizational programs vary according to the economic conditions that are confronted contributes to a paradox for most organizations. Since total rationality is not an assumption of this analysis, it can be safely assumed that an organization cannot be sure of exactly what contribution each of its parts makes to the whole. For example, research and development can be viewed as one of the luxuries that should go when an organization faces some hard times. But by concentrating on the production and distribution of what R&D has done in the past, the organization may miss the development of a new product that would be of great long-run benefit. People in health-related research sponsored by the federal government have claimed that cutbacks in these activities have come at a time when crucial breakthroughs are about to be made. Here again, the decision is made on the economic ground that other activities are of greater importance. Tragic (and sometimes humorous) examples such as these could be given for probably every kind of organization. Periods of economic difficulty do force organizations to evaluate their priorities and trim off excess fat, if any is found. As in the case of the communication process, the criteria by which the evaluations are accomplished are the key variables.

Economic conditions surrounding organizations improve and decline with the organizations responding to the situation. In their responses in any situation, the important factor of competition is present. Economic competition can be most easily seen in business organizations, where success is measured in the competitive marketplace. While the competition is not "pure," it is still an evident part of the value systems in a private-enterprise economy. What is less evident, but equally real, is economic competition among and within organizations outside the business sphere.

From repeated experiences in government agencies at several levels, it is clear that competition is fierce during budget season (Wildavsky 1964). Government agencies are all competing for part of the tax revenues, which constitute a finite "pot." Organizations that rely on contributions from members, such as churches, are also affected by the general economic conditions, since the contributors have more or less income available. An interesting research question is the extent to which the severity of economic competition varies among organizations in all sectors of society. It seems almost equal, regardless of the organization's major emphases.

Demographic Conditions

Demography is another factor. The number of people served, and their age and sex distributions, make a great deal of difference to all organizations. As a general rule, an organization can predict its probable "market" for the future from information in census data, but population shifts are less predictable and make the organization more vulnerable. In a society where race, religion, and ethnicity are important considerations, shifts in these aspects of the demographic condition must also be considered. The most striking examples of the importance of demographic change come from organizations located in the central cities of growing metropolitan areas. Businesses, schools, and police departments have different clientele from what they once had, even though the organizations themselves might not reflect this. At least in the short run, it is the urban poor and minority-group members who suffer the consequences. The organizations themselves, however, eventually undergo transitions (usually painful) as they begin to realize that their clientele has become different and that they themselves must change.

Ecological Conditions

Related to the demographic scene is the general *ecological situation* surrounding an organization. The number of organizations with which it has contacts and relationships and the environment in which it is located are components of the organization's social ecological system. In an urban area, an organization is much more likely to have contacts with a myriad of other organizations than is one in a rural area. Since the density of other organizations around any particular organization varies widely, the potential for relationships also varies.

Shifting from social ecology to the physical environment, the relationships between organizations and ecological conditions become more evident because of the recent concerns about the total ecological system. It is increasingly clear that organizations have effects on the environment, as is abundantly demonstrated by the various organizations that pollute and the others that fight pollution.

A more subtle point is that the environment affects organizations. Factors such as climate and geography set limits on how they allocate resources. Transportation and communciation costs rise if an organization is distant from its market or client. Even such mundane items as heating and cooling expenses must be considered limits on an organization. Although these factors are generally constants, since only in unusual circumstances are there significant changes, these conditions cannot be ignored in a total organizational analysis involving comparisons between organizations.

Cultural Conditions

The environmental conditions discussed thus far are fairly easily measured in terms of "hard" indicators of the degree to which they are present or absent. A more difficult task is to determine the extent to which they actually affect the organizations in a social system. For the present it has to be assumed that they make a difference, even though we cannot specify which is more important than the others in particular situations. Other conditions in the external environment that are vitally important are more difficult to measure. The first of these is the *culture* surrounding an organization. The experiences of multinational firms provide common-sense examples of the importance of cultural differences. Unless the values and behaviors of the indigenous population are understood and appreciated, such projects are likely to fail.

While the influence of the culture is now an accepted fact, it is not clear whether culture overrides other factors in determining how an organization is shaped and operates. There is evidence suggesting that organizations at an equivalent technological level—for example, at the same degree of automation of production—are quite similar in most respects, as was indicated in the chapter on structure. The basic problem is to sort out the influences of these various environmental factors as they impinge on the organization. Unfortunately, not enough is yet known for such fine distinctions to be made. The various factors discussed so far probably interrelate in their organizational effects in a rather complex interaction pattern. For example, it appears that the more routine and standardized the technology, the less the impact of cultural factors. The production of children's toy automobiles is probably carried out in similar organizations in Hong Kong, London, Japan, Switzerland, or Tonka, Minnesota. When one moves to less routinized technological operations, such as local government, the administration of justice, or highway construction, the impact of culture is likely to be higher.

The complexity of the issue can be seen when it is realized that we are dealing with only two of the variables we have discussed in these examples. If the other factors are added, the picture is much more difficult to comprehend. As research proceeds and some quantitative measures of the variables discussed become available, the complex interactions will be more understandable.

In its impact on organizations, culture is not a constant, even in a single setting. Values and norms change as events occur that affect the population involved. If they involve conditions relevant to the organization, these shifts are significant for it. Newspaper editorials, letters to the editor, and other colorations of reports in the mass media indicate how values can change in regard to particular organizations or types of organizations. These value shifts may precede or accompany political shifts, which would have a more direct kind of impact. Changes in consumer tastes represent another way that cultural conditions can affect organizations. Examples of this are easily found; a dramatic one is that of the contrasting experiences with the Edsel and Mustang cars by the Ford Motor Company.

Another approach to analyzing environment dimensions has been developed by Aldrich (1979, pp. 63–70). His approach can be intertwined with the distinctions among the environmental elements just considered.

Environment Capacity

The capacity of an environment refers to its "richness" or "leanness," or the level of resources available to an organization. According to Aldrich:

Organizations have access to more resources in rich environments, but such environments also attract other organizations. Stockpiling and hoarding of resources is probably not as prevalent in rich as in lean environments. Lean environments also promote cut-throat competitive practices, and apart from rewarding organizations capable of stockpiling and hoarding, lean environments reward efficiency in the use of resources. Two alternatives are open to organizations in lean environments: move to a richer environment, or develop a more efficient structure. The latter alternative can be accomplished by improving operating practices, merging with other organizations, becoming more aggressive vis-à-vis other organizations, or moving to a protected subenvironment through specialization. (p. 63)

Examples of such organizational responses are evident in many different cases. American Airlines moved its corporate headquarters from New York City to Dallas. Although the terms rich and lean environment were not used, the reasons given for the move essentially had that meaning, with the airline citing access to qualified personnel and more modern facilities as reasons for the move. At times, some of the responses which Aldrich suggests are not possible. Legal requirements, for example, may prevent merger because of the threat of monopoly. In such cases, as Pfeffer and Nowak (1976) point out, organizations may engage in joint ventures. Joint ventures involve the investment of resources from several organizations in a single large project, such as the Concorde airplane developed by France and England.

Environmental Homogeneity-Heterogeneity

This dimension refers to the degree of similarity or differentiation within a population of organizations, individuals, or other social units. According to Aldrich, a homogeneous environment is simpler for organizations, since standardized ways of responding can be developed. Many organizations attempt to make their environment more homogeneous by limiting the kinds of clients served, markets entered, and so on. Social service organizations consistently attempt to make their environment homogeneous by referring clients that do not fit within their operations to other social service organizations. The result of this, of course, is that the most difficult clients get referred and referred and referred.

Environmental Stability-Instability

This refers to the extent of turnover of elements or parts of the environment. Stability, like homogeneity, permits standardization. Instability leads to unpredictability, which organizations resist. Any aspect of an organization's environment can be stable or unstable, whether it be economic, legal, or technological conditions.

Environmental Concentration-Dispersion

Concentration or dispersion in the environment involves the distribution of the elements in the environment. Are they located in one place or are they scattered across a large area? It is easier for an organization to operate with a more concentrated environment, as in the case of customers or clients.

Domain Consensus-Dissensus

Organizations claim a domain or market. This dimension refers to the degree to which these claims are recognized or disputed by other parties, such as governmental agencies. If all interested parties agree that a particular organization has the right and obligation to operate in a particular way in a particular area, there is domain consensus. This is the dimension that involves organizational "turf."

It is evident that the very nature of private enterprise involves domain dissensus. It is also evident that many business firms seek to achieve consensus by having protective legislation or regulations passed in their behalf. Import quotas and tariffs are examples of this. In the public sector, organizations, there are domain fights as new organizations are created, threatening the existence of older participants in an area. Many of the failures of governmental social service programs can be attributed to domain fights with entrenched agencies that did not cooperate with new programs, such as Model Cities.

Environmental Turbulence

This is the most difficult of Aldrich's dimensions to understand, since the idea of turbulence seems a great deal like instability. Turbulence here means that there is a great deal of causal interconnection among the elements in the environment. In a turbulent environment there is a high rate of environmental interconnection. An economic shift has political and technological ramifications in a turbulent environment. The movement of business firms from the Northeast to the Sun Belt in the United States is an example of such turbulence. These moves have lowered the tax base in the Northeast, forcing raises in the tax rates to maintain essential and nonessential services which in turn leads to additional decisions to move. The effect of such moves spin off into other sectors, such as education, health, and social services.

It would be possible to merge the two sets of dimensions that have been identified. Thus, technological conditions could be analyzed in terms of homogeneity, capacity, stability, and so on. A 7×6 matrix could be constructed to demonstrate all the possibilities. This will not be done, however, since this would simply be an exercise of little relevance to reality. As will be seen shortly, organizations tend to simplify the complexity of their environments. While all of the dimensions that we have identified are important from an analytical standpoint, they are not used this way in practice.

Before turning to an analysis of how the environment is perceived by the organization, one other distinction about the environment should be made. Jurkovich (1974) developed a typology of organizational environments that is similar to Aldrich's in many ways. Jurkovich includes a consideration that has thus far been neglected—whether the environment itself is organized. This can be seen to be important in instances of consumers, where organized consumers can be more threatening to an organization than nonorganized individuals. Rather obviously, most environmental pressures come from other organizations in the form of government agencies, competing organizations, cultural organizations, and the like. When we examine interorganizational relationships in the next chapter, the specific linkages between organizations and their counterparts will be analyzed in detail. Here it is sufficient to note that whether the environmental elements are organized or not is a consideration that should not be overlooked.

THE PERCEPTION OF THE ENVIRONMENT

We have been proceeding as though the environment is something "out there" beyond the organization, which anyone in the organization can readily spot and identify. It would be handy if this were the case but it is not. The environment comes into the organization as information and like all information, is subject to the communications and decision-making problems which have been identified.

People have different positions in organizations. Some people are designated as "gate keepers" (Nagi 1974) or "boundary spanners" who are designated to admit certain information that is relevant to the organization. Their perceptions are influenced by their positions within the organization (Leifer and Huber 1977). Of course, the very definition of where the organization stops and the environment begins is open to question.

Starbuck (1976) has pointed out that different positions are at an organization's boundaries, depending on what the activity at the moment is. At times it is the switchboard operator, while at other times it is the president or chief executive officer.

According to Starbuck (pp. 1078–80), an organization *selects* those aspects of the environment with which it is going to deal. The selection process is affected by the selection processes of other organizations with which it is in contact. At the same time, of course, interorganizational linkages are affected by environmental pressures (Provan, Beyer, and Kruytbosch 1980). In this manner, organizations go about constructing or inventing their environments. Meyer (1975a) finds that the scope of the domain or environment claimed or selected by organizations has an impact on its operations. Narrow domain claims are associated with stability and broad and inconsistent claims with loss of functions. Broad claims coupled with technological capacity and newness lead to domain expansion. Meyer concludes that domain claims actually seldom contract.

Contemporary organizational theory has been stressing perceived uncertainty in the environment (Duncan 1973; Leifer and Huber 1977). It is equally important to stress the fact that much of the environment that is perceived is actually certain, rather than uncertain. Colleges and universities, for example, face a certain demographic profile of the number and distribution of potential students. Business firms face a rather certain environment of governmental regulations. The environment is thus both uncertain and certain; the key factor is the perceptions of this and the resultant actions.

Just as the perceptions of individuals are shaped by their experiences, so, too, are organizations. Starbuck maintains (1976, pp. 1080–81) that organizations are *more* realistic than individuals because of their constant comparisons with and sharing personnel among comparable organizations. Whether or not this is the case has not yet been demonstrated. It must be remembered that the perceivees of the environment are themselves individuals, with all of their (our) idiosyncracies in perception. McNeil (1978) claims that organizational managers seek to extend their power in the environment. If this is the case, then their actions and those of their organizations will be based on power acquisition and their perceptions will reflect this power orientation.

THE IMPACT OF THE ENVIRONMENT ON THE ORGANIZATION

What do all of these environmental factors, however selected and perceived, do to organizations? There are several answers. In the first place, organizations vary in their vulnerability to environmental pressures (Jacobs 1974). The more dependent an organization is on its environment, the more vulnerable it is. An organization with strong financial resources is less vulnerable to economic fluctuations than is one with no reserves. In the 1970s and early 1980s, petroleum manufacturers were highly dependent and vulnerable to political shifts in their sources of raw materials and their markets. These firms attempt to manipulate their environment by stabilizing the political conditions.

When an organization is vulnerable, it reacts to the environment. Several studies have shown that strong environmental pressures are related to increased formalization and a general "tightening" of the organization (see Freeman 1973; Khandwalla 1972; Boddewyn 1974; and Pfeffer and Leblebici 1973). It is odd that the environmental pressures do this, since in many ways the loosely coupled organization is more adaptive to the environment and is more likely to develop innovations that might be beneficial over the long run (Weick 1976). Organizations that are vulnerable to the environment, of course, face a greater risk of failure if an innovation happens not to be successful.

There are more measures of environmental impact than vulnerability alone. To focus only on this feature logically leads to a Darwinian conclusion that a natural selection process would occur, with only the fittest surviving. This natural selection approach has become a dominant aspect of organizational theory (Aldrich and Pfeffer 1976; Aldrich 1979) and will be considered in detail in the last chapter.

Every organization is dependent on its environment to some degree. Each adapts internal strategies to deal with the perceived pressures (Snow and Hrebreniak 1980). Contingency theory strongly suggests that there is no single best way to cope with environmental pressures. The specific stance that an organization takes derives from choices that are made within it. This decision-making process is a political one in the sense that different particular options are supported by different factions within the decision-making structure. The option finally selected is a consequence of the power of individuals and groups that support it. That environmental pressures often tighten the organization may be a consequence of the fact that this is the option that powerful segments of organizations have traditionally taken. It may not be the one most useful for the organization, of course.

Among the strategies that organizations develop for dealing with their environments, a critical one is to attempt to shape the environment itself. As noted earlier, Hirsch (1975) has shown that the typical pharmaceutical manufacturing firm has been more successful than the typical firm in the phonograph record industry largely because the pharmaceutical firms have been able to control relevant aspects of their environments. The pharmaceutical firms could exert control over pricing and distribution, patent and copyright laws, and external opinion leaders. This control of the environment was a source of greater profitability. Organizations attempt to gain and maintain power over environmental conditions that are of strategic importance to them. In a situation of scarce resources, organizations may also resort to illegal acts such as price-fixing or other activities to restrain trade. Thus, like the development of internal organizational power in which successful coping with strategic contingencies is linked to the development of power, so in its interactions with the environment the organization must be able to cope with and control external strategic and important contingencies.

SUMMARY AND CONCLUSIONS

Throughout the present analysis we have identified other environmental impacts on the structure and process of organizations. Pfeffer and Salancik (1978) suggest that organizations are *controlled* by environmental contingencies. Others, such as McNeil (1978) and Perrow (1979) suggest the opposite—that organizations control the environment. The truth of the matter probably lies somewhere between these extremes. Some organizations are controlled at some times; others control at some times. It is quite possible that an organization could move from one position to another, gaining or losing power in the environment. American automobile manufacturers appear to have lost significant power as regulation, competition, and apparent ineptitude have occurred. Regulation and competition are environmental controls; ineptitude is not. By the same token, banks and other financial institutions seem to have retained their power and are not in a controlled situation. Part of the reason for this is the pattern of interorganizational linkages which they have been able to develop, as will be demonstrated in the next chapter.

In this chapter we have examined some of the impacts of the environment on organizations. We also noted the impact of the environment on the development of organizations and considered the various dimensions of the environment. The analysis has been on the general environment of organizations. In the next chapter we will consider the *specific* environment of organizations—other organizations.

12

Interorganizational Relationships

All organizations have relationships with other organizations. Some are relatively trivial, while others are of central importance for the parties involved. Some sets of relationships have strong societal impacts, while others do not. Before moving to an analysis of interorganizational relationships, let us consider some of these variations.

Most organizations have vending machines of one sort or another. Coffee, candy, cigarettes, soda, and so on are available for employees at the drop of several coins. For the employing organization, the contract with the vending machine company is probably a rather trivial factor in their overall operations. For the vending machine company, a particular contract may be trivial or crucial, depending upon the scope of their operations and the size of a particular contract.

Colleges and universities engage in many forms of interorganizational linkages. One of the more conspicuous ones is the National Collegiate Athletic Association. The NCAA has strong jurisdiction over men's intercollegiate sports. Aldrich (1979 pp. 337–40) and Stern (1981) have documented the manner in which the NCAA rose to its position of power. Stern's work suggests that there is more close monitoring of successful teams than of less successful ones. Interorganizational linkages such as the NCAA are designed to equalize the power among the organizations involved.

Clients of social service organizations are vitally affected by interorganizational relationships. A common practice is client referral. Theoretically, if one agency is unable to provide the needed services for a particular client, the individual is referred to an appropriate agency for service. What happens in practice is that clients that are easily treated or provided services tend not to be referred, while the more difficult ones are referred, with the most difficult cases sometimes eventually "falling between the cracks" of the referring set of organizations.

At the societal level there has been a long standing concern with the actual and potential power of the "military-industrial complex." This refers to interorganizational patterns linking the military with industry into a powerful set of organizations which can dominate other spheres of life.

Organizational theorists have increasingly recognized the importance of interorganizational relationships. Cook (1977) has neatly summarized this growing awareness. She notes (62–63):

> During the past decade there has been growing interest among organizational theorists in organization environment relations (cf. Dill, 1958; Emery and Trist, 1965; Lawrence and Lorsch, 1967; Maniha and Perrow, 1965; Pfeffer, 1972a; Simpson and Gulley, 1962; Terreberry, 1968; Thompson and McEwen, 1958; Duncan, 1972; Aldrich, 1974) and interorganizational relations (cf. Reid, 1964; Aiken and Hage, 1968; Braito et al., 1972; Clark, 1965; Evan, 1966; Guetzkow, 1966; Levine and White, 1961; Litwak and Hylton, 1962; Pfeffer, 1972b, Thompson, 1967; Turk, 1970, 1973; Warren, 1967; Warren, Rose and Bergunder, 1974; Aldrich, 1972, 1974; Marrett, 1971; Allen, 1974; Benson, 1975; Lehman, 1975). Several factors account for this trend. First, organizational theorists have recently begun to conceptualize organizations as "open," adaptive systems rather than "closed" systems (cf. Thompson, 1967; Katz and Kahn, 1966). According to Buckley, "that a system is open means, not simply, that it engages in interchange with the environment, but that the interchange is an essential factor underlying the system's viability" (1967:50). Thus, the environment has been defined as an important element for those who adopt the open systems model, not only as the social context in which organizations exist, but also as an important determinant of organizational structure and process.
>
> A second contributing factor to this development in organizational theory has been the growing awareness on the part of organizational theorists that previous research on organizations (primarily case studies of single organizations) does not adequately provide an understanding of the complex social structure of rapidly changing urban communities (cf. Etzioni, 1960; Turk, 1970, 1973; Warren, 1967, 1974). Not only is the environment becoming more complex and turbulent (Terreberry, 1968), but the web of organizations within communities is becoming increasingly complex, interrelated, and extensive (Turk, 1973). Previous theoretical perspectives have provided few guidelines for analyzing the effects of these factors upon organizational life. These realities have prompted increasing concern over the duplication of organizational efforts, overlapping domains of organizational activity, coordination of diverse elements within a community, and the integration of and control over various organizational functions, especially with reference to organizations in the social service sector (cf. Reid, 1964; Warren, 1967; Warren, Rose and Bergunder, 1974; Zald, 1969; Baker and O'Brien, 1971;

Lehman, 1975). Theorists have begun to conceptualize cities and communities as networks of organizations or "aggregates of organizations which appear, disappear, change, merge, and form relations with one another" (Turk, 1970:1), and research efforts have been mounted to assess the utility of this approach for investigation of macrosociological phenomena. Turk (1970:16) has suggested that the evidence concerning the fruitfulness of this approach is sufficient to prompt the question, "Is the organization not the proper unit in the analysis of modern, large scale social systems?"

The answer to this question from our perspective is a resounding *Yes.* Cook has identified the major roots of the current interest in interorganizational relationships. In our analysis, we will not be concerned with the issues of cities and communities, but rather with interorganizational phenomena in their own right. In order to do so, we will first examine the variety of forms of interorganizational relationships that can be identified. We will also identify various levels of analysis which can be utilized in the analysis of interorganizational relationships.

FORMS AND LEVELS OF ANALYSIS OF INTERORGANIZATIONAL RELATIONSHIPS

There is general agreement that interorganizational relationships have three basic forms. These are illustrated in Figure 12-1.

The dyad or pairwise relationship is the simplest form of interorganizational relationship and has probably received the most attention in empirical research. The interorganizational set idea was derived from Merton's (1957) analysis of role sets. Evan (1966) and Caplow (1964) introduced the organizational set idea into the literature. The emphasis is on a focal agency (FA in Figure 12-1) and its dyadic relationships with other organizations. As Van de Ven and Ferry (1980) note, it is possible to trace the impact of changes in one dyadic relationship as they affect other pairwise relations within the set.

Figure 12-1   Forms of interorganizational relationships

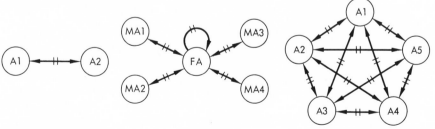

a. Pairwise or Dyadic   b. Interorganizational Set   c. Interorganizational Network
   Interorganizational
   Relationship

Source: Van de Ven and Ferry 1980, p. 298.

Aldrich (1979) has introduced a variation on the organizational set. This is the action set, which is composed of "a group of organizations formed in a temporary alliance for a limited purpose" (p. 280). According to Aldrich, "action sets may have their own formalized agreements, internal division of labor, behavioral norms vis-á-vis other organizations, and clearly defined principles for the recruitment of new members" (p. 281).

Interorganizational networks are more inclusive. They consist "of all organizations linked by a specified type of relation, and (are) constructed by finding the ties between all organizations in a population" (Aldrich 1979, p. 281). Van de Ven and Ferry (1980) define the network as "the total pattern of interrelationships among a cluster of organizations that are meshed together in a social system to attain collective and self-interest goals or to resolve specific problems in a target population" (p. 299). The Van de Ven and Ferry approach stresses the network in areas such as social or health service delivery within a community and would include all of the organizations in that network of service delivery. The Aldrich approach is different in that it does not concern itself with collective goals or target groups, but focuses instead on linkages, such as financial or other resource transactions. Personnel or client flows would be the linkages in the Aldrich scheme. In reality, an empirical analysis would probably find a close overlap between the two approaches, since organizations linked by resource flows in the health care area would also probably be those identified following the Van de Ven and Ferry framework.

Before turning to the issue of levels of analysis among these patterns of interorganizational relationships, it should be noted that an analyst can focus on a variety of dimensions within these forms. Figures 12-2, 12-3, 12-4, and 12-5 demonstrate the complexity that exists when the organizational set concept is used.

The example is drawn from research on the social-control system for problem youth.[1] Figure 12-2 indicates the organizations in interaction with a focal organization, in this case the police. The frequency of the interaction is also indicated. Figure 12-3 indicates the degree of formalization of the relationship; the Figure 12-4 indicates whether it is cooperative or conflictual.

These figures include only a few variables and a few members of the organization set. The complexity of the relationships is indicated by the fact that frequent interactions do not necessarily mean highly formalized or cooperative relations. In addition, it can be seen in Figure 12-4 that cooperation and conflict can exist in the same relationship. The organizations cooperate on some issues but conflict on others.

Another meaning implicit in the idea of the organization set is indicated in Figure 12-5, where the major linkages for the police are seen to be with other law-enforcement agencies. While these relationships are based on contacts in regard to law-enforcement problems, they are also a major basis by which the focal police department determines how well it is doing.

---

[1] The research was conducted by the author and John P. Clark with support by NIMH Grant #2RO MH17508-03MH8.

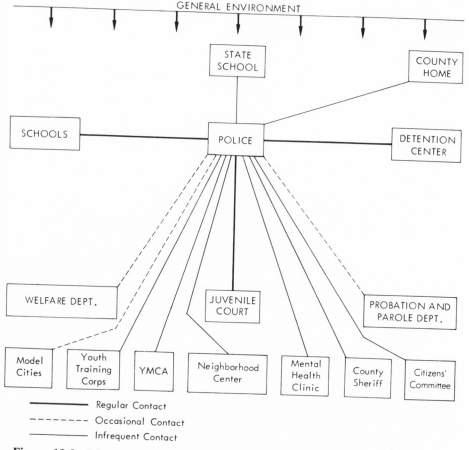

GENERAL ENVIRONMENT

STATE SCHOOL

COUNTY HOME

SCHOOLS

POLICE

DETENTION CENTER

WELFARE DEPT.

JUVENILE COURT

PROBATION AND PAROLE DEPT.

Model Cities | Youth Training Corps | YMCA | Neighborhood Center | Mental Health Clinic | County Sheriff | Citizens' Committee

——————— Regular Contact

– – – – – – – Occasional Contact

——————— Infrequent Contact

Figure 12-2 The organization set and interaction frequency

Organizations use other organizations of the same type both for comparison purposes and as a source of new ideas.

The analysis of interorganizational relationships is complex. Not only does an organization like the police have relationships with the sets of organizations depicted in Figures 12-2 through 12-5, but they also have multiple other sets of relationships. Each organization must purchase goods and services. Many of these organizations have concerns other than problem youths. The welfare department, for example, is also involved in financial assistance programs with linkages to federal, state, and local organizations as well as citizen's groups.

There is yet another form of interorganizational relationship. This is the joint venture (Pfeffer and Nowak 1976). This form entails the creation of a new organizational entity by organizations joining in a partnership.

243

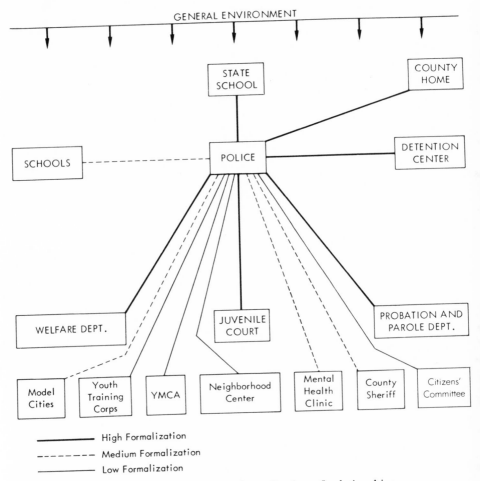

GENERAL ENVIRONMENT

STATE SCHOOL

COUNTY HOME

SCHOOLS

POLICE

DETENTION CENTER

WELFARE DEPT.

JUVENILE COURT

PROBATION AND PAROLE DEPT.

Model Cities

Youth Training Corps

YMCA

Neighborhood Center

Mental Health Clinic

County Sheriff

Citizens' Committee

——————— High Formalization

- - - - - - - Medium Formalization

——————— Low Formalization

Figure 12-3 The organization set and formalization of relationships

The joint venture is a means by which illegal mergers can be avoided, but yet permits joint-capital investment on the part of the organizations involved. Pfeffer and Nowak note that joint ventures may occur in profit and nonprofit sectors. Among profit seeking organizations, oil and gas exploration efforts are a common form of joint venture, as the participating organizations, which have both competitive and symbiotic relationships among themselves, seek to reduce environmental uncertainty and reduce the risks for each participant. Joint ventures among nonprofit organizations are exemplified by alliances formed among private colleges. These alliances are a means by which they can achieve competitive advantages over independent colleges.

The joint venture is a good place to begin to analyze the issue of *level* of analysis. In the case of the joint venture, one could focus attention on the newly created entity *or* the participating organizations *or* both. This is the case of all forms of interorganizational interaction. In the case of the dyad, for example, the focus of interest can be on the organizations involved, on the relationship itself, or on the environment in which the dyadic relationship is based. One could also focus on the individuals involved, such as boundary personnel. We will not be concerned with individuals in the present analysis. Schmidt and Kochan (1977), for example, focused on the motivations of the organizations to participate in interorganizational relationships. Hall et al. (1977) focused on the quality of relationships among the organizations that they studied.

When the analysis is focused on sets or networks, more complexity is introduced, since the focus can be on the set or network, a focal organization within the constellation, other organizations, the relationships themselves, or the environment in which all this is occurring. Provan,

Figure 12-4 The organization set and conflict–cooperation

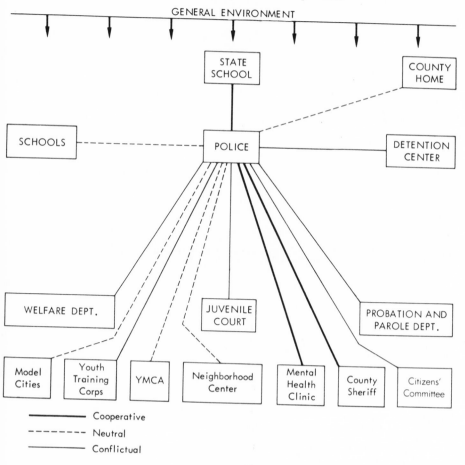

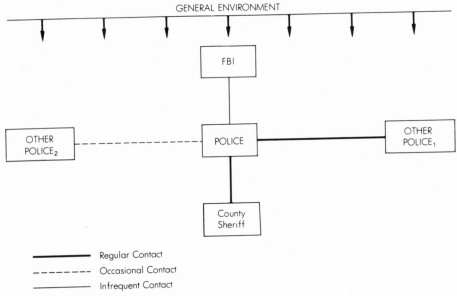

GENERAL ENVIRONMENT

FBI

OTHER
POLICE₂

POLICE

OTHER
POLICE₁

County
Sheriff

——————— Regular Contact

– – – – – – – Occasional Contact

——————— Infrequent Contact

Figure 12-5   Another type of organization set

Beyer, and Kruytbosch (1980) examined the linkages with environmental elements that modify power relationships within an organizational set. Klonglan et al. (1976) studied the relationship between organizational characteristics and interorganizational relationships at different levels of government, such as the country or state levels. The focus here is on the manner in which organizational characteristics are related to interorganizational patterns. Turning the analysis in another direction, Metcalf (1976) found that interorganizational relationships serve organizations as they adapt for their own needs. Interorganizational relationships provide a means of adapting to, rather than merely responding to, environmental pressures. Interorganizational analysis is thus a complex and potentially confusing enterprise, since various studies have had different foci, with less clarity on the level of analysis than would be desirable.

A major difficulty in interorganizational analyses is the ordering among the units of investigation. Using a simplified set of distinctions among the environment, the organizations involved, and the qualities of the relationships, we can identify the following alternatives:

ENVIRONMENT⟶ORGANIZATIONS ⟶ RELATIONSHIPS
ORGANIZATIONS ⟶ RELATIONSHIPS ⟶ ENVIRONMENT
RELATIONSHIPS ⟶ ORGANIZATIONS ⟶ ENVIRONMENT
ORGANIZATIONS ⟶ ENVIRONMENT ⟶ RELATIONSHIPS
ENVIRONMENT ⟶ RELATIONSHIPS ⟶ ORGANIZATIONS
RELATIONSHIPS ⟶ ENVIRONMENT ⟶ ORGANIZATIONS

Each alternative represents a possible assumption about causal ordering, with the situation made more complicated by the possibility of feedback loops for each alternative. Unfortunately, we do not have the answer regarding optimal ordering. The reason for this is that each component is interactive with the others. We probably have an extended example of the chicken-versus-egg argument here, with causal priority difficult to establish and probably not worth the effort, since each component does affect and is effected by the other. As will be seen below, an analytical framework will be presented which attempts to introduce order to this situation, but the framework is primarily heuristic.

Analyses of interorganizational relationships have overwhelmingly been oriented to the delivery of human services such as health care, employment service, youth-serving organizations, welfare organizations, and the like. The reason for this has been the belief that interorganizational coordination would lead to improved service delivery and lower costs. Federal and state research support and programs reflected this emphasis and researchers in the area responded to these emphases. This has led to an underemphasis on interorganizational interactions in the private sector. Reve and Stern (1979) note that interorganizational analyses have missed marketing interactions in distribution networks, with their use of power and the pressures of conflict. In a similar manner, labor-management relationships have not been analyzed from the perspective of interorganizational relationships.

Hage (1980) has considered interorganizational relationships in the private sector. He notes that joint ventures are an important interorganizational form here. Also important are interlocking boards of directors, although, as Hage notes (p. 459), it is unclear exactly how much power such boards actually have. Other forms of interactions in the private sector include trade associations, coalitions for purposes of actions in regard to the government, such as lobbying, joint research efforts, and the publication of trade journals. Until we have more analyses in the private sector, our knowledge about interorganizational relationships will be incomplete. For the moment, we will have to rely upon existing evidence in order to begin to understand such relationships.

A FRAMEWORK FOR INTERORGANIZATIONAL ANALYSIS[2]

The focus of this chapter is on interorganizational relationships themselves, rather than on the participating organizations. The analysis is primarily inductive, based on research findings in the area. While the actual amount of research has been less than the general level of attention paid to interorganizational relationships, the research enables us to develop a means of understanding interorganizational relationships which is not based on conjecture. We will consider characteristics of the general

[2] This framework was developed in conjunction with NIMH Order No. 80MO 10551901D. Joseph P. Morrissey and Michael Lindsey collaborated on this project.

environment that appear to be important, specific situational factors affecting relationships, the bases of the relationships, resource flows in relationships, actual transactions, and finally outcomes of the relationships.

General Environmental Characteristics

We earlier identified dimensions of organizational environments. These same dimensions are critical for interorganizational relationships. Thus, technological, legal, political, economic, demographic, ecological, and cultural conditions have been identified. Hall et al. (1977) have identified legal mandates as an important basis for interaction. The cultural conditions in a community could support or repress interorganizational relationships. Additional research is needed to determine exactly how these environmental dimensions affect interorganizational patterns.

Aldrich (1979) approached the environment along a different set of dimensions. He identified environmental capacity, homogeneity-heterogeneity, stability-instability, concentration-dispersion, consensus-dissensus, and turbulence as the critical environmental dimensions.

Turbulence has been identified as an important factor because it refers to the increasing causal interconnection among the elements in the environment. This means that there is a greater rate of interconnection among the organizations in a system (Emery and Trist 1965; Terreberry 1968). As turbulence increases, we would expect a higher rate of interorganizational relationships.

Environmental complexity would play a similar role, as the number of activities and situations in the environment rise with increasing complexity. Aldrich (1979) argues that organizations deal with complexity by specializing in a limited range of activities. This, in turn, leads to a loosely coupled system in which links among organizations are necessary for organizational survival. Aldrich's emphasis on survival suggests that organizations are not tightly bound to each other, but only to the extent that they need each other for survival. This is too limited a view of the importance of the environment, since other characteristics, such as legal or economic situations may lead to tighter binding than would simply be caused by complexity.

Homogeneity-heterogeneity would have an impact on the range of organizations that have interactions, with a heterogeneous environment having the capability for a wider range of interactions. Aldrich (1979) suggests that a heterogeneous environment leads to a proliferation of organizational programs, which may contribute to a higher level of interorganizational interaction. Environmental capacity, in Aldrich's terms, is similar to the economic dimension, but also includes other resource bases. There are contradictory interpretations of the impact of environmental capacity. Galaskiewicz and Shatin (1980) report that poor neighborhoods draw fewer social service organizations and thus fewer interorganizational linkages. Aiken and Hage (1968) report that a shortage of resources draws organizations together. Turk (1973) found that the scale of municipal government was related to the development of interorganizational relationships. A rich environment may provide the organization with resources that permit it to engage in interorganizational relationships that it otherwise might not.

The stability-instability factor also appears to have mixed consequences. Galaskiewicz and Shatin report that stable clientele provide certainty for organizations and thus less need for interaction. Aldrich (1979) suggests that stability may permit the development of formalized or routinized relationships.

The concentration-dispersion dimension appears to be more straight-forward. Aldrich (1979) reports that concentration of manpower agencies contributes to interagency interactions. Similarly, the consensus-dissensus dimension also appears to have a one-directional relationship with inter-organizational interactions, with domain consensus, which will be discussed in more detail later, contributing to interactions.

Quite obviously, more research is needed to determine the patterns of relationships between the environment, interorganizational relationships, and the organizations involved. Such research is difficult to accomplish, since environmental qualities have to be measured over time as do interorganizational relationships. The problem of causal ordering referred to above also presents severe analytical problems. Despite these problems, a full understanding of interorganizational relationships is impossible without an adequate conceptualization and eventual measurement of these general environmental properties.

Situational Factors

Properties of the environment have been analyzed as being crucial for interorganizational relationships. The specific situations in which inter-organizational relationships take place have received attention also, but with less analytical clarity. The situational factors that will be discussed represent preconditions for interaction.

Awareness   It has long been recognized that organizations operate in a "field" of other organizations (Warren 1967). Less recognized is the fact that organizations vary in their awareness of the field around them. Awareness refers to both the recognition of other organizations and the recognition by organizational representatives that their organization is interdependent with other organizations in their field.

Interorganizational relationships do not occur automatically. A good part of interorganizational theory is predicated on the assumption that interorganizational relationships will not occur unless there is awareness of potential or actual interdependence among the organizations involved (Levine and White 1961; Litwak and Hylton 1962; Levine, White, and Paul 1963). Klonglan et al. (1976) have suggested that there is a form of hierarchy of awareness. First is a general awareness of the existence of other organizations and their activities. The next level involves mutual acquaintance among the directors of the organizations. The focus on directors is probably too narrow, since acquaintances among staff members would be of great importance in some instances. The next levels of awareness involve specific interactions and joint board membership among directors. We will deal with these issues separately, since they involve interactions and are a step beyond simple awareness.

Van de Ven and Ferry (1980) approach awareness from a different perspective. They suggest that there are two levels of awareness. At the more general level is the extent to which boundary spanners in organizations are knowledgeable about the goals, services, and resources present in other organizations. This awareness provides identification of alternative sources of services and resources. According to Van de Ven and Ferry, higher levels of awareness are likely to result in higher levels of interaction.

The second level of awareness involves interpersonal ties among organizational personnel (Boje and Whetten 1979). These can involve old school ties, membership in common professional organizations, membership in common religious or fraternal organizations, simple friendships, or contacts that are based solely on work bases. Galaskiwicz and Shatin (1980) report that interpersonal ties are crucial for interorganizational relationships at periods of environmental turbulence. It is possible to develop sociometric measures of such acquaintanceships (Rogers 1974). A higher level of interpersonal ties is seen to be linked to higher levels of interorganizational interaction. Overlooked in most analyses of such ties is their quality. Quite obviously, friendship will yield a different form of interorganizational relationship than will animosity. Interorganizational relationships are based on much more than the qualities of the individuals involved, but this factor should not be overlooked.

Domain Consensus-Dissensus   The domain issue has already been discussed in terms of Aldrich's (1979) analysis of the dimensions of the general environment of organizations. The domain issue has particular salience in interorganizational relationships. Unfortunately, several meanings are embedded in the usage that the concept has received.

One meaning has a simple spatial referent. The domain is the geographical area served by an organization, such as the "service area" or "catchment area" used by neighborhood health centers or community mental health centers. In these spatial cases the issue of domain is usually settled in advance, with domain not really an issue except for potential clients who may reside on a border of two organizations' domains.

A more important meaning of domain concerns the level of agreement about role or task differentiation among the organizations involved in interorganizational relationships (Levine et al. 1963). The roles organizations play relative to one another, in terms of their programs and services and the clients to be served, may be critical issues for the organizations involved. Aldrich (1979) views domain consensus in this manner, in terms of the degree to which an organization's claim to a specific domain is disrupted or recognized by another organization. Molnar (1978) focused on whether or not organizational dyads served common clients, while Van de Ven and Ferry (1980) considered clients, services, and funding sources as indicators of organizations sharing similar domains. Two issues are intertwined here. First is the issue of consensus or agreement on domain, while the second involves the commonness of the domain. It is quite possible that organizations could claim the same domain with consensus or dissensus.

Another aspect of the domain issue involves ideological considerations. Analysts such as Benson et al. (1973), Boje and Whetten (1979), Hall et al. (1977), Mulford (1980), and Schmidt and Kochan (1977) have grappled with this issue. Ideological issues can involve the compatibility of the goals of the organizations involved, conformity in terms of treatment ideologies in social service organizations, or compatibility in terms of understanding the nature of the issues faced. The ideological issue becomes important in practice. For example, police agencies typically have a different ideology toward problem youth than do social welfare agencies. These differences, which can be severe or mild, affect the qualities of interactions among the organizations.

Levine and White (1961) have argued that domain consensus must exist before exchange relationships among agencies are possible. Molnar (1978) suggests that organizations with intersecting domains tend to be more interdependent than those that do not share domains, with intersecting domains contributing to interorganizational relationships. Others, such as Schmidt and Kochan (1977) and Hall et al. (1977) have argued that interorganizational relationships do not depend on domain consensus. These authors do suggest that the level of consensus does affect the qualities of relationships but not their existence. Cook (1977) has suggested that exchange relationships do not depend on such consensus.

The various forms of consensus are important for interorganizational relationships. There is agreement that consensus will lead to more positive relationships among the organizations involved. Whether this is desirable or not, of course, depends upon the context.

Geographical Proximity   The distribution of organizations in space has received relatively little attention in the literature on organizations in general. Geographical proximity refers to the spatial distance between organizations or their subunits. It has been noted that distance can facilitate or inhibit interactions (Broskowski 1980). It is more difficult to establish or maintain relationships across distances, for organizations and for individuals. It can also be noted that the type of unit involved in an interorganizational relationship interacts with the spatial issue. Modern communication techniques permit rapid information flows across space, but clients or staff members would be more difficult to transfer.

Reid (1969), Schermerhorn (1975), Boje and Whetten (1979), and Halpert (1981) have suggested that the decision to coordinate with another organization is easier if the organizations involved are physically close to one another. Proximity promotes familiarity of domains. In many communities several city or county agencies might be housed in the same building. This proximity would facilitate interactions in comparison with organizations that are spread throughout some geographical area.

Localized Dependence   Related to the issue of geographical proximity is the degree to which organizations are dependent upon a local area for their resources. Galaskiewicz (1979) and Maas (1979) have examined this factor. Their concern has been with the extent to which needed resources are obtained only from a local area versus a more widely dispersed resource base. If organizations with localized dependence are successful in commanding these localized resources, they are seen as more powerful or central in the network of organizations in a community. If, on the other hand, there is high localized dependency with relatively weak access to resources, the organization is much more vulnerable to the power of other organizations.

Size The final situational factor is the size of the actual or potential set or network of organizations. Most analyses have focused on the actual number of organizations in a network (Van de Ven and Ferry 1980). Size is a situational factor in that at any given time there are a finite number of organizations available for interactions. In general, the number of organizations in a relationship is related to the complexity faced by any single organization. It is also likely that large numbers of relationships weaken the quality of the relationships (John 1977; Caragonne 1978; Agranoff and Pattahas 1979). An increase in the number of organizations in a relationship affects dependencies, domains, and the potential rewards or resources for participating in the relationships. Again, the analogy with individuals is appropriate here. Many ties reduce the likelihood of each of the ties being strong, so that a greater proportion of linkages in a large network would be more superficial than in a smaller network. While weak ties among individuals have been shown to have great importance for their job seeking (Granovetter 1973), there is no solid evidence regarding the impact of different forms of ties among organizations. It would appear that a large set or network would have the potential for dissipating resources and actions, but it could also lead to a situation in which there were many alternatives for an organization, in terms of resource acquisition, client flows, and the like.

Caplow (1964) has demonstrated the manner in which the number of relationships increases exponentially as group size increases. The same thing would occur among organizations. The number of organizations in a relationship or potentially available thus is an important situational factor for interorganizational relationships.

Bases of Interaction

Interorganizational relationships do not just happen. They occur in an environment and in a situational context. They also occur for some reason. We will identify four reasons or bases for contact here. They range from ad hoc situations to those which are mandated by law or regulation. The outcome from each basis is likely to be different for the organizations involved and for the relationship itself.

Ad Hoc Bases Relationships have an ad hoc basis when there is little or no previous patterning in the relationships among organizations. A specific need, problem, or issue may arise among two or more organizations. In the social service area, a client with an unusual problem may trigger one organization to call up another to get an opinion or to make a referral. Ad hoc bases are the least important for interorganizational relationships, since they tend to be one-shot operations. If an ad hoc situation repeats itself or more elements enter the relationships among the agencies involved, other bases for a continued relationship will develop.

Exchange Bases The exchange basis for interorganizational relationships has been the dominant orientation toward such relationships since Levine and White's (1961) seminal paper. According to Levine and White, exchange is "any voluntary activity between two organizations which has consequences, actual or anticipated, for the realization of their respective goals or objectives" (p. 120). Cook (1977) has extended this formulation beyond the two-party implication of Levine and White. She examines exchange within networks of organizations and incorporates power differentials among organizations into her formulation. The exchange idea incorporates the notion that organizations must acquire resources and that exchange is the major mechanism by which this occurs (Thompson 1967; Jacobs 1974; Benson 1975).

The exchange basis can be seen as a form of bargaining in which each organization seeks to maximize its advantage in acquiring resources from another organization (Schmidt and Kochan 1977). Although the exchange formulation seems to imply that this is bargaining among equals, modern exchange theory, as exemplified by Cook's work, does not make that assumption. Power differences among organizations are taken into account. Schmidt and Kochan (1977) argue that even in a situation in which there is a great imbalance of power, the powerful organization which seeks to interact with a weaker organization can do so because of the power difference. The exchange is unequal, but the participants do engage in resource exchange. The exchange basis emphasizes the importance of resource acquisition for the organizations involved. It also contains an implication of rationality, as the organizations seek to maximize their gains in interaction. All of the problem associated with decision making in organizations must be considered in exchange interactions, since decisions here cannot be assumed to be any more rational than decisions made in other spheres of organizational actions.

Exchange is an important basis for interorganizational interactions. It becomes less of a factor, however, when the interactions between organizations become formalized.

Formalized Agreements Marrett (1971) defines formalization as the degree to which the interdependency among organizations is given official sanction by the parties involved. This official sanction or recognition (Aldrich 1979) is typically written down and may be legally or contractually binding (Van de Ven and Ferry 1980). A formal agreement is based on exchange. Once the agreement is signed or otherwise authorized, it throws the relationship into a different light, since interactions are based on a specified pattern rather than ongoing through the exchange process at each interaction episode.

In a study of organizations concerned with problem youths, Hall et al. (1977) found that the presence of a formal agreement between organizations was related to the frequency and importance of interactions to a greater degree than to other bases of interaction. They also found that an organization did not need to evaluate other organizations when a formal agreement was in place. Apparently, the presence of a formal agreement is based on frequent and important interactions among organizations, with the agreement serving to simplify interactions, since each interaction does not have to be weighed in terms of its contributions to the organizations involved. The organizations have agreed to interact and the interactions take place.

Another basis for interaction has a very different source than agreements among the organizations involved. In many instances, interactions among organizations are mandated from outside the interacting parties.

Mandatedness   This basis for interorganizational relationships has received increasing attention in recent years. Mandatedness refers to the extent to which relationships are governed by laws or regulations. These laws or regulations are imposed on the relationship by legislative or administrative rulings. For example, laws regarding unemployment compensation may require a public employment agency to interact with a welfare department in order to determine client eligibility. Such interaction may or may not have occurred without a mandate present. Halpert (1981) points out that a mandated relationship may place an organization in a contradictory position. Compliance with the mandate may disrupt established procedures. At the same time, it may be necessary for the organization if it is to receive financial support.

The importance of a mandate for interorganizational relationships has been identified by Schmidt and Kochan (1977) and Hall et al. (1977). Hall et al. (1977, 1978) and Molnar and Rogers (1979) suggest that mandated relationships may lead to conflict, since organizations may be forced to interact even with domain dissensus, interpersonal animosities among members, and so on.

Mandated interactions do not guarantee that interactions will take place. Unless there is some sort of enforcement mechanism, organizations may ignore a mandate. Since mandates are typically associated with some type of resource flow and with monitoring, they usually do in fact serve as an important basis for interorganizational interactions. It is quite possible that an organization can receive contradictory mandates (Gardner and Snipe 1970). This means that an organization will have to try to serve several mandates at one time along with its own orientations from an exchange perspective. It may seek to interact with one organization but be forced to interact with one or more other organizations. Again, this moves the analysis of interorganizational interactions still further from a basis of pure rationality.

Mandated interactions should continue to receive attention in research and practice. Interorganizational interactions outside of the area of human services would appear to be frequently based on some sort of mandate. Governmental regulatory agencies are mandated to interact with business firms. City and county government agencies are mandated to interact with state and federal level agencies. While exchange considerations enter into the passage of laws and regulations through the process of lobbying and the give and take of policy formulation, the presence of a strong and enforced mandate leads to interorganizational relationships of a different form than those which evolve from ongoing exchanges. In this section we have examined ad hoc, exchange, formalized agreement, and mandated bases of interorganizational interactions. Each basis has a different outcome. At the same time, all interorganizational interactions involve something passing between the organizations involved. We will now turn to a consideration of the resources which flow between organizations.

Resource Flows

Regardless of the environment, the situational factors, and the bases of interactions, interorganizational interactions have a content, and it is to this that we now turn. Exchange theory properly focuses on resource exchange, and we will examine resource interdependency among organizations. The flow of resources vary in their intensity, so that this quantitative aspect of interactions will be examined. We will then turn to the issue of joint programs, where organizations, in addition to exchanging resources, also engage in activities together. Finally, we will deal with the issue of interlocking boards of directors. This is a form of resource that has received a great deal of attention. It is placed in this section because of the potential contribution it makes to resource flows.

Resource Interdependence   Situations in which two or more organizations are dependent upon one another for the resources each has access to or controls are the basis of resource interdependency. Resources take a variety of forms. Galaskiewicz and Marsden (1978) examined inflows and outflows of information, money, and social support in their interorganizational analysis. Molnar (1978) also identified information, but added other resources in terms of funds, facilities, and personnel. He also suggested that organizations that have intersecting domains tend to be more interdependent. Mulford (1980) adds equipment and meeting rooms to the list of resources which could be exchanged. Clients can also be seen to be a resource in this context (Boje and Whetten 1979).

It has long been recognized that organizations are seldom capable of controlling all of the resources they require (Levine and White 1961; Litwak and Hylton 1962). An interorganizational division of labor can develop in which the participating organizations specialize by providing a particular service in return for a particular resource they need (Aldrich 1979). Each organization becomes dependent upon the other in this type of situation. Organizations tend to resist dependence and to attempt to make other organizations dependent upon them (Benson 1975). As will be seen below, the development of interlocking boards has been viewed as a means by which dependence can be reduced.

It is unclear what the direction of resource flows means in terms of interdependence. On one hand, a great outflow of some resource, such as money, could indicate great dependence, since the organization involved would appear to have to buy needed goods or services. On the other hand, money outflow may make other organizations more dependent upon the organization in question if this is their only source of funds. The exact meaning of resource interdependence requires a comprehensive understanding of the overall interorganizational patterning before the meaning of the interdependence can be determined. Nonetheless, resources are the contents of the many transactions among organizations.

Intensity The level of resource investment required of the organizations involved in interorganizational relationships determines the intensity of the relationship (Marrett 1971; Aldrich 1979). For service organizations, the higher the level of referrals, services provided, staff support, facilities and other resources, the greater the intensity of the relationship. Implicit in the consideration of intensity is the question of the relative proportion of an organization's resources that are invested into the relationship. The higher the proportion, the more intense the relationship.

Van de Ven and Ferry (1980) emphasize the importance of information flows in the determination of intensity. In their view, information is an important commodity in an interaction and should be treated as distinct from other forms of resources.

The more intense the relationship, the more important it is for the organizations involved. The relationships that any organization has vary in their intensity, from the casual to the all consuming. The former makes little difference, while the latter has the potential to actually consume the organization if all of its efforts involve interorganizational relationships and if these relationships use up all of its resources.

Intensity is sometimes confused with or combined with the frequency of interactions. This appears to be a bad mix, since frequent interactions can be casual, but a really intense interaction can be infrequent. For this reason, we will consider frequency in another context. Dyadic relationships, networks, and organizational sets can all vary in their degree of intensity. For example, during a period of crisis, such as that experienced in Atlanta, Georgia, in 1980 and 1981, with the kidnapping and killing of black children, relationships between police agencies, levels of government, and citizens' groups are extremely intense. In a noncrisis situation, relationships will be less intense. The impact of intensity is both network wide and organization specific.

Joint Programs Aiken and Hage (1968) and Mulford and Mulford (1980) have identified joint programs as a particular type of resource flow. Here the emphasis is not simply on resource flows in terms of interdependency, but on substantial resource commitment and collaboration. Aiken and Hage (1968) found that joint programs were of particular importance to the welfare and health organizations that they studied. They appeared to be more salient than client, personnel, or financial support flows. Joint programs were not "minor incidents" in the lives of the organizations. Some had been in existence for over twenty years (p. 919). Aiken and Hage also found that joint programs tended to foster other joint programs, since the interorganizational relationships grew in scope and depth.

Joint programs involve an investment of resources and an intense relationship. They also involve purposive actions in regard to some issue which is jointly confronted. Joint programs can involve a particular type of client or treatment program in the services sector or a new area of exploration in the area of raw materials, as in the case of joint ventures (Pfeffer and Nowak 1976). The important difference between joint programs and other forms of interactions is that the actions are purposive and not just responsive to environmental pressures.

Director Interlocks Interlocking boards of directors have been the subject of commentary and research for a long time. Pennings (1980b) notes that U.S. Supreme Court Justice Louis Brandeis warned in 1913 that such interlocks contain many evils, such as the suppression of competition. Pennings goes on to note that contemporary analyses of interlocks run the gamut from analyses of board interlocks as the means by which elites maintain societal control to sober scholarly analyses of the manner in which organizations attempt to control uncertainties by such interlocks. There is a large volume of literature on this topic, which Pennings covers well, and which will not be repeated here.

Director interlock refers to a situation in which an officer or director of one organization is a member of the board of directors of another organization. Another form of interlock is when members of two organizations are on the board of a third organization (Burt, Christman, and Kilburn 1980).

Burt, Christman, and Kilburn (1980), Burt (1980), and Pennings (1980b) note that interlocks are a means by which organizations can attempt to manage uncertainty in their environments. Interlocks provide access to resources and can influence decisions. Aldrich (1979) notes that there are instances in which interlock occurs because an organization demands representation on another organization's board, thus lowering the autonomy of the latter organization.

Hage (1980 p. 95) notes that the actual power of boards of directors is quite limited in that their power is to ratify or defeat what the chief executive officer and his or her administration propose to do. Quite frequently, the executive officer and the administration have greater knowledge than members of the board and can thus control the situation. At the same time, boards of directors can remove top administrative officers (James and Soref 1980; Bauer 1981). In my view, the power of boards of directors is an empirical issue. They can be viewed as simply another type of resource flow, which they probably are in most cases, or as a means of elite domination of organizations, which they probably are in a limited number of cases.

In order to understand the consequences of interlocks of boards of directors, Pennings' (1980 pp. 188–91) findings will be summarized (see also Burt 1980). Of the 797 largest American business firms, only 62 have no interlocks with the remaining 735 firms. Financial firms are disproportionately represented in the interlocks. Interlocks are most common in concentrated industries where monopolies almost exist in the first place. Financial firms avoid interlocks with firms that appear risky, instead seeking interlocks with those that are not risky. Well-interlocked firms were found to have greater economic effectiveness. This was particularly the case with firms that rely on equity financing and which were capital intensive. The relationships between interlocks and economic effectiveness were strongest for effective organizations. Apparently, financial firms do not want to get involved with operations that they perceive as performing poorly. Pennings views these patterns of interlocks as persuasive attempts by financial firms to enhance their position with solvent firms that will be reliable customers for loans, bonds, and other forms of debt. It is a technique by which financial firms acquire good customers.

Pennings' findings are hardly radical, but they are in keeping with what we understand about the ways in which organizations seek to acquire resources and enhance their position in their environment. It should be stressed that organizations in the public sector engage in the same kinds of activities through boards of trustees, advisory boards, and the like. Zald (1970b) demonstrated the importance of Boards for the YMCA. An examination of the Board of any college or university would reveal similar linkages into important segments of the organization's environments. Provan, Beyer, and Kruytbosch (1980) have shown the importance of board interlocks in the operation of the United Way.

Director interlocks are a means by which the resources important to organizations and their relationships flow between organizations. They are separately identified here, because they may be hidden from analyses at the level of official transactions between organizations. Board interlock is also an additional resource for the organizations involved. Any serious effort at understanding interorganizational relationships should examine the board memberships of the interacting parties, whether in dyads, sets, or networks.

The flow of resources and joint programs are the content of interorganizational relationships. Our analysis will now turn to a consideration of the various dimensions of interorganizational transactions.

Transaction Forms

Interorganizational relationships are interaction processes between organizations and within networks and sets. In the analysis that follows, we will build on Marrett's identification (1971) and Aldrich's (1979) discussion of the critical dimensions of interorganizational relationships. We will first note how the interactions can be structured and then turn to the transaction processes themselves.

Interaction Formalization   We have already noted the fact that organizations can have formalized agreements among themselves which can govern their interrelationships. These agreements are in place prior to the succeeding interactions. There is another aspect of formalization that can serve to structure the interactions. This is the presence of an intermediary organization which serves to coordinate or control interorganizational interactions.

Warren (1967) analyzed Community Decision Organizations and Mott (1968) studied a coordinating council, both of which represent the type of formalization under consideration here. Councils of Churches, Chambers of Commerce, Welfare Boards, and other such mediating and coordinating organizations serve to structure the relationships among organizations. As Van de Ven and Ferry (1980) suggest, the power of these formalizing agencies can be more or less binding, so that it is important to consider the degree of interaction formalization. In some cases, the intermediary organization's decisions are binding, while in other cases they are merely advisory. An example of this variation can be seen in Pfeffer and Long's (1977) analysis of organizations affected by the United Fund. They found that the power of the United Fund was inversely related to the capabilities of the member organizations obtaining funds from alternative sources. Those agencies which were highly dependent upon the United Fund would have their interactions more formalized and controlled than those with less dependence.

Interaction Standardization Marrett (1971) and Aldrich (1979) identify two aspects of standardization. First is the degree to which the resources interchanged are standardized. If organizations agree to exchange particular types of clients or personnel, high standardization is present. Low standardization would occur when the units are heterogeneous. High standardization would result in more routinized interactions, with less time and energy devoted to sorting and classifying the units that are exchanged or transferred.

The second form of standardization involves the procedures used in the transactions. Low standardization would be represented by procedures based on a case-by-case decision process, while high standardization would be exemplified by similar procedures being used over a period of time. When high standardization is present, there are likely to be forms and checklists that are routinely filled out as the transaction occurs. Aldrich (1979) suggests that larger and more complex organizations are more likely to standardize their transactions than are smaller and less complex organizations. A common example of standardization is the assignment of academic credits for students transferring from a community college to a four-year college. The large college or university is more likely to have developed procedural standardization for determining transferable credits. The credits themselves are examples of unit standardization.

Importance Interorganizational relationships vary in their importance for the interacting organizations. Hall et al. (1977, 1978); Klonglan and Paulson (1971) and Schmidt and Kochan (1977) have focused on this dimension. The Hall et al. (1978) study found that the importance of interaction was a strong predictor of the frequency of interaction. The idea of importance contains two elements. The first is the importance of another organization to the work of a focal organization, while the second is the importance of the interaction itself. In either case, importance is a major contributor to the generation of interorganizational relationships. Importance has been examined at the dyadic level and not at the set or network levels, but the pattern would appear to be the same. At the network level, if all mental health organizations in the network perceived that the other organizations and the interactions themselves were important, the interactions themselves would take place with greater frequency.

Hall et al. (1977) reports that important interactions are likely to lead to formalized agreement among the organizations interacting.

Frequency As noted above, frequency of interaction and intensity are sometimes viewed synonymously. We view frequency as a component of the transactions among organizations, with intensity as a component of the resource flow among organizations. While importance and frequency are closely associated, there is not a necessary relationship between the processes. A once-a-year budget meeting may be more important than weekly casual contacts. In general, however, important relationships are frequent relationships. Hall et al. (1978) found that frequent interactions were related to high levels of both coordination and conflict. This suggests that frequent interactions tend to involve more elements of the organizations involved than do infrequent interactions. Marrett (1971), Aldrich (1979), and Van de Ven and Ferry (1980) all suggest that there is a strong linkage between frequency and intensity. Frequent interactions contribute to heightened resource flows. It should be noted that interactions can have high or low frequency on the basis of voluntary exchange, formal agreements, or mandates.

Reciprocity Reciprocity refers to the symmetry of the transactions among organizations. Resources can flow to both parties equally or in an imbalanced fashion. Baty, Evan, and Rothermel (1971) have examined faculty personnel flows among graduate schools of business. They found that the flows were not reciprocal, with prestigious schools of business sending out more faculty members in the form of new Ph.D.'s than they received. In this case, the lack of reciprocity contributed to the power of the sending schools, since the less powerful schools were dependent upon the more powerful. When there is mutual dependence, organizations will attempt to maintain reciprocal relationships.

Power Of all the interorganizational transaction processes, power has received the most attention. Power in an interorganizational situation is equivalent to that in the intraorganizational situation—the ability of one party to have another party do what the other party would not otherwise do (Dahl 1957). The power variable has been used in a variety of ways, and we will try to disentangle the various approaches that have been suggested.

One dominant theme is based on resources, with power being viewed as the possession of resources which enables an organization to use those resources to gain the compliance of others (Burt 1977; Aldrich 1979). Building on Emerson's (1962) work, which sees power as residing in dependency, analysts have argued that parties in a power relationship are tied to each other by the dependence of one party on the other, or perhaps by mutual dependence. Power lies in asymmetrical dependence.

Using Blau's (1964) work as a starting point, Aldrich (1979) examined the manner in which social service organization administrators deal with the power dependency issue. Four alternatives were suggested. First, an organization can build up its own resource base and thus reduce dependence. Secondly, the organization can seek alternative sources for needed resources, thus limiting dependency. Thirdly, an organization can use coercive force to make the other organization surrender resources without complying with its demands. This is the conflict situation as exemplified by the strike. Finally, the organization can essentially withdraw from the situation by modifying its goals or technologies. If these alternatives are not available or are not chosen, dependency will continue, with the organization having less power than the organization with which it is interacting.

Halpert (1974), using a modification of French and Raven's (1968) analysis of power bases, identified expert, referent, reward, coercive, legal, and community power bases of interorganizational power. He saw possession of these power bases or resources as the source of organizational power in interorganizational transactions.

The approach to interorganizational power discussed here has been primarily applied to dyadic relationships. Network analysts have frequently substituted the notion of *centrality* for power. Centrality refers to the relative position of an organization in a network of organizations, with those more central being viewed as having more power (Boje and Whetten 1979; Galaskiewicz 1979). Information and resource flows can be traced in networks. In a totally decentralized network, there is equal participation by all organizations, with perfect symmetry or reciprocity and no power differences. As Aldrich (1979) notes, this is a rare situation, since networks are typically integrated by a centrally located organization.

There is yet another aspect to interorganizational power. There are some interorganizational situations in which the issue of exchange is not a consideration and network centrality is determined in advance. This is the situation in which power relationships are determined in advance of any interactions. In a network of organizations in which all receive their resources from a central source, such as a government agency, the power relationships are predetermined. Some bargaining will occur, but the relationship is set in advance. Organizations that are designated as information clearinghouses would have a similar power role. As in the case of power within organizations, the present hierarchy of power must not be overlooked, although it has been by interorganizational analysts.

Cooperation   Cooperation is a process in which organizations pursue their own goals and thus retain autonomy, while at the same time orienting their actions toward a common issue outcome (Mulford 1980; Warren, Rose, and Bergunder 1974). We are distinguishing cooperation from coordination, since the latter process involves the pursuit of a common goal. Coordination will be considered later. Cooperation is typically viewed as a form of voluntary interaction (Maas 1979) and would be found in instances of exchange or voluntary-agreement-based relationships. Klonglan and Paulson (1971) note that cooperation can involve personnel interchange. Aiken and Hage (1968) viewed cooperation in terms of products and services for clients. The cooperation process involves a rather small investment on the part of the organizations involved, but it does mean that they have to take each other's actions into account.

Conflict   Interorganizational conflict is an oppositional process in which one party attempts to block or thwart the activities of another party. As Galtung (1965) notes, conflict can occur at the individual and collective level and within and between social systems. For the analysis here, we are concerned with interorganizational conflict, whether it be interpersonal or collective in basis. Interpersonal conflict is relatively easy to understand. Collectively based conflict is more complex and refers to situations in which the organization as a whole is involved in the conflict. An example here is Sebring's analysis (1977) of university-state government interactions in which past unsuccessful encounters led to present conflicts.

Conflict can take several forms in interorganizational transactions. Some conflict is regulated, as in competition, while other conflict takes place outside of a regulatory base. As in the case of intraorganizational processes, conflict can also be based on power differences or on domain disputes (Molnar and Rogers 1979). It can also be based on ideological grounds. Halpert (1981) documents the manner in which police agencies are in conflict with other social service organizations, primarily because of their differing philosophies.

The correlates of conflict are not well understood. A major reason for this is a pervasive belief that conflict is a process to be avoided. This belief appears to be misguided. Guetskow (1966) and Assael (1969), have suggested that conflict and its resolution can have long-run benefits for interorganizational relationships. Zeitz (1980) argues that conflict is system-integrative and -disintegrative. The resolution of old conflicts sets the stage for new conflicts in a dialectic manner. Hall, Clark, and Giordano (1979) found that conflict was related to interaction frequency and to interactions based on both formal agreements and mandates. They do not see agreements or mandates as the cause of conflicts, but rather interpret this relationship as being based on the fact that agreements and mandates are found in situations that are important to the parties involved. This study also found that conflict was related to power differences. While noting that resource acquisition can be an important source of conflict, the study found that conflict also existed between organizations which had very different resource bases, such as different levels of government, as when city agencies are in conflict with county agencies.

Conflict Resolution   Inasmuch as there are few Hundred Years Wars among organizations, it is safe to conclude that most conflicts are resolved. Van de Ven and Ferry (1980), drawing on earlier works by Blake and Mouton (1964), Lawrence and Lorsch (1967), Burke (1970), and Filley, House, and Kerr (1976) identified four conflict resolution techniques that take place at the interorganizational level. The issues can be ignored or avoided; the issues can be smoothed over by playing down differences and emphasizing common interests; the issues can be openly confronted with differences worked through as in the case of collective bargaining; or the issues can be submitted to some hierarchical power, either in the form of some party at a higher administrative level or an outside party which is given power over the situation. Aldrich (1979) suggests two other alternatives—contracting or expanding the organizational boundary. Contraction involves removing the organization from some aspect of its domain and thus conflict resolution, while expansion permits an organization to encompass the conflicting other organization. Aldrich's suggestions are particularly relevant in the competitive situation.

Conflict resolution has been found to be a major contribution to coordination (Hall et al. 1978). Interorganizational relationships are complex, if this is the case. It will be remembered that in this study conflict was based on interaction frequency and the importance of the interactions. These factors contribute to conflict, conflict resolution, and coordination. It is impossible to understand the outcomes of interorganizational interactions without considering conflict and its resolution.

Coordination   Coordination has had an interesting role in interorganizational analyses. Probably most studies have had coordination as an explicit or implicit dependent variable, on the assumption that somehow coordination was good for any clients involved, could cut costs, and was good in its own right. That assumption is now under serious question.

Coordination involves a process of concerted decision making or action in which two or more organizations participate with some sort of deliberate adjustment to one another (Warren, Rose, and Bergunder 1974). A key factor here is the idea that the transactions are deliberate and involve a goal which is collective. This is a major point of differentiation from cooperation. Aiken et al. (1975) subsume cooperation under coordination, but I prefer to keep the processes analytically distinct.

Gans and Horton (1975) identified two forms of coordination in social service organizations. Administrative coordination involves fiscal issues, personnel practices, and planning and programming. Joint budgeting and joint planning exemplified coordinated administrative practices. Coordinated direct service activities would involve such things as case conferences or a case coordinator. The coordination transaction process is complex in that administrative matters could be highly coordinated, with service coordination in a shambles.

In my view, coordination is a process and not an outcome of interorganizational relationships. It may or may not be desirable. Basing his comments on Warren et al.'s (1974) analysis of urban reform movements, Perrow (1979) makes the following comments in regard to coordination:

> What, then, about the lack of coordination? Little was needed; there was an overall consensus as to who should do what, a division of labor or of sectors, and new formal coordination mechanisms did not increase the efficiency of the agencies. As others have pointed out, coordination has costs associated with it, as well as presumed benefits, and there may be substantial gains with redundant, uncoordinated activity and substantial costs with coordination which eliminates back-up facilities. (p. 235)

The Warren et al. study also found that new agencies designed to enhance coordination and innovation actually accomplished little. We thus view coordination as one form of interorganizational transaction. We are concerned with the outcomes of interorganizational relationships, and we turn to this in the final section.

Outcomes

The outcome issue is simple and complex. Its simplicity is that it lies in the eyes and minds of the beholders. Van de Ven and Ferry (1980, p. 327) have devised a simple set of questions to determine if other organizations have carried out their commitments, the relationships have been productive, the time and effort spent in the relationships was worthwhile, and the degree of satisfaction with which relationships are viewed.

The complexity of the outcome issue is that there are multiple eyes and minds which can make this assessment. This is an identical problem with the issue of organizational effectiveness, which will be considered in the next chapter. The perceived effectiveness of interorganizational interactions can be assessed from the standpoint of participants within each organization, the organization as a whole, clients served or disserved, the community in which the interactions take place, or legislative or administrative decision makers who have jurisdiction over the particular dyads, sets, or networks in question. The outcome issue is thus one of political power, resource dependence, and moral choice. Outcomes which are good for one organization may be bad for another; clients may benefit, but the organizations may suffer; relationships may be cost effective, but damaging to organizations and clients. Analyses of interorganizational relationships must keep these considerations in mind.

SUMMARY AND CONCLUSIONS

In this chapter we have attempted to provide an overview of the topic of interorganizational relationships. We have identified the various forms of interorganizational relationships, such as dyads, sets, and networks. We have also concerned ourselves with the level-of-analysis issue and have considered the difficulty in ordering the relationships among organizational, environmental, and interorganizational relationship levels. We then presented a framework for analyzing interorganizational relationships, beginning with general environmental considerations, then moving to specific situational factors, bases of interaction, resource flows, transaction forms, and, finally, outcomes. Whether or not this framework is useful or not will lie in its applicability.

Most of the research on which this analysis has been based was carried out in social service organizations, with the exception of the materials on director interlocks. We clearly need an expanded data base from a broader range of organizations. The analysis contained relatively little reference to the organizations involved in interactions. Little is actually known of this linkage. Aiken and Hage's work is among the few which have considered this issue and their data base is extremely limited, although Hage (1980) has attempted to extrapolate from this data base to some hypotheses regarding interorganizational relationships. We also suffer from a shortage of information about the individuals involved in interorganizational interactions. There is some limited information on boundary spanners, but this role may actually be a peripheral one, with much greater importance found in the individuals who are on interlocking boards or who interpret and decide upon the information brought by boundary spanners.

The area of interorganizational relationships is thus one of great research potential. There is a general belief that the relationships are important, even though this has not yet been really demonstrated. There is also a general belief that interorganizational relationships contribute to organizational effectiveness, the topic of the next chapter.

V

Organizational Effectiveness and Organizational Theory

In this final section we deal with two topics that have been central to the entire analysis. We basically study organizations for two reasons. One is to understand how and why organizations are effective or ineffective. We may want to make them more or less effective from an economic, political, or moral perspective. It is now well recognized that the various parties concerned with any single organization can have contrasting and conflicting views on its effectiveness. We are not neutral about the organizations with which we deal as workers, clients, customers, or publics. I don't want to be abused by any organization, public or private. I also want the organizations in which I participate as a member to do well. Doing well is to be effective. My perspective on effectiveness, however, varies with my position in the organization. I see effectiveness differently as a faculty member than I saw it when I was a vice president of my university. I have different perspectives about the other organizations of which I am a part. As a member of the public, I also care about the present and future effectiveness of private and public organizations that affect our society. I would like to see organized crime go out of existence, but I want to see our public schools thrive.

There is thus this practical and personal reason to study organizations. The second reason for studying organizations is more abstract. The ideal of organizational scholars is to develop organizational theory. We want to be able to understand and predict our subject matter. Some, such as Hage (1980), opt for a deductive system. The approach taken here, as evidenced by the emphasis on empirical research findings, is inductive. The theoretical approach which will be developed in the last chapter is based on the research which has been considered throughout this analysis. This is not meant to be the final word on organizational theory, since ongoing research will continue to modify the directions which are suggested. Nonetheless, the final chapter will serve as a means of summarizing much of what has been presented.

13

Organizational Effectiveness

There have been several recent and generally excellent attempts to bring the literature on organizational effectiveness together. There are several competing models of effectiveness in the literature which have served as the bases for these analyses. In the present chapter, these models will be analyzed and their strengths and weaknesses highlighted. Inherent in the models and in the debates between the models is the idea that organizational effectiveness as a concept contains *contradictions*. With this in mind, a contradiction model of effectiveness will be developed, which is designed to encompass the insights that previous models have identified.

For practitioners and scholars who concentrate on organizational analysis, organizational effectiveness has been a dominant explicit and implicit point of departure. Benson (1977) suggests that this reflects the administrative-technical orientation of people who study organizations. They wish to find ways to adjust organizations to enhance effectiveness. Benson notes that while many studies deal with effectiveness in a direct and highly visible way, even those studies which do not focus on effectiveness tend to deal with it implicitly, as an underlying or background orientation.

Not everyone is concerned with organizational effectiveness in this manner. There are many important social issues which are basically attempts to prevent organizational effectiveness. Opponents of nuclear energy development and generation and of abortion are essentially against the effectiveness of the organizations that provide electricity and abortions. Ironically, the success of these oppositional efforts depends upon the effectiveness of the oppositional organizations.

269

The present analysis is an attempt to decompose the concept of organizational effectiveness and to expose and examine the contradictions inherent in the concept and its applications. The purpose is to provide a sounder basis for research, theory, and practice. It is hoped that the analysis will be more than administrative-technical and that it will be informative for individuals concerned with altering the directions that organizations take.

Before beginning the analysis, I would like to describe an organization that apparently does *not* conform to the model to be presented here. The purpose of the description is to highlight some of the issues to be considered at a later point and to demonstrate that most of our conceptualizations of effectiveness are much too simplistic.

The organization to be described is a small automobile dealership. It sells and services Saabs, Swedish cars of somewhat unique design and styling which are also relatively expensive. By every indicator that is commonly used and by every effectiveness model that is currently in vogue, this is an effective organization. It makes a profit. It provides customers with good service at prices that are at times startlingly low. The workers have high morale and work diligently. The customers are happy, with most on a first-name basis with the owner of the dealership. The cars perform well and meet governmental safety and environmental protection criteria.

What is the secret of success here? There actually appear to be several such secrets. In the first place, the organization is quite small, with no more than twenty individuals involved in sales, service, and clerical work. The head of the service department is also the owner and major salesperson. There seem to be no disputes about what the appropriate goals of the organization are. Resources are apparently brought into the organization with little difficulty, since people either like Saabs or they do not, which makes for little intensive competition, especially since there are relatively few dealerships in the surrounding area. The various individuals and groups that are connected to the dealership as workers or customers appear to have compatible interests and there are few fights about overcharging or work being done that was not needed. There are no external pressures on the organization to change its policies. Although I have no direct evidence, it would appear that other organizations with which this one has contact would judge it to be quite effective, the only exception being organizations that are growth- or volume-oriented, who would view this operation as not aggressive enough.

This example contains many elements that will enter the later discussion. The organization's *goals* are being met. It is able to acquire and utilize sufficient *resources* to insure organizational survival. Its *personnel* and *clientele* are satisfied. There is *agreement* among participants, within the organization at different levels in the organization and between members and nonmembers on what the organization is doing and how it is doing it. Finally, the organization is apparently serving the best interests of the *community*, since it provides a relatively fuel-efficient and safe automobile.

On the latter point some might argue that the private automobile itself is socially harmful, but that argument can wait for a moment.

While this appears to be a model organization, it is too atypical to really be of much use. It is too small and noncomplex. There is little differentiation among its personnel. Its clientele is self-selected and quite homogeneous. Its goals are few and limited. It does not have much community impact. In short, it is not like most organizations.

The auto dealership example does contain the core elements which must be considered in regard to effectiveness. These are the goals, resources, personnel, clientele, and community in which the organization is embedded. The basic point of this analysis is that *there are contradictions within and between these elements.*

The introduction of the notion of contradictions is not a new one in organizational analyses. Benson (1977) emphasizes dialectical processes in organizations. Heydebrand (1977) documents the fact that the very nature of organizations is one of contradiction, such as the activity of organizing versus organization itself or traditional hierarchical control versus new forms of control, such as professionalization. These recent emphases on contradictions build on aspects of organizational reality which have largely been ignored by organizational theorists of the 1960s and 1970s. Labor-management and staff-line conflicts are essentially inherent in organizations and contribute to the kinds of contradictions which will be included in our examination of organizational effectiveness.

THE CONTRADICTION MODEL: AN INTRODUCTION

Before getting into the specifics of the contradiction model of effectiveness that is to be introduced here, it should be made clear that the approach to be taken forces the analysis of effectiveness away from attempts to conceive of overall effectiveness. A contradiction model means the uncompromised acceptance of the fact that it is folly to try to conceptualize organizations as effective or ineffective (Campbell 1977). This approach agrees with the urgings of Hannan and Freeman (1977b) and Kahn (1977) that effectiveness not be used as a scientific concept.

While there is agreement that effectiveness as an overall concept has little or no utility, it would be a major mistake to simply ignore issues and findings that have been developed in regard to effectiveness. This seeming contradiction can be resolved if a contradiction model of effectiveness is used. Put very simply, a contradiction model of effectiveness will consider organizations to be more or less effective in regard to the variety of goals which they pursue, the variety of resources which they attempt to acquire, the variety of constitutents inside and outside of the organization whether or not they are part of the decision-making process, and the variety of time frames by which effectiveness is judged. The idea of variety in goals, resources, and so on is key here, since it suggests that an organization can be effective in some aspects of its operations and less so on others.

The contradiction idea has its roots in the research project on organi-

272 ORGANIZATIONAL EFFECTIVENESS

zations that deal with problem youths which was discussed in the previous chapter. It was found that these organizations had multiple and conflicting goals. One set of organizations in the study were juvenile detention centers. These organizations had the goals, among others, of "maintaining secure custody" and "providing healthy living arrangements." On the face of it, these are incompatible goals, since secure custody would be optimized by simply locking the youths in cells, which is hardly a healthy living arrangement. Other research, such as Kochan et al. (1976), has also pointed to the issue of multiple and conflicting goals.

The example of contradictory goals noted above comes from the public sector. It is frequently believed that goals here are more amorphous and contradictory than those in the private sector. Unfortunately, the picture here is also one of contradictions. At first glance, the goal idea seems simplest in the case of profit-making organizations. Indeed, much of the research on effectiveness has used this type of organization because of goal clarity. The readily quantifiable profit goal is not such a simple matter, however. It is confounded by such issues as the time perspective (long-run or short-run profits); the rate of profit (in terms of returns to investors); the important issue of survival and growth in a turbulent and unpredictable environment that might in the short run preclude profit making; the intrusion of other values, such as providing quality products or services or benefiting humankind; and the firm's comparative position vis-á-vis others in the same industry. Even the nature of profit itself has multiple meanings. It can involve return on stockholders' equity, return on total capital, sales growth, earnings-per-share growth, debt-to-equity ratio, and net-profit margin. These are not well correlated (Forbes 1973) which alone makes the idea of goals extremely complex.

The goal approach has another complication. In its simplest form, the goal model implies that if an organization has a certain goal, it will organize itself in such a way as to maximize or optimize the attainment of that goal. It is well known, by now, that there are limitations on the rationality of human actors and that decisions within organizations tend to be less than optimal. (March and Simon 1958). Even with these qualifications, it is generally assumed that organizations operate under "norms of rationality" (Thompson 1967). The complication is that what might be at least minimally rational at one point in time may not be so at another.

This complication frequently occurs because of situations beyond organizational control, as seen in the following example. The example is based around the safety of the DC-10 aircraft, which after a tragic crash, was the subject of intensive examination and testing for parts subject to failure. The aircraft were grounded several times, creating complications for the airlines involved and for travelers.

This is not the point of the example, however. The point is that a contradiction occurs when what was once a seemingly rational decision becomes highly questionable at a later point in time, as events occur that upset the premises of the original decision. If an airline decided to make a major investment in DC-10s and to base its profitable long-range flights on this aircraft, it was a rational decision at the time. By utilizing only one type of aircraft, maintenance and inventory costs are reduced and ground facilities can be standardized. This contributes to increased profit and the decision seems to be a clear victory for the goal model and rationality. Then the whole picture changes, and the victory is turned into a highly problematic situation, since regardless of the outcome of the examination of the DC-10s, income was lost while the planes were grounded, and potential passengers shifted to other airlines that fly other aircraft. As will be developed in more detail later, it is impossible to consider organizations without considering the context in which they are operating. This, by the very nature of the context, creates the potential for contradictions with the goal model.

The DC-10 example can be used to illustrate another aspect of the contradiction model. Two groups argued forcefully for the grounding. These were the associations of airline passengers and the union representing flight attendants. Thus, both some clientele and some organizational members had different views of effectiveness than the airline officials or the Federal Aviation Agency, which sought to keep the planes flying.

The fact that different individuals and groups have different perspectives on effectiveness should not be surprising, and it is recognized to some extent in the literature on effectiveness (Pennings and Goodman 1977; Keeley 1978). The contradiction model that is being proposed here makes the differences among organizational constituents an explicit part of the model.

Before moving to another aspect of the model, it should be noted that not all constituents are equal. Within the organization, the obvious fact of differential power at different hierarchical levels means that the effectiveness views of those at the top carry more weight than the views of those at the bottom. Similarly, different departments within an organization have different amounts of power, based on their resources and centrality for organizational operations. The more powerful the *external* group, the more likely that its views on effectiveness will be heeded by organizational decision makers.

Another component of the contradiction model involves the acquisition of resources by the organization. If resource acquisition is viewed simplistically as only bringing in financial resources, little contradiction is evident. Organizations also require personnel, political support, and public support. Financial resource acquisition is frequently tied to the acquisition of these other forms of support. For example, in New York State, programs for the treatment of mental illness and mental retardation were at one time administered by a single state agency. Due to a series of events, advocates for the mentally retarded-developmentally disabled became well organized and highly vocal in support of more and better services for their constituents. The mentally ill did not have this strong set of advocates. The mental retardation advocates pushed the state legislature, the executive branch, and the mental health agency itself for more resources for the retarded, while the professional staff of the agency continued to want to see the resource level for mental illness maintained and strengthened.

This conflict contributed to the splitting up of the agency into separate and separately budgeted agencies dealing with the two types of clients. Financial resource acquisition, in this case, was directly linked to political resource acquisition.

Resource acquisition also contains the potential for contradictions. Some school systems, for example, having funding approved for activities such as interscholastic sports or driver education but not for items such as counseling or the library. Business firms in the oil industry can be successful in acquiring financial resources, but lose media and political support on charges of excess profits.

The analysis of effectiveness has led to the development of several models of effectiveness. Each emphasizes a different aspect of the overall issue and each provides important insights.

MODELS OF ORGANIZATIONAL EFFECTIVENESS

The System-Resource Model

The choice of the system-resource model as the first effectiveness model to be examined is based on the fact that an extensive analysis of the environmental-organizational interface has been presented. This model was developed by Yuchtman and Seashore (1967; Seashore and Yuchtman 1967). Katz and Kahn's (1978) approach, which is somewhat different, has not received the attention that the Yuchtman-Seashore version has; it raised many of the issues critical in theoretical developments regarding the environment.

Yuchtman and Seashore began by noting that variables concerning organizational effectiveness could be ordered into a hierarchy. At the top of the hierarchy is some ultimate criteria which can only be assessed over time. An example of such an ultimate criterion would be the optimum use of opportunities and resources found in the environment. In terms of the natural selection or resource dependence models, ultimate criteria would be survival or death.

Next come penultimate criteria. According to Seashore and Yuchtman (1967), they have the following characteristics: "They are relatively few in number; they are 'output' or 'results' criteria referring to things sought for their own value; they have trade-off value in relation to one another; they are in turn wholly caused by partially independent sets of lesser performance variables; their sum in some weighted mixture over time wholly determines the ultimate criterion. These criteria would be factorially independent of one another, although probably correlated in observed performances; also some of the component variables would be universal, others unique to certain classes of organizations" (pp. 378–79).

The next level of variables involve the subsidiary variables. These are many in number, some of which would refer to subgoals or means for achieving goals, while others would be in terms of organizational states or processes. The relationships among these variables would take many forms—positive and negative correlation, independence, causal, covarying, interacting, and so on. They would be related to the penultimate criteria in the form of being overlapping, but distinguishable subsets. These subsidiary variables would have short time frames and represent transitory states or processes within the organization.

Yuchtman and Seashore believed that the ultimate criterion was an unmeasurable construct and chose to focus in on the penultimate criteria. They then sought to investigate, through statistical testing:

1. Whether there is a set of penultimate performance variables, factorially pure, that account for much of the total variance in performances.

2. Whether the factors are strongly correlated with, and therefore potentially caused by, sets of subsidiary variables representing organizational states and processes, but not goals.

3. Whether the set of factors is constant across a number of similar organizations (not tested in the present analysis).

4. Whether this set of factors is constant over some span of time.

5. Whether the performance of a single organization is variable over time within the set of constant factors.

6. Whether the conceptual content of the factors suggest that some of them may be universal, others unique. (p. 380)

Yuchtman and Seashore had a unique data set with which to test their ideas. The data came from seventy-five independent insurance agencies in the United States. Data were available over an eleven-year period, with three time periods used in the study. The nature of the insurance business is such that extensive records are kept, and Seashore and Yuchtman had some two hundred variables with which to work, of which they utilized seventy-six.

Based on a principal component solution, orthogonally rotated, factor analysis, ten factors or penultimate criteria were identified which accounted for about 70 percent of the total variance in performance. The factors were extremely stable over the eleven-year period, even though the relationships among the factors varied at different time periods.

The factors did have different time frames, with some being very stable over time and others having cyclic or phasic effects. For example, three of the factors were extremely stable over the eleven-year period. "Business volume" referred to issues such as agency manpower, number of policies in force, and number of new sales. The stability is explained by the fact that once people are committed to buying life insurance, they tend to keep buying from the same agency. "Market penetration," or the extent to which the agency had captured a share of the local market, can be similarly viewed as success leading to success. "Business Mix" referred to the presence of both large and small policies and individual and employee benefit policies. It was also linked to previous successes.

Three of the factors were much more time specific. These were the "youthfulness of members," "productivity of new members," and "rate of manpower growth." Apparently these organizations would take in numbers of new young agents at one point in time and then not take many in during the next time period.

The rest of the factors were intermediate in their stability over time. These factors included "production costs," or measures of overhead expenses in regard to sales, "maintenance costs," or the costs involved in maintaining accounts, "management emphasis," or the managers' personal commission, and "member productivity," or the new business generated per agent. According to Seashore and Yuchtman, these internal performance criteria adjust somewhat over the shorter term in the interests of longer term patterns.

Seashore and Yuchtman then go on to test their notion of subsidiary variables and their predicted relationship with the penultimate variables. In order to do this, they utilized data from a survey taken at one point in time (1961). One of the more interesting findings was that there is an apparent lag in the kinds of social-psychological variables considered in the survey. The survey tapped such factors as perceptions of managerial supportiveness, quality of upward communication, and the nature of managerial power. They found relatively few significant relationships between the subsidiary and penultimate variables in the same year as the survey, but many more when the subsidiary variables were correlated with the penultimate variables for the following year.

This finding is interesting in two ways. First, it is instructive methodologically, since it points up the potential problems faced in cross-sectional analyses. Important relationships may be disguised or unobserved when data from only one point in time are used. Secondly, the finding suggests a causal relationship, with managerial behavior in one year leading to performance results in a second year. Seashore and Yuchtman did not test another possible causal relationship—that performance in the year preceding the survey led to the managerial behavior uncovered in the survey, but their findings on the importance of time-series analyses is an important one.

A second finding from this phase of the analysis was that each predictor was related to some of the penultimate performance variables but not to others. According to Seashore and Yuchtman, this is in line with their prediction that the subsidiary variables would be sorted into subsets having causal relationships with the higher order performance variables.

The final finding in this analysis is most interesting. They determined that some of the lower order variables have strong positive relationships with some performance variables and strong negative relationships with others. Managerial supportiveness, for example, was found to affect high business volume, acquisition and retention of manpower, market penetration, and the youthfulness of the work force. Supportiveness was also negatively related with productivity per agent. This kind of finding strongly suggests that both predictor and outcome variables be treated as sets of variables, since focusing just on pairs of variables could lead to misleading results.

Seashore and Yuchtman conclude that these findings lead to a definition of effectiveness of an organization as the "*ability to exploit its environment in the acquisition of scarce and valued resources to sustain its functioning*" (p. 393). Their reasoning is that while some of the penultimate criteria found could be construed as goals, such as business volume and market penetration, others, such as youthfulness of members or high proportion of new members, could not.

Another conclusion is that resource acquisition must be viewed as relative to the capacity of the environment. Some organizations operate in rich environments, while others act on poorer ones. They also note that their definition stresses the ability to utilize the environment, rather than maximum utilization of the environment, since maximum utilization could lead to the total depletion of resources.

Seashore and Yuchtman conclude their argument by noting that all of the penultimate criteria uncovered in their research probably could not be generalized to all organizations, but that some of them could be. They suggest that the systems-resource approach is preferable to the goal approach, since, in their view, imputing goals to organizations is teleological.

In an interesting extension and twist of the Seashore-Yuchtman position, Molnar and Rogers (1976) measured the amount of resources coming into and flowing out of a set of public agencies. They found that inflow was related to outflow, as might be expected. They also viewed the distribution of resources from a public organization as an appropriate effectiveness indicator.

The Seashore-Yuchtman argument is persuasive. It does contain some problem areas, however. For instance, it is actually a question of semantics whether or not growth in business volume is viewed as only one form of resource acquisition or as a goal. The relatively stable penultimate criteria discussed by Seashore and Yuchtman can easily be viewed as goals or constraints on the decisions made by the insurance firms in question. The less stable criteria, such as youthfulness of members, could actually turn out to be predictor variables for these sorts of organizations. It is well known, for example, that young men and women who enter the life insurance sales occupation have good success at first, selling to relatives and friends. This would appear to be a means by which a goal, such as sales volume, could be achieved.

It should also be noted that resource acquisition does not just happen but is based on what the organization is attempting to achieve, namely its goals. This is in line with our earlier discussion of decision making, in which decisions are made on the basis of perceived environmental conditions and organizational goals. It appears reasonable to argue that resources are seldom acquired just for their own sake but rather in reference to the paths selected by the power coalitions in the organization. Scott (1977, p. 67) suggests that Seashore and Yuchtman implicitly recognize this point when they suggest that criteria for determining effectiveness must be identified. Scott also suggests that the Seashore-Yuchtman formulation is overly narrow in that it only utilizes the interests of the organizational directors. In the case of insurance firms, potential customers could withhold resources, but there are many forms of organizations in which potential customers do not have this option.

Campbell (1977, p. 44) notes an additional problem with the kind of approach taken by Yuchtman and Seashore. While factor analysis is a fine methodological tool, it does not arrange the factors in the form of a hierarchy. Campbell is suggesting that some of the penultimate criteria may be more important than others, and thus that choices may have to be made among the criteria. In the case of the insurance firms, this could take the form of having to choose between increasing business volume or increasing market penetration. When stated in these terms, the argument moves awfully close to a goal-modeling format. Before turning to the goal model, it should be noted that the Seashore and Yuchtman formulation, which has not generated any coherent line of research (Goodman and Pennings 1977, p. 4), does sensitize us to the critical importance of organization-environment transactions.

The Goal Model

The goal model of effectiveness is both simple and complex. In its simple version, effectiveness has been defined as the "degree to which [an organization] realizes its goals" (Etzioni 1964, p. 8). Complexity occurs as soon as it is realized that most organizations have multiple and frequently conflicting goals. Kochan, Cummings, and Huber (1976) have pointed out that structural differentiation in organizations is related to goal diversity and goal incompatibility. Since most organizations do exhibit structural diversity, such multiplicity and incompatibility can almost be taken as a given for organizations. This makes the goal model difficult to use, but does not automatically destroy its utility.

Before dealing specifically with the model, some aspects of the nature of the goals should be noted. Goals involve intents and outcomes and serve as constraints on decision making. Organizational goals by definition are creations of individuals, singly or collectively. At the same time, the determination of a goal for collective action becomes a standard by which the collective action is judged. The collectively determined, commonly based goal seldom remains constant over time. New considerations imposed from without or within deflect the organization from its original goal, not only changing the activities of the organization, but also becoming part of the overall goal structure. The important point is that the goal of any organization is an abstraction distilled from the desires of members and pressures from the environment and internal system.

Thinking of goals as abstract values has the utility of indicating the reason why organizational members do not just act on their feelings or whims of a particular day. At the same time, it is a mistake to take as the abstraction the official goal statements of the organization. Perrow (1961) has analyzed this situation nicely. He notes that official goals are "the general purposes of the organization as put forth in the charter, annual reports, public statements by key executives and other authoritative pronouncements." Operative goals, on the other hand, "designate the ends sought through the actual operating policies of the organization; they tell us what the organization actually is trying to do, regardless of what the official goals say are the aims" (p. 855).

In one of the early studies in the tradition of modern organizational theory, Blau (1955) found that two employment agency units, which had the same official goals, actually were very different in what they really were attempting to accomplish. One unit was high competitive, with members striving to outproduce each other in terms of the numbers of individuals placed. In the other unit, cooperation and quality of placement was stressed.

In discussing this point, Perrow notes (1961):

> Where operative goals provide the specific content of official goals, they reflect choices among competing values. They may be justified on the basis of an official goal, even though they may subvert another official goal. In one sense they are a means to official goals, but since the latter are vague or of high abstraction, the 'means' become ends in themselves when the organization is the object of analysis. For example, where profit making is the announced goal, operative goals will specify whether quality or quantity is to be emphasized, whether profits are to be short run and risky or long run and stable, and will indicate the relative priority of diverse and somewhat conflicting ends of customer service, employee morale, competitive pricing, diversification, or liquidity. Decisions on all of these factors influence the nature of the organization and distinguish it from another with an identical official goal. (pp. 855–56)

Operative goals may be linked directly to official goals. At the same time, operative goals can develop which are unrelated to official goals. Perrow goes on to note:

> Unofficial operative goals, on the other hand, are tied more directly to group interests, and while they may support, be irrelevant to, or subvert official goals, they bear no necessary connection with them. An interest in a major supplier may dictate the policies of a corporate executive. The prestige that attaches to utilizing elaborate highspeed computers,may dictate the reorganization of inventory and accounting departments. Racial prejudice may influence the selection procedures of an employment agency. The personal ambition of a hospital administrator may lead to community alliances and activities which bind the organization without enhancing its goal achievement. On the other hand, while the use of interns and residents as "cheap labor" may subvert the official goals of medical education, it may substantially further the offical goal of providing a high quality of patient care. (p. 856)

Operative goals are thus a derivation of and distillation from official goals. They are developed and modified through ongoing interaction patterns within organizations. They are more than just the results of interpersonal interactions, however. They persist beyond the life of a particular interaction and become the standards by which the organization's actions are judged and around which decisions are made. Even though operative goals are developed in concrete interactions, they, like official goals, are abstractions, since they become standards by which actions and decisions are judged. (For additional discussion of these points, see Price 1972.)

The discussion of the development of operative goals suggests that goals change over time. There are three reasons for changes in the goals of organizations. First, organizations are in *direct* interaction with the environment. Thompson and McEwen (1958) presented a framework for understanding goal shifts as a result of such interaction. Organizational goal setting is affected by competitive, bargaining, co-optative and coalitional relationships with the environment. Competition occurs when the rivalry between two organizations is mediated by a third party, as in the case of business firms competing for the same customers. Competition also occurs in the public sector as government agencies compete for a share of the tax dollar (Wildavsky 1964). Competition affects the goal structure as the organization shapes its action to try to insure continued support. In this regard, of course, the goal model can be seen to encompass at least some aspects of the systems resource model.

Bargaining also involves resources, but in a different manner. The organization is in direct interaction with suppliers, customers, and other organizations. In a bargaining situation, an organization has to "give" a little in order to get what it desires. Thompson and McEwen note the example of a university which bargains the right to name a building for a substantial gift to build the building. Police agencies will bargain with offenders to receive information about other offenders. Bargaining is more subtle than direct competition, but it also affects the structure of goals.

Co-optation is "the process of absorbing new elements into the leadership or policy-determining structure of an organization as a means of averting threats to its stability or existence" (Thompson and McEwen 1958, p. 27). The classic study of co-optation is Selznick's (1966) analysis of the development of the Tennessee Valley Authority. The TVA shifted its emphases as segments of the community were brought into its decision-making system. Burt et al. (1980) have shown that business firms engage in co-optation as they engage in situations in which there are market constraints. Co-optation is a two-way street, of course, with both co-opters and co-optees being affected by the action.

Coalition is the actual combining of two or more organizations. This is the most extreme form "of environmental conditioning of organizational goals" (Thompson and McEwen 1958, p. 28). In this case, the organizations in the coalition cannot set goals unilaterally.

Shifts in organizational goals as a result of direct interactions with other organizations in a focal organization's environment emphasizes the importance of dealing with operative, rather than official goals. A reliance on just official goals would miss these sometimes subtle, sometimes dramatic shifts. This kind of analysis also indicates the importance of looking at organizational effectiveness over time, since a cross-sectional analysis might be done just prior to a significant shift and thus be essentially meaningless.

Goals can also change as a result of *internal* organizational changes. We have already noted the importance of power coalitions within organizations. These power coalitions can shift, sometimes as a result of external pressures, but also because of internal dynamics. Michels' (1949) classic study of the development of oligarchy in political parties and labor unions is illustrative of this. The goals of the rank and file tend to give way to those of the elites. Organizations may begin to emphasize goals which are easily quantifiable, at the expense of those which are not so easily quantified. Universities look at the number of faculty publications, rather than the more difficult to measure goal of classroom teaching; business firms look at output per worker, rather than "diligence, cooperation, punctuality, loyalty, and responsibility" (Gross 1968, p. 295). If organizations do begin to emphasize that which is easily quantifiable, then there is a shift of goals in that direction. Internally generated goal shifts take place as a result of decisions made within the organization. While such decisions can reflect external pressures, they can also be a result of power shifts within the organization that are basically unrelated to external pressures. The "old guard" retires, new coalitions are formed, and old arrangements disintegrate. These can occur independently of environmental forces. Jenkins (1977) notes that goal shifts are possible when there is slack in the organization and it is secure. He found that staff interactions guided by a new professional ideology and strong purposive commitments contributed to major and radical goal shifts within the National Council of Churches in the United States. He also suggests that threats to the organization's domain would probably lead to a more conservative stance.

The final source of goal shifts lies outside the organization and involves *indirect* pressures from the environment. Economic conditions can become altered. Technological developments must be accommodated. Values shift. Organizational goals are adjusted to these environmental conditions. The classic study of this form of goal shift is Sills' (1957) analysis of the March of Dimes organization, which had been oriented around the treatment of individuals who suffered the crippling effects of polio. The development of safe vaccines, a technological development, essentially eliminated the need for the continued existence of the organization, until it shifted its goals to include other crippling diseases.

Another example of this form of goal shift can be seen among colleges and universities as the demographic composition of the population shifts. There is no longer a growing supply of young people, but there is of older people. Higher educational organizations are now including nontraditional students as major recruitment targets, with "seminars for seniors" and a wide array of continuing education programs. The demographic shifts are beyond the control of the organizations involved, as are the other sources of indirect pressure from the environment. Although organizations can try to influence values, manipulate the economy to their advantage, and keep up with technological developments, there are many situations that are simply beyond organizational control. At various times, the United States has faced shortages of gasoline. Organizations, even petroleum firms, have no control over the actions of oil-producing nations.

Thus, the environment can have an indirect, but still crucial role in the determination of goal shifts.

Thus far, the analysis has suggested that organizations have multiple goals. These goals may be contradictory. They may also shift. The analysis will now turn to a consideration of how goals can be used in analyzing effectiveness.

GOALS AND EFFECTIVENESS

As noted earlier, the most simple use of the goal model suggests that an organization is effective to the degree to which it achieves its goals. According to Campbell (1977):

> The goal-centered view makes a reasonably explicit assumption that the organization is in the hands of a rational set of decision makers who have in mind a set of goals that they wish to pursue. Further, these goals are few enough in number to be manageable and can be defined well enough to be understood. Given that goals can be thus identified, it should be possible to plan the best management strategies for attaining them. Within this orientation, the way to assess organizational effectiveness would be to develop criterion measures to assess how well the goals are being achieved.

Unfortunately, for organizations and their analysts, the matter is not that simple. Hannan and Freeman (1977b) have examined the goal model and have pinpointed some of the problems with its use. They begin their analysis by pointing out that it would be unsatisfactory to totally drop the goal concept, since goals are part of the defining characteristics of organizations. They go on to note, however, that a first and major difficulty with the goal approach is that there is likely to be a multiplicity of organizational goals. This occurs even among the publicly legitimated or official goals, as has already been noted. Hannan and Freeman comment: "Virtually all public agencies and bureaus have very many public goals. For example, the number and diversity of goals of agencies like the Department of Health, Education, and Welfare (HEW) and the Department of Commerce boggle the imagination" (pp. 111–12).

Such boggling is compounded when private or operative goals are entered into the analysis. Making the situation even more complicated is that organizational subunits can and do develop their own goals. As discussed earlier, the more complex the organization, the more complex its goal structure. The multiplicity of goals is a difficult problem in and of itself.

According to Hannan and Freeman, the second broad problem with goals involves their specificity (p. 113). Universities have the very general goals of advancing the store of useful knowledge; police agencies have the goal of protecting the public. These broad goals become much more specific in actual operations, with the more specific goals taking a variety of possible forms. For the police, for example, protecting the public could be approached from the standpoint of putting more officers on foot patrol, cracking down on prostitution, putting more officers in plainclothes operations, or making public relations statements. Within the organization, units can move into divergent directions which are consistent with the broader goal but which could interfere with each other.

The third problem with goals involves the *temporal dimension* (Hannan and Freeman 1977b). They note:

> Should we consider the short run or the long run or both? The many published empirical studies that employ cross-sectional data on samples of organizations (see, for example, Lawrence and Lorsch 1967) tacitly take the short-run perspective. Whether or not this is appropriate depends on the nature of the goals function for each organization. To the extent that the goals function stresses quick return on investment (as in many business ventures, disaster relief organizations, military field units, and so on) the short-run outcomes should be given highest priority. For those organizations that orient toward continued production (for example, many other types of business ventures, universities, research and development organizations, and so on) the year-to-year fluctuations in performance should be discounted and the average performance over longer periods emphasized. (p. 113)

Hannan and Freeman note that different levels in the hierarchy can employ different time frames, making the situation even more complex. They do not deal with the fact that different units within the same organization can also have different time frames as Lawrence and Lorsch (1967) found in their interdepartmental comparisons.

Hannan and Freeman suggest that the goal approach be retained in organizational analyses, by using goals in a manner similar to which individual preferences are used in microeconomics. They note that such preferences are not measured directly.

> Their role (more precisely, the role of hypotheses regarding preference functions or indifference curves) is to permit the formulation of testable hypotheses relating prices and consumer behavior.
>
> Many of the problems we have listed are also problems in the conceptualization and measurement of individual preferences. The point is that these difficulties do not impede the use of unmeasured preferences in the formulation of individual preference theories with strong empirical implications. The same could be true of organizational goals. Goals and environmental configurations together determine organizational behavior. We suggest treating goals as unmeasured causal variables and using propositions involving goals to derive falsifiable propositions relating environmental chracteristics and organizational behavior. (p. 115)

As will be seen, in the contradiction model being developed here, we do not leave goals as unmeasured, but do attempt to deal with some of the issues raised in Hannan and Freeman's analysis.

284   Organizational Effectiveness

Hannan and Freeman also deal with the second part of the goal model, which is organizational performance or output. Outcome assessment is difficult for several reasons. First is the time perspective used. An outcome that is successful for the short run could be disastrous for the long run. The test of this idea requires longitudinal data of the sort that is not readily available. Another problem in outcome assessment involves "bounding systems" (Hannan and Freeman 1977b, p. 116), or the problem in distinguishing the effects of events both inside and outside of the organization. The issue here is that it is very difficult to determine what activity within an organization contributes to some outcome. It is equally difficult to specify if this outcome is a result of organizational actions or the result of some external force. Hannan and Freeman note that the quality of the input of an organization affects the quality of the output. Many social service organizations, for example, select clients (inputs or external forces) who appear to have good chances of success in the treatment which the organization provides. More problematic clients are referred elsewhere or simply passed around the social service system. This sort of situation makes the assessment of the outcome of the social service organization difficult, since it is difficult to disentangle organizational-versus-input effects.

The same problem can be seen in business firms. Almost all firms have a personnel or industrial relations department. Very few, if any, can specify the contributions of such departments to outcomes, even though there is a general belief that the quality of the services provided by personnel are important.

The problem is made even more complicated by the fact that while both input quality and the contribution of units within organizations can be understood as contributors to performance, so too can the ability of the organization to control the quality of inputs. Control of environmental factors is an outcome of organizational actions. As noted in the discussion of the resource-dependence model, organizations attempt to build up demands for their outputs. Success here means higher performance. Hannan and Freeman conclude:

> Once we acknowledge that all these factors are subject to organizational strategy and action, we are faced with a serious methodological problem. All of the variables that appear in the conventional analyses are endogenous, that is, causally dependent on other variables in the model. For example, the quality of inputs may be a function of the expenditure on inputs, which is a function of output performance. If none of these factors is causally prior, or exogenous, it is extremely difficult to obtain unique estimates of any relevant causal effects in the system. In the technical language of econometrics, the system is underidentified. To remedy this situation one must make a considerable number of strong assumptions concerning the details of the causal structure. Unfortunately, the existing theories of organizational performance (and effectiveness) do not provide a basis for these assumptions. (p. 122)

Hannan and Freeman conclude their argument by suggesting that effectiveness be dropped as a scientific concept, since comparisons across organizations cannot be made to construct and test abstract theories of organizations. They then suggest that effectiveness considerations remain valid in terms of engineering or social criticism. By this they mean that effectiveness can be used in the administrative technical sense by individuals interested in engineering or in managing organizations toward public or private goals. Social criticism can be accomplished by demonstrating that organizations are not doing what they claim to be doing or that they are not doing it well enough. In the contradiction model which will be developed here, the intent will be to permit effectiveness considerations to remain at the scientific level.

Scott (1977) has identified additional problems with the goal approach. He suggests that goals have been used in three ways in effectiveness analyses. First, they can be viewed as sources of incentives for organizational participants. Secondly, they can be approached as guides to participants' efforts. This is similar to the approach being taken here. The third aspect of goals is that "they provide criteria for identifying and appraising selected aspects of organizational functioning. In short, we must analytically distinguish between goals employed to motivate or direct participants' behavior, on the one hand, and goals used to set criteria for the evaluation of participants' or the entire organization's behavior, on the other" (p. 66). This distinction between goals for motivation and direction and goals for evaluative purposes is a useful one. Although we have emphasized the fact that goals must be incorporated into the decision-making framework, effectiveness concerns pull the analysis in the direction of the evaluative-criteria side of the goal formulation.

There are additional problems with the goal model. Reimann (1975) has noted that the goal model of effectiveness contains the problem that an organization cannot be effective if this means attainment of all or most of its goals. Multiplicity and contradictions among goals must be recognized in any utilization of goals in effectiveness studies.

We have not dealt with the issue of who or which parties are to judge the performance of organizations in regard to goals, where goals are used. As will be developed in detail at a later point, the views of different organizational constituents can vary widely and should be considered, as they will be in the contradiction model. In the next section we will deal specifically with attempts to conceptualize effectiveness in terms of the satisfaction of organizational participants. One approach that has been promising, based around the goal model, has been to ask persons in superordinate positions about the effectiveness of organizational units which are subordinate to them. This approach is quite useful for performance assessments of organizational subunits. It also could be used in situations where organizations within a single political jurisdiction, such as state, country, or city organizations, are being examined. In reality, such effectiveness judgments are made at the time of budget allocations, but that process contains more than effectiveness considerations.

The approach of asking superordinates about the effectiveness of subordinates has been used with success by Mahoney and Weitzel (1969) and Duncan (1973). This approach has revealed the fact that even superordinates stress different goals. Mahoney and Weitzel note:

> General business managers tend to use productivity and efficient performance. These high-order criteria refer to measures of output, whereas lower-order criteria tend to refer to characteristics of the organization climate, supervisory style, and organizational capacity for performance. The research and development managers, on the other hand, use cooperative behavior, staff development, and reliable performance as high-order criteria; and efficiency, productivity, and output behavior as lower-order criteria. (p. 362)

Effectiveness thus lies in the eye and mind of the beholder, with the important qualification that some beholders are more powerful than others. Before turning to an examination of participant-satisfaction approaches to effectiveness, which deal specifically with this issue, one final research finding regarding the goal model will conclude this section. Molnar and Rogers (1976) attempted to determine if measures of effectiveness from the goal model were related to measures of effectiveness from the systems-resource model. They found only weak relationships among the measures from the two approaches, suggesting again that effectiveness must be approached with full awareness of the contradictions inherent in organizations and in effectiveness.

Participant-Satisfaction Models

In this section we will examine models of effectiveness that, in various ways and at various levels, utilize individuals as the major frame of reference. The emphasis in these models is *not* satisfaction in terms of morale or some other psychological state of the individual. This is frequently a component of the goal model, seeing morale as just one of several goals. Rather, in these models the emphasis is on individual or group judgments about the quality of the organization.

Barnard (1938) set the tone for participant satisfaction models with his analysis of organizations as cooperative, incentive-distributing devices. "Individuals contributed their activities to organizations in return for incentives, the contribution of each in the pursuit of his particularistic ends being a contribution to the satisfaction of the ends of others. Barnard regarded the motives of the individuals participating in organizations as the critical determinants. Only if these were satisfied, could the organization continue to operate" (Georgiou 1973, p. 300). Organizational success was not viewed in terms of goals being achieved, but rather through its capacity to survive through being able to gain enough contributions from the members by providing sufficient rewards or incentives.

Georgiou (1973), building on the work of Barnard, has developed what he labels as a "counter-paradigm" to the goal model (see also, Samuel 1979). According to Georgiou:

Thus, the essential thrust of the counter paradigm is that the emergence of organizations, their structure of roles, division of labor, and distribution of power, as well as their maintenance, change, and dissolution can best be understood as outcomes of the complex exchanges between individuals pursuing a diversity of goals. Although the primary focus of interest lies in the behavior within organizations, and the impact of the environment on this, the reciprocal influence of the organization on the environment is also accommodated. Since not all of the incentives derived from the processes of organizational exchange are consumed within the interpersonal relations of the members organizational contributors gain resources with which they can influence the environment. (p. 308)

The implication of Georgiou's argument for effectiveness is that incentives within organizations must be adequate for maintaining the contributions of organizational members and must also contain a surplus for developing power capabilities for dealing with the environment. A basic problem with this argument is that it does not disclose how the incentives are brought into the organization in the first place. If a major incentive is money, this must be secured. To be sure, money is brought into the organization through exchanges with the environment, but it appears that the systems-resource approach or a goal model dealing with profit is necessary prior to considering individual inducements.

Cummings (1977) approaches effectiveness from a slightly different perspective. He states:

One possibly fruitful way to conceive of an organization and the processes that define it is as an instrument or an arena within which participants can engage in behavior they perceive as instrumental to their goals. From this perspective, an effective organization is one in which the *greatest percentage of participants* perceive themselves as free to use the organization and its subsystems as instruments for their own ends. It is also argued that the greater the degree of perceived organizational instrumentality by *each* participant, the more effective the organization. Thus, this definition of an effective organization is entirely psychological in perspective. It attempts to incorporate both the number of persons who see the organization as a key instrument in fulfilling their needs *and*, for each person, the degree to which the organization is so perceived. (pp. 59–60)

According to this approach, factors such as profitability, efficiency, and productivity are necessary conditions for organizational survival and not ends in themselves. The organization must acquire enough resources in order to permit it to be instrumental for its members. In a rather related approach, Steers (1977) argues that more effective organizations are those in which the members agree with the goals of the organization and thus work more consistently to achieve them.

Approaching organizational effectiveness from the perspective of individuals and their instrumental gains or their goals has three major problems. The first problem, which is particularly the case for Steers' approach, is that individuals have varying forms of linkages to the organizations of which they are a part. As Etzioni (1961, 1975) has demonstrated, people's involvement in organizations can be alienative, calculative, or moral. These different forms of involvement preclude the possibility of individual and goal congruence in many types of organizations. Continuing for a moment with a criticism of Steers' approach, it does not appear to be unfair to note that many personnel in most organizations are probably unaware of the organizations' official *or* operative goals, so that agreement becomes a moot point.

The more basic problem in these psychological formulations is that by focusing on instrumentality for individuals, the activities or operations of the organization as a whole, or by subunits, is missed. While the instrumentality approach is capable of being generalized across organizations, it misses the fact that organizational outputs do something in society. They are consumed, enjoyed, and are environmentally harmful. They affect other organizations and people in and out of other organizations as much as people within a focal organization. The psychological approach also downplays the reality of conflicts among goals and decisions that must be made in the face of environmental pressures. The problem is basically one of overlooking a major part of organizational reality. For example, Angle and Perry (1981) found a positive relationship between workers' commitment to the organization and such effectiveness indicators as adaptability, turnover, and tardiness. No such relationship was found with the effectiveness indicators of operating costs and absenteeism. By reducing effectiveness considerations to the individual level, the point is missed that there can be conflicts between desirable outcomes, such as lowered operating costs and lowered turnover.

A third problem with this form of individualistic approach is that it misses the fact that individuals outside the organization are affected by what organizations do. Stipak (1979), for example, found little relationship between objective service delivery indicators and citizen evaluation. Giordano (1976, 1977) found that the "clients" of a juvenile justice system network had clearly different views of the effectiveness of organizations such as the police, courts, and probation departments than the members of these agencies had. This is hardly surprising, of course, since the clients in this case were juveniles who had had trouble with the law. Nonetheless, a client perspective on effectiveness would seem to be a critical component of any comprehensive effectiveness analysis.

Keeley (1978) has tried to overcome the problems of just focusing on the reactions of internal organizational actors by proposing a "social justice" approach to effectiveness. Building on the work of Rawls (1971), Keeley suggests that a guiding principal for organizational evaluation might be "maximization of the least advantaged participants in a social system" (p. 285). Keeley then proposes that this approach could be operationalized by minimizing the *regret* that participants experience in their interactions with the organization. Keeley recognizes the difficulties associated with the actual application of this approach, but claims that this approach actually contains an optimization principle that goal models do not contain. It is possible to specify the manner in which group regret can be minimized across organizations. It is not possible to specify how goal attainment can be optimized across organizations, given the diversity of goals.

Keeley concludes:

> Finally, the social-justice model—specifically the minimization of regret principle—manages to balance participant interests in an ethical, yet pragmatic, fashion. It may seem perverse to focus on regretful organizational participants rather than on those, possibly more in number, who enjoy the outcomes of cooperative activity. But the point is that generally aversive system consequences ought not, and in the long run, probably will not be tolerated by some participants so that positive consequences can be produced for others. Systems that minimize the aversive consequences of interaction are, therefore, claimed to be more just as well as more stable in the long run. (p. 290)

One can disagree with the practicality of Keeley's approach from the standpoint of the difficulties in determining levels of regret for all system participants—after all, the cost of surveys is extremely high and not all participants probably realize that they are participants—but the point on ethicality is one that should remain fixed in effectiveness modeling.

Constraints, Goals, and Participants

Pennings and Goodman (1977) have made a major contribution to the literature on effectiveness. They approach participants by introducing the concept of the dominant coalition. In order to show how Pennings and Goodman bring participants into effectiveness determination, it is necessary to trace their theoretical argument. Their approach is very similar to the contradiction model used in the present analysis.

Pennings and Goodman begin their argument by defining effectiveness: "Organizations are effective if relevant constraints can be satisfied and if organizational results approximate or exceed a set of referents for multiple goals" (p. 160).

The idea of constraints involves conditions or requirements that must be satisfied if an organization is to be effective. Constraints involve policies or procedures, set in advance. They guide decision making and behavior in the organizations. Examples of constraints are "maintaining market share at a certain percentage, maintaining quality at a certain level, and not doing business in foreign countries requiring political kickbacks" (p. 160).

Organizational goals refer to desired end states or objectives specified by the dominant coalition. Pennings and Goodman are explicit in their inclusion of multiple goals. Both constraints and goals are used in the assessment of effectiveness, but there are important differences between the two concepts. Goals receive special attention and concern from the dominant coalition. They are closely related to the motivations of the dominant coalition. Interestingly, goals and constraints can be on the same dimension or area of activity, but the difference lies in the attention paid by the dominant coalition. Pennings and Goodman state:

> Whether achieving a particular quantity or quality level is a goal or constraint depends partially on which is more central to the organization's dominant coalition. For example, some U.S. universities emphasize the number of students enrolled as a constraint for quality of academic excellence, whereas other universities emphasize high enrollment but are constrained by the need of maintaining a minimum level of academic excellence. (p. 161)

A second difference between goals and constraints is that "goals may or may not approximate a referent, whereas constraints must be satisfied as a necessary condition of organizational effectiveness. Degrees (or the relative amount) of organizational effectiveness can be assessed by the degree to which a goal approximates or exceeds a referent" (p. 161). This is a complicated set of ideas and requires some discussion. Referents are the standards against which constraints and goals are weighed or evaluated. They involve the dominant coalition's standards of evaluation. Constraints must be met if an organization is to be effective, but just meeting the constraint does not mean effectiveness. Achieving a goal on top of the constraint is effectiveness. Pennings and Goodman use the example of a business firm that wants to increase its profits (a goal) and at the same time maintain the quality of service (a constraint). A failure in maintaining quality of service would contribute to ineffectiveness, but exceeding the quality of service standard would not lead to effectiveness. Only by increasing its profitability would the organization be effective. Effectiveness is based on the degree to which the goal is achieved.

Interestingly, Pennings and Goodman do not bring in resources as constraints. It would appear that the systems resource and goal models could be nicely joined in constraint-goal terminology. Certainly resources are required and the resource level required for operations is a constraint on the organization. This may be the most appropriate usage of the systems-resource model, *viewing resources as important constraints that must be satisfied before movements toward goals can be realized.*

Pennings and Goodman recognize the fact that there are multiple goals and constraints and that the time frame for these is not constant. They also recognize that for each constraint or goal there may be multiple referents. They do not note that different referents for a single goal or constraint may have contradictory elements, as will be demonstrated later. They do note that effectiveness must always be measured after the fact.

An important contribution of the Pennings-Goodman formulation is the recognition that organizations have internal and external constituencies (see also Katz and Kahn 1978). These are the components of the dominant coalition that decides goals and determines constraints. Effectiveness criteria are defined by the dominant coalition on the basis of consensus agreements that are achieved. Consensus is achieved by negotiation among the parties involved. This is not a simple process, since the various constituencies have differing and multidimensional preferences.

The process of achieving consensus has the effect of focusing attention on the goals, constraints, and referents. It also forces the dominant coalition to consider alternative arrangements among these elements, adjusting levels of constraints so that goals might be achieved, or altering goals in the face of constraints that cannot be adjusted. Pennings and Goodman view organizations as being made up of multiple constituencies that influence the setting of constraints, goals, and referents. The internal dominant coalition determines the forms and emphases that these take. According to Pennings and Goodman, "although constituencies may hold many referents and constraints with which to evaluate the organization, it is only to the extent that these constraints and referents can be imposed on the organization that they become useful tools for assessing effectiveness" (p. 171).

The approach to be taken in the contradiction model is quite similar to that of Pennings and Goodman. A major difference is the utilization of resources as constraints. Another important difference is that while the Pennings-Goodman formulation stresses consensus achieved in the dominant coalition, the contradiction model will not assume consensus. To be sure, decision have to be made, but there may be times when the consensus that is achieved for a particular decision is so tenuous that it is very short lived, and the decision is soon reversed. The contradiction model stresses the fact that the various constituencies of an organization may have irreconcilable differences and that effectiveness for one party may be the opposite for another.

The Pennings-Goodman approach is difficult to apply on a comparative basis (Seashore 1977, p. 189). Unless referents can be constructed that are generically alike and comparable, it will be difficult to do anything in the way of cumulative research. Seashore believes that this is possible and that significant criterion variables can be developed. This is the point of view of the present approach as well.

The Pennings-Goodman formulation is much more comprehensive than the other participant satisfaction models discussed in this section. The importance they attribute to the consensus achieved through the dominant coalition led to its placement here. The placement here is also based on the importance given to the political process in effectiveness determination. Both systems-resource and goal modeling tend to imply rational decision making, with strategies adopted on the basis of how best to acquire resources or survive to maximize goal attainment. The present approach also assumes that decisions will be made on the basis of some degree of rationality, but tempered with the political facts of organizational life.

Social-Function Models

Social-function models are based on the issue of what organizations do to or for the society of which they are a part. Most representative of this approach is Parsons' (1960) analyses of organizations. According to Parsons, all social systems must solve four basic problems (pp. 183–86). The first is *adaptation*, or the accommodation of the system to the reality demands of the environment, coupled with the active transformation of the external situation. The second problem is *goal achievement*, or the defining of objectives and the mobilization of resources to obtain them. Third is *integration*, or establishing and organizing a set of relations among the member units of the system that serve to coordinate and unify them into a single entity. The last problem is *latency*, or the maintenance over time of the system's motivational and cultural patterns.

These "pattern variables" are designed to be applicable for all social systems. Organizations are part of the goal-achievement system of society. At the same time, organizations can be viewed as social systems in their own right and must deal with the four basic problems. Thus, in one sense, effectiveness can be conceptualized on the basis of how well these problems are resolved. Mulford et al. (1976–77) operationalized these problems and found that there were strong intercorrelations among them in terms of how well a set of noneconomic organizations achieved integration, goal achievement, and so forth.

Parsons' approach has been criticized on several grounds. Blau and Scott (1962) suggest that his "extremely abstract conceptions yield a theoretical scheme devoid of a system of propositions from which specific hypotheses can be derived; in short that he has only developed a theoretical framework and not a substantive theory" (p. 40). Mouzelis (1967) notes that while some groups may be served by an organization, others may not—this is a basic problem of functional analysis. Conceptualizing and measuring societal functions served, while considering the interests of all parties involved, has thus far not been accomplished.

Despite these problems, interest in societal functions served by organizations remains an issue. Perrow (1977) follows this tradition in an interesting manner. He first notes that most studies of effectiveness are what he calls the "variable analysis" type (p. 96). This type of study involves trying to isolate those variables which are somehow related to measures of effectiveness. This is in the administrative-technical tradition. In place of this form of analysis, Perrow suggests that analysts engage in two other types of effectiveness studies—"gross-malfunctioning analysis" and "revelatory analysis." Both involve the question of effectiveness for whom?

Gross-malfunctioning analysis is proposed as a method to isolate poorly operating organizations with an eye toward improving their services or products. This is proposed as an alternative to the common practice of looking at high performance organizations and trying to find the correlates of this high performance. Revelatory analysis deals more precisely with the effectiveness-for-whom question. Perrow views organizations as

intentional human constructions but not necessarily rational systems guided by official goals; as bargaining arenas, rather than cooperative systems; as systems of power rather than crescive institutions reflecting cultural norms; and as resources for other organizations and groups rather than closed systems. If we define organizations, then, as intentional human constructions wherein people and groups compete for outputs of interest to them under conditions of unequal power, we have posed the issue of effectiveness quite differently than in the other two perspectives. We now have to ask, what does the organization produce? (p. 101)

In answer to this question, Perrow notes that human service organizations, such as hospitals, prisons, schools, welfare organizations, and the like have outputs which are more critical than the services provided to clients. Employment opportunities, segregation and control of people who are thought to be deviant or of the wrong age to be part of society, business opportunities for legitimate businesses, and markets for organized crime are some of the major outputs of such social service organizations. Perrow also suggests that concerns with morale should be recast in terms of the ways in which individuals can use the organization to their own advantage. Perrow believes that revelatory analysis would

reveal what most managers know but social scientists cannot afford to acknowledge, namely, that complex social systems are greatly influenced by sheer chance, accident, luck; that most decisions are very ambiguous, preference orderings are incoherent and unstable, efforts at communication and understanding are often ineffective, subsystems are very loosely connected, and most attempts at social control are clumsy and unpredictable. (p. 103)

Perrow is suggesting two things here. First, organizations should not be analyzed with preconceived notions about what the function of the organization is. In a sense, he is calling for a recognition of both manifest and latent functions (Merton 1949), although these terms are not used. He is also calling for an explicit recognition of the parties involved in organizational operations and their stake in the survival of the organization. The fact that different groups have different stakes suggests that an approach to organizations that looks at decisions and actions as a simple ordering around goals or environmental pressures is naive.

The effectiveness-for-whom issue must remain in any effectiveness formulation. If nothing else, this is the contribution of those who view effectiveness from the societal function perspective. That different parties are affected in different ways by organizational actions should be clear. Actions that are successful in one direction may be unrelated to actions in another direction. Alexander and Buchholz (1978) have shown, for example, that corporate social responsibility is unrelated to the stock-market performance of the corporations. Efforts in one arena may have little impact in another.

There is a final aspect of societal-functioning analysis that should be mentioned. Organizations are embedded in environments, as has been amply documented. If organizations attempt to alter their impact on those who are being affected, this can only be done within the parameters of general social trends. Child (1976) has shown that demands for greater participation on the part of workers, which is seen as a means of strengthening democracy generally, face opposition from the sheer fact that organizations are growing and becoming more bureaucratized and centralized. The potential societal function is thus blunted by trends that seem incapable of being reversed.

TOWARD A CONTRADICTION MODEL

Many of the elements of the proposed contradiction model have already been outlined. This section will present some additional reasons why such a model appears to be the one which, in the long run, will be most useful for effectiveness analysis.

The first reason for considering the appropriateness of a contradiction model is that previous investigators have used highly contradictory indicators—and have found equally contradictory evidence—in their studies of effectiveness. For example, Campbell and others (1974) found some *thirty* different criterion measures of effectiveness that have appeared in the effectiveness literature. Rohrbaugh and Quinn (1980) have attempted to reduce these thirty measures to a single measure, but this may gloss over the contradictions among them.

In another review of the literature, Cameron (1978) looked at the types and sources of effectiveness criteria that have been used. There are four types of criteria in this formulation. First, organizational aspects can be considered in terms of whether goal accomplishment, resource acquisition, or internal organizational processes are the focus. Second, the criteria can be organization-specific or more universal. Third, the criteria can take the form of normative prescriptions or of descriptions of effective organizations. Finally, the criteria can be dynamic or static.

There are three sources of criteria in this formulation. First is the constituencies being considered. These can involve the dominant coalition, many levels of constituencies within the organization, or external constituencies. Second, the level of the source of criteria should be considered. This refers to whether the criteria come from the super-system or society, from the organization as a whole, from subunits, or from individuals. Finally, the source of criteria can be from organizational records of performance or from the perceptions of persons concerned with organizational performance.

Figure 13-1 shows a cross tabulation of both the nature and sources of criteria. It also shows where various previous investigations fit into Cameron's scheme.

Cameron's own findings, from colleges and universities, are that effectiveness is a multiple-domain phenomenon. Effectiveness in one domain does not mean effectiveness in another. In discussing the results of his research, Cameron concludes:

> Effectiveness in one domain may not necessarily relate to effectiveness in another domain. For example, maximizing the satisfaction and growth of individuals in an organization . . . may be negatively related to high levels of subunit output and coordination. . . . Specifically, publishing a large number of research reports may be a goal indicating a high level of effectiveness to

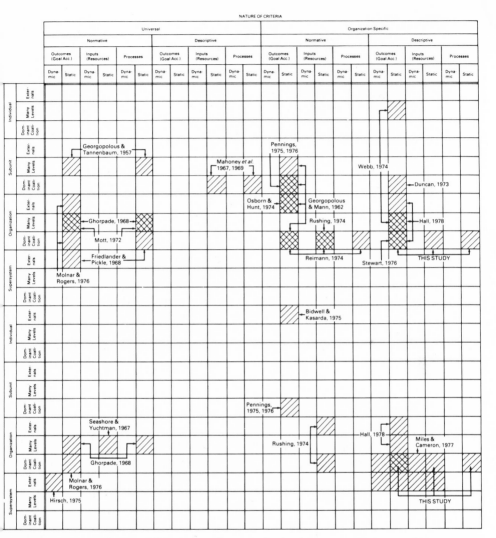

Figure 13-1 Selections of sources and types of criteria for 21 empirical studies of organizational effectiveness

Source: Cameron 1978, p. 608.

faculty members (on an individual level) while indicating low effectiveness at the subunit or organizational level (e.g., poor teaching quality, little time with students, little personal attention for students, graduate student teaching instead of professors) to legislators and parents of undergraduates. (p. 625)

Cameron's analysis and findings come close to the contradiction model. Effectiveness must be considered from the standpoint of multiple constituencies. Cameron does not, however, indicate that different constituencies have differing levels of power over the organization. He also does not get at the fact that the pressures on an organization change over time, with some goals being stressed more at one time than another or one environmental issue taking precedence over another for a time phase and then fading from significance. The general conclusion, however, is very close to that which is being developed here.

There is another aspect to the work of Cameron and Campbell which should be noted. Both writers have demonstrated that there have been multiple approaches to effectiveness in the literature. If we make the rather reasonable assumption that these writers are in contact with reality as they construct it, then the fact that effectiveness is multifaceted and involves multiple domains should have been evident for a long time. Effectiveness cannot be approached in a unitary way. A realization of the contradictory nature of effectiveness is essential if organizational analysis is to proceed.

The Contradiction Model

The model which we have been developing is intended to be applicable across all organizations. This is stated with full recognition of the problems associated with specifying boundary and levels of analysis (Hannan and Freeman 1977b). Quite obviously, reasarch and practice must take into account the type of organization being considered as well as the place of the organization in its larger constellation. Nonetheless, the model proposed is designed to sensitize analysts to the critical issues involving effectiveness. Specific applications can take the boundary and level of analysis issues into account and, it is hoped, build a cumulative set of findings.

The model itself is as follows:

1. *Organizations face multiple and conflicting environmental constraints.*
The constraints which organizations face have a variety of sources. Seashore (1977) has noted that these may be imposed on the organization, bargained for, discovered, or self-selected. Imposed constraints are those over which the organization has little or no control. Benson (1977) has commented on the fact that these imposed constraints frequently contain contradictions. Taxes and governmental regulations are the examples that come most immediately to mind here, but the matter is more complex than this. Large and powerful organizations have an important role in shaping taxation and regulatory legislation. In hearings before the U.S. Senate in 1979, representatives of business-interest groups were the first and most dominant people to testify on regulatory reform legislation. Only at the very end of the hearings did representatives of public-interest groups have the opportunity to testify on environmental, rate, and health and safety regulations.

Despite the politics of lobbying, it is reasonable to conclude that governmental regulations are in fact imposed on most organizations, because once they are enacted, they are designed to be implemented across the board. Thus, affirmative action, pollution control, income tax, and specific legal rate structures affect all organizations within the classes of organizations for which legislation is designed. In the Senate hearings noted above, the business firms claimed that regulatory requirements were a major cause of inflation and were prohibitively expensive. The issue for the present analysis is not whether regulations and tax programs are cost effective or socially beneficial or not, but that they are imposed constraints on organizations, which may contribute to or detract from organizational performance.

Imposed constraints are not just based on governmental actions. Private-sector actions can also impose constraints. For example, a computer manufacturer may develop a new and improved computer with a new language. If an organization must update its computing capabilities and chooses the improved model offered by the computer manufacturer in question, it is constrained to force all of its personnel using the computer to learn the new language. A simpler example in the private sector is when a major supplier goes out of business. Whether publicly or privately based, the constraints imposed upon an organization are critical for it. They serve as limits to action.

Constraints based on bargaining arise from competition or anticipated competition. Business firms have shares of markets which they may or may not try to expand. Their share of the market serves as an important constraint on their volume of production or service output. Colleges and universities develop tacit or explicit agreements with one another regarding the appropriate scope of each other's "turf."

Constraints which are discovered are most easily exemplified in extractive industries, as when a well goes dry or a vein of ore runs out. Discovered constraints occur in other settings, however. When an organization suddenly finds out that it is spending more on fuel costs than had been budgeted and is faced with the necessity of cutting back its operations or raising prices, it is a discovered constraint. It should be noted that in regulated industries, rate hikes may not be directly tied to rising costs.

Self-imposed constraints almost have the characteristics of goals. According to Seashore (1977, p. 188), they reflect the individuality of members of the dominant coalition. This is exemplified by the news industry. Molotch and Lester (1975) demonstrated that there were significant differences between newspapers in the amount of news space given to an oil spill in California. Editorial policy imposes a constraint on the organization in terms of what is determined to be newsworthy and what is not. In the case of the Molotch-Lester analysis, editorial policy is also shaped by the constraints of external political and economic pressures. Other forms of self-imposed constraints can be an insistence upon only producing high quality goods or services or attempting to dupe the public.

Regardless of the source of the constraints, their conflicting nature must be stressed. Efforts designed to permit the organization to meet one constraint may operate against the meeting of another. Universities are confronted with requirements (constraints) dealing with the use of funds received from federal grants and contracts. Meeting these constraints, through personnel assignments, may prevent them from meeting others.

As a specific example, on my campus, decisions had to be made as to where personnel vacancies can be filled. If personnel are hired to meet federal audit requirements, it means that other personnel are not hired. This means that another constraint cannot be met, such as the demand for more security officers to allay pressures from people who fear assault. Limitations on the overall staffing level of the university forced the university to confront the contradictions faced by the opposing constraints.

As a general rule, the larger and more complex the organization, the greater the range and variety of environmental constraints that it will face. The source can be external or internal, but the constraints are important factors that must be considered as decisions are made. Such consideration can be done on the basis of more or less sophisticated decision-making modes. Regardless of the decision-making approach or style that is used, an organization has to consider the environment, recognize and order the constraints that it confronts, and attempt to predict the consequences of the directions chosen or not chosen.

2. *Organizations have multiple and conflicting goals.*

It may seem that this point requires little additional elaboration, since the earlier discussion of goals provided the background necessary for this conclusion. The discussion here will focus on the implications of multiple and conflicting goals in the actual operation of organizations.

It has been emphasized that goals serve as constraints on decision making. If a business firm has the goals of profit making, high return on investment, and growth, it is faced with the situation of deciding between return on investment and growth. Return on investment involves the distribution of profits to stockholders, while growth requires reinvestment of profit into research and development or the development of new markets. It should be noted that decisions surrounding goals are directly related to organizational resources. Resource acquisition and goals are closely related matters, even though the goal and resource-acquisition models have been portrayed as having real contrasts. In actual operation, there is a close connection between these phenomena.

The ways in which this close connection operates can be seen in an actual decision-making situation that was recently faced in my university. SUNY Albany, like the rest of the SUNY system and many other colleges and universities in the United States, was faced with a budget cut. The university was informed that it would have to trim a specified number of positions from its personnel roster. It was up to each campus to determine where these cuts should be made. Each vice president prepared a list of positions that could be cut. Each vice president also argued vehemently about the merits of cutting positions in the *other* vice-presidential areas, in order to protect the positions in his own area.

This situation is one in which power might be assumed to be the most critical variable. Indeed, earlier research (Pfeffer and Salancik 1974) suggests that this is exactly the case. Hills and Mahoney (1978) report a similar finding, with the modification that in times of affluence, decisions are more likely to be made by workload or bureaucratic criteria, while in times of adversity, decisions would be made on the basis of power coalitions. The SUNY situation was certainly one of adversity.

At the same time, goals did not just disappear from the situation. Issues such as the emphasis on research in the university, needs for continued recruitment and retention of highly qualified faculty and students to achieve the goal of being a first-rate university, and reiterations of the importance of having a safe and attractive campus environment were voiced and served as much more than rhetoric. In the end, the cuts made were based on decisions that involved power coalitions *and* goals. In this particular university, a great deal of time and effort goes into an annual review of goals and priorities, so that the example may not be typical, but it would appear that such situations are not all that unique.

The actual outcome of the cuts was that some faculty lines, some administrative lines, and some support lines (custodial, security, bus drivers, and so on) were cut. The cuts were not made on the basis of a simple formula, such as seniority or an across-the-board formula. Rather, each cut was analyzed from the standpoint of the impact it would have on the campus.

Coulter (1979) has argued that behavior and attitudes of organizational members and internal organizational process may contribute to effectiveness but should not be confused with it. Thus, it is with the political processes in regard to decision making. Pfeffer and Salancik (1974) and Hills and Mahoney (1978) are correct in their conclusions that power coalitions are major factors in issues such as budgetary decisions. Such coalitions are critical to the process of decision making. Simply stopping with the process, however, is a mistake, since the content of what the coalitions decide is missed. Part of that content is a concern with the goals of the organization involved—which to stress and which to downplay—and the relationships between goals and the acquisition of resources are considerations that are an important part of a comprehensive and contradiction-based approach to effectiveness.

3. *Organizations have multiple and conflicting external and internal constituencies.*

The strict meaning of constituency involves a population within a legislative district, but that is not the sense in which the term is used here. Here the term refers to the people affected by an organization. These are the customers or clients of an organization, those people who are not customers or clients but are affected by an organization, and members of an organization. By using the term constituency, there is no implication of the degree to which the people are organized. The degree of organization can vary widely. On the one hand are such organized groups as welfare-rights organizations, nuclear-power opponents, and labor unions. On the other hand there are people who are totally unaware of each other's relationship with a particular organization. Any consideration of effectiveness should also include those individuals who are unaware of the fact that they are being affected by an organization, such as people whose health has been endangered by unrevealed dumping of pollutants.

There is relatively little evidence in regard to the manner in which external constituencies react to organizations. In a study of banks, Schneider, Parkington, and Buxton (1980) found that workers and customers had quite similar perceptions of the services rendered. They attributed this to the fact that boundary personnel in banks serve as facilitators for the customers they meet. Katz et al. (1975) found general satisfaction with government services. Christenson and Sachs (1980) found that large size was negatively related to perceived quality of service in public organizations. The reactions of constituencies is undoubtedly linked to the basis of their interactions with organizations. The Katz et al. study found that agencies of constraint generated much more dissatisfaction than did helping agencies. Clients and customers do have reactions to the organizations with which they interact. A complete analysis of the range of reactions is yet to be done. It would be most interesting to determine the forces which lead constituents to organize against an organization and why some such movements are successful while others are not, but that is beyond the scope of the present analysis. Rather obviously, however, organized constituents have a greater impact on the organization itself than do unorganized constituents.

Before leaving the issue of external constituencies it should be noted that organizations can do actual damage to their constituencies. Dangerous toys can be intentionally or unintentionally produced and marketed. Educational programs can create unattainable expectations. Pollutants can be dumped. Wars can be waged. Organizations are not benign, and effectiveness assessments should reflect this.

External constituencies, particularly when they are organized, could be considered as a component of environmental constraints, but it seems preferable to consider them separately here, since they have the capacity to react to a particular organization. The environmental constraints discussed earlier are best viewed as being composed of factors that impinge upon all of the organizations of a particular type or in a particular area. External constituencies do not necessarily have the same perspectives on a particular organization. Stockholders, as an important form of constituency, want profits, while the recipients of pollutants may not.

There is more evidence and even a form of consensus in regard to internal constituencies. It is now common to consider effectiveness from the perspective of the dominant coalition and to analyze the manner in which groups within the organization achieve power within such coalitions (Pennings and Goodman 1977). Organizations can be viewed as arenas in which power struggles are a dominant activity.

While organizations certainly are political, there is a tendency for the literature on topics such as dominant coalitions to portray organizations as in continual power struggles, with the participants actively and constantly seeking more power for themselves, their department, or their level in the hierarchy. Such a portrayal may be too dynamic. It ignores the presence of a preestablished hierarchy in most organizations. Such a hierarchy sets the rules for the exercise of power. in most organizations most of the time, the existing hierarchy is undisturbed. While dramatists and novelists have captured well the intricacies of such power struggles, the fact of the matter appears to be that these are rare occurrences, with existing power arrangements accepted as legitimate. A comprehensive and contradiction-based approach to effectiveness recognizes both stability and internal conflict.

4. All organizations have multiple and conflicting time frames.
There are three important temporal considerations in regard to effectiveness. Hannan and Freeman (1977b) have noted that goals have a temporal dimension. They state (1977b):

> To the extent that the goals function stresses quick return on investment (as in many business ventures, disaster relief organizations, military field units, and so on) the short-run outcomes should be given the highest priority. For those organizations that orient toward continued production (for example, many other types of business ventures, universities, research and development organizations, and so on), the year-to-year fluctuations in performance should be discounted and the average performance over longer periods emphasized.
>
> The conceptual problem is that we do not know how organizations discount time. Two organizations with the same goals operating with the same structure in the same environment may place a very different emphasis on speed of return on investment. One organization may capitalize on some situations in a way that increases both the probability of quick favorable outcomes and the risk of long-term decline. The other may eschew the quick return in favor of long-term security. . . . The analyst must also know the premium placed on speed of return. (pp. 113–14)

Hannan and Freeman go on to note that the time frame may differ with different levels in the organization, with higher levels generally taking a longer time perspective than lower levels. Lawrence and Lorsch (1967) have documented the difference in time perspective across organizational divisions. These inter- and intraorganizational differences in time perspectives regarding goals force the analyst and practitioner to refer back to the constituency issue, since it is critical to understand whose time frame is being considered. There is no easy resolution to the time frame issue. Within the organization it is a matter of the political process inherent in decision making. For the outside observer, the selection of a time frame is dependent upon the nature of the question being asked.

The second aspect of the time frame issue involves environmental constraints. Organizational environments shift over time, and constraints that were critical at one point in time fade as new issues arise. Hannan and Freeman (1974, 1977a) have suggested that organizations can adopt a specialized structure designed to fit a specific environment or a more generalized structure that is not ideally suited for any one environment, but does moderately well in a variety of environments.

There is another way in which environmental constraints can be approached. The *degree* of environmental constraint on an organization will vary over time. At some points in time, organizations appear to do little else than attempt to cope with such constraints. At other times, the environment is more benign. In the later situation, more attention can be given to matters such as goals and goal attainment. There is no easy way to capture this variation in environmental intensity, except by attempting to determine the manner in which constituents shape their decisions and actions.

The final element of the temporal issue involves the history of the organizations in question. Stinchcombe's (1965) analysis of the development of organizational forms and the population-ecology approach to organizations (Aldrich and Pfeffer 1976) deal with this issue. Simply put, new organizations face more of a struggle than do older organizations. In a similar way, organizations in an industry or sector which is experiencing decline have different problems than those in a growth industry or sector. The analyst or practitioner must be aware of the place of the organization in terms of its own history and of its industry or sector.

The temporal dimension of effectiveness is essentially one of judgment. Decisions must be made in terms of the frame of reference for analysing goal attainment, the nature and phasing of environmental constraints, and the historical situation of the organization. Failing to recognize this can lead the analyst and practitioner to incorrect conclusions. For the analyst, the result is a poor study; for the practitioner, it is organizational decline or death.

We have considered contradictions in environmental constraints, goals, constituents, and time. These are the realities constructed in and for all organizations (Benson 1977). They are the basis for judgment and action (Pfeffer 1977). They lead to the conclusion that *no organization is effective.* Instead, organizations can be viewed as effective (or ineffective) to some degree in terms of specific constraints, goals, constituents, and time frames. The analysis will now conclude with some practical issues in the study of effectiveness.

Some Practical Applications

When considering the issue of practical applications from a contradiction model, the first conclusion that must be reached is that efforts to be effective must always involve less than total rationality. It is now a matter of faith in organizational theory that organizations do not optimize in their decision making, but rather satisfice (March and Simon 1958). Further, Simon (1957) emphasizes that people have important limits to their rationality. They may intend to be rational, but they cannot perceive the consequences of their actions, and the range of alternatives available, nor can they rank the range of alternatives in a reasonable order of preference. More recently March and Olsen (1976) have stressed the fact that there is a high degree of goal ambiguity in organizations and that this further deflects from rationality. Thus, even when a goal model is stressed, limitations on people's capabilities and the complexities of the situation itself make it impossible for organizations to make the kinds of decisions among alternatives that would lead to optimal effectiveness.

The analysis presented here goes beyond these considerations and has emphasized the fact that there are compromises which must be made among pressing constraints, goals, constituents and time frames. The ordering of the compromises is based on power relationships and coalitions within the organizations, coupled with external pressures. This is done within a framework of realization that if once an action is selected, others are not possible, particularly with constant or diminishing resources. Before considering these matters further, it is imperative that a relatively neglected topic be addressed—the fact that there are some constraints over which organizations can have no control.

Constraints Beyond Organizational Control

Organizations attempt to control those constraints which they perceived to be central to them. Devices such as industrial vertical integration, utilization of boards of directors, political intervention, and advertising are all efforts to reduce environmental uncertainty or shape the environment to the benefit of the organization. At the same time, some events are uncontrollable.

A simple example of this is the weather. If an organization is dependent upon particular weather patterns, it can do little in regard to the forces of nature. Cloud seeding has yet to become truly feasible and no device has been developed to control the external temperature. Agricultural organizations are subject to droughts, floods, and prolonged hot or cold spells. Winter recreational organizations, such as ski resorts, suffer when there is no snow and warm temperatures. A bad year in 1980 brought the demise of some areas due to weather. Organizations that are weather prone can engage in activities that minimize the influence of the forces of nature, such as building up reserves of food goods or manufacturing man-made snow (even this does not work if the temperature is above freezing), but these organizations face a basically uncontrollable constraint.

More complex examples come in the forms of world political and economic shifts. As petroleum costs rise and supplies lessen, petroleum users are affected. While it can be argued that oil firms and some financial institutions are capable of controlling even these phases of their environments, this point seems exaggerated when the total scope of international political, economic, social, and military arrangements are considered. For the vast majority of private and public organizations, such control is out of the question. The organizations must be viewed simply as the recipient, though not necessarily passive, of externally derived forces.

There are other, less dramatic, forces than the sweep of world events that are important for organizations, but which they cannot control. These include such things as demographic patterns and local or regional economic developments. Colleges and universities, for example, are faced with a demographic situation in which there are simply fewer people of the traditional college-attending ages. Many states are cutting back their support for higher education and some of these same colleges and universities must cope with that. It is interesting to note that these organizations must cope with certainty rather than uncertainty in these situations.

Uncontrollable events and forces affect organizations. They are part of the constraint package that is faced. What is important for the discussion here is that they cannot be manipulated. They are conditions to which organizations must adjust as they deal with other constraints, goals, constituents, and time frames. There is another class of phenomena which is largely outside the control of organizations—the mandated situation.

Mandated Situations

Mandated situations involve contingencies that are imposed upon organizations from other organizations. They typically involve economic or regulatory phenomena. On the economic side, for example, costs of energy, which may or may not be related to the world-wide energy situation, are passed on to or imposed upon energy customers. In most energy-related or, more generally, monopolized situations, the receiving organization can do little more than receive. There are not alternative sources typically, but if there are, they too have raised their prices equally. Noneconomic examples include the vast array of federal and state regulations that are imposed on organizations, with little or no input from the organizations involved. At the present time, for example, colleges and universities are developing plans for the implementation of the previously mentioned revised federal regulations on amount of time and effort spent on federally supported grants and contracts. Since almost all colleges and universities receive federal funds, it is a widespread issue. The regulations have some very confusing elements. Countless (and at times pointless) numbers of meetings have been held at these colleges and universities on the techniques by which these revised regulations will be implemented. The point here is not this particular regulation but that there are mandated situations over which the receiving organizations have no control. They are the imposed constraints which were discussed earlier. As a practical matter, they cannot just be ignored, since to do so would mean the loss of federal funds.

Internally Generated Mandates

Some mandates which organizations face arise from traditions or norms developed within organizations or from bargaining with employee groups. Union contracts, tenure rules, and organizational histories are examples here. Organizations do not have a complete range of decisions open to them. While it might appear advantageous and even rational for a university to close down a department with very few students, no majors, and an unproductive faculty, this is seldom done, except under very dire economic conditions calling for "retrenchment." Even here, severe mandates generated by union contracts operate. In the New York State system, the union contract specifies that retrenched employees from one campus have the first crack at positions open in their specialty on another campus in the system. This, in turn, potentially limits the decision-making freedom of the second campus.

Another example of this sort of internally generated mandate is the automobile industry in the United States. As of the early 1980s, the industry is in very bad shape. There are a number of reasons which have been suggested for this, including low-priced foreign competition, low quality standards, and poor management. Another reason is the force of tradition within the companies which led them to continue to do business as usual, in this case continuing to produce large, fuel-inefficient automobiles.

The discussion thus far has focused on the limitations faced by organizations as they confront uncontrollable contingencies and externally and internally mandates. There are situations in which these conditions create opportunities where they did not previously appear to exist. Suppose, for example, that a highly fuel-efficient automobile engine has been developed. At the time of its development, it was too expensive for successful competition. Rising fuel prices could make it economically viable. A market could be entered, where none existed before. A nonhypothetical example of this sort of phenomenon can be seen from demographic patterns. The high birth rate during the 1940s baby boom was a constraint that schools had to face in later decades. The decline in the birth rate continues to be a constraint for educational organizations, but the people born during the boom are now providing an opportunity for industries and services which serve young adults. Increases in longevity have provided the consumers for the old-age industry. The constraints and mandates discussed thus far have the potential for opportunities as well as limitations for organizations. The world in which organizations operate is not totally composed of constraints and mandates over which organizations have no control. There are situations which are potentially manipulable.

Environmental Constraints that Are Potentially Manipulable

Organizations attempt to manipulate their environment. It is well recognized that a major task of top management is enhancing the position of their organization in the environment. Analyses of interlocking corporate boards of directors have suggested that such interlocking can serve four major external functions (Aldrich 1979, p. 297). The selection of directors can be a means by which financial, legal, or other information or expertise can be brought to the organization. Directors can also be selected with the intent of facilitating the organization's search for capital or other resources. This is the primary reason that bank officials are so heavily represented on the corporate boards across the array of business firms. Community leaders on the boards of hospitals or colleges serve to bring in the resource of legitimacy. Board composition can also serve a political function. The selection of the appropriate director can assist in coping with federal and state agencies, since the presence of politically powerful individuals or representatives of politically powerful groups can serve to blunt vigorous governmental actions. Finally, board composition has been viewed as a means by which the interests of powerful external organizations are served, such as banks, insurance companies, or controlling blocks of family interests.

Interlocking directorates do not create certainty for the organizations involved. There is some evidence (Burt, Christman, and Kilburn 1980; Pennings 1980b) that certain patterns of interlocks may contribute to higher profitability for the organizations studied, but no claim has been made that the results of these analyses explain all of the variance in profit.

The fact that the environment is only potentially manipulable can be seen in Hirsch's (1975) analysis of the pharmaceutical and popular music industries. The pharmaceutical industry had great success in protecting itself from competition by securing the passage of state and federal legislation. It also was successful in getting organized medicine, through the American Medical Association, to permit the industry to advertise drugs by brand names, rather than by their generic name. Prescriptions were made by brand, rather than compound. Hirsch suggested that the popular music (record) industry had a quite similar structure to begin with, but was unable to obtain protective legislation and exclusive rights to the profits possible whenever a song was played on the radio. The popular music industry lobbied and used other techniques to try to protect itself, but was unable to and had severe problems as musical tastes changed along with the many other cultural changes in the 1960s. One industry was successful, while the other was not.

This is an area of uncertainty for organizations. If someone were to come up with a *certain* technique for controlling the environment, as the early and later monopolists have, every organization would adopt it. Antimonopoly laws are specifically designed to prevent environmental control. Organizations attempt to control as much as they legally can or as much as they can without being caught.

The discussion thus far has focused on the private sector. Public organizations also seek to control their environment. The public budgetary process is one in which resources are sought for organizational mainte-nance and growth. Public organizations send messages to their constituents and others. These messages are designed to protect the organization and further its interests. Altheide and Johnson (1980) suggest that this "prop-aganda" may be quite detrimental to the public in many instances.

In this section the argument has been that organizations engage in a variety of activities designed to manipulate their environment in their favor. Whether through interlocking boards of directors, purchasing suppliers, seeking to have favorable legislation passed, or through prop-aganda, the attempt is to manipulate the environment on behalf of the organization. These efforts only have the potential for success, since other organizations with other purposes are interacting with the same compo-nents of the environment. Organizations can be most sure of the conse-quences of their actions when the organization itself is considered.

Organizational Characteristics

Organizations have the capability of being structured and restructured in accordance with the outcomes of decision making and political processes within their own boundaries. Much of the thinking that has emerged from the contingency model (Lawrence and Lorsch 1967) has dealt directly with this issue. The basic notion is that their are multiple organizational forms which are most likely to be successful, depending upon the situations which the organization is confronting (see Becker and Neuhauser 1975, for an example of this kind of analysis). One of the major tasks of top management is to determine what the most appropriate organizational form is for various situations. It is not uncommon to find business firms in rapidly changing technological fields to have no formal tables of organization or organizational charts because the organization is in a constant change mode.

Organizations are not totally flexible. Union contracts, custom, and laws mediate against total self-determination. Nonetheless, it is possible to structure or restructure organizations to bring about greater adaptability or rigidity or more or less participation in the decision-making process. The organizational form is most subject to organizational control of all of the factors affecting effectiveness that we have considered. Whether or not organizational form is most crucial for organizational effectiveness is uncertain. It would appear that ultimate survival might well be a function of factors beyond organizational control (Whetten 1980). The more controllable a particular situation is, perhaps the less important it is. It is quite clear that controlling the relevant environment, over time and across conditions, and structuring the organization to acquire sufficient resources and to pursue and move to accomplish major goals, is a key to any consideration of effectiveness.

SUMMARY AND CONCLUSION

This chapter has been an attempt to make some sense out of the critical area of organizational effectiveness. Conceptual and methodological contradictions in the analysis of effectiveness have been presented and a contradiction model was developed. The model contains key elements for the resource-acquisition and goals models and is an attempt to combine them in a manner which retains their key insights but adds the important factor of inherent contradiction. Organizational effectiveness will remain as the major concern for organizational practitioners and analysts. Ignoring the contradictions will not advance knowledge or practice. Ignoring the fact that there are factors beyond organizational control or which are only potentially manipulable will also not contribute to theory or practice. It is only when theorists and practitioners realize the limited range of options open to organizations, as they confront constraints and mandates and attempt to move toward goal achievement and cope with the issues of multiple constituents and conflicting time frames, that both usable and theoretically interesting developments will take place.

In the next and final chapter we will consider organizational theory. It will be a short chapter, because many of the issues have already been considered in this chapter and throughout the analysis.

14

Organizational Theory

The objectives of this chapter are limited. We are going to examine some traditional and contemporary theories about organizations and suggest what appears to be a fruitful way of conceptualizing organizations. In many ways the entire book has been about organizational theory, as linkages among major structural, processual, environmental, and inter-organizational factors have been traced. No attempt at summarizing and pulling all of these findings together will be attempted.

At the outset it should be noted that there are two theoretical traditions that will *not* be considered. The reason for this is that they are treated better elsewhere than they could be treated here. The first tradition to be omitted focuses on the individual and his or her interpretations and actions within the organization. This is largely the domain of organizational psychology (see Weick 1979), but has also been addressed with strong insights by sociologists such as Silverman (1971) and Albrow (1980). A major thrust of these writers is that organizational reality is constructed and interpreted by individuals in the course of their interactions in organizations. The perspective which has been presented here agrees wholeheartedly.

The second tradition is the radical or neo-Marxian perspective, which deals with organizations as instruments through which the power of elites or the state is transmitted and magnified. Writers such as Braverman (1974) have described the manner in which the modern organization controls workers through technological change. Excellent overviews of both of these traditions can be found in Burrell and Morgan (1979), Clegg and Dunkerly (1980), and Salaman and Thompson (1980). Interestingly, all of these works are British. Benson (1977) has presented a concise statement of the Marxian perspective in an American journal. Form (1981) has provided some evidence that refutes this perspective, but the ultimate test of the utility of the Marxian perspective will be based on additional empirical research. By and large, this has yet to be accomplished.

Our analysis of organizational theory will begin with a categorization of traditional organizational theory, based largely around the work of Pugh (1966). Champion (1975) and Scott (1981) provide different, but largely compatible systematizations of traditional theories. Pugh refers to these alternative theories as management theory, structural theory, group theory, individual theory, technology theory, and economic theory.

THEORETICAL TRADITIONS

Management theory has been largely derived from practicing managers who have attempted to put their experiences on paper for the benefit of other practitioners. The major representatives of this approach are Fayol (1949), Urwick (1947), Gulick and Urwick (1937), Mooney and Reilly (1931), and Taylor (1911). (Pugh places Taylor in another category, but he is as easily and more traditionally placed here.) These writers have offered numerous prescriptions on how organizations ought to be set up for maximum productivity and efficiency. Their major concern has been with principles of specialization, hierarchical arrangements, delegation of authority and responsibility, span of control, and the arrangement of organizational subunits.

Because these authors are concerned with getting the most out of the organization and its employees, they attempt to develop techniques that are applicable to all organizations. They suggest, for example, that "each five to six workers . . . need one first line supervisor; every six first line supervisors, and hence, every forty workers, need one second line supervisor, and so on" (Etzioni 1964, p. 23). Various principles of specialization are offered, such as by purpose, process, clientele, or geographical concentration.

Management theory has been criticized on many grounds. The nature of the specialization within an organization can be affected by the general culture in which the organization is found, the kinds of personnel employed, the availability of personnel, and the restrictions imposed by labor legislation and union contracts. Management theory tends to ignore or oversimplify the motivations of all levels of employees, assuming at one extreme that all manual workers should be viewed as extensions of the machines with which they are working, or, at the other extreme, that higher level employees should be guided solely by job descriptions. These writers also assume only one type of authority—that based on hierarchical position. The role of expertise is almost totally ignored or is assumed to coincide perfectly with position.

A more basic problem with this approach is highlighted by Pugh:

The . . . difficulty with management theorists, particularly the common sense ones, is that not being scientists, their statements do not have sufficient precision to enable crucial experiments to be undertaken to test their validity. This is their attraction for the layman, since the proverbs appear to be wise and true for all occasions. But scientific statements are precisely *not* true for *all* occasions, and it is an integral part of the process of science to look for occasions for which they are not true. A scientific hypothesis is essentially a falsifiable statement. When the statements of the management theorists are subject to the same scrutiny, and attempts made to operationalize them, it is usually found that they do not stand up to such analysis very well. (p. 238)

Pugh then notes that the proverb, "Increased specialization will lead to greater efficiency," sounds fine, but the basis for specialization remains unspecified.

Etzioni (1964) pinpoints the difficulties inherent in this approach when he raises the questions: "Take, for example, building missiles for military use. Should the missile program be assigned to one branch of the armed forces or all three, since missiles can be used on land, sea, and air? Should we have a single missile force because all missile-building requires a common fund of knowledge? Should we build a number of different regional forces because some missiles are built for Europe's defense and some for U.S. defense?" (p. 24).

Thus, while management theorists deal with issues that are central to the understanding of organizations, their treatment is insufficiently based in reality. While the theorists themselves have real experiences that serve as the basis for their own formulations, the generalizability and basis for the formulations are highly suspect. Since management theory is in many ways a very specific form of the closed-system perspective, it suffers from the same weaknesses of that perspective, which will be discussed later.

Structural theorists are the next group identified by Pugh.

Regularities in such activities as task allocation, the exercise of authority, and coordination of function are developed. Such regularities constitute the organization's structure, and sociologists have studied systematic differences in structure related to variations in such factors as the objectives of ownership, geographical location, and technology of manufacture, which produce the characteristic differences in structure of a bank, a hospital, a mass production factory or a local government department. (p. 239)

Weber, of course, is identified most closely with this approach in his discussions of bureaucracy. Later examinations of the extent to which organizations do or do not conform to the bureaucratic model are in the structuralist tradition, including, of course, Pugh's own work.

The major problem in the utilization of the structuralist approach appears to be due to historical developments within the field of organizational analysis itself. Many earlier studies that have become "classics" in their own right came to the justified conclusion that when the pure bureaucratic model is applied to real organizations it leads to a whole series of dysfunctions. (See for example, Selznick 1966; Gouldner 1954;

and Merton 1957.) These dysfunctions exist at both the organizational and individual behavior levels. In retrospect, it is not surprising that there are differences in power among organizational subunits, that some tasks cannot be organized in the same way as other tasks within the organization, or that individuals may overconform to rules and procedures. If organizational structure is assumed to be based only on the bureaucratic model, the structuralist approach is certainly a dead-end street. If, on the other hand, variations in structure are assumed and the sources of variations can be pinpointed, the structuralist approach remains a relevant component for organizational analysis. Burns and Stalker (1961) and Lawrence and Lorsch (1967) have demonstrated rather clearly that major differences in structure are related to environmental, technological, and internal considerations. These differences are also related to organizational effectiveness.

Pugh points out that the traditional structuralist approach does not take the individual and his motivations and contributions to the organization into consideration. The individual is assumed to be "programmed into" appropriate organizational behaviors. Here again this may have been the case in the past. Few contemporary analysts ignore the individual. He is considered in conjunction with the other factors that are significant for understanding organizations. Organizational structure is one of these factors.

Using just one structural yardstick, whether it be the bureaucratic model or anything else, is clearly rather futile. At the same time, the past misuse of the structural approach should not result in its dismissal. The structuralist approach will remain as one of the important and powerful tools, because structural regularities are an important contributor to the differences between organizations.

Partially as a reaction to an extreme emphasis on structure and partly from its own impetus, the third school of theorists, the *group theorists*, arose. Mayo (1933), who directed the now famous (or infamous, depending on one's point of view) Hawthorne studies, and Lewin (1951) and his associates, who followed up with further research, are most directly responsible for, and advocates of, this approach. The major premise of this set of theorists is that the work group exerts a tremendous amount of influence on individual behavior, overriding both the organizationally based norms and the individual's own predispositions. Some of the principal conclusions from this approach are:

> The amount of work carried out by a worker is determined not by his physical capability but by his social capacity; non-economic rewards are most important in the motivation and satisfaction of workers, who react to their work situations as groups and not as individual; the leader is not necessarily the person appointed to be in charge, informal leaders can develop who have more power; the effective supervisor is "employee-centered" and not "job-centered," that is, he regards his job as dealing with human beings rather than with the work; communication and participation in decision making are some of the most significant rewards which can be offered to obtain the commitment of the individual. (Pugh 1966, p. 241)

These findings, which are correct to some degree for all organizations, have been taken as the basis for an overall organizational theory and also for many prescriptions on how managers ought to manage and how organizations ought to organize. (See, for example, Likert 1961 and McGregor 1960.) But there are several drawbacks to this use. Foremost is that there is contradictory evidence on group bases of behavior as compared with individual or organizational bases for behavior. (For a particularly devastating critique of the major empirical basis for this perspective, see Carey 1967, pp. 403–16.) Under some conditions, the factors that seem to be the major determinants of behavior are the exact opposite of what the group theorists propose. Pugh (p. 241) points out that these theorists have ignored the important dimension of power in organizational relationships. The evidence used as the basis of the approach comes largely from case studies, and these case studies, according to Lawrence and Lorsch (1967, pp. 179–82), have generally been carried out in organizations that would provide support for the group theorists' perspective. The group theorists argue that organizational theory ought to be built around the concept of the group and its effects on the individual and on his or her behavior in the organization. The group and the processes of group interaction become tools for better organizations, management, and, in the long run, society, according to this perspective. But because this approach ignores many other highly salient factors, it cannot stand alone as an organizational theory. But the findings of the research and the perspective taken do contribute to our overall understanding of organizations and thus must be incorporated in any form of systematic overview that is taken.

The next set of theorists is also concerned with the individual—in this case, as an individual. Pugh labels as *individual theorists* those who focus their major concern upon individuals and their predispositions, reactions, and personality within the organizational setting. A basic issue in such an approach is what view of personality is taken. On the one hand are those of a psychoanalytical bent who see organizations as staffed by members with varying kinds of relationships to their parents, and who, acting in a continual state of development, behave in organizations on the basis of their individual predispositions alone. Others, such as Maslow (1956) and Herzberg, (1959), view the organization as a means of providing the individual with a set of rewards of varying levels of satisfaction, with the implication that organizations should continually attempt to provide members with the highest (self-growth and self-development) level of motivation and reward possible. While these and other such approaches to individual personality contain elements of plausibility, they have not been sufficiently documented with empirical evidence to allow their total acceptance as the final theory of personality. More important for our purposes, they obviously ignore or totally discount the impact of organizational, wider societal, and, generally, even group influences on individual behavior.

The work of March and Simon (1958), a modern classic in the field of organizations, utilizes the individual perspective. They regard the organization as a set of individuals engaged in the decision-making process. While they recognize the importance of organizational constraints on the decision-making process, their framework is built on individual motivations. Their important discussion of the "cognitive limits on rationality" is at the individual psychological level, with important organizational modifiers such as hierarchical and task differentiation. Too frequently, sociologists tend to assume that individual differences are randomly distributed and therefore do not matter in their analyses. The viewpoint taken here is that they do in fact matter.

The next perspective is represented by the *technology theorists*. Much of the gist of this approach has already been examined, with its implication that technology is a major factor in the development and form of organizations.

The final set of theorists considered by Pugh is that of the *economic theorists*. Their approach typically uses business firms as its basis, but the ideas can be extended to other organizational forms. The basic premise in this perspective is that the organization is an active participant in the economic process, seeking to enhance its position and make economically sound (rational) decisions. Much of the work in this area is an attempt to specify how economically rational decisions can be made under conditions of psychological and sociological variations (Cyert and March 1963).

The approach is valuable because it forces the organizational analyst, and particularly the sociologist, to pay attention to economic factors. At face value, economic factors are important to organizations simply as necessary for survival, but they are too often ignored in organizational analyses. It is true that we have no clear understanding of the exact role that economic factors play. If too much attention is given to such factors, many of the dangers of an overly rational view of organizations come into play. If they are ignored, an important component is eliminated.

This overview of traditional organizational theory suggests that many of the issues that have been identified in the past remain important for contemporary theory. As will be seen, contemporary theory is dominated by a concern with environmental considerations. A major exception is Hage (1980), whose elaborate theoretical scheme includes a strong emphasis on internal organizational structures and processes. Hage's work contains some 23 premises and 174 hypotheses, rendering it impossible for summarization here. The test of its utility will come in future use.

CONTEMPORARY ORGANIZATIONAL THEORIES

As noted in the chapter on the environment and throughout much of the analysis in this book, the environment is a major research and conceptual emphasis in contemporary organizational theory. This emphasis is, in some ways, a reaction to several decades of research which concentrated on the internal structural attributes of organizations and to seemingly endless controversies over what factors determined structure, such as size versus technology. Much of this research was carried out as though organizations operated in a closed system, with little or no input from the organizational environment.

Another reason for the emphasis on environments is the clear realization that organizations, like individuals are not islands unto themselves. Other organizations provide inputs, regulate operations, and consume outputs. More general societal conditions, such as the state of the economy, availability of energy, population shifts, and the political climate also affect organizations, as we have seen.

The concern with the environment led to the development of *contingency theory*. This theory emerged from Lawrence and Lorsch's (1967) seminal work which has been discussed. Later writers such as Galbraith (1973; 1977), Becker and Neuhauser (1975), and Negandhi and Reimann (1973a; 1973b), developed the basic ideas further. According to Scott (1981 p. 114) contingency theory can be summarized in the following manner: "The best way to organize depends on the nature of the environment to which the organization must relate." Thus, in Lawrence and Lorsch's study the successful plastics firms were those that were differentiated to deal with an uncertain and changing environment.

Contingency theory has been heavily criticized as being tautological. It has also been criticized as not being a theory, since no explanation is made regarding why or how a best way to organize develops. Katz and Kahn (1978 p. 249) suggest that the idea of a best way to organize for a particular environment ignores political considerations, such as demands for collective bargaining, for a minimum wage, or for a union contract. Katz and Kahn note that high efficiency could be the result of paying low wages, inducing workers to work long hours, or to work harder. Pfeffer and Salancik (1978) have noted the importance of consumers and regulators for organizational operations. Despite these problems, contingency theory remains an important part of the literature on organizations. Perhaps its greatest contribution has been to emphasize the importance of the environment for organizations. This environmental focus has come to dominate contemporary organizational theory.

The Natural-Selection Model

The most extreme version of utilizing environmental factors to explain organizational phenomena is the *natural-selection* or *population-ecology* model (Aldrich and Pfeffer 1976; Hannan and Freeman 1977a; Aldrich 1979; Kasarda and Bidwell 1979). This approach "posits that environmental factors select those organizational characteristics that best fit the environment" (Aldrich and Pfeffer, p. 79).

The natural-selection model is concerned primarily with organizational change or transformation. According to Aldrich and Pfeffer, the model differs from Campbell's (1969) analysis of systemic evolution in that no assumption of progression is made. The natural selection model does not assume that changes are necessarily in the direction of more complex or better organizations. The direction of change in organizations is toward a better fit with the environment.

According to Aldrich and Pfeffer, the natural-selection model does not deal with single organizational units, but is concerned with populations of organizations. Organizations that have the appropriate fit with the environment are selected over those that do not fit or fit less appropriately.

Following Campbell, Aldrich and Pfeffer suggest that there are three stages in the natural-selection model. The first stage is when variations occur in organizational forms. These variations can be planned or unplanned. Once variations have occured, the second stage, selection, occurs. The analogy here is to organic evolution in which some mutations work and others do not. Organizational forms that fit are selected over those that do not. The final stage is retention. The forms that are selected are "preserved, duplicated, or reproduced" (p. 81). Aldrich (1979) notes that retention takes place, in the contemporary situation, through devices such as business schools that train future organizational managers and executives. The training contains lessons learned from organizational forms that have been successful or selected.

Organizational forms fill *niches* in the environment. Niches are "distinct combinations of resources and other constraints that are sufficient to support an organizational form" (p. 28). The notion of niches raises the fascinating possibility that there are unfilled niches "out there" just waiting for the right organizational form. Aldrich (p. 112) suggests that home video games and pocket electronic calculators were examples of unfilled niches being filled, but these are poor examples, since they are not organizational forms, but are simply consumer products. A better example of a once unfilled, but now filled niche is the conglomorate corporation, in which a set of unrelated industries are brought together under a single ownership. This was a new organizational form that was selected by the environment as appropriate.

Aldrich and Pfeffer identify some problems with the natural-selection model. The sources of the original variations are not specified. Managerial processes within organizations are ignored. Inasmuch as only the successful organizational forms will survive in the long run, the processes by which the fit between the organization and the environment is achieved can be ignored. The model also has the problem of being analogous to economic theories which assume perfect competition. Perfect competition does not exist in almost all instances.

Van de Ven (1979) provides some additional criticisms of this model as it was developed by Aldrich. Van de Ven suggests that the notion of "fit" between the environment and organizations is unclear. According to Van de Ven, Aldrich appears to use fit as

either an *unquestioned axiom* or an *inductive generalization* in a causal model that asserts that organizational environment determines structure because effective or surviving organizations adopt structures that fit their environmental niches relatively better than those that do not survive. To avoid a tautology, the proposition implicitly reduces to the hypothesis that organizational survival or effectiveness moderates the relationship between environment and structure. (p. 323)

This is interesting, because effectiveness is scarcely mentioned in the natural-selection modeling efforts.

Van de Ven goes on to criticize the natural-selection model for drawing too heavily on analogies with biological systems. This approach is ill-founded, since it does not deal with human decisions and motives. Ethical problems are ignored and the whole process is viewed as inevitable. Van de Ven notes that research on small groups has also dealt with the variation-selection-retention process without slipping to the biological analogy level.

Van de Ven also criticizes the model because of its down-playing of strategic choices made on behalf of organizations. The variations in forms that occur have some source and, according to Van de Ven, it is the strategic choices made within organizations. The idea of strategic choice will be incorporated in the next theoretical perspective to be analyzed.

There is an additional aspect of choice which is not considered in the natural-selection model. Grafton (1975) has noted that some federal agencies have been created as last resort responses to socioeconomic or technological difficulties. These agencies fill a niche, to be sure, but the niche is defined by governmental decision makers.

There is another troublesome aspect of the natural-selection model. Organizations are not inert masses, even though they seem so at times. Even organizations that are seemingly inert have an impact by their very inertia, but this is not the point. The point is that organizations do things. They transform inputs into outputs. These outputs have an impact on the society. Individuals, groups, and other organizations respond to organizational outputs. We are harmed and benefited by organizational outputs. In this sense we are the environment of organizations. If we act toward organizations by support or opposition, and if we have power or can influence power holders, the environment responds to organizations. The natural-selection model, as developed by Aldrich, recognizes the role of the state in organizational creation, but the general aura of the natural-selection model is one of an environment that is not filled with human actors, but is rather an unfeeling, uncaring, condition in which organizations must operate. Perrow (1979, p. 243) has also noted that the model removes power, conflict, disruption, and social class variables from the analysis of social processes.

These criticism of the natural-selection model are not intended to suggest that it has no utility. The utility of the model is in two areas. As some sort of "ultimate test" of effectiveness, survival is a positive indication and organizational death a negative indication. The natural-selection model can thus give an historical perspective that other approaches do not. It does not work well, however, with large contemporary private and public organizations that are guaranteed survival for the short and even medium range of time (Aldrich and Pfeffer 1976, p. 88). The natural-selection model is also useful as a sensitizing concept to the importance of environmental factors. If an organizational form is in a period of growth or decline, because of an expanding or shrinking niche, any model must take that into consideration. Medical technology in developed countries has now permitted many people to live until old age, with the infirmities that this brings. The organizational form of the hospital is inappropriate for the aging individual who is not faced with a life-threatening emergency. The new organizational form of the hospice appears to be filling the niche that was created. Evaluations of hospices will have to take the survival and growth potential into account.

The Resource-Dependence Model

The natural-selection model downplays the role of organizational actors in determining the fate of organizations. Aldrich and Pfeffer (1976) suggest that there is an alternative model, which they label the resource-dependence model, which brings organizational decisions and actions back into consideration. Pfeffer and Salanick (1978) elaborate the basic model. This model also retains the environment as a critical influence on organizations, but in a slightly different manner. The discussion that follows relies heavily on Aldrich and Pfeffer's analysis, with some additions and extensions.

The resource-dependence model has strong ties to what has been labeled the political-economy model of organizations (Wamsley and Zald 1973; Benson 1975) and the dependence-exchange approach (Hasenfeld 1972; Jacobs 1974). The model also incorporates the contingency theory (Lawrence and Lorsch 1967; Becker and Neuhauser 1975) approach to organizations, although Aldrich and Pfeffer do not note this. The basic premise of the resource-dependence model is that decisions are made within organizations. These decisions are made within the internal political context of the organization. The decisions deal with environmental conditions faced by the organization. Another important aspect of the model is that organizations attempt to deal actively with the environment. Organizations will attempt to manipulate the environment to their own advantage. Rather than being passive recipients of environmental forces, and the natural-selection model implies, organizations will make strategic decisions about adapting to the environment. Pfeffer and Salanick (1978) emphasize the role of management in this process.

No organization is able to generate all of the various resources that it needs. Similarly, not every possible activity can be performed within an organization to make it self-sustaining. Both of these conditions mean that organizations must be dependent on the environment for resources. Even seemingly self-sustaining organizations, such as isolated monasteries, must recruit new members or they will go out of existence. The resources that are needed can be in the form of raw materials, finances, personnel, or services or production operations that the organization cannot or does not perform for itself. The sources of resources in the environment are other organizations, with the exception being extractive industries which have the potential of owning the raw-material physical base. Even these organizations are dependent on other organizations for other resources. The fact that resources are obtained from other organizations means that the resource-dependence model can be thought of as an interorganizational resource-dependence model, since the resources come from other organizations.

Since the resource-dependence model portrays the organization as an active participant in its relationship with the environment, it also contains the idea that the administrators of organizations "manage their environments as well as their organizations, and the former activity may be as important, or even more important, than the latter" (Aldrich and Pfeffer 1976, p. 83). This is what Parsons (1960) called the institutional level of operations, in which the organization is linked to the social structure by its top executives.

A key element of the resource-dependence model is strategic choice (Chandler 1962; Child 1972b). This concept implies that a decision is made among a set of alternatives in regard to the strategy that the organization will utilize in its dealings with the environment. The assumption is that the environment does not force the organization into a situation in which no choice is possible. The organization is faced with a set of possible alternatives in dealing with the environment. Aldrich and Pfeffer note that the criteria by which choices are made and by which structures are determined are both important and problematic. There is not just one optimal structure or course of action. The resource-dependence model stresses the importance of internal power arrangements in the determination of the choices made. Both internal power arrangements and the demands of external groups are central to the decision-making process. Pfeffer and Salanick (1978) suggest that organizational management can take symbolic, responsive, or discretionary roles in response to environmental demands. The resourse-dependence model does not include the idea of goals as part of the decision-making process, which is an oversight that will be addressed at a later point in the discussion.

As has been noted, the resource-dependence model suggests that organizations are, or attempt to be, active in affecting their environment. This contributes to the variation among organizations, since variations are the result of "conscious, planned responses to environmental contingencies. Organizations attempt to absorb interdependence and uncertainty, either completely, as through merger (Pfeffer 1972b), or partially, as through cooperation (Pfeffer 1972a; Allen 1974) or the movement or personnel among organizations (Pfeffer and Leblebici 1973)" (Aldrich and Pfeffer 1976, p. 87). The conglomorate corporation is a striking example of variation in organizational form brought about by strategic choice.

The resource-dependence model also deals with the selection process, which was central to the natural-selection model. Instead of viewing selection solely from the standpoint of the environment selecting appropriate organizational forms, the resource-dependence model considers the ways in which organizations deal with their environments to insure that they survive. The environment is still the key factor, however. Aldrich and Pfeffer (p. 89) argue that the environment provides many of the constraints, uncertainties, and contingencies faced by organizations. As Hickson et al. (1971) have shown, organizational units that have the capability of dealing with constraints, uncertainties, and contingencies are those that obtain the most power within the organization. The power distribution within the organization is critical in determining the nature of the choices made, thus linking the environment to the choices made through the power process operating within the organization. The emphasis on power within the organization is a necessary one, since decisions are made in a political context. The resource-dependence model emphasizes interunit power differentials and tends to ignore hierarchical power differences. Hierarchical power differences must be considered in any analysis of strategic choice, since such differences can override interunit power struggles. It is quite possible that interunit power developments, as between marketing and production departments, have a crucial role in determining who rises in the hierarchy, but once the hierarchy is set, the power of the positions at the top of the organization would appear to be most central to the strategic decisions that are made. Regardless of the source of the power, of course, the strategic choices remain tied to environmental pressures. Again, it should be noted, the idea of goals is not included in the model in terms of decision making.

Aldrich and Pfeffer (1976), building on the work of Child (1972b), note that there are three ways in which strategic choices operate in terms of the environment. The first is that decision makers in organizations do have autonomy. This autonomy is much greater than would be suggested by a strict adherence to environmental determinism. The autonomy of the decision makers is reflected in the fact that more than one kind of decision can be made about the environmental niche being occupied—more than one kind of structure is suitable for given environments. In addition, organizations can enter or leave niches. This is illustrated by the fact that business firms can decide to try new markets or abandon old ones. Similarly, many colleges and universities are attempting to expand their niches, obviously in the face of decreasing demand by traditional students, by offering more and more courses and programs designed for nontraditional, older students.

The second way in which strategic choices are made about the environment involves attempts to manipulate the environment itself. Business firms attempt to create a demand for their products; they may also enter into arrangements with other firms to regulate competition, legally or illegally. Operating through the political process, business firms may also secure the passage of tariffs or quotas to restrict competition from foreign firms. Organizations in the public sector do essentially the same thing when they expand or fight for the retention of their jurisdiction. The various attempts that Presidents Nixon and Carter made to reorganize the federal government in the United States met with impassioned and successful resistance on the part of the agencies to be affected. The decision makers in these agencies exercised strategic choice about their environment.

The third way in which the strategic choices are made about the environment is based on the fact that particular environmental conditions are perceived and evaluated differently by different people. This point is a crucial one which requires some elaboration. Silverman (1971) and

Benson (1977) have stressed the point that the "reality" of organizations is a social construction. Organizational actors define reality in terms of their own background and values. Kanter (1977) has documented the manner in which recruitment policies for executives in a large business firm resulted in the firm's having executives of very homogeneous backgrounds. Kanter suggests that this permits the executives to have a great deal of trust in each other, since they will experience things in the same ways and, by implication, make the same kinds of decisions.

These are not new ideas. Thomas (1923) noted that if men define situations as real, they are real in their consequences. Weber (1947) also stressed the importance of subjective reality. While contemporary writers such as Silverman and Benson emphasize reality construction within organizations, the same point holds for the construction of the reality of the environment. The environment is perceived, interpreted, and evaluated by human actors within the organization. The perception becomes the reality and environmental conditions are only important as they are perceived by organizational decision makers. Different actors can perceive the same phenomenon quite differently. The point here is that the environment is acted upon by organizational decision makers on the basis of their perceptions, interpretations, and evaluations. While there may be commonality because of homogeneity of background within an organization, and even this will not be perfect, there will not be commonality between organizations. Thus, different organizations will act differently toward the same environmental conditions, if the perceptions are different. In this regard, Starbuck (1976) has pointed out that the critical question is the extent to which organizational perceptions vary from objective indicators of environmental conditions.

Aldrich and Pfeffer correctly note that there are limitations on the range of choices which are available to organizational decision makers. There may be legal barriers which prevent an organization from moving into a particular area. Economic barriers also exist. Some projects may be too expensive. Markets can be so dominated by a few firms that it is impossible for a new, small firm to enter.

In addition to barriers that preclude certain decisions, decisions to attempt to alter the environment may not be possible for many organizations. Small organizations, for example, have much less power than large organizations in terms of their capabilities of modifying their environments. A small state college has much less impact on the educational environment than does Harvard University.

As suggested in the discussion of perceptions of the environment, organizations can also be limited in their array of possible choices by the homogeneity of their personnel. To the extent that personnel have similar backgrounds and training, choices will tend to be similar.

The final aspect of the resource-dependence model is the manner in which the retention of organizational forms takes place. Aldrich and Pfeffer are less clear about the mechanisms which operate in regard to the resource-dependence model. They do suggest, however, several mechanisms that organizations utilize that result in the retention of previously successful adaptations. In many ways, these retention mechanisms represent tactical decisions about how the organization is to operate once the strategic decisions have been made.

One such retention device is bureaucratization. Organizations develop documentation and filing systems. These examples from the organizational past serve as precedents for the organizational present. The development of organizational policy serves the same function. Records and policies can provide the framework and content for decisions to be made. This provides continuity for the organization and ensures that past forms are retained. In addition, role specialization and standardization, with related job descriptions, also ensure that policies are followed. Another important characteristic of bureaucracy, advancement based on performance, also aids in continuity. If people are advanced up through the system, their experiences will be quite common and they will react in ways similar to the ways in which people have reacted in the past. Finally, the bureaucratic mechanism of a hierarchial structure also helps the retention process. The power of those at the top of the organization is viewed as legitimate. Authority is exercised and each decision is not questioned. As Perrow (1979) has noted, bureaucratization is probably the most efficient form of administration, and all organizations will move toward this form if they seek efficiency.

In addition to the organizational form of bureaucracy, and the policies and procedures governing individuals which arise from it, people are also socialized on a more informal basis into behavioral patterns that are deemed appropriate. Aldrich and Pfeffer (1976), in their discussion of this socialization process note: "As part of this process, expectations concerning actions and attitudes appropriate to that position are communicated. Persons entering an organization are socialized (Dornbusch 1955), and as an outcome of this socialization process the culture of the organization is transmitted to new members" (p. 97). Part of the culture of the organization involves folk wisdom and operating "rules of thumb" that persist over time.

Finally, the leadership structure of organizations tends to be consistent over time. As has been noted, people are screened and filtered as they move to the top of organizations. The screening and filtering is done by people already at the top of the organization and they are very likely to select people who are like themselves.

> Furthermore, since the promotion of leaders is based on their experience and expertise in dealing with critical organizational contingencies, to the extent that the definition of organizational uncertainties remains the same, similarity in leadership characteristics is further assured. Organizations that are marketing-oriented, such as consumer goods companies, may tend to promote people with sales or marketing experience, who because of similar backgrounds and socialization, will have fairly similar ideas about organizational policy. (Aldrich and Pfeffer 1976, p. 98)

There are thus several mechanisms which insure that organizational forms that have been successful will be retained. The thrust of the resource-dependence model is on the manner in which organizations deal with environmental contingencies. For the purposes of the present analysis, this approach is incomplete, since the idea of goals is sidestepped. This reduces the utility of the model.

Bringing Goals Back In

The idea of organizational goals has been central in most conceptualizations of organizations, as has been documented. In this section, the problems associated with using *only* a goal model for organizational analysis will not be considered. The purpose here is to bring organizational goals into the resource-dependence perspective and broaden that perspective into what I believe is a more useful model of organizations. Simply put, organizational goals are another element which are considered as strategic choices are made about organizational futures. The resource-dependence model ignores goals, but this seems counter to the reality of actual decision making.

As an oversimplified example, suppose that an organization has profit as its only goal. As decisions are made about environmental constraints, the goal is not ignored, but rather it enters the decision-making process. The organization attempts to adjust to the environmental constraints *and* protect its profitability. It does not simply react to the environment.

The approach taken here is an extension of the Weberian (1947) stance that humans are social actors. Organizational decision makers (actually all organizational members) do create the reality of the situations organizations face in their own minds. Part of the reality construction includes sets of ideas about where the organization is going. This is mixed into the decision-making process.

The approach does not make assumptions about the rationality involved, nor does it take a simplistic view that organizations are instruments designed to carry out goals. Rather, the approach adds goals back into the reasons that organizations act as they do. Goals are part of the culture of organizations and part of the mind sets of decision makers. Organizations, like the individuals who comprise them, are purposive creatures. The purposiveness can be overcome by external pressures, to be sure, and the organization may die or have to drastically alter its operations. The models which emphasize the environment are correct in pointing out the importance of the environment for the birth and death of organizations. They err, however, in departing totally from goal considerations.

Mohr's (1973) analysis of goals is particularly useful in understanding the relevance of goals for organizational analyses. Building on the work of Cartwright and Zander (1968), Mohr first notes that there are three possible kinds of goals. First, individuals in a group or organization have goals for themselves. The individuals also have goals for the group or organization. Finally, there are the goals *of* the organization. The first two types of goals are held by individuals, while the last is held collectively. The last two types are of interest to the organizational analyst.

According to Mohr, goals involve both *intent* and *outcomes*. The intent is based on the consensus of intent among organizational members, while the outcome involves both "transitive" externally oriented or functional goals and "reflexive" internally oriented institutional goals. It is important to stress that Mohr is referring to the intents and outcomes sought by the organizational members. They are in the minds of the members. Mohr is very aware that the determination of goals is no easy task. We have noted the manner in which goals can be determined and some of the problems associated with the determination of goals.

In building toward a definition of organizational goals, Mohr first notes that there are program goals. A political scientist, Mohr is making reference to programs within governmental agencies, but organizations in the private sector also have programs as parts of their complex set of activities. A program goal is "the collective intent of program members to bring about some specific state of the program itself or of its environment." An organizational goal, then is "the goal of a program occurring within the organization and under its auspices whose direct referent is either the organization itself as an institution or some aspect of the organization's environment" (p. 475).

Mohr suggests that transitive and reflexive goals are coequal, but it would appear that one type could be stressed more than the other at different points in an organization's life. The emphasis on multiple goals makes this interpretation necessary, as does the fact that environmental pressures are not constant.

Mohr's emphasis on consensus is somewhat confusing. He notes that in large, federated organizations only those at the very top of the organization are aware of the transitive goals and that some individuals may barely have heard of the programs to which they do not belong. This is true to be sure, but this weakens Mohr's idea of consensus, which has the unintended possible implication that some sort of vote is taken at every decision point.

Preferable to the idea of consensus is that of the *dominant coalition*. In discussing the dominant coalition, in relation to effectiveness, Pennings and Goodman (1977) note that it comprises a direct and indirect

representation or cross-section of horizontal constituencies (that is, subunits) and vertical constituencies (such as employees, management, owners, or stockholders) with different and possibly competing expectations. Consensus about the importance of the various criteria of effectiveness is hypothesized to be a function of the relative weights that the various constituencies carry in the negotiated order which we call organization. Consensus among members of the dominant coalition can be employed as a vehicle for obtaining effectiveness data. For example, how important is market share versus employee satisfaction? What should be the trade-off between research and development, between teaching and research, between patient care, medical research, and physicians' education? And so on. The consensus of the coalition allows the identification of such effectiveness criteria. These criteria may have different degrees of importance for the different constituencies in the dominant coalition; but somehow the preferences and expectations are aggregated, combined, modified, adjusted, and shared by the members of the dominant coalition. By invoking the concept of dominant coalition it is possible to preserve the notion of organizations as rational decision making entities. (p. 152)

Pennings and Goodman's term "effectiveness criteria" has the same meaning, for the purposes here, as goals. Their emphasis on the dominant coalition reintroduces the idea that decisions made in organizations are made within a political context. Their emphasis on rationality is correct, but perhaps overstated. If we return for the moment to the environmental-based models, it can be seen that things happen around an organization which cannot be foreseen. And, there may be competing external pressures *or* internal issues which cannot be rationally resolved because of their clearly contradictory nature. Nonetheless, the Pennings and Goodman approach is useful as an extension of Mohr's emphasis on organizational goals.

The importance of goals should be approached from another standpoint. Simon (1964) argues that the idea of organizational goals is a reification, or a case of "treating it as a superindividual entity having an existence and behavior independent of the behavior of its members" (p. 2). The analysis here accepts such reification as necessary and correct. Interestingly, Simon then goes on to note:

In the decision-making situations of real life, a course of action, to be acceptable, must satisfy a whole set of requirements, or constraints. Sometimes one of these requirements is singled out and referred to as the goal of the action. But the choice of one of the constraints, from many, to a large extent is arbitrary. For many purposes it is more meaningful to refer to the whole set of requirements as the (complex) goal of the action. This conclusion applies both to individual and organizational decision making. (p. 7)

Thus, to Simon and for our purposes here, goals are constraints for organizational decision making. So too are the environmental constraints discussed in the earlier section.

Nondecisions and Organizational Actions

The discussion thus far has emphasized the importance of decision making in organizations. Both the environment and organizational goals serve as constraints on organizational decision making and help to shape the paths that organizations take. The combination of these approaches makes it seem as though organizations are constantly making decisions and that this is the key to understanding how and why organizations operate.

There are two ways in which a total reliance upon the decision-making approach is misleading. First, there are important instances which involve nondecisions. These are instances in which the decision makers in organizations decide not to make a decision and proceed in the direction that was being pursued. Markets are not entered, projects are not begun, innovations are not adopted, or regulations are not passed. These are decisions to be sure, based on the environmental-goal mix that has been described. By noting the importance of nondecisions in this manner, however, it is possible to see that organizations are remarkably stable. In commenting upon the natural-selection model, Perrow (1979) notes that

in most areas of economic power—railroads, auto manufacturing, oil production and marketing, steel production—there are very few organizations and they are of the same kind. There are three major U.S. auto manufacturers, and while organizational theorists could pour over the differences among them (if they bothered to study them), in species terms they are very similar. In the social world, then, a different kind of logic seems to be working. There is not much variation among units; a few giant organizations dominate the many small ones; the giant ones rarely die (there is little negative selection); and in the public sector, efficiency and adaptation are not effectiveness criteria—we simply do not let schools and garbage collectors go out of business. (p. 242)

The point here is not another criticism of the natural-selection model but to indicate that these large organizations do go on as they have, in many areas of operation, not making decisions nor enduring severe environmental pressures.

There is another aspect to this point. Much of what occurs in organizations is based on *precedent*. Using a very different example, the role of precedent can be illustrated. My son recently graduated from the sixth grade. The elementary school is quite small, with only two classes at each grade level, and hardly of the scope of the auto manufacturer. The graduation had the usual elements—band and orchestral pieces, choral renditions, speeches, and the awarding of diplomas. The procedures used were those that had been used in the past. There are formal and informal records kept regarding what happens as sixth-grade graduations and the precedent is repeated year after year. As teachers come and go, they are told what their predecessors did. The form stays largely the same, although the content may vary.

The point of this little example is that even in small and simple organizations there are many ongoing activities that are guided by precedent. In larger, more complex organizations, the same point would appear to be true, even to a greater extent, as records are kept, procedures are formalized, and position descriptions developed to guide the behavior of individual role incumbents. Many and probably most of the activities of organizations are of this ongoing type. Automobiles continue to be made; patients are admitted, treated, and released from hospitals; insurance premiums are credited to accounts; sacrements are performed in churches; and tax forms are processed.

It is these ongoing activities that are at the heart of organizations. They are less exciting than points of decision or environmental crises. They are less dramatic than the formation or death of an organization. Yet they are the bases of organizations. Any organizational model which ignores them misses a critical component.

These ongoing activities may or may not be goal oriented. They also may or may not be oriented toward the environment. Some organizational activities are totally support activities. The men and women who mow the lawns at my university neither contribute to the goal nor adapt the organization to the environment, except insofar as mown grass somehow might appeal to a legislator or private donor, yet the lawns continue to be mown. The payroll department processes pay checks and may contribute more directly to a goal of morale among employees, if such a goal exists.

In this review of the state of contemporary organizational theory, the natural-selection, resource-dependence, and goal models of organizations have been stressed, with the ongoing activity emphasis added. The importance of decision making and the manner in which decision makers construct and negotiate reality has been noted. Decisions are made in a political context within organizations and are affected by power positions and power coalitions in and out of the organizations. Organizations are viewed as dynamic entities, but with continuity of activities due to precedent. No attempt has been made to weight the strength of these various components, since the importance of goals, environmental pressures, ongoing activities, and decision making will vary according to the particular contingencies being faced at a particular point in time. Our view is that the goals, environmental pressures, ongoing activities, and decisions made may be contradictory, both within and between these categories. Organizational members do create an order out of them, but this order is subject to constant recreation due to changing circumstances.

SUMMARY AND CONCLUSIONS

This review of organizational theory has been brief. In examining traditional theories, the attempt was to illustrate some of the considerations that have long concerned organizational analysts. The review of contemporary theory was an attempt to extend the dominant models on the basis of the considerations contained throughout the analysis in this book. The perspective presented here is based on my understanding of the nature of organizations and the nature of organizational theory. The approach is consistent with the reality that I perceive and have attempted to portray in these pages.

References

Administrative Science Quarterly 1965 10, (June) Entire Issue.

Administrative Science Quarterly 1969 14, (December) Entire Issue.

AGRANOFF, R., AND A. PATTAHAS 1979 *Dimensions of Services Integration: Service Delivery, Program Linkages, Policy Management, Organizational Structure.* Human Services Monograph Series 13, Project SHARE, DHEW Publication No, 02-76-130. Washington, D.C.: U.S. Government Printing Office.

AIKEN, MICHAEL, ROBERT DEWAR, NANCY DITOMASO, JERALD HAGE, AND GERALD ZEITZ. 1975 *Coordinating Human Services.* San Francisco: Jossey Bass.

AIKEN, MICHAEL, AND JERALD HAGE 1966 "Organizational Alienation: A Comparative Analysis," *American Sociological Review,* 31, no. 4 (August), 497–07.

————. 1968 "Organizational Interdependence and Interorganizational Structure," *American Sociological Review,* 33, no. 6 (December), 912–30.

ALBROW, M. C. 1970 *Bureaucracy.* London: Pall Mall.

ALDRICH, HOWARD E. 1972a "Technology and Organizational Structure: A Reexamination of the Findings of the Aston Group," *Administrative Science Quarterly,* 17, no. 1 (March), 26–43.

————. 1972b "Reply to Hilton: Seduced and Abandoned," *Administrative Science Quarterly,* 17, no. 1 (March), 55–57.

————. 1972c "An Organization—Environment Perspective on Co-operation and Conflict in the Manpower Training System," in *Conflict and Power in Complex Organizations,* ed. ANANT NEGANDHI. Kent, Ohio: Center for Business and Economic Research.

————. 1974 "The Environment as a Network of Organizations: Theoretical and Methodological Implications." Paper presented at the International Sociological Association Meetings, Toronto, Canada.

————. 1979 *Organizations and Environments.* Englewood Cliffs, N.J.: Prentice-Hall, Inc.

ALDRICH, HOWARD E., AND JEFFREY PFEFFER 1976 "Environments of Organizations," *Annual Review of Sociology,* Vol. 2. Palo Alto, Ca.: Annual Review Inc.

ALEXANDER, ERNEST R. 1974 "Decision Making and Organizational Adaptation: A Proposed Model." Mimeographed. Eighth World Congress of Sociology, Toronto.

————. 1979 "The Design of Alteratives in Organizational Contexts," *Administrative Science Quarterly,* 24, no. 3 (September), 382–04.

ALEXANDER, GORDON J., AND ROGER A. BUCHHOLZ 1978 "Corporate Social Responsibility and Stock Market Performance," *Academy of Management Journal,* 21 no. 3 (September), 479–86.

ALLEN, MICHAEL PATRICK 1974 "The Structure of Interorganizational Elite Cooptation: Interlocking Corporate Directorates," *American Sociological Review,* 39, no. 3 (June), 393–96.

————. 1976 Management Control in the Large Corporation: Comment on Zeitlin," *American Journal of Sociology,* 81, no. 4 (January), 885–94.

ALLEN, MICHAEL PATRICK, SHARON K. PANIAN, AND ROY E. LOTZ 1979 "Managerial Succession and Organizational Performance: A Recalcitrant Problem Revisited," *Administrative Science Quarterly,* 24, no. 2 (June), 167–80.

ALTHEIDE, DAVID L., AND JOHN M. JOHNSON 1980 *Bureaucratic Propaganda.* Boston: Allyn and Bacon, Inc.

ALUTTO, JOSEPH, AND JAMES A. BELASCO 1972 "A Typology for Participation in Organizational Decision Making," *Administrative Science Quarterly,* 17, no. 1 (March), 117–25.

ANDERSON, THEODORE, AND SEYMOUR WARKOV 1961 "Organizational Size and Functional Complexity," *American Sociological Review,* 26, no. 1 (February), 23–28.

ANGLE, HAROLD L. AND JAMES L. PERRY 1981 "An Empirical Assessment of Organizational

Commitment and Organizational Effectiveness," *Administrative Science Quarterly*, 26, no. 1 (March), 1–14.

ANTONIO, ROBERT J. 1979 "Domination and Production in Bureaucracy," *American Sociological Review*, 44, no. 6 (December), 895–912.

ARGYRIS, CHRIS 1969 "On the Effectiveness of Research and Development Organizations," *American Scientist*, 56, no. 4 (July), 344–55.

———. 1972 *The Applicability of Organizational Sociology*. London: Cambridge University Press.

———. 1973 "Personality and Organization Theory Revisited," *Administrative Science Quarterly*, 18, no. 2 (June), 141–67.

ARONOWITZ, STANLEY 1973 *False Promises*. New York: McGraw-Hill Book Company.

ASSAEL, HENRY 1969 "Constructive Role of Interorganizational Conflict," *Administrative Science Quarterly*, 14, no. 4 (December), 573–82.

ATHANASSIADES, JOHN C. 1974 "On Investigation of Some Communication Patterns of Female Subordinates in Hierarchial Organizations," *Human Relations*, 27, no. 2 (March), 195–209.

AZUMI, KOYA, AND CHARLES J. MCMILLAN 1974 "Subjective and Objective Measures of Organizational Structure." Mimeo, *American Sociological Association*, New York.

BACHARACH, SAMUEL B., AND EDWARD J. LAWLER 1980 *Power and Politics in Organizations*. San Francisco: Jossey-Bass.

BAKER, FRANK, AND GREGORY O'BRIEN 1971 "Intersystem Relations and Coordination of Human Service Organizations," *American Journal of Public Health*, 61, no. 1 (January), 130–37.

BALDRIDGE, J. VICTOR, AND ROBERT A. BURNHAM 1975 "Organizational Innovation: Individual, Organizational, and Environmental Impacts," *Administrative Science Quarterly*, 20, no. 2 (June), 165–76.

BALES, ROBERT F. 1953 "The Equilibrium Problem in Small Groups," in *Working Paper in Theory of Action*, eds. TALCOTT PARSONS, ROBERT F. BALES, AND EDWARD SHILS, New York: The Free Press.

BALES, ROBERT F., AND PHILIP E. SLATER 1955 "Role Differentiation in Small Decision Making Groups," in *Family Socialization and Interaction Processes*, eds. TALCOTT PARSONS AND ROBERT BALES. New York: The Free Press.

BARNARD, CHESTER I. 1938 *The Function of the Executive*. Cambridge, Mass.: Harvard University Press.

BARON, JAMES N., AND WILLIAM T. BIELBY 1980 "Bringing the Firms Back In: Stratification, Segmentation and the Organization of Work," *American Sociological Review*, 45, no. 5 (October), 737–65.

BARTON, ALLEN H. 1961 *Organizational Measurement*. New York: College Entrance Examination Board.

BATY, GORDON, WILLIAM EVAN, AND TERRY ROTHERMEL 1971 "Personnel Flows as Interorganizational Relations," *Administrative Science Quarterly*, 16, no. 4 (December), 430–43.

BAUER, DOUGLAS 1981 "Why Big Business is Firing the Boss" *New York Times Magazine* (March 8), 22–25, 79–91.

BAVELAS, ALEX 1959 "Communication Patterns in Task Oriented Groups," *Journal of the Acoustic Society of America*. 22, no. 6 (November), 725–30.

BECKER, SELWYN W., AND DUNCAN NEUHAUSER 1975 *The Efficient Organization*. New York: Elsevier.

BENSON, J. KENNETH 1975 "The Interlocking Network as a Political Economy," *Administrative Science Quarterly*, 20, no. 2 (June), 229–49.

———. 1977 "Innovation and Crisis in Organizational Analysis," *Sociological Quarterly*, 18, no. 1 (Winter), 3–16.

BENSON, J. KENNETH, JOSEPH T. KUNCE, CHARLES A. THOMPSON, AND DAVID L. ALLEN 1973 *Coordinating Human Services*. Columbia, Mo.: University of Missouri, Regional Rehabilitation Institute.

BERLE, ADOLPH A., AND GARDINER C. MEANS 1932 *The Modern Corporation and Private Property*. New York: The Macmillan Company.

BEYER, JANICE M., AND HARRISON M. TRICE 1979 "A Reexamination of the Relations between Size and Various Components of Organizational Complexity," *Administrative Science Quarterly*, no. 1 (March), 48–64.

BIERSTEDT, ROBERT 1950 "An Analysis of Social Power," *American Sociological Review*, 15, no. 6 (December), 730–38.

BIGGART, NICOLE WOOLSEY 1977 "The Creative—Destructive Process of Organizational Change: The Case of the Post Office," *Administrative Science Quarterly*, 22, no. ? (September), 410–26.

BLAKE, RICHARD R., AND JANE S. MOUTON 1964 *The Managerial Grid*. Houston: Gulf Publishing Co.

BLAU, JUDITH R., AND WILLIAM McKINLEY 1979 "Ideas, Complexity, and Innovation," *Administrative Science Quarterly*, 24, no. 2 (June), 200–19.

BLAU, PETER M. 1955 *The Dynamics of Bureaucracy*. Chicago: University of Chicago Press.

——. 1964 *Exchange and Power in Social Life*. New York: John Wiley and Sons, Inc.

——. 1968 "The Hierarchy of Authority in Organizations," *American Journal of Sociology*, 73, no. 4 (January), 453–67.

——. 1970 "Decentralization in Bureaucracies," in *Power in Organizations*, ed. MAYER N. ZALD. Nashville, Tenn.: Vanderbilt University Press.

——. 1972 "Interdependence and Hierarchy in Organizations," *Social Science Research*, 1, no. 1 (April), 1–24.

——. 1973 *The Organization of Academic Work*. New York: John Wiley and Sons, Inc.

——. 1974 *On the Nature of Organizations*. New York: John Wiley and Sons, Inc.

BLAU, PETER M., AND W. RICHARD SCOTT 1962 *Formal Organizations*. San Francisco: Chandler Publishing Co.

BLAU, PETER M., WOLF HEYDEBRAND, AND ROBERT E. STAUFFER 1966 "The Structure of Small Bureaucracies," *American Sociological Review*, 31, no. 2 (April), 179–91.

BLAU, PETER M., AND RICHARD A. SCHOENHERR 1970 "A Formal Theory of Differentiation in Organizations," *American Sociological Review*, 35, no. 2 (April), 201–18.

—— AND RICHARD A. SCHOENHERR 1971 *The Structure of Organizations*. New York: Basic Books.

BLAUNER, ROBERT 1964 *Alienation and Freedom*. Chicago: University of Chicago Press.

BODDEWYN, JOHN 1974 "External Affairs: A Corporate Function in Search of Conceptualization and Theory," *Organization and Administrative Sciences*, 5, no. 1 (Spring), 67–106.

BOJE, DAVID M., AND DAVID A. WHETTEN 1979 "Centrality and Attributions of Influence in Interorganizational Networks." Unpublished paper. Urbana: University of Illinois.

BOULDING, KENNETH E. 1964 "A Pure Theory of Conflict Applied to Organizations," in *Power and Conflict in Organizations*, ed. ROBERT L. KAHN AND ELISE BOULDING. New York: Basic Books, Inc.

BRAITO, RITA, STEVEN PAULSON, AND GERALD KLONGLAN 1972 "Domain Consensus: A Key Variable in Interorganizational Analysis." In *Complex Organizations and Their Environments*, eds. MERLIN BRINKERHOFF AND PHILLIP KUNZ. Dubuque, Iowa: William C. Brown.

BRAVERMAN, HARRY 1974 *Labour and Monopoly Capital*. New York: Monthly Review Press.

BREWER, JOHN 1971 "Flow of Communication, Expert Qualifications, and Organizational Authority Structure," *American Sociological Review*, 36, no. 3 (June), 475–84.

BRINKERHOFF, MERLIN B. 1972 "Hierarchial Status, Contingencies, and the Administrative Staff Conference," *Administrative Science Quarterly*, 17, no. 3 (September), 395–407.

BROSKOWSKI, ANTHONY 1980 "Literature Review on Interorganizational Relationships and Their Relevance to Health and Mental Health Coordination." Tampa, Fla.: Northside Community Mental Health Center (Final Report) NIMH Contract #278-00300P.

BROWN, JOHN L., AND RODNEY SCHNECK 1979 "A Structural Comparison Between Canadian and American Industrial Organizations," *Administrative Science Quarterly*, 24, no. 1 (March), 24–47.

BROWN, M. CRAIG 1981 "Administrative Succession and Organizational Performance: One More Look at the Recalcitrant Problem of the Succession Effect." Mimeographed. Albany: SUNY-Albany.

BROWN, RICHARD HARVEY 1978 "Bureaucracy as Praxis: Toward a Political Phenomenology of Formal Organizations," *Administrative Science Quarterly,* 23, no. 3 (September), 365–82.

BUCHER, RUE 1970 "Social Process and Power in a Medical School," in *Power in Organizations,* ed. MAYER N. ZALD. Nashville: Vanderbilt University Press.

BUCKLEY, WALTER 1967 *Sociology and Modern Systems Theory.* Englewood Cliffs, N.J.: Prentice-Hall, Inc.

BURACK, ELMER H. 1967 "Industrial Management in Advanced Production Systems: Some Theoretical Concepts and Preliminary Findings," *Administrative Science Quarterly,* 12, no. 4 (December), 479–500.

BURKE, RONALD J. 1970 "Methods of Resolving Superior-Subordinate Conflict: The Constructive Use of Subordinate Differences and Disagreements," *Organizational Behavior and Human Performance,* 5 (4), (July), 393–411.

BURNS, TOM 1967 "The Comparative Study of Organizations," in *Methods of Organizational Research,* ed. VICTOR H. VROOM. Pittsburgh: University of Pittsburgh Press.

BURNS, TOM, AND G. M. STALKER 1961 *The Management of Innovation.* London: Tavistock Publications.

BURRELL, GIBSON, AND GARETH MORGAN 1979 *Sociological Paradigms and Organizational Analysis.* London: Heinemann.

BURT, RONALD S. 1977 "Power in a Social Typology," *Social Science Research,* 6 (Winter), 1–83.

————. 1980 "Cooptive Corporate Action Networks: A Reconsideration of Interlocking Directorates Involving American Manufacturing," *Administrative Science Quarterly* 25, no. 4 (December), 557–82.

BURT, RONALD S., KENNETH P. CHRISTMAN, AND HAROLD C. KILBURN, JR. 1980 "Testing a Structural Theory of Corporate Cooptation: Interorganizational Directorate Ties as a Strategy for Avoiding Market Constraints on Projects," *American Sociological Review,* 45, no. 5 (October), 821–41.

CAMERON, KIM 1978 "Measuring Organizational Effectiveness in Institutions of Higher Education," *Administrative Science Quarterly,* 23, no. 4 (December), 604–32.

CAMPBELL, DONALD 1969 "Variation and Selective Retention in Socio-Cultural Evolution," *General Systems: Yearbook of the Society for General Systems Research* 16:69–85.

CAMPBELL, JOHN P. 1977 "On the Nature of Organizational Effectiveness," in *New Perspectives on Organizational Effectiveness,* eds. PAUL S. GOODMAN AND JOHANNES M. PENNINGS San Francisco: Jossey-Bass.

CAMPBELL, JOHN P., AND OTHERS 1974 *The Measurement of Organizational Effectiveness.* Final Report, Navy Personnel Research and Development Center Contract N 00022-73-C-0023. Minneapolis: Personnel Decisions.

CAPLOW, THEODORE 1964 *Principles of Organization.* New York: Harcourt Brace Jovanovich.

CARAGONNE, P. 1978 "Service Integration: Where Do We Stand?" Paper prepared for the 39th National Conference on Public Administration, April, at Phoenix, Arizona.

CAREY, ALEX 1967 "The Hawthorne Studies: A Radical Criticism," *American Sociological Review,* 32, no. 3 (June), 403–16.

CARPER, WILLIAM B., AND WILLIAM E. SNIZEK 1980 "The Nature and Types of Organizational Taxonomies: An Overview," *Academy of Management Review,* 5, no. 1 (January), 65–75.

CARTWRIGHT, DORWIN 1965 "Influence, Leadership, and Control." in *Handbook of Organizations,* ed. JAMES G. MARCH. Chicago: Rand McNally and Co.: 1–47.

CARTWRIGHT, DORWIN, AND A. ZANDER 1968 "Motivational Processes in Groups: Introduction," in *Group Dynamics* (3rd ed.), ed. D. CARTWRIGHT AND A. ZANDER. New York: Harper and Row.

CARZO, ROCCO, JR., AND JOHN N. YANOUZAS 1969 "Effects of Flat and Tall Organizational Structures," *Administrative Science Quarterly,* 14, no. 2 (June), 178–91.

CHAMPION, DEAN J. 1975 *The Sociology of Organizations.* New York: McGraw-Hill, Book Company.

CHANDLER, A. D., JR. 1962 *Strategy and Structure.* Cambridge, Mass.: MIT Press.

CHILD, JOHN 1972a "Organizational Structure and Strategies of Control: A Replication of the Aston Study," *Administrative Science Quarterly*, 17, no. 2 (June), 163–77.

———. 1972b "Organizational Structure, Environment, and Performance: The Role of Strategic Choice," *Sociology*, 6, no. 1, 1–22.

———. 1973 "Strategies of Control and Organizational Behavior," *Administrative Science Quarterly*, 18, no. 1 (March), 1–17.

———. 1976 "Participation, Organization, and Social Cohesion," *Human Relations*, 29, no. 5 (May), 429–51.

CHILD, JOHN, AND ROGER MANSFIELD 1972 "Technology, Size and Organizational Structure," *Sociology*, 6, no. 3 (September), 369–93.

CHRISTENSON, JAMES A., AND CAROLYN E. SACKS 1980 "The Impact of Government Size and Number of Administrative Units on the Quality of Public Service," *Administrative Science Quarterly*, 25, no. 1 (March), 89–101.

CLARK, BURTON 1956 *Adult Education in Transition*. Berkeley: University of California Press.

———. 1965 "Interorganizational Patterns in Education," *Administrative Science Quarterly*, 10, no. 3 (September), 224–37.

CLEGG, STEWART, AND DAVID DUNKERLY 1980 *Organization, Class, and Control*. London. Routledge and Kegan Paul.

COHEN, MICHAEL D., JAMES G. MARCH, AND JOHN P. OLSEN 1972 "A Garbage Can Model of Organizational Choice," *Administrative Science Quarterly*, 17, no. 1 (March), 1–25.

COLEMAN, JAMES S. 1974 *Power and the Structure of Society*. New York: W. W. Norton and Company.

COMSTOCK, DONALD, AND W. RICHARD SCOTT 1977 "Technology and the Structure of Subunits: Distinguishing Individual and Work Group Effects," *Administrative Science Quarterly*, 22, no. 2, (June), 177–202.

COOK, KAREN S. 1977 "Exchange and Power in Networks of Interorganizational Relations." *Sociological Quarterly*, 18, no. 1 (Winter), 62–82.

CORWIN, RONALD 1973 *Reform and Organizational Survival: The Teacher Corps as an Instrument of Educational Change*. New York: John Wiley and Sons, Inc.

COSER, LEWIS 1966 *The Functions of Social Conflict*. New York: The Free Press.

———. 1967 *Continuities in the Study of Social Conflict*. New York: The Free Press.

COULTER, PHILLIP B. 1979 "Organizational Effectiveness in the Public Sector: The Example of Municipal Fire Protection," *Administrative Science Quarterly* 24, no. 1 (March), 65–81.

CRAIG, JOHN G., AND EDWARD GROSS 1970 "The Forum Theory of Organizational Democracy: Structural Guarantees as Time Related Variables," *American Sociological Review*, 35, no. 1 (February), 19–33.

CRITTENDEN, ANN 1978 "Philanthropy, The Business of the Not-so-Idle Rich" *New York Times* (July 23) Section F. 3–5.

CROZIER, MICHAEL 1964 *The Bureaucratic Phenomenon*. Chicago: University of Chicago Press.

———. 1973 *The Stalled Society*, trans. RUPERT SWYER. New York: The Viking Press.

CUMMINGS, LARRY L. 1977 "The Emergence of the Instrumental Organization." In *New Perspectives on Organizational Effectiveness*, eds. PAUL S. GOODMAN AND JOHANNES M. PENNINGS. San Francisco: Jossey-Bass.

CYERT, RICHARD, AND JAMES MARCH 1963 *A Behavioral Theory of the Firm*. Englewood Cliffs, N.J.: Prentice-Hall, Inc.

DAFT, RICHARD L., AND SELWYN W. BECKER 1978 *Innovation in Organizations: Innovation Adoption in School Organizations*. New York: Elsevier.

DAFT, RICHARD L., AND PATRICIA J. BRADSHAW 1980 "The Process of Horizontal Differentiation: Two Models," *Administrative Science Quarterly*, 25, no. 3 (September), 441–56.

DAHL, ROBERT 1957 "The Concept of Power," *Behavioral Science*, 2, no. 3 (July), 201–15.

DAHRENDORF, RALF 1959 *Class and Class Conflict in Industrial Society*. London: Routledge and Kegan Paul.

DALTON, MELVILLE 1959 *Men Who Manage*. New York: John Wiley and Sons, Inc.

DEWAR, ROBERT D., AND JERALD HAGE 1978 "Size, Technology, Complexity and Structural Differentiation: Toward a Theoretical Synthesis," *Administrative Science Quarterly*, 23, no. 1 (March), 111–36.

DEWAR, ROBERT D., DAVID A. WHETTEN, AND DAVID BOJE 1980 "An Examination of the Reliability and Validity of the Aiken and Hage Scales of Utilization, Formalization, and Task Routineness," *Administrative Science Quarterly*, 25, no. 1, (March), 120–28.

DILL, WILLIAM R. 1958 "Environment as an Influence on Managerial Autonomy," *Administrative Science Quarterly*, 2, no. 1 (March), 409–43.

————. 1965 "Business Organizations." In *Handbook of Organizations*, ed. JAMES G. MARCH. Chicago: Rand McNally and Co.

DONALDSON, LEX, AND MALCOLM WARNER 1974 "Bureaucratic and Electoral Control in Occupational Interest Associations," *Sociology*, 8, no. 1 (January), 47–59.

DORNBUSCH, SANFORD M. 1955 "The Military Academy as an Assimilating Institution," *Social Forces*, 33, no. 4 (May), 316–21.

DORNBUSCH, SANFORD M., AND W. RICHARD SCOTT 1975 *Evaluation and the Exercise of Authority*. New York: Basic Books.

DOWNS, ANTHONY 1967 *Inside Bureaucracy*. Boston: Little, Brown, and Company.

DOWNS, GEORGE W., JR., AND LAWRENCE B. MOHR 1976 "Conceptual Issues in the Study of Innovation," *Administrative Science Quarterly*, 21, no. 4 (December), 700–714.

DRUCKER, PETER 1973 *The Practice of Management*. New York: Harper and Row.

DUBICK, MICHAEL A. 1978 "The Organizational Structure of Newspapers in Relation to Their Metropolitan Environment," *Administrative Science Quarterly*, 23, no. 3 (September), 418–33.

DUBIN, ROBERT 1965 "Supervision and Productivity: Empirical Findings and Theoretical Considerations." In *Leadership and Productivity*, eds. ROBERT DUBIN, GEORGE HOMANS, FLOYD MANN, AND DELBERT MILLER. San Francisco: Chandler Publishing Co.

DUNCAN, ROBERT B. 1972 "Characteristics of Organizational Environments and Perceived Environmental Uncertainty," *Administrative Science Quarterly*, 17, no. 3 (September), 313–27.

————. 1973 "Multiple Decision-Making Structures in Adapting to Environmental Uncertainty: The Impact on Organizational Effectiveness," *Human Relations*, 26, no. 3 (June), 273–91.

EITZEN, D. STANLEY, AND NORMAN R. YETMAN 1972 "Managerial Change, Longevity and Organizational Effectiveness," *Administrative Science Quarterly*, 17, no. 1, (March), 110–18.

EMERSON, RICHARD M. 1962 "Power-Dependence Relations," *American Sociological Review*, 27, no. 1 (February), 31–40.

EMERY, F. E., AND E. L. TRIST 1965 "The Causal Texture of Organizational Environments," *Human Relations*, 18, no. 1 (February), 21–32.

ETZIONI, AMITAI 1960 "New Directions in the Study of Organizations and Society." *Social Research*, 27, no. 2 (Summer) 223–8.

————. 1961 *A Comparative Analysis of Complex Organizations*. New York. The Free Press.

————. 1964 *Modern Organizations*. Englewood Cliffs, N.J.: Prentice-Hall, Inc.

————. 1965 "Dual Leadership in Complex Organizations," *American Sociological Review*, 30, no. 5 (October), 688–98.

————. 1968 *The Active Society: A Theory of Societal and Political Processes*. New York: The Free Press.

————. 1975 *A Comparative Analysis of Complex Organizations* (rev. ed.). New York: The Free Press.

EVAN, WILLIAM 1966 "The Organization Set: Toward a Theory of Interorganizational Relations," in *Approaches to Organizational Design*, ed. JAMES THOMPSON. Pittsburgh: University of Pittsburgh Press.

FARBERMAN, HARVEY A. 1975 "A Criminogenic Market Structure: The Automobile Industry," *The Sociological Quarterly*, 16, no. 4 (Autumn), 438–57.

FAYOL, HENRI 1949 *General and Industrial Management*. London: Sir Isaac Pitman.

FENNELL, MARY C. 1980 "The Effects of Environmental Characteristics on the Structure of Hospital Clusters," *Administrative Science Quarterly*, 29, no. 3 (September), 489–510.

FIEDLER, FRED E. 1967 *A Theory of Leadership Effectiveness.* New York: McGraw Hill Book Company.

———. 1972 "The Effects of Leadership Training and Experience: A Contingency Model Explanation," *Administrative Science Quarterly,* 17, no. 4 (December), 453–70.

FILLEY, ALAN C., AND ROBERT J. HOUSE 1969 *Managerial Processes and Organizational Behavior.* Glenview, Ill.: Scott, Foresman and Company.

FILLEY, ALLEN C., ROBERT J. HOUSE, AND STEVEN KERR 1976 *Managerial Process and Organizational Behavior.* Glenview, Ill.: Scott, Foresman and Company.

FORBES 1973 "The Numbers Game: The Larger the Company, the More Understanding the Accountant?" 112, no. 1 (July), 33–35.

FORM, WILLIAM 1981 "Resolving Ideological Issues on the Division of Labor" in HUBERT M. BLALOCK, JR. (ed.), *Theory and Research in Sociology.* New York: The Free Press.

FOX, FREDERICK V., AND BARRY M. STAW 1979 "The Trapped Administrator: Effects of Job Insecurity and Policy Resistance upon Commitment to a Cause of Action," *Administrative Science Quarterly,* 24, no. 3 (September), 449–71.

FREEMAN, JOHN H. 1973 "Environment, Technology, and the Administrative Intensity of Manufacturing Organizations," *American Sociological Review,* 38, no. 6 (December), 750–63.

———. 1979 "Going to the Well: School District Administrative Intensity and Environmental Constraints," *Administrative Science Quarterly,* 24, no. 1 (March), 119–33.

FREEMAN, JOHN H., AND MICHAEL T. HANNAN 1975 "Growth and Decline Processes in Organizations," *American Sociological Review,* 40, no. 2 (April), 219–28.

FREIDSON, ELIOT 1973 *The Professions and Their Prospects.* Beverly Hills, Cal.: Sage Publications, Inc.

FRENCH, JOHN R. P., AND BERTRAM RAVEN 1968 "The Bases of Social Power," in *Group Dynamics* (3rd. ed.), ed. DORWIN CARTWRIGHT AND ALVIN ZANDER. New York: Harper and Row.

FRENCH, WENDELL 1969 "Organizational Development: Objectives, Assumptions, and Strategies," *California Management Review,* 12, no. 2 (Winter): 23–34.

GALASKIEWICZ, JOSEPH 1979 "The Structure of Community Organizational Networks," *Social Forces,* 57, no. 4 (June), 1346–64.

GALASKIEWICZ, JOSEPH, AND PETER J. MARSDEN 1978 "Interorganizational Resources Networks: Formal Patterns of Overlap," *Social Science Research,* 7, no. 2 (June) 89–107.

GALASKIEWICZ, JOSEPH, AND DEBORAH SHATIN 1980 "Leadership and Networking Among Neighborhood Human Service Organizations." Revised paper read at the INSNA Conference on New Directions in Structural Analysis, March 1978.

GALBRAITH, JAY 1973 *Designing Complex Organizations.* Reading, Mass.: Addison-Wesley Publishing Company.

———. 1977 *Organization Design.* Reading, Mass.: Addison-Wesley-Publishing Company.

GALBRAITH, JOHN KENNETH 1974 "The U.S. Economy is Not a Free Market Economy," *Forbes,* 113, no. 10 (May), 99.

GALTUNG, JOHAN 1965 "Institutionalized Conflict Resolution: A Theoretical Paradigm," *Journal of Peace Research,* 2, no. 4 348–96.

GAMSON, WILLIAM, AND NORMAN SCOTCH 1964 "Scapegoating in Baseball," *American Journal of Sociology,* 70, no. 1 (July), 69–72.

GANS, SHELDON P., AND GERALD T. HORTON 1975 *Integration of Human Services: The State and Municipal Levels.* New York: Praeger Publications.

GARDNER, ELMER A., AND JAMES N. SNIPE 1970 "Toward the Coordination and Integration of Personal Health Service," *American Journal of Public Health,* 60, no. 11 (November): 2068–78.

GEORGIOU, PETRO 1973 "The Goal Paradigm and Notes Toward a Counter Paradigm," *Administrative Science Quarterly,* 18, no. 3 (September), 291–310.

GIORDANO, PEGGY C. 1974 "The Juvenile Justice System: The Client Perspective." Ph.D. dissertation, University of Minnesota.

———. 1976 "The Sense of Injustice: An Analysis of Juveniles' Reaction to the Justice System," *Criminology,* 14, no. 1 (May), 93–112.

————. 1977 "The Clients Perspective in Agency Evaluation," *Social Work*, 22, no. 1 (January), 34–39.

GLISSON, CHARLES A. 1978 "Dependence of Technological Routinizations on Structural Variables in Human Service Organizations," *Administrative Science Quarterly*, 23, no 3 (September), 383–95.

GOFFMAN, IRVING 1959 *The Presentation of Self in Everyday Life*. New York: Doubleday.

GOODMAN, PAUL, AND JOHANNES PENNINGS 1977 *New Perspectives on Organizations' Effectiveness*. San Francisco: Jossey-Bass.

GORDON, GERALD, AND SELWYN BECKER 1964 "Careers, Organizational Size and Succession," *American Journal of Sociology*, 70, no. 2 (September): 216–222.

GOULDNER, ALVIN, ed. 1950 *Studies in Leadership*. New York: Harper and Row.

GOULDNER, ALVIN 1954 *Patterns of Industrial Bureaucracy*. New York: The Free Press.

————. 1962 "Comment," *American Journal of Sociology*, 67, no. 1 (July), 54–56.

GRAFTON, CARL 1975 "The Creation of Federal Agencies," *Administration and Society*, 7, no. 3 (November), 328–65.

GRANOVETTER, MARK 1973 "The Strength of Weak Ties," *American Journal of Sociology*, 78, no. 6 (May), 1360–80.

GROSS, EDWARD 1968 "Universities as Organizations: A Research Approach," *American Sociological Review*, 33, no. 4 (August), 518–43.

GRUSKY, OSCAR 1961 "Corporate Size, Bureaucratization, and Managerial Succession," *American Journal of Sociology*, 67, no. 3 (November), 355–59.

————. 1963 "Managerial Succession and Organizational Effectiveness," *American Journal of Sociology*, 69, no. 1 (July), 21–31.

————. 1964 "Reply," *American Journal of Sociology*, 70, no. 1 (July), 72–76.

————. 1970 "The Effects of Succession: A Comparative Study of Military and Business Organization," in *The Sociology of Organizations*, ed. Oscar Grusky and George Miller. New York: The Free Press.

GUEST, ROBERT 1962 "Managerial Succession in Complex Organizations," *American Journal of Sociology*, 68, no. 1 (July), 47–54.

GUETZKOW, HAROLD 1965 "Communications in Organizations," in *Handbook of Organizations*, ed. James G. March. Chicago: Rand McNally and Company.

————. 1966 "Relations Among Organizations," in *Studies in Behavior in Organizations: A Research Symposium*, ed. R. V. BOWERS. Athens, Ga.: University of Georgia Press.

GULICK, LUTHER, AND LYNDALL F. URWICK, eds. 1937 *Papers on the Sciences of Administration*. New York: Institute on Public Administration, Columbia University.

GUSFIELD, JOSEPH R. 1955 "Social Structure and Moral Reform: A Study of the Woman's Christian Temperance Union," *American Journal of Sociology*, 61, no. 3 (November), 221–32.

————. 1963 *Symbolic Crusade*. Urbana, Ill.: University of Illinois Press.

HAAS, J. EUGENE, RICHARD, H. HALL, AND NORMAN J. JOHNSON 1966 "Toward an Empirically Perceived Taxonomy of Organizations," in *Studies on Behavior in Organizations*, ed. Raymond V. Bowers. Athens, Ga.: University of Georgia Press.

HAGE, JERALD 1965 "An Axiomatic Theory of Organizations," *Administrative Science Quarterly*, 10, no. 3 (December), 289–320.

————. 1974 *Communications and Organizational Control*. New York: John Wiley and Sons, Inc.

————. 1980 *Theories of Organizations*. New York: John Wiley and Sons, Inc.

HAGE, JERALD, AND MICHAEL AIKEN 1967a "Relationship of Centralization to other Structural Properties," *Administrative Science Quarterly*, 12, no. 1 (June), 72–91.

————. 1967b "Program Change and Organizational Properties," *American Journal of Sociology*, 72, no. 5 (March), 503–19.

————. 1969 "Routine Technology, Social Structure, and Organizational Goals," *Administrative Science Quarterly*, 14, no. 3 (September), 366–77.

————. 1970 *Social Change in Complex Organizations*. New York: Random House, Inc.

HAGE, JERALD, MICHAEL AIKEN, AND CORA BAGLEY MARRETT 1971 "Organizational Structure and Communications," *American Sociological Review*, 36, no. 5 (October), 860–71.

HAGE, JERALD, AND ROBERT DEWAR   1973   "Elite Values Versus Organizational Structure in Predicting Innovation," *Administrative Science Quarterly*, 18, no. 3 (September), 279–90.

HALBERSTAM, DAVID   1972   *The Best and the Brightest.* New York: Random House, Inc.

HALL, RICHARD H.   1961   "An Empirical Study of Bureaucratic Dimensions and their Relation to Other Organizational Characteristics." Ph.D. dissertation, Ohio State University.

————.   1962   "Intraorganizational Structural Variation: Application of the Bureaucratic Model," *Administrative Science Quarterly*, 7, no. 3 (December), 295–308.

————.   1963   "The Concept of Bureaucracy," *American Journal of Sociology*, 69, no. 1 (July), 32–40.

————.   1968   "Professionalization and Bureaucratization," *American Sociological Review*, 33, no. 1 (February), 92–104.

————.   1975   *Occupations and the Social Structure* (2nd ed.). Englewood Cliffs, N.J.: Prentice-Hall, Inc.

————.   1981   "Technological Policies and Their Consequences." In *Handbook of Organizational Design*, eds. Paul H. Nystrom and William C. Starbuck (eds.). London: Oxford University Press.

HALL, RICHARD H., JOHN P., CLARK, AND PEGGY C. GIORDANO   1979   "The Extent and Correlates of Interorganizational Conflict." Mimeographed. Albany: SUNY-Albany.

HALL, RICHARD H., JOHN P. CLARK, PEGGY GIORDANO, PAUL JOHNSON, AND MARTHA VAN ROEKEL   1977   "Patterns of Interorganizational Relationships," *Administrative Science Quarterly*, 22, no. 3 (September), 457–74.

————.   1978   "Interorganizational Coordination in the Delivery of Human Services" in Lucien Karpik (ed.) *Organization and Environment: Theory, Issues and Reality.* Beverly Hills, Cal.: Sage Publications, Inc.

HALL, RICHARD H., J. EUGENE HAAS, AND NORMAN JOHNSON   1967a   "An Examination of the Blau-Scott and Etzioni Typologies," *Administrative Science Quarterly*, 12, no. 2 (June), 118–39.

————.   1967b   "Organizational Size, Complexity, and Formalization," *American Sociological Review*, 32, no. 6 (December), 903–12.

————.   1972   "Reply to Weldon," *Administrative Science Quarterly*, 17, no. 1 (March), 79–80.

HALL, RICHARD H. AND CHARLES R. TITTLE   1966   "Bureaucracy and Its Correlates," *American Journal of Sociology*, 72, no. 3 (November), 267–72.

HALPERT, BURTON P.   1974   *An Empirical Study of the Relationship Between Power, Conflict, and Cooperation on the Interorganizational Level.* Doctoral dissertation, Department of Sociology, University of Minnesota.

————.   1981   "Antecedent Conditions Which Facilitate or Inhibit Coordination." in *Interorganizational Coordination*, eds. David L. Rogers and David A. Whetten. Ames, Iowa University of Iowa Press.

HANNAN, MICHAEL T., AND JOHN H. FREEMAN   1977a   "The Population Ecology of Organizations," *American Journal of Sociology*, 82, no. 5 (March) 929–64.

————.   1977b   "Obstacles to Comparative Studies," in *New Perspectives on Organizational Effectiveness*, eds. Paul S. Goodman and Johannes Pennings. San Francisco: Jossey-Bass.

HART, DAVID K., AND WILLIAM G. SCOTT   1975   "The Organizational Imperative," *Administration and Society* 7, no. 3 (November) 259–285.

HASENFELD, YEHESKEL   1972   "People Processing Organizations: An Exchange Approach," *American Sociological Review*, 37, no. 3 (June), 256–63.

HAWLEY, AMOS H.   1968   "Human Ecology." in *International Encyclopedia of the Social Sciences*, ed. D. L. Sills. New York: The Macmillan Company.

HAWLEY, W. E., AND L. D. ROGERS   1974   *Improving the Quality of Urban Management.* Beverly Hills, Cal: Sage Publications.

HEILBRONER, ROBERT   1974   "Nobody Talks about Busting General Motors in 500 Companies," *Forbes*, 113, no. 9 (May), 61.

HEISE, DAVID R.   1972   "How Do I Know My Data? Let Me Count the Ways." *Administrative Science Quarterly*, 17, no. 1 (March), 58–61.

HELLER, FRANK A.   1973   "Leadership Decision Making and Contingency Theory," *Industrial Relations*, 12 no. 2 (May), 183–199.

HELMICH, DONALD, AND WARREN B. BROWN 1972 "Succession Type and Organizational Change in the Corporate Enterprise," *Administrative Science Quarterly*, 17, no. 3 (September), 371–81.

HERMAN, JEANNE B., RANDALL B. DUNHAM, AND CHARLES HULIN 1975 "Organizational Structure, Demographic Characteristics, and Employee Responses," *Organizational Behavior and Human Performance*, 13, no. 2 (April), 206–32.

HERZBERG, FREDERICK, BARNARD MAUSNER, AND BARBARA SYNDERMAN 1959 *The Motivation to Work*. New York: John Wiley and Sons, Inc.

HEYDEBRAND, WOLF V. 1973 *Comparative Organizations: The Results of Empirical Research*. Englewood Cliffs, N.J.: Prentice-Hall, Inc.

————. 1977 "Organizational Contradictions in Public Bureaucracies: Toward a Marxian Theory of Organizations," *The Sociological Quarterly*, 18, no. 1 (Winter) 83–107.

HICKS, ALEXANDER, ROGER FRIEDLAND, AND EDWIN JOHNSON 1978 "Class Power and State Policy: The Case of Large Business Corporations, Labor Unions, and Governmental Redistribution in the American States," *American Sociological Review*, 43, no. 3 (June), 302–15.

HICKSON, DAVID J. 1966 "A Convergence in Organizational Theory," *Administrative Science Quarterly*, 11, no. 2 (September), 224-237.

HICKSON, DAVID J., DEREK S. PUGH, AND DIANA C. PHEYSEY 1969 "Operational Technology and Organizational Structure: An Empirical Reappraisal," *Administrative Science Quarterly*, 14, no. 3 (September), 378–97.

HICKSON, DAVID J., C. A. HININGS, C. A. LEE, R. E. SCHNECK, AND J. M. PENNINGS 1971 "A 'Strategic Contingencies' Theory of Interorganizational Power," *Administrative Science Quarterly*, 16, no. 2 (June), 216–29.

HICKSON, DAVID J., C. R. HININGS, C. J. MCMILLAN, AND J. P. SCHWITTER 1974 "The Culture Free Context of Organizational Structure: A Tri-National Comparison," *Sociology*, 8 no. 1 (January), 59–80.

HILLS, FREDERICK S., AND THOMAS A. MAHONEY 1978 "University Budgets and Organizational Decision Making," *Administrative Science Quarterly*, 23, no. 3 (September), 454–65.

HILTON, GORDON 1972 "Causal Inference Analysis: A Seductive Process." *Administrative Science Quarterly*, 17, no. 1 (March), 44–54.

HININGS, C. R., D. J. HICKSON, J. M. PENNINGS, AND R. E. SCHNECK 1974 "Structural Conditions of Interorganizational Power," *Administrative Science Quarterly*, 17, no. 1 (March), 22–44.

HIRSCH, PAUL M. 1975 "Organizational Effectiveness and the Institutional Environment," *Administrative Science Quarterly*, 20, no. 3 (September), 327–44.

HIRSCHMAN, ALBERT O. 1972 *Exit, Voice, and Loyalty*. Cambridge, Mass.: Harvard University Press.

HOFSTEDE, GEERT H. 1972 *Budget Control and the Autonomy of Organizational Units*. Proceedings of the First International Sociological Conference on Participation and Self-Management, Zagreb, Yugoslavia.

HOLDEN, CONSTANCE 1980 "Innovation—Japan Races Ahead as U.S. Falters," *Science*, 210, no. 4471 (November), 751–54.

HOLDAWAY, EDWARD A., JOHN F. NEWBERRY, DAVID J. HICKSON, AND R. PETER HERON 1975 "Dimensions of Organizations in Complex Societies: The Educational Sector," *Administrative Science Quarterly*, 20, no. 1 (March), 37–58.

HOLLANDER, EDWIN P., AND JAMES W. JULIAN 1969 "Contemporary Trends in the Analysis of Leadership Processes," *Psychological Bulletin*, 71, no. 5 (May), 387–97.

HOUGLAND, JAMES G., JON M. SHEPARD, AND JAMES R. WOOD 1979 "Discrepancies in Perceived Organizational Control: Their Decrease and Importance in Local Churches," *The Sociological Quarterly*, 20, no. 1 (Winter), 63–76.

HOUGLAND, JAMES G., AND JAMES R. WOOD 1980 "Control in Organizations and Commitment of Members," *Social Forces*, 59, no. 1 (September), 85–105.

INKSON, J., DEREK S. PUGH, AND DAVID J. HICKSON 1970 "Organizational Context and Structure: An Abbreviated Replication," *Administrative Science Quarterly*, 15, no. 3 (September), 318–29.

IVANCEVICH, JOHN M., AND JAMES H. DONNELLY, JR. 1975 "Relation of Organizational Structure to Job Satisfaction, Anxiety, Stress, and Performance," *Administrative Science Quarterly*, 20, no. 2 (June), 272–80.

JACOBS, DAVID 1974 "Dependency and Vulnerability: An Exchange Approach to the Control of Organizations," *Administrative Science Quarterly*, 19, no. 1 (March), 45–59.

JAMES, DAVID R., AND MICHAEL SOREF 1981 "Profit Constraints on Managerial Autonomy: Managerial Theory and the Unmaking of the Corporate President," *American Sociological Review* 46, no. 1 (February), 1–18.

JANOWITZ, MORRIS 1960 *The Professional Soldier*. New York: The Free Press.

————. 1969 *Institution Building in Urban Education*. New York: Russell Sage Foundation.

JENKINS, J. CRAIG 1977 "Radical Transformation of Organizational Goals," *Administrative Science Quarterly*, 22, no. 4 (December) 568–86.

JERMIER, JOHN M., AND LESLIE J. BERKES 1979 "Leader Behavior in a Police Command Bureaucracy: A Closer Look at the Quasi-Military Model," *Administrative Science Quarterly*, 24, no. 1 (March), 1–23.

JOHN, D. 1977 *Managing the Human Service System: What Have We Learned from Services Integration?* Project SHARE Monograph Series. Rockville, Md. National Institute of Mental Health.

JULIAN, JOSEPH 1966 "Compliance Patterns and Communication Blocks in Complex Organizations," *American Sociological Review*, 31 (June), no. 3 382–89.

JURKOVICH, RAY 1974 "A Core Typology of Organizational Environments," *Administrative Science Quarterly*, 19, no. 3 (September), 380–89.

KAHN, ROBERT L. 1977 "Organizational Effectiveness: An Overview," in *New Perspectives on Organizational Effectiveness*, ed. Paul S. Goodman and Johannes M. Pennings. San Francisco: Jossey-Bass.

KAHN, ROBERT L., DONALD M. WOLFE, ROBERT P. QUINN, J. DIEDRICK SNOEK, AND ROBERT A. ROSENTHAL 1964 *Organizational Stress: Studies in Role Conflict and Ambiguity*. New York: John Wiley and Sons, Inc.

KAMENS, DAVID H. 1977 "Legitimating Myths and Educational Organizations: The Relationship Between Organizational Ideology and Formal Structure," *American Sociological Review*, 42, no. 2 (April), 208–19.

KANTER, ROSABETH MOSS 1977 *Men and Women of the Corporation*. New York: Basic Books.

KAPLAN, ABRAHAM 1964 "Power in Perspective," in *Power and Conflict in Organizations*, ed. Robert L. Kahn and Elise Boulding. New York: Basic Books.

KASARDA, JOHN D. 1973 "Effects of Personnel Turnover, Employee Qualifications, and Professional Staff Ratios on Administrative Intensity and Overhead," *The Sociological Quarterly*, 14, no. 3 (Summer), 350–58.

KASARDA, JOHN D., AND CHARLES E. BIDWELL 1979 "A Human Ecological Theory of Organizational Structuring" in Michael Micklin and Harvey M. Choldin (eds.) *Sociological Human Ecology: Contemporary Issues and Applications*. New York: Academic Press.

KATZ, DANIEL 1964 "Approaches to Managing Conflict," in *Power and Conflict in Organizations*, ed. Robert L Kahn and Elise Boulding. New York: Basic Books.

KATZ, DANIEL, BARBARA A. GUTEK, ROBERT L. KAHN, AND EUGENIA BARTON 1975 *Bureaucratic Encounters*. Ann Arbor, Mich.: Institute for Social Research.

KATZ, DANIEL, AND ROBERT L. KAHN 1966 *The Social Psychology of Organizations*. New York: John Wiley and Sons, Inc.

————. 1978 *The Social Psychology of Organizations* (Rev. ed). New York: John Wiley and Sons, Inc.

KAUFMAN, HERBERT 1971 *The Limits of Organizational Change*. University, Ala.: University of Alabama Press.

KEEGAN, WARREN J. 1974 "Multinational Scanning: A Study of the Information Sources Utilized by Headmasters Executives in Multinational Companies," *Administrative Science Quarterly*, 19, no. 3 (September), 411–21..

KEELEY, MICHAEL 1978 "A Social Justice Approach to Organizational Evaluation," *Administrative Science Quarterly*, 23, no. 2 (June), 272–292.

KHANDWALLA, PRADIP N. 1972 "Environment and Its Impact on the Organization," *International Studies of Management and Organization*, 2, no. 3 (Fall), 297–313.

KIMBERLY, JOHN R. 1975 "Environmental Constraints and Organizational Structure: A Comparative Analysis of Rehabilitation Organizations," *Administrative Science Quarterly*, 20, no. 1 (March), 1–19.

337

————. 1976 "Organizational Size and the Structuralist Perspective: A Review Critique, and Proposal," *Administrative Science Quarterly*, 21 no. 4 (December), 577–97.

————. 1980 "Initiation, Innovation, and Institutionalization in the Creation Process," in *The Organizational Life Cycle*, ed. John R. Kimberly, Robert H. Miles, and Associates. San Francisco: Jossey-Bass.

KIMBERLY, JOHN R., AND ROBERT A. MILES, AND ASSOCIATES 1980 *The Organizational Life Cycle*. San Francisco: Jossey-Bass.

KLATZKY, SHEILA 1970a "The Relationship of Organizational Size to Complexity and Coordination," *Administrative Science Quarterly*, 15, no. 4 (December), 428–38.

————. 1970b "Organizational Inequality: The Case of Public Employment Agency," *American Journal of Sociology*, 76, no. 3 (November), 474–91.

KLONGLAN, GERALD E., AND STEVEN K. PAULSON 1971 *Coordinating Health Organizations: The Problem of Cigarette Smoking*. Final report submitted to the National Clearinghouse for Smoking and Health, United States Public Health Service.

KLONGLAN, GERALD E., RICHARD D. WARREN, JUDY M. WINKELPLECK, AND STEVEN K. PAULSON 1976 "Interorganizational Measurement in the Social Services Sector: Differences by Hierarchical Level," *Administrative Science Quarterly*, 21 no. 4 (December), 675–87.

KOCHAN, THOMAS A., GEORGE P. HUBER, AND LARRY C. CUMMINGS 1975 "Determinants of Interorganizational Conflict in Collective Bargaining in the Public Sector," *Administrative Science Quarterly*, 20, no. 1 (March), 10–23.

KOCHAN, THOMAS A., LARRY C. CUMMINGS, AND GEORGE P. HUBER 1976 "Operationalizing the Concepts of Goals and Goal Incompatibility in Organizational Behavior Research," *Human Relations*, 29, no. 6 (June), 527–44.

KOHN, MELVIN 1971 "Bureaucratic Man: A Portrait and Interpretation," *American Sociological Review*, 36, no. 3 (June), 461–74.

KOHN, MELVIN L., AND CARMI SCHOOLER 1973 "Occupational Experience and Psychological Functioning: An Assessment of Reciprocal Effects," *American Sociological Review*, 38, no. 1 (February), 97–118.

————. 1978 "The Reciprocal Effects of Substantive Complexity of Work and Intellectual Flexibility: A Longitudinal Assessment," *American Journal of Sociology*, 84, no. 1 (July), 1–23.

KORNHAUSER, WILLIAM 1963 *Scientists in Industry*. Berkeley: University of California Press.

KRIESBERG, LOUIS 1962 "Careers, Organizational Size and Succession," *American Journal of Sociology*, 68, no. 3 (November), 355–59.

————. 1964 "Reply." *American Journal of Sociology*, 70, no. 2 (September), 223.

LAMMERS, CORNELIUS J. 1967 "Power and Participation in Decision Making," *American Journal of Sociology*, 73, no. 2 (September), 201–16.

————. 1975 "Self-Management and Participation: Two Concepts of Democratization in Organizations," *Organization and Administrative Sciences*, 5, no. 4 (Winter), 35–53.

LAWLER, EDWARD E., AND LYMAN W. PORTER 1967 "The Effect of Performance on Job Satisfaction." *Industrial Relations*, 7, no. 1 (October) 20–28.

LAWRENCE, PAUL R., AND JAY W. LORSCH 1967 *Organization and Environment*. Cambridge, Mass.: Harvard University Press.

LAZARSFELD, PAUL S. AND HERBERT MENZEL 1961 "On the Relationship between Individual and Collective Properties" in Amitai Etzioni ed., *Complex Organizations: A Sociological Reader*. New York: Holt, Rinehart & Winston, Inc.

LEAVITT, HAROLD J. 1951 "The Effects of Certain Communications Patterns on Group Performance," *Journal of Abnormal and Social Psychology*, 46, no. 1 (January), 38–50.

LEHMAN, EDWARD W. 1975 *Coordinating Health Care: Explorations in Interorganizational Relations*. Beverly Hills, Calif.: Sage Publications.

LEIFER, RICHARD, AND GEORGE P. HUBER 1977 "Relations Among Perceived Environmental Uncertainty, Organizational Structure, and Boundary Spaning Behavior," *Administrative Science Quarterly*, 22, no. 2 (June), 235–47.

LENSKI, GERHARD 1963 *The Religious Factor*. Garden City, N.Y.: Doubleday & Company, Inc., Anchor Books.

LEVINE, SOL, AND PAUL E. WHITE 1961 "Exchange as a Conceptual Framework for the Study of Interorganizational Relationships," *Administrative Science Quarterly*, 5, no. 1 (March), 583–610.

LEVINE, SOL, PAUL E. WHITE, AND BENJAMIN D. PAUL 1963 "Community Interorganizational Problems in Providing Medical Care and Social Services," *American Journal of Public Health*, 53 (8), (August), 1183–95.

LEWIN, KURT 1951 *Field Theory in Social Science*. New York: Harper.

LIEBERSON, STANLEY, AND JAMES F. O'CONNOR 1972 "Leadership and Organizational Performance: A Study of Large Corporations," *American Sociological Review*, 37, no. 2 (April), 117–30.

LIKERT, RENSIS 1961 *New Patterns of Management*. New York: McGraw-Hill Book Company.

LINCOLN, JAMES R. 1979 "Organizational Differentiation in Urban Communities: A Study in Organizational Ecology," *Social Forces*, 57, no. 3 (March), 915–30.

LINCOLN, JAMES R., AND GERALD ZEITZ 1980 "Organizational Properties from Aggregate Data," *American Sociological Review*, 45, (June), 391–405.

LINCOLN, JAMES R., JON OLSON, AND MITSUYO HANADA 1978 "Cultural Effects on Organizational Structure: The Case of Japanese Firms in the United States," *American Sociological Review*, 43, no. 3 (December), 829–47.

LINDBLOM, CHARLES E. 1959 "The Science of Muddling Through," *Public Administration Review*, 19, no. 2 (Spring), 78–88.

LIPSET, SEYMOUR MARTIN 1960 *Agrarian Socialism*. Berkeley and Los Angeles: University of California Press.

LIPSET, SEYMOUR MARTIN, MARTIN A. TROW, AND JAMES S. COLEMAN 1956 *Union Democracy*. New York: The Free Press.

LITWAK, EUGENE 1961 "Models of Organizations Which Permit Conflict," *American Journal of Sociology*, 76, no. 2 (September), 177–84.

LITWAK, EUGENE, AND LYDIA HYLTON 1962 "Interorganizational Analysis: A Hypothesis on Coordinating Agencies," *Administrative Science Quarterly*, 6, no. 1 (March), 395–420.

LORSCH, JAY, AND JOHN MORSE 1974 *Organizations and Their Members*. New York: Harper and Row.

MAAS, MERIDEAN LEONE 1979 "A Formal Theory of Organizational Power." Doctoral dissertation, Department of Sociology, Iowa State University.

MAHONEY, THOMAS A., AND WILLIAM WEITZEL 1969 "Managerial Models of Organizational Effectiveness," *Administrative Science Quarterly*, 14, no. 3 (September) 357–65.

MAHONEY, THOMAS A., PETER FROST, NORMAN F. CRANDALL, AND WILLIAM WEITZEL 1972 "The Conditioning Influence of Organizational Size on Managerial Practice," *Organizational Behavior and Human Performance*, 8, no. 2 (October), 230–41.

MANIHA, JOHN K., AND CHARLES PERROW 1965 "The Reluctant Organization and the Aggressive Environment," *Administrative Science Quarterly*, 10, no. 3 (September), 238–57.

MANNS, CURTIS L., AND JAMES G. MARCH 1978 "Financial Adversity, Internal Competition, and Curricular Change in a University," *Administrative Science Quarterly*, 23, no. 4 (December), 541–52.

MANSFIELD, ROGER 1973 "Bureaucracy and Centralization: An Examination of Organizational Structure," *Administrative Science Quarterly*, 18, no. 4 (December), 77–88.

MARCH, JAMES G., AND HERBERT A. SIMON 1958 *Organizations*. New York: John Wiley and Sons, Inc.

MARCH, JAMES G., AND JOHN P. OLSEN 1976 *Ambiguity and Choice in Organizations*. Bergen, Norway: Universtesforlaeet.

MARGLIN, STEPHEN A. 1974 "What Do Bosses Do? The Origins and Functions of Hierarchy in Capitalist Production," *The Review of Radical Political Economics* 6, no. 2 (Summer), 60–112.

MARRETT, CORA BAGLEY 1971 "On the Specification of Interorganizational Dimensions," *Sociology and Social Research*, 56, no. 1 (October), 83–99.

——. 1980 "Influences on the Rise of New Organizations: The Formation of Women's Medical Societies," *Administrative Science Quarterly*, 25, no. 2 (June), 185–99.

MARSH, ROBERT M. AND HIROSHI MANNARI 1981 "Technology and Size as Determinants the Organizational Structure of Japanese Factories," *Administrative Science Quarterly* 26, no. 1 (March), 32–57.

MARTIN, PATRICIA YANCEY 1979 "Size in Residential Service Organizations," *The Sociological Quarterly*, 20, no. 4 (Autumn), 569–79.

MASLOW, ABRAHAM 1956 *Eupsychian Management*. Homewood, Ill: Richard P. Irwin.

MAURICE, MARC, FRANCOISE SELLIER, AND JEAN-JACQUES SILVESTRE 1980 "The Search for a Societal Effect in the Production of Company Hierarchy: A Comparison Between France and Germany." Paper translated from *Revue Francoise de Socialogie*, (June 1979).

MAYO, ELTON 1933 *The Human Problems of Industrial Civilization*. New York: The Macmillan Company.

MCGREGOR, DOUGLAS 1960 *The Human Side of Enterprise*. New York: McGraw-Hill Book Company.

MCKELVEY, BILL 1975 "Guidelines for the Empirical Classification of Organizations," *Administrative Science Quarterly*, 20, no. 4 (December), 509–25.

——. 1978 "Organizational Systematics: Taxonomic Lessons from Biology," *Management Science*, 24, no. 13 (September) 1428–40.

MCMILLAN, CHARLES J. 1973 "Corporations without Citizenship: The Emergence of Multinational Enterprise," in *People and Organizations*, ed. Graeme Soloman and Kenneth Thompson, (eds.), London: Longman Group Limited.

MCMILLAN, CHARLES J., DAVID J. HICKSON, C. R. HININGS, AND R. E. SCHNECK 1973 "The Structure of Work Organizations Across Societies." *Academy of Management Journal*, 16, no. 4 (December), 555–69.

MCNEIL, KENNETH 1978 "Understanding Organizational Power: Building on the Weberian Legacy," *Administrative Science Quarterly*, 23, no. 1 (March), 65–90.

MCNEIL, KENNETH, AND RICHARD E. MILLER 1980 "The Profitability of Consumer Protection: Warranty Policy in the Auto Industry," *Administrative Science Quarterly*, 25, no. 3 (September), 407–27.

MCNEIL, KENNETH, AND EDMOND MINIHAN 1977 "Regulation of Medical Devices and Organizational Behavior in Hospitals," *Administrative Science Quarterly*, 22, no. 3 (September), 475–90.

MECHANIC, DAVID 1962 "Sources of Power of Lower Participants in Complex Organizations," *Administrative Science Quarterly*, 7, no. 3 (December), 349–64.

——. 1963 "Methodology of Organizational Studies" in Harold J. Leavitt (ed.) *The Social Science of Organizations*. Englewood Cliffs, N.J.: Prentice-Hall, Inc.

MELCHER, ARLYN L. 1975 *Structure and Process of Organizations: A Systems Approach*. Englewood Cliffs, N.J.: Prentice-Hall, Inc.

MELTZER, LEO, AND JAMES SALTER 1962 "Organizational Structure and the Performance and Job Satisfaction of Physiologists," *American Sociological Review*, 27, no. 3 (June), 351–62.

MERTON, ROBERT K. 1957 *Social Theory and Social Structure*. Glencoe, Ill.: Free Press.

METCALF, J. L. 1976 "Organizational Strategies and Interorganizational Networks," *Human Relations*, 29 (4), (April) 327–43.

MEYER, JOHN W., AND BRIAN ROWAN 1977 "Institutionalized Organizations: Formal Structure as Right and Ceremony," *American Journal of Sociology*, 83, no. 2 (September), 340–63.

MEYER, MARSHALL W. 1968a "Automation and Bureaucratic Structure," *American Journal of Sociology*, 74, no. 3 (November), 256–64.

——. 1968b "Two Authority Structures of Bureaucratic Organization," *Administrative Science Quarterly*, 13, no. 2 (September), 211–18.

——. 1971 "Some Constraints in Analyzing Data on Organizational Structures," *American Sociological Review*, 36, no. 2 (April), 294–97.

——. 1972 "Size and the Structure of Organizations: a Causal Analysis," *American Sociological Review*, 37, no. 4 (August), 434–40.

——. 1975a "Organizational Domains," *American Sociological Review*, 40, no. 5 (October), 599–615.

──────. 1975b "Leadership and Organizational Structure," *American Journal of Sociology,* 81, no. 3 (November), 514–42.

MEYER, MARSHALL W., AND ASSOCIATES 1978 *Environments and Organizations.* San Francisco: Jossey-Bass.

MEYER, MARSHALL W., AND M. CRAIG BROWN 1977 "The Process of Bureaucratization," *American Journal of Sociology,* 83, no. 2 (September), 364–85.

MICHELS, ROBERT 1949 *Political Parties.* Glencoe, Ill.: Free Press.

MILES, RAYMOND E., CHARLES C. SNOW, AND JEFFREY PFEFFER 1974 "Organization-Environment: Concepts and Issues," *Industrial Relations,* 13, no. 3 (October), 244–64.

MILETI, DENNIS S., DAVID S. GILLESPIE, AND J. EUGENE HAAS 1977 "Size and Structure in Complex Organizations," *Social Forces,* 56, no. 1 (September), 208–17.

MILLER, GEORGE A. 1967 "Professionals in Bureaucracy, Alienation Among Industrial Scientists and Engineers," *American Sociological Review,* 32, no. 5 (October), 755–68.

MILLER, JON, SANFORD LABOWITZ, AND LINCOLN FRY 1975 "Inequalities in the Organizational Experiences of Woman and Men," *Social Forces,* 54, no. 2 (December), 365–81.

MILNE, R. S. 1970 "Mechanistic and Organic Models of Public Administration in Developing Countries," *Administrative Science Quarterly,* 15, no. 1 (March), 57.

MINTZBERG, HENRY 1979 *The Structuring of Organizations.* Englewood Cliffs, N.J.: Prentice-Hall, Inc.

MOCH, MICHAEL K. 1976 "Structure and Organizational Resource Allocation," *Administrative Science Quarterly,* 21, no. 4 (December), 661–74.

MOCH, MICHAEL K., AND EDWARD V. MORSE 1977 "Size, Centralization, and Organizational Adoption of Innovation," *American Sociological Review,* 42, no. 5 (October), 716–25.

MOHR, LAWRENCE B. 1971 "Organizational Technology and Organizational Structure," *Administrative Science Quarterly,* 16, no. 4 (December), 444–51.

──────. 1973 "The Concept of Organizational Goal," *American Political Science Review,* 67, no. 2 (June) 470–81.

MOLNAR, JOSEPH J. 1978 "Comparative Organizational Properties and Interorganizational Interdependence," *Sociology and Social Research,* 63, no. 1 (October), 24–48.

MOLNAR, JOSEPH J., AND DAVID L. ROGERS 1976 "Organizational Effectiveness: An Empirical Comparison of the Goal and System Resource Approaches," *The Sociological Quarterly,* 17, no. 3 (Summer) 401–13.

──────. 1979 "A Comparative Model of Interorganizational Conflict," *Administrative Science Quarterly,* 24, no. 3 (September), 405–24.

MOLOTCH, HARVEY, AND MARILYN LESTER 1975 "Accidental News: The Great Oil Spill as Local Occurrence and National Event," *American Journal of Sociology,* 81, no. 2 (September), 235–60.

MOONEY, JAMES D. AND ALLAN C. REILLY 1931 *Onward Industry!* New York: Harper and Row.

MORRIS, ROBIN 1972 "Is the Corporate Economy a Corporate State?" *The American Economic Review,* 62, no. 1 (March) 103–19.

MOTT, BASIL J. F. 1968 *Anatomy of a Coordinating Council.* Pittsburgh: University of Pittsburgh Press.

MOUZELIS, NICOS P. 1967 *Organization and Bureaucracy: An Analysis of Modern Theories.* Chicago: Aldine.

MULDER, MAUK, AND HENKE WILKE 1970 "Participation and Power Equalization," *Organizational Behavior and Human Performance,* 5, no. 5 (September), 430–48.

MULFORD, CHARLES L. 1980 "Dyadic Properties as Correlates of Exchange and Conflict Between Organizations," Unpublished Paper, Department of Sociology, Iowa State University, (October).

MULFORD, CHARLES L., GERALD E. KLOUGLEN, RICHARD D. WARREN, AND JANET B. PADGITT 1976–77 "A Multidimensional Evaluation of Effectiveness in a Non-Economic Organization," *Organization and Administrative Sciences,* 7, no. 4 (Winter), 125–43.

MULFORD, CHARLES L. AND MARY ANN MULFORD 1980 "Interdependence and Intraorganizational Structure for Voluntary Organizations," *Journal of Voluntary Action Research* 9, no. 1–4, 20–34.

NAGI, SAAD Z. 1974 "Gate-Keeping Decisions in Service Organizations: When Validity Fails," *Human Organization*, 33, no. 1 (Spring), 47–58.

NEEDLEMAN, MARTIN L., AND CAROLYN NEEDLEMAN 1979 "Organizational Crime: Two Models of Criminogenesis," *The Sociological Quarterly*, 20, no. 4 (Autumn), 517–28.

NEGANDHI, ANANT R., AND BERNARD C. REIMANN 1972 "A Contingency Theory of Organization Re-examined in the Context of a Developing Country," *Academy of Management Journal*, 15, no. 2 (June), 137–46.

———. 1973a "Correlates of Decentralization: Closed and Open System Perspectives," *Academy of Management Journal*, 16, no. 4 (December), 570–82.

———. 1973b "Task Environment, Decentralization and Organizational Effectiveness," *Human Relations*, 26, no. 2 (April), 203–14.

NELSON, JOEL I. 1966 "Clique Contacts and Family Orientations," *American Sociological Review*, 31, no. 5 (October), 663–72.

New York Times 1981 (April 28): Section A, p. 8, Col. 3.

ODIONE, GEORGE S. 1965 *Management by Objectives*. New York: Pitman Publishing Corporation.

O'REILLY, CHARLES A. III, AND KARLENE H. ROBERTS 1974 "Information Filtration in Organizations: Three Experiments," *Organizational Behavior and Human Performance*, 11, no. 2 (April), 253–65.

OUCHI, WILLIAM G. 1977 "The Relationship Between Organizational Structure and Organizational Control," *Administrative Science Quarterly*, 22, no. 1 (March), 95–113.

OUCHI, WILLIAM G., AND ALFRED M. JAEGER 1978 "Social Structure and Organizational Type," in *Environments and Organizations*, ed. MARSHALL W. MEYER AND ASSOCIATES. San Francisco: Jossey-Bass.

OUCHI, WILLIAM G., AND JERRY B. JOHNSON 1978 "Types of Organizational Control and Their Relation to Emotional Well-Being," *Administrative Science Quarterly*, 23, no. 2 (June), 293–317.

OUCHI, WILLIAM G., AND MARY ANN MAGUIRE 1975 "Organizational Control: Two Functions," *Administrative Science Quarterly*, 20, no. 4 (December), 559–69.

PALUMBO, DENNIS J. 1969 "Power and Role Specificity in Organizational Theory," *Public Administration Review*, 29, no. 3 (May–June), 237–48.

PARKE, E. LAUCK, AND CURT TAUSKY 1975 "The Mythology of Job Enrichment: Self-Actualization Revisited," *Personnel*, 52, no. 5 (September), 12–21.

PARSONS, TALCOTT 1960 *Structure and Process in Modern Society*. New York: The Free Press.

PEABODY, ROBERT L. 1962 "Perceptions of Organizational Authority: A Comparative Analysis," *Administrative Science Quarterly*, 6, no. 1 (March), 463–82.

PEARSON, JESSICA S. 1978 "Organizational Response to Occupational Injury and Disease: The Case of the Uranium Industry" *Social Forces* 57, no. 1 (September), 23–41.

PENNINGS, JOHANNES M. 1973 "Measures of Organizational Structure: A Methodological Note," *American Journal of Sociology*, 79, no. 3 (November), 686–704.

———. 1980a "Environmental Influences on the Creation Process," in *The Organizational Life Cycle*, eds. JOHN R. KIMBERLY, ROBERT H. MILES, AND ASSOCIATES. San Francisco: Jossey-Bass.

———. 1980b *Interlocking Directorates*. San Francisco: Jossey-Bass.

PENNINGS, JOHANNES M., AND PAUL S. GOODMAN 1977 "Toward a Workable Framework," in *New Perspectives on Organizational Effectiveness*, eds. PAUL S. GOODMAN AND JOHANNES M. PENNINGS. San Francisco: Jossey-Bass.

PERROW, CHARLES 1961 "The Analysis of Goals in Complex Organizations," *American Sociological Review*, 26, no. 6 (December) 688–99.

———. 1967 "A Framework for the Comparative Analysis of Organizations," *American Sociological Review*, 32, no. 2 (April), 194–208.

———. 1970a. "Departmental Power and Perspective in Industrial Firms," in *Power in Organizations*, ed. MAYER N. ZALD. Nashville, Tenn.: Vanderbilt University Press.

———. 1970b *Organizational Analysis*. Belmont, Cal.: Wadsworth Publishing Co.

———. 1972 *Complex Organizations: A Critical Essay*. Glenview, Ill.: Scott Foresman and Co.

———. 1977 "Three Types of Effectiveness Studies," in *New Perspectives on Organizational*

Effectiveness, eds. PAUL S. GOODMAN AND JOHANNES M. PENNINGS. San Francisco: Jossey-Bass.

————. 1979 *Complex Organizations: A Critical Essay* (2nd ed.). Glenview, Ill.: Scott, Foresman and Company.

PERRUCCI, ROBERT, AND MARC PILISUK 1970 "Leaders and Ruling Elites: The Interorganizational Bases of Community Power," *American Sociological Review*, 35, no. 6 (December), 1040–57.

PETER, LAURENCE J., AND RAYMOND HULL 1969 *The Peter Principle*. New York: William Brown & Co., Inc.

PETERSON, RICHARD A. 1970 "Some Consequences of Differentiation," in *Power in Organizations*, ed. MAYER ZALD. Nashville, Tenn.: Vanderbilt University Press.

PFEFFER, JEFFREY 1972a "Merger as a Response to Organizational Interdependence," *Administrative Science Quarterly*, 17, no. 3 (September), 328–94.

————. 1972b "Size and Composition of Corporate Boards of Directors," *Administrative Science Quarterly*, 17, no. 2 (June), 218–28.

————. 1976 "Beyond Management and Worker: The Institutional Function of Management," *Academy of Management Review*, 1, no. 2 (April), 36–46.

————. 1977 "Power and Resource Allocation in Organizations," in *New Directions in Organizational Behavior*, eds. BARRY STAW AND GERALD SALANCIK. Chicago, Ill.: St. Clair Press.

————. 1978 "The Micropolitics of Organizations," in *Environments and Organizations*, eds. MARSHALL W. MEYER AND ASSOCIATES. San Francisco: Jossey-Bass.

———— 1981 *Power in Organizations*. Marshfield, Mass.: Pitman Publishing Company.

PFEFFER, JEFFREY, AND HUSEIN LEBLIBIEI 1973 "The Effect of Competition on Some Dimensions of Organizational Structure," *Social Forces*, 52, no. 2 (December), 268–79.

PFEFFER, JEFFREY, AND ANTHONY LONG 1977 "Resource Allocation in United Funds: Examination of Power and Dependence," *Social Forces*, 55, no. 3 (March), 776–90.

PFEFFER, JEFFREY, AND WILLIAM L. MOORE 1980 "Average Tenure of Academic Department Heads: The Effects of Paradigm, Size, and Departmental Demography," *Administrative Science Quarterly*, 25, no. 3 (September), 387–406.

PFEFFER, JEFFREY, AND PHILLIP NOWAK 1976 "Joint Ventures and Interorganizational Dependence," *Administrative Science Quarterly*, 21, no. 3 (September), 398–418.

PFEFFER, JEFFREY, AND GERALD R. SALANCIK 1974 "Organizational Decision Making as a Political Process: The Case of a University Budget," *Administrative Science Quarterly*, 19, no. 2 (June) 135–151.

————. 1978 *The External Control of Organizations: A Resource Dependence Perspective*. New York: Harper and Row.

PFEFFER, JEFFREY, GERALD R. SALANCIK, AND HUSEYIN LEBLEBICI 1978 "Uncertainty and Social Influence in Organizational Decision Making" in *Environments and Organizations*, eds. MARSHALL W. MEYER AND ASSOCIATES. San Francisco: Jossey-Bass.

PINDER, CRAIG C., AND LARRY F. MOORE 1979 "The Resurrection of Taxonomy to Aid the Development of Middle Range Theories of Organizational Behavior," *Administrative Science Quarterly*, 24, no. 1 (March), 99–118.

PONDY, LOUIS R. 1967 "Organizational Conflict: Concepts and Models," *Administrative Science Quarterly*, 12, no. 1 (September), 296–320.

————. 1969 "Varieties of Organizational Conflict," *Administrative Science Quarterly*, 14, no. 4 (December), 499–505.

————. 1970 "Toward a Theory of Internal Resource Allocation," in *Power in Organizations*, ed. MAYER N. ZALD. Nashville, Tenn.: Vanderbilt University Press.

PRICE, JAMES L. 1968 *Organizational Effectiveness: An Inventory of Propositions*. Homewood, Ill.: Richard D. Irwin, Inc.

————. 1971 "The Study of Organizational Effectiveness," *The Sociological Quarterly*, 13, no. 1 (Winter), 3–15.

————. 1972 *Handbook of Organizational Measurement*. Lexington, Mass.: D. C. Heath and Company.

343

————. 1977 *The Study of Turnover*. Ames, Iowa: Iowa State University Press.

PROVAN, KEITH G., JANICE M. BEYER, AND CARLOS KRUYTBOSCH 1980 "Environmental Linkages and Power in Resource-Dependence Relations Between Organizations," *Administrative Science Quarterly*, 25, no. 2 (June), 200–25.

PUGH, DEREK S. 1966 "Modern Organization Theory: A Psychological and Sociological Study," *Psychological Bulletin*, 66, no. 21 (October) 235–51.

PUGH, DEREK S., DAVID J. HICKSON, AND C. R. HININGS 1969 "An Empirical Taxonomy of Work Organizations," *Administrative Science Quarterly*, 14, no. 1 (March), 115–26.

PUGH, DEREK S., DAVID J. HICKSON, C. R. HININGS, K. M. LUPTON, K. M. MCDONALD, C. TURNER, AND T. LUPTON 1963 "A Conceptual Scheme for Organizational Analysis," *Administrative Science Quarterly*, 8, no. 3 (December), 289–315.

PUGH, DEREK S., D. J. HICKSON, C. R. HININGS, AND C. TURNER 1968 "Dimensions of Organizational Structure," *Administrative Science Quarterly*, 13, no. 1 (June), 65–105.

————. 1969 "The Context of Organizational Structures," *Administrative Science Quarterly*, 14, no. 1 (March), 91–114.

QUINN, ROBERT E. 1977 "Coping with Cupid: The Formation, Impact, and Management of Romantic Relationships in Organizations," *Administrative Science Quarterly*, 22, no. 1 (March), 30–45.

RANSON, STEWART, BOB HININGS, AND ROYSTER GREENWOOD 1980 "The Structuring of Organizational Structures," *Administrative Science Quarterly*, 25, no. 1 (March), 1–17.

RAPHAEL, EDNA 1967 "The Anderson-Warton Hypothesis in Local Unions: A Comparative Study," *American Sociological Review*, 32, no. 5 (October), 768–76.

RAWLS, J. 1971 *A Theory of Justice*. Cambridge, Mass.: Harvard University Press.

REID, WILLIAM J. 1964 "Interagency Coordination in Delinquency Prevention and Control," *Social Service Review*, 38, no. 4 (December), 418–28.

————. 1969 "Inter-organizational Coordination in Social Welfare: A Theoretical Approach to Analysis and Intervention," in *Readings in Community Organization Practice*, eds. RALPH M. KRAMER AND HENRY SPECT. Englewood Cliffs, N.J.: Prentice-Hall, Inc.

REIMANN, BERNARD C. 1975 "Organizational Effectiveness and Management's Public Values: A Canonical Analysis," *Academy of Management Journal*, 18, no. 2 (June) 224–41.

REVE, TORGER AND LOUIS W. STERN 1979 "Interorganizational Relations in Marketing Channels" 1979 *Academy of Management Review*, 4, no. 3 (July), 405–16.

ROBBINS, STEPHEN P. 1974 *Managing Organizational Conflict: A Nontraditional Approach*. Englewood Cliffs, N.J.: Prentice-Hall, Inc.

ROBERTS, KARLENE H., CHARLES L. HULIN, AND DENISE M. ROUSSEAU 1978 *Developing an Interdisciplinary Science of Organizations*. San Francisco: Jossey-Bass.

ROBERTS, KARLENE H., CHARLES A. O'REILLY III, GENE E. BRETTON, AND LYMAN W. PORTER 1974 "Organizational Theory and Organizational Communications: A Communications Failure?" *Human Relations*, 27, no. 4 (May), 501–24.

ROETHLISBERGER, FRITZ J., AND WILLIAM J. DICKSON 1939 *Management and the Worker*. Cambridge, Mass.: Harvard University Press.

ROGERS, DAVID L. 1974 "Towards a Scale of Interorganizational Relations Among Public Agencies," *Sociology and Social Research*, 59, no. 1 (October), 61–70.

ROHRBAUGH, JOHN, AND ROBERT E. QUINN 1980 "Evaluating the Effectiveness of Public Organizations: A Method for Developing a Single Index," *Journal of Health and Human Resource Administration*, 2, no. 3, 343–54.

ROSENBAUM, JAMES E. 1979 "Organizational Career Mobility: Promotion Chances in a Corporation During Periods of Growth and Contraction," *American Journal of Sociology*, 85, no. 1 (July), 21–48.

ROSENGREN, WILLIAM 1964 "Communications, Organizations, and Conduct," *Administrative Science Quarterly*, 9, no. 2, (June), 70–90.

ROSNER, M., B. KAUČIČ, A. S. TANNENBAUM, M. VIANELLO, AND G. WEISER 1973 "Worker Participation and Influence in Five Countries," *Industrial Relations*, 12, no. 2 (May), 200–12.

ROSOW, JEROME M., ed. 1974 *The Worker and the Job: Coping with Change*. Englewood Cliffs, N.J.: Prentice-Hall, Inc.

ROTHSCHILD-WHITT, JOYCE 1979 "The Collectivist Organization: An Alternative to Rational Bureaucratic Models," *American Sociological Review*, 44, no. 4 (August), 519.

RUBIN, I. 1979 "Loose Structure, Retrenchment and Adaptability in the University." Paper presented at the Midwest Sociological Society meetings, Minneapolis.

RUS, VELJKO 1972 "The Limits of Organized Participation," in *Proceedings of the First International Conference on Participation and Self-Management.* (Vol. 2). Zagreb, Yugoslavia.

RUSHING, WILLIAM A. 1968 "Hardness of Material as Related to Division of Labor in Manufacturing Industries," *Administrative Science Quarterly*, 13, no. 2 (September), 224–45.

———. 1976 "Profit and Nonprofit Orientations and the Differentiation-Coordination Hypothesis for Organizations: A Study of Small General Hospitals," *American Sociological Review*, 41, no. 4 (August), 676–91.

SALAMAN, GRAEME, AND KENNETH THOMPSON, eds. 1980 *Control and Ideology in Organizations.* Cambridge, Mass.: MIT Press.

SALANCIK, GERALD R., AND JEFFREY PFEFFER 1974 "The Bases and Use of Power in Organizational Decision Making: The Case of a University," *Administrative Science Quarterly*, 19, no. 4 (December), 453–73.

———. 1977 "Constraints on Administrator Discretion: The Limited Influence of Mayors on City Budgets," *Urban Affairs Quarterly*, 12, no. 4 (June), 475–98.

SALES, STEPHEN M. 1969 "Organizational Role as a Risk Factor in Coronary Disease," *Administrative Science Quarterly*, 14, no. 3 (September), 325–37.

SAMUEL, YITZHAK 1979 "An Exchange and Power Approach to the Concept of Organizational Effectiveness." Mimeographed. Department of Sociology and Anthropology, Tel-Aviv University, Israel.

SANFORD, R. NEVITT 1964 "Individual Conflict and Organizational Interaction," in *Power and Conflict in Organizations*, eds. ROBERT L. KAHN AND ELISE BOULDING. New York: Basic Books, Inc.

SCHEFF, THOMAS J. 1961 "Control over Policy by Attendants in a Mental Hospital," *Journal of Health and Human Behavior*, 2, no. 2 (Summer), 93–105.

SCHERMERHORM, JOHN R., JR. 1975 "Determinants of Interorganizational Cooperation," *Academy of Management Journal*, 18, no. 4 (December), 846–56.

SCHLESINGER, JOSEPH A. 1965 "Political Party Organization," in *Handbook of Organizations.* ed. JAMES G. MARCH. Chicago: Rand McNally and Co.

SCHMIDT, STUART M., AND THOMAS A. KOCHAN 1972 "Conflict: Toward Conceptual Clarity," *Administrative Science Quarterly*, 17, no. 3 (September), 371–81.

———. 1977 "Interorganizational Relationships: Patterns and Motivations," *Administrative Science Quarterly*, 22, no. 2 (June), 220–34.

SCHNEIDER, BENJAMIN, JOHN J. PARKINGTON, AND VIRGINIA M. BUXTON 1980 "Employee and Customer Perspectives of Service in Banks," *Administrative Science Quarterly*, 25, no. 2 (June) 252–67.

SCHOLLHAMMER, HANS 1971 "Organization Structures of Multinational Corporations," *Academy of Management Journal*, 14, no. 3 (September), 345–65.

SCHUMAN, HOWARD 1971 "The Religious Factor in Detroit: Revisited," *American Sociological Review*, 36, no. 1 (February), 48–50.

SCOTT, W. RICHARD 1964 "Theory of Organizations," in *Handbook of Modern Sociology*, ed. ROBERT E. L. FARRIS. Chicago: Rand McNally and Co.

———. 1977 "Effectiveness of Organizational Effectiveness Studies," in *New Perspectives on Organizational Effectiveness*, eds. PAUL S. GOODMAN AND JOHANNES M. PENNINGS. San Francisco: Jossey-Bass.

———. 1981 *Organizations: Rational, Natural, and Open Systems.* Englewood Cliffs, N.J.: Prentice-Hall, Inc.

SCOTT, WILLIAM G. 1974 "Organizational Theory: A Reassessment," *Academy of Management Journal*, 17, no. 2 (June), 242–54.

SEASHORE, STANLEY E. 1977 "An Elastic and Expandable Viewpoint," in *New Perspectives on Organizational Effectiveness*, eds. PAUL S. GOODMAN AND J. M. PENNINGS. San Francisco: Jossey-Bass: 185–92.

SEASHORE, STANLEY E., AND YUCHTMAN, EPHRAIM 1967 "Factorial Analysis of Organizational Performance," *Administrative Science Quarterly*, 12, no. 3 (December), 377–95.

SEBRING, ROBERT H. 1977 "Health Councils as a Strategy for Community Change," *Journal of the Community Development Society*, 18, no. 1 (Spring), 74–85.

SEILER, LAUREN H. AND GENE F. SUMMERS 1979 "Corporate Involvement in Community Affairs," *The Sociological Quarterly*, 20, no. 3 (Summer), 375–86.

SELZNICK, PHILIP 1957 *Leadership in Administration*. New York: Harper and Row.

——. 1960 *The Organizational Weapon*. New York: The Free Press.

——. 1966 *TVA and the Grass Roots* (HARPER TORCHBOOK, ed.). New York: Harper and Row.

SILLS, DAVID L. 1957 *The Volunteers*. New York: The Free Press.

SILVERMAN, DAVID 1971 *The Theory of Organizations: A Sociological Framework*. New York: Basic Books.

SIMON, HERBERT A. 1957 *Administrative Behavior*. New York: The Free Press.

——. 1957 *Models of Men, Social and Rational*. New York: John Wiley and Sons, Inc.

——. 1964 "On the Concept of Organizational Goal," *Administrative Science Quarterly*, 9, no. 1 (June), 1–22.

SIMPSON, RICHARD L. 1969 "Vertical and Horizontal Communication in Formal Organizations," *Administrative Science Quarterly*, 14, no. 3 (September), 188–96.

SIMPSON, RICHARD L., AND WILLIAM GULLEY 1962 "Goals, Environmental Pressures, and Organizational Characteristics," *American Sociological Review*, 27, no. 3 (June), 344–50.

SNOW, CHARLES C., AND LAWRENCE G. HREBINIAK 1980 "Strategy, Distinctive Competence and Organizational Performance," *Administrative Science Quarterly*, 25, no. 2 (June), 317–36.

STARBUCK WILLIAM H. 1976 "Organizations and Their Environments," in *Handbook of Industrial and Organizational Psychology*, ed. MARVIN D. DUNNETTE. Chicago: Rand McNally and Co.

STAW, BARRY M. AND EUGENE SZAWJKOWSKI 1975 "The Scarcity-Munificence Component of Organizational Environments and the Commission of Illegal Acts," *Administrative Science Quarterly*, 20, no. 3 (September), 345–54.

STEERS, R. M. 1977 *Organizational Effectiveness: A Behavioral View*. Pacific Palisades, Cal.: Goodyear.

STERN, ROBERT N. 1981 "Competitive Influences on the Interorganizational Regulation of College Athletics," *Administrative Science Quarterly*, 26, no. 1 (March), 15–32.

STINCHCOMBE, ARTHUR L. 1959 "Bureaucratic and Craft Administration of Production," *Administrative Science Quarterly*, 4, no. 2 (September), 168–87.

——. 1965 "Social Structure and Organization," in *Handbook of Organizations*, ed. JAMES G. MARCH. Chicago: Rand McNally and Co.

STIPAK, B. 1979 "Citizen Satisfaction with Urban Services: Potential Misuse as a Performance Indicator," *Public Administration Review*, 39, no. 1 (January) 46–52.

STOGDILL, RALPH 1974 *Handbook of Leadership: A Survey of Theory and Research*. New York: The Free Press.

STOLZENBERG, ROSS M. 1978 "Bringing the Boss Back In: Employer Size, Employee Schooling and Socioeconomic Achievement," *American Sociological Review*, 43, no. 6 (December), 813–28.

STYSKAL, RICHARD A. 1980 "Power and Commitment in Organizations: A Test of the Participation Thesis," *Social Forces*, 57, no. 4 (June), 925–43.

SWIGERT, VICTORIA LYNN AND RONALD A. FARRELL 1980–81 "Corporate Homicide: Definitional Processes in the Creation of Deviance," *Law & Society Review* 15, no. 1 (Fall), 163–82.

TANNENBAUM, ARNOLD S. 1965 "Unions," in *Handbook of Organizations*, ed. JAMES G. MARCH. Chicago: Rand McNally and Company.

——. 1968 *Control in Organizations*. New York: McGraw-Hill Book Company.

TANNENBAUM, ARNOLD S., BOGDAN KAUČIČ, MENOCHEN ROSNER, MINO VIANELLO, AND GEORGE WIESER 1974 *Hierarchy in Organizations*. San Francisco: Jossey-Bass.

TAUSKY, CURT 1978 *Work Organizations: Major Theoretical Perspectives*, 2/E. Itasca, Ill.: F. E. Peacock Publishers, Inc.

346

TAYLOR, FREDERICK W. 1911 *Principles of Scientific Management.* New York: Harper and Row.

TAYLOR, JAMES C. 1971 "Some Effects of Technology in Organizational Change," *Human Relations,* 24, no. 2 (April), 105–23.

TERKEL, STUDS 1974 *Working.* New York: Pantheon Books.

TERREBERRY, SHIRLEY 1968 "The Evolution of Organizational Environments," *Administrative Science Quarterly,* 12, no. 4 (March), 590–613.

THOMAS, W. I. 1923 *The Unadjusted Girl.* Boston: Little Brown and Co.

THOMPSON, JAMES D. 1967 *Organizations in Action.* New York: McGraw-Hill Book Company.

THOMPSON, JAMES D., AND WILLIAM MCEWEN 1958 "Organizational Goals and Environment: Goalsetting As An Interaction Process," *American Sociological Review,* 23, no. 1 (February), 23–31.

THOMPSON, VICTOR 1961 *Modern Organizations.* New York: Alfred A. Knopf, Inc.

———. 1965 "Bureaucracy and Innovation," *Administrative Science Quarterly,* 10, no. 1 (June), 1–20.

TOYNBEE, ARNOLD 1974 "As I See It," *Forbes,* 113, no. 7 (April), 68.

TRACY, PHELPS, AND KOYA AZUMI 1976 "Determinants of Administrative Control: A Test of a Theory with Japanese Factories," *American Sociological Review,* 41, no. 1 (February), 80–94.

TURK, HERMAN 1970 "Interorganizational Networks in Urban Society: Initial Perspectives in Comparative Research," *American Sociological Review,* 35, no. 1 (February) 1–18.

———. 1973 "Comparative Urban Structure from an Interorganizational Perspective," *Administrative Science Quarterly,* 18, no. 1 (March), 37–55.

UNITED STATES SENATE 1979 Committee on Government Affairs, Hearings on S.262, S.755, S.445, S.93, 96th Congress, 1st Sess.

URWICK, LYNDALL F. 1947 *The Elements of Administration.* London: Sir Isaac Pitman.

USEEM, MICHAEL 1979 "The Social Organization of the American Business Elite and Participation of Corporate Directors in the Governance of American Institutions," *American Sociological Review,* 44, no. 4 (August), 553–72.

VAN DE VEN, ANDREW H. 1976 "Equally Efficient Structural Variations Within Organizations." in *The Management of Organization Design: Research and Methodology,* eds. L. PONDY, D. SLEVEN, AND R. KILLMAN. New York: Elsevier Publishing Company.

———. 1979 "Howard E. Aldrich: Organizations and Environments," *Administrative Science Quarterly,* 24, no. 2 (June) 24, 320–26.

VAN DE VEN, ANDREW H., AND ANDRE DELBECQ 1974 "A Task Contingent Model of Work Unit Structure," *Administrative Science Quarterly,* 19, no. 2 (June), 183–97.

VAN DE VEN, ANDREW H., ANDRE L. DELBECQ, AND RICHARD KOENIG, JR. 1976 "Determinants of Coordination Modes Within Organizations," *American Sociological Review,* 41, no. 2 (April), 322–38.

VAN DE VEN, ANDREW H., DENNIS EMMETT, AND RICHARD KOENIG, JR. 1974 "Frameworks for Inter-Organizational Analysis," *Organization and Administrative Sciences,* 5, no. 1 (Spring), 113–29.

VAN DE VEN, ANDREW H., AND DIANE L. FERRY 1980 *Measuring and Assessing Organizations.* New York: John Wiley and Sons.

VOLLMER, HOWARD M., AND DONALD L. MILLS, eds. 1966 *Professionalization.* Englewood Cliffs, N.J.: Prentice-Hall, Inc.

WAGER, L. WESLEY 1972 "Organizational 'Linking-Pins': Hierarchical Status and Communicative Roles in Interlevel Conferences," *Human Relations,* 25, no. 4 (September), 307–26.

WALKER, CHARLES R., AND ROBERT GUEST 1952 *The Man on the Assembly Line.* Cambridge, Mass.: Harvard University Press.

WALTON, RICHARD E. 1980 "Establishing and Maintaining High Commitment Work Systems," in *The Organizational Life Cycle.* eds. JOHN R. KIMBERLY, ROBERT H. MILES, AND ASSOCIATES. San Francisco: Jossey-Bass.

WAMSLEY, GARRY L. 1970 "Power and the Crisis of the Universities," in *Power in Organizations,* ed. MAYER N. ZALD. Nashville, Tenn.: University of Tennessee Press.

347

WAMSLEY, GARRY, AND MAYER N. ZALD 1973 *The Political Economy of Public Organizations.* Lexington, Mass.: D.C. Heath and Company.

WARREN, DONALD I. 1968 "Power, Visibility, and Conformity in Formal Organizations," *American Sociological Review,* 33, no. 6 (December), 951–70.

WARREN, ROLAND 1967 "The Interorganizational Field as a Focus for Investigation," *Administrative Science Quarterly,* 12, no. 3 (December), 396–419.

WARREN, ROLAND, STEPHEN ROSE, AND ANN BERGUNDER 1974 *The Structure of Urban Reform.* Lexington, Mass.: D. C. Heath and Co.

WARRINER, CHARLES K. 1956 "Groups Are Real: A Reaffirmation," *American Sociological Review,* 21, no. 9 (October), 549–54.

———. 1979 "Empirical Taxonomics of Organizations: Problematics in Their Development." Mimeographed. Lawrence, Kans: University of Kansas.

———. 1980 "Organizational Types: Notes on the 'Organizational Species' Concept" Mimeographed. Lawrence, Kan.: Department of Sociology, University of Kansas.

WARRINGER, CHARLES K., RICHARD H. HALL, AND BILL McKELVEY 1981 "The Comparative Description of Organizations: A Research Note and Invitation," *Organizational Studies,* 2, no. 2 (April).

WEBER, MAX 1947 *The Theory of Social and Economic Organization.* Trans. A. M. Parsons and T. Parsons. New York: The Free Press.

WEICK, KARL 1976 "Educational Organizations as Loosely Coupled Systems," *Administrative Science Quarterly,* 21, no. 1 (March), 1–19.

———. 1979 *The Social Psychology of Organizing 2/e.* Reading, Mass.: Addison-Wesley Publishing Company.

WEINER, NAN 1977 "Situational and Leadership Influence on Organizational Performance," Mimeographed. Columbus, Ohio: College of Administrative Science, The Ohio State University.

WELDON, PETER D. 1972 "An Examination of the Blau-Scott and Etzioni Typologies: A Critique," *Administrative Science Quarterly,* 17, no. 1 (March), 76–78.

WHETTEN, DAVID A. 1978 "Coping with Incompatible Expectations: An Integrated View of Role Conflict," *Administrative Science Quarterly,* 23, no. 2 (June), 254–71.

———. 1980 "Sources, Responses and Effects of Organizational Decline," in *The Organizational Life Cycle,* eds. JOHN R. KIMBERLY AND ROBERT H. MILES AND ASSOCIATES. San Francisco: Jossey-Bass.

WHETTEN, DAVID A., AND HOWARD ALDRICH 1979 "Organization Set Size and Diversity: People-Processing Organizations and Their Environments," *Administration and Society,* 11, no. 3 (November), 251–81.

WHETTEN, DAVID A., AND EUGENE SZWAJKOWSKI 1978 "Relational Variables in Interorganizational Research: Conceptual and Methodological Issues." Working Paper. College of Commerce and Business Administration, University of Illinois.

WILDAVSKY, AARON 1964 *The Politics of the Budgetary Process.* Boston: Little Brown and Company.

WILENSKY, HAROLD 1967 *Organizational Intelligence: Knowledge and Policy in Government and Industry.* New York: Basic Books, Inc.

WOOD, JAMES R. 1975 "Legitimate Control and Organizational Transcendence," *Social Forces,* 54, no. 1 (September), 199–211.

WOODWARD, JOAN 1958 *Management and Technology.* London: Her Majesty's Stationery Office.

———. 1965 *Industrial Organizations: Theory and Practice.* London: Oxford University Press.

Work in America 1973 Cambridge, Mass.: MIT Press.

YARMOLINSKY, ADAM 1975 "Institutional Paralysis," *Daedalus,* 104, no. 1 (Winter), 61–67.

YUCHTMAN, EPHRAIM, AND STANLEY SEASHORE 1967 "A System Resource Approach to Organizational Effectiveness," *American Sociological Review,* 32, no. 6 (December), 891–903.

YUKL, GARY A. 1981 *Leadership in Organizations.* Englewood Cliffs, N.J.: Prentice-Hall, Inc.

ZALD, MAYER N. 1969 "The Structure of Society and Social Service Integration," *Social Science Quarterly,* 50, no. 3 (December), 577–67.

ZALD, MAYER N., ed. 1970a *Power in Organizations.* Nashville, Tenn.: Vanderbilt University Press.

———. 1970b *Organizational Change: The Political Economy of the YMCA.* Chicago: University of Chicago Press.

———. 1970c "Political Economy: A Framework for Comparative Analysis," in *Power in Organizations,* ed. MAYER N. ZALD. Nashville, Tenn.: Vanderbilt University Press.

ZALKIND, SHELDON, AND TIMOTHY W. COSTELLO 1962 "Perceptions: Some Recent Research and Implications for Administration," *Administrative Science Quarterly,* 7, no. 2 (September), 218–35.

ZALTMAN, GERALD, ROBERT DUNCAN, AND JONNY HOLBECK 1973 *Innovations and Organizations.* New York: Wiley Interscience.

ZEITLIN, MAURICE 1974 "Corporate Ownership and Control: The Large Corporation and the Capitalist Class," *American Journal of Sociology,* 79, no. 5 (March), 1073–119.

———. 1976 "In Class Theory of the Large Corporation: Response to Others," *American Journal of Sociology,* 81, no. 4 (January), 894–903.

ZEITZ, GERALD 1980 "Interorganizational Dialectics," *Administrative Science Quarterly,* 25, no. 1 (March), 72–78.

ZWERMAN, WILLIAM L. 1970 *New Perspectives on Organization Theory.* Westport, Conn.: Greenwood Publishing Company.

Name Index

Thompson, James D., 32, 64, 74, 177-180, 240, 253, 272, 280, 347
Thompson, Kenneth, 309, 345
Thompson, Victor, 106-107, 347
Tittle, Charles R., 61, 335
Toynbee, Arnold, 25, 347
Tracy, Phelps, 222, 347
Trice, Harrison M., 68, 80, 328
Trist, E.L., 64, 240, 248, 332
Trow, Martin A., 176, 339
Turk, Herman, 240-241, 248, 347
Turner, C., 80, 81, 85, 97-98, 102, 344

United States Senate, 296, 347
Urwick, Lyndall F., 309, 347
Useem, Michael, 22, 347

Van Roekel, Martha, 335
Vianello, Mino, 344, 346
Vollmer, Howard M., 79, 141, 347

Walton, Richard E., 106, 347
Wamsley, Gary, 132-133, 317, 347-348
Warkow, Seymour, 61, 84-85, 328
Warner, Malcolm, 58, 332
Warren, Donald I., 137, 348
Warren, Richard D., 338, 341
Warren, Roland, 240, 249, 258, 261, 263, 348
Warriner, Charles K., xiii, 35, 41, 42, 45, 47, 348
Weber, Max, 28-29, 56, 131, 133, 134, 219, 310, 320, 322, 348

Weick, Karl, 120-121, 215, 237, 308, 348
Weiner, Nan, 174, 348
Weiser, George, 344, 346
Weitzel, William, 286, 339
Weldon, Peter D., 43, 348
Whetten, David A., 51, 98, 120-121, 221, 250, 251, 255, 261, 307, 329, 348
White, Paul E., 241, 249, 253, 259, 339
Wildavsky, Aron, 280, 348
Wilensky, Harold, 185, 197, 348
Wilke, Henke, 138, 341
Winkelpleck, Judy M., 338
Wolfe, Donald M., 337
Wood, James R., 136, 348
Woodward, Joan, 61, 64, 167, 348
Work in America, 6, 348

Yanouzas, John N., 197, 330
Yarmolinsky, Adam, 120, 348
Yetman, Norman R., 172, 332
Yuchtman, Ephraim, 274-278, 346, 348
Yukl, Gary A., 162, 348

Zald, Mayer N., 148-149, 162, 240, 258, 317, 348-349
Zalkind, Sheldon, 190-192, 349
Zaltman, Gerald, 211-213, 215, 349
Zander, Alvin, 322, 330
Zeitlin, Maurice, 174, 349
Zeitz, Gerald, 39, 51, 119, 262, 327, 339, 349
Zwerman, William L., 64, 349

Subject Index

Aston group, 58, 61, 66, 147
Authority, 81-82, 133-134
Authority, perception, 137-138

Boards of Directory, 21-23, 257-258
Boundaries, 29, 31, 32-33
Boundary Spanners, 72-73
Bureaucracy, 6-7, 56, 96
Bureaucracy, Roman, 21

Centralization, 50-55, 56, 99-100, 114-126
Change, 10-12, 207-216
  nature of, 208
  organizations as agents, 12-18
  organizations as resistors, 18-21
  organizations as weapons, 14-15
  process, 209-210
  resistance to, 208-209
Classification, see types of organizations
Cliques, 142-143
Coalitions, 142-143
Collectivist, democractic organization, 33-35
Communications, 138-139, 184-205
  bases, 187-189
  distortion, 186, 191
  horizontal, 198-202
  importance, 184-187

individual factors, 190-192
  organizational factors, 192-202
  problems, 202-205
  vertical, 192-198
Communities, 9-10
Competition, 70, 120
Complexity, 50, 56, 61-62, 68, 76-94
  consequences, 84-86
  variations in, 76-78, 83-84
Compliance, 136-137
Conflict, 7, 35, 89-90, 91, 151-157
  bases, 152-153
  situations, 153-155
  in society, 18
Conformity, 137
Constituents, 270, 273, 289-291, 299-301
Control, 86-90
Co-optation, 13
Coordination, 86-90, 196
Crime, organizational, 23, 24
Cultural Conditions, 17
Customers and Clients, 6-7

Decentralization, 13, 74
Decision Making, 31, 38, 66, 69, 73-75, 113-114, 148, 176-183, 324-326
Definitions, 28-33
Dependency, 143-145

354